American Militarism and Anti-Militarism
in Popular Media, 1945–1970

American Militarism and Anti-Militarism in Popular Media, 1945–1970

LISA M. MUNDEY

McFarland & Company, Inc., Publishers
Jefferson, North Carolina, and London

Library of Congress Cataloguing-in-Publication Data

Mundey, Lisa M., 1975–
    American militarism and anti-militarism in popular media,
1945–1970 / Lisa M. Mundey.
        p.   cm.
    Includes bibliographical references and index.

    ISBN 978-0-7864-6650-4
    softcover : acid free paper ∞

    1. Mass media and war — United States.   2. War in mass
media.   3. War and society — United States.   4. Militarism —
Social aspects — United States — History — 20th century.
5. Popular culture — United States — History — 20th century.
I. Title.
P96.W352U5565 2012
303.6'6097309045 — dc23   2011052294

British Library cataloguing data are available

On the cover: (top) George C. Scott in the 1970 *Patton*; (bottom)
anti-draft and anti-war student protesters inWashington, D.C.,
1965 (both photographs from the Michael Ochs Archives/Getty
Images)

Front cover design by Rob Russell

Manufactured in the United States of America

McFarland & Company, Inc., Publishers
   Box 611, Jefferson, North Carolina 28640
      www.mcfarlandpub.com

TABLE OF CONTENTS

PREFACE

This book focuses on the unique aspects of American militarism and anti-militarism in the early decades of the Cold War. During this era, the military appeared frequently in popular culture, particularly on television, in Hollywood movies, and in comic books, three of the areas upon which I focused this study. Although other elements of American culture could be included, I chose these mediums for their popularity. I also decided to focus on direct images of the military rather than genres like the Western, which often implicitly stand in for the military in pop culture. I included military recruiting ads in the study as an indication of the images military officials (or their advertising agencies) wanted the public to see or thought would appeal to their target audience: young men and women in their late teenage years and early 20s, who were also the group most frequently surveyed by the Pentagon about their attitudes toward the military and military service. Images alone, however, do not tell the whole story. I track conservative opinions and perceptions in Henry Luce's *Life* and *Time* magazines and liberal views in the *New Republic*. Gallup polls, Department of Defense surveys, and other polling data offer insight into more general American public opinions with respect to the military, the draft, contemporary military conflicts, and other areas of American military policy. Taken together, we can discern general public attitudes, beliefs, and perceptions toward the military, the growing militarization, and the persistent anti-militarism in American culture in the first two and a half decades of the Cold War.

Scholars characterize the early decades of the Cold War as an era of rising militarism in the United States. Though scholars differ as to the extent militarism pervaded American society, they point to the growing American military establishment, the peacetime draft, and other developments as evidence that America militarized during this period. Rather than rely on the definitions offered by scholars, it is important to understand how Americans of the post–World War II era understood militarism.

When Americans living during the early Cold War used the term "militarism" it was often in reference to the authoritarian regimes the nation had fought against in World War II. Americans believed that militarist nations deployed their armies aggressively to expand power, that in a militarist nation the military possessed power outside of civilian authority or constitutional limits, that they had a national emphasis on maintaining military preparedness during peacetime, and that the military imposed regimentation and other military values upon civilian society. As a result of the specific World War II context of this definition, most Americans did not consider the large force structure, technological advances, or other elements of American Cold War defense policy as akin to the militarism of the former Nazi or Japanese regimes. Indeed, Americans of the post–World War II era considered themselves anti-militaristic. In America, anti-militarism included a preference for citizen-soldiers instead of regulars, civilian control of the military, volunteerism rather than conscription, and individualism over regimentation.

Adopting the definitions of militarism and anti-militarism used by Americans in the early Cold War offers insights into how the public could embrace more militaristic national security policies yet continue to perceive themselves as fundamentally anti-militaristic. Sometimes anti-militarism is explicit, as in a fear of the regulars launching a coup d' état, or more implicit, as in poking fun at the military or having an anti-authoritarian characterization of the military. Negative portrayals of the regulars and praise for citizen-soldiers in popular culture is anti-militaristic (and in some cases outright anti-military) by this Cold War era definition. A focus on individualism over regimentation in the characterization or portrayal of the armed forces is anti-militaristic. Romanticizing or glorifying combat as ennobling, exciting, desirable, or redemptive is militaristic. Aggressive use of force or pre-emptive war is also militaristic, as is a state of perpetual vigilance or preparedness to go to war at a moment's notice during peacetime. Few portrayals of the military in American popular culture fall clearly on the side of militarism, and fewer still show Americans participating in overt aggression. As a result, scholars cannot simply characterize the entire era as militarized because there are degrees of militarism and anti-militarism in American culture, shifting over time. An understanding of growing militarism in American culture requires a more nuanced interpretation that accounts for continuing anti-militaristic self-perceptions within American society. Moreover, the militarism of the 1945–1970 period differs in many ways from the militarism in American culture after 1980. In order to understand the changes in American culture after the shift toward the All Volunteer Force in 1973, we should first understand the militarism and continued anti-militarism in American culture after World War II.

I have traveled across the United States to pull sources together for this project, including the UCLA Film and Television Archives (before many of the TV shows ended up on DVD and Netflix); the Browne Popular Culture Library at Bowling Green State University, which has an excellent collection of comic books; and the National Archives and Records Administration in College Park, Maryland. I thank the friendly and knowledgeable staff who assisted me in finding the materials I needed for this project. I would not have been able to conduct this research without the Colonel Peter Cullen Military History Fellowship and travel grants from the Institute of Military History and Twentieth Century Studies. A Faculty Development Grant from the University of St. Thomas helped me to finish the manuscript.

I thank all those who have helped me through the process. A few deserve particular gratitude: Mark P. Parillo guided me through the project's early stages. Brian M. Jones offered support and feedback on the manuscript. Thanks to William M. Donnelly, who collected materials from the National Archives for me and has read this manuscript in many forms. He not only offered insightful comments but kept me honest in the details. All lingering mistakes are mine and mine alone. I appreciate the assistance of my colleagues at the University of St. Thomas. Last but not least, thank you to my friends and family, particularly my husband, Mike, who offered support and encouragement through the whole project.

INTRODUCTION

One evening in December 1962, American television viewers tuned in to watch a show set in the backwaters of the World War II Pacific Theater. A PT boat commander and his crew — all citizen-soldiers—created a sanctuary from the regular Navy on a small South Pacific island. A sign on the dock proclaimed: "All armed forces personnel keep off— Girls come on in!" When the base's commanding officer threatened to turn the island into an officers' club, the sailors protested by declaring that their haven is "a democracy run by the men for the men." They aimed to take action to protect it. Dressed in blackout clothes and wearing face paint, the crew approached the main post in rubber boats and sabotaged the building supplies, blaming the mayhem on the Japanese. When the base commander persisted in building his club on their island, the crew staged a fake Japanese "attack," which they immediately thwarted. A visiting admiral recommended a citation for the brave sailors and ordered the club moved to the main post for safety. The crew returned to their refuge, happy to enjoy their oasis and ignore inconvenient Navy regulations.[1]

The above episode of the lighthearted comedy series *McHale's Navy* aired well into an era of American culture that scholars consider already militarized. According to public-opinion polls, contemporary observations, television, comic strips, and motion pictures, however, Americans retained some anti-militarist sentiments and perceived themselves as anti-militaristic during the first decades of the Cold War.

Defining Terms

Scholars characterize the early decades of the Cold War as an era of rising militarism in the United States. While there are many definitions of militarism, a commonly cited one is by Alfred Vagts, who characterizes it as a system of ranking "military institutions and ways above the ways of civilian life, carrying military mentality and modes of acting and decision into the civilian sphere."[2] A scholar of the American anti-militarist tradition, Arthur Ekirch, Jr., defines militarism as "a society in which war, or preparation for war, dominates politics and foreign policy. Soldiers and military-minded civilians become a governing elite dedicated to expanding the military establishment and inculcating martial values."[3] Michael Sherry deliberately chose a term — militarization — that differs from Vagts's definition of militarism, as the U.S. does not fit Vagts's concept. Sherry argues that, starting in the 1930s, a process of militarization began to dominate American life, which he defines as "the process by which war and national security became consuming anxieties and provided the memories, models, and metaphors that shaped broad areas of national life."[4] Ekirch agrees with Sherry that American militarism is distinctive. He argues that the Cold War "made possible a new type of militarism unrecognizable to those who looked for its historic characteristics. Militarism might now be clothed in a civilian uniform and imposed upon a people who accepted a permanent warfare economy as not more than a way to full employment and a welfare state."[5] Richard H. Kohn acknowledges that militarism during the Cold War was "less noticeable and pervasive" than during World War II, but he argues that it was during the Cold War era that militarization became permanently entrenched.[6]

Other scholars chart militarism in popular culture. Christian Appy applies the term "sentimental militarism" to describe 1950s culture, which included the ideas that "U.S. soldiers are peace-loving citizen soldiers, the fight is on behalf of women and loved ones at home ... and the military is a melting pot of democratic values."[7] J. Fred MacDonald, Stephen Whitfield, and David L. Robb maintain that any positive portrayal of the military is pro-military government propaganda. For these three scholars, only an outright rejection of the military as an institution constitutes a non-militaristic interpretation.[8] Carl Boggs and Tom Pollard assert that "the film industry has adeptly transformed the horrors of warfare into vast commodified spectacles that help empower the U.S. war system as it moves along the path of global domination."[9] Many of these definitions of militarism become so broad as to encompass any reference to the military or to war. Americans of the early Cold War did not have such a broad understanding of militarism. Indeed, some of what scholars are defining as "militarization" or "sentimental militarism" properly belongs to the historical American definition of anti-militarism.

Americans of the post–World War II era understood militarism in reference to the authoritarian regimes the nation had fought against in World War II. Americans believed that militarist nations deployed their armies aggressively to expand power and that the military became the model for these societies.[10] In reference to Nazi Germany, the military became a "state within a state" outside of constitutional and civilian authority. Further, the German army imposed values of obedience, duty, and collective sacrifice on its society. For the Nazis, war itself was ennobling.[11] Additionally, peacetime military preparedness led to militarism. Americans, therefore, understood militarism to include the aggressive use of a military force; the military's possession of power outside of civilian authority or constitutional limits; the military's imposition upon society of regimentation or values that could undermine democracy and a national emphasis on maintaining military preparedness during peacetime. As a result of the specific World War II context of this definition, most Americans did not consider the large force structure, technological advances, or other elements of American Cold War defense policy as akin to the militarism of the former Nazi or Japanese regimes. Indeed, the U.S. had a long anti-militarist identity.

The United States was founded, in part, on the principle of anti-militarism. Anti-militarism is not pacifism or the total rejection of war. As Ekirch explains that "the antimilitarist may accept war and armies as a sometimes necessary evil," but he also considers large, draftee armies "as a threat to the preservation of civil institutions of government."[12] In America, anti-militarists have traditionally favored non-aggressive and non-preventive war, preferred citizen-soldiers over regulars, asserted civilian control of the military, chose volunteerism over conscription, and favored individualism over regimentation.[13] Anti-militarism in American culture began in the colonial era as a fear of central power and standing armies, which led to the establishment local militias, citizen-soldiers called to arms in an emergency.[14] Early Americans generally disliked military professionals. By relying on citizen-soldiers, Americans wanted to guarantee civil liberties and constitutional authority. Militia also proved less expensive than funding full-time regulars. While colonial militia originated as a system of universal male military service, it evolved into a voluntary arrangement.[15] The colonial heritage bequeathed upon subsequent generations a reliance on volunteer citizen-soldiers, a distrust of military regulars, and civilian control of a small standing military force.

During the nineteenth century, the militia system developed into a social fraternity infused with a "martial spirit" but still centered on the ideals of volunteerism and individualism. At the turn of the century, American citizen-soldiers continued their voluntary associations but adhered more strongly to professional standards of efficiency and preparedness.[16] The National Guard, the self-proclaimed heir of the citizen-soldier tradition, evolved from a system of local, independent, volunteer organizations in the nineteenth century to a national, federally-funded military force in the early twentieth century.[17] The trajectory of the American military system moved toward greater professionalism, but Americans remained convinced that the military of a democracy fundamentally differed from that of an authoritarian state.

One final definition is needed. The term "citizen-soldier" attained a broad definition in post–World War II America. Americans most often applied the term "citizen-soldier" to the members of the National Guard or reserve forces. During and after World War II, however, they also referred to draftees both in wartime and peacetime as citizen-soldiers rather than regulars.[18] In the Cold War era, Americans invoked the term "citizen soldier" to describe any American in uniform. It was a catch phrase for the soldiers— regular or reserve — of a democracy rather than the soldiers of an authoritarian state.[19] Adopting these definitions used by Americans in the early Cold War offers insights into how the public could embrace more militaristic national security policies yet continue to perceive themselves as fundamentally anti-militaristic.

Overview

In the minds of most Americans living in the first two decades after the Second World War, the United States remained firmly anti-militarist. Anti-militarist sentiment proved bipartisan, as both Democrats and Republicans expressed it. American military policy at the end of World War II followed a familiar American anti-militarist tradition: President Harry Truman ordered a massive demobilization of the military and of the war economy to return to peacetime status. Most of the 16 million men and women who served in uniform during the war returned home and returned to civilian lives. In fact, so many stayed out of uniform that the Pentagon scrambled to fill billets for occupation duty. Congress extended the draft in order to meet these postwar manpower needs. Congress continued to extend the draft because too few Americans volunteered to serve despite survey polls that suggested Americans thought a larger military was necessary to oppose the emerging threat from the Soviet Union. Americans supported militarist policies but did not want to participate in the policies firsthand. Nevertheless, presidential administrations from that of Harry Truman through Lyndon Johnson relied on large reserve forces and temporary military service through the draft. As George Flynn explains, "Equally important in rationalizing the draft was that it overcame dangers to the state inherent in maintaining a mass army. Drafting civilians could secure the state against militarism because by infusing the armed forces with a leaven of civilians, the state insured itself against right-wing coups."[20] The same rationale explains widespread support for mandatory training in the Reserve Officers Training Corps at American colleges and universities through the 1950s. In the minds of university administrators, civilian institutions of higher learning civilianized the military rather than vice versa.[21] Of course, the opposite argument was made during the late 1960s when the Vietnam-era draft came under attack as anti-democratic by infringing on individual freedom and liberty. By this time, both the political left and right abandoned their support for the draft, and President Richard Nixon subsequently created the All Volunteer Force in 1973.

Hollywood reflected American fatigue with combat at the conclusion of World War II. Hollywood temporarily abandoned war films because audiences had tired of the war. Poll data and contemporary observations show that Americans did not necessarily perceive World War II in favorable terms. Veterans in the filmmaking business revived the genre in 1949 to pay tribute to the men who served in World War II. They made three films that became classics: *Battleground*, *Twelve O'Clock High*, and *Sands of Iwo Jima*. Many of the subsequent films and television shows depicting World War II stemmed from the initial postwar wave of films. These later portrayals adopted similar characterizations and themes. Although rarely present in mainstream presentations, gender, race, and ethnicity did occasionally play a role in these stories. As other scholars have deftly explored the racial and gender issues of this era, with some exceptions, they are not included as main themes here.[22]

Before the 1980s, recruiting advertising tended toward mass mainstream audiences with what recruiters considered universal themes. There was less emphasis on niche markets or themes targeting specific audiences, though there were some, such as nursing for women.[23] Recruiting ads most often appeared in mainstream periodicals appealing to middle America: *Life*, *Saturday Evening Post*, *Collier's*, and similar publications. Military advertising often focused on how military service would help prepare one for civilian jobs and meet life goals. Air Force and Navy recruiters also emphasized technical training and skills with the latest cutting-edge technology. Even during the war years of the Korean and Vietnam conflicts, recruiting advertising predominantly focused on education and training rather than combat. For women, recruiting advertising showed the military as basically civilian in nature, if not in name, and military service as a patriotic vacation.

North Korea's invasion of South Korea in June 1950 upset the post–World War II return to peacetime normalcy. President Truman committed American forces to the Korean peninsula and used the crisis to expand the active duty military force. The Pentagon increased draft calls and mobilized American reserve forces, including the involuntary recall of many World War II veterans—including some women—for another war. Truman limited the scope of the Korean War to prevent a wider war with China or the Soviet Union, a decision that did not necessarily play well in the media or with the troops. Truman also faced a public relations nightmare when the popular Korean theater commander, General Douglas MacArthur, began to agitate publicly for a wider war with China, even after it was clear the Truman administration wanted no such expanded conflict. The president removed MacArthur from command in order to maintain firm civilian control of the military.

Portrayals of the Korean War in popular culture proved dark and conflicted. *The Steel Helmet* (1951) and *The Bridges at Toko-Ri* (1955) contained overtly anti-war interpretations of the conflict. *Pork Chop Hill* (1959) did not present the kind of "good war" that was becoming the cultural narrative for World War II stories. Comic books, too, depicted Korea as filled with devastation and moral ambiguities until these themes were squashed by the censorship embedded in the 1955 Comics Code. The conflicted images of the Korean War created opportunities for dark and anti-militarist portrayals of World War II to appear on the silver screen as well, stories like *From Here to Eternity* (1953) and *Mister Roberts* (1955).

Most military television comedies of the late 1950s and 1960s adhered to implicit anti-militarist themes by spoofing active-duty military life. These shows paralleled themes in long-running comic strips like *Beetle Bailey* and *Sad Sack*. By lampooning typical military life, they appealed to audiences who had military experience and could appreciate the absurdity of some aspects of military life. Female versions of these spoofs, anti-militarist comics, television comedies, and Hollywood movies delighted audiences as well. Even if these stories did not reject the military as an institution, they certainly showed a healthy skepticism about it. Discipline, regimentation, and unthinking obedience to authority were hardly the order of the day. The Cuban Missile Crisis reinforced anti-militarism in American culture, as seen in the 1964 anti-nuclear and anti-professional military films *Fail Safe*, *Dr. Strangelove*, and *Seven Days in May*. The crisis also inspired television producers to set new series in the World War II era, which increasingly appeared as a clear-cut, unambiguous victory, unlike the tension of the Cold War.

Some films, comics, and television shows in the 1950s and 1960s were respectful of the military and presented more glorified images of the military and of warfare, yet privileged the image of the citizen-soldier rather than the long serving regulars. Though the emphasis on citizen-soldiers began with the movies created during World War II, it gained permanency as part of the cultural narrative during the 1950s and became the dominant characterization of American servicemen and women by the early– and mid–1960s. World War II Medal of Honor recipient Audie Murphy's autobiographical film, *To Hell and Back* (1955), exemplifies the good war and the citizen-soldier imagery of the more militarized interpretations of that war. Still, audiences had mixed reactions to these films, comics, and television shows, too, suggesting that audiences did not automatically accept the images presented to them about the military. It appears that children and teenagers were more accepting of glorified images of war than adults were.

The influence of veterans on the opinions and attitudes of friends and family should not be underestimated. In 1954, there were 20 million veterans in a population of just over 163 million Americans, one of the highest percentages of veterans in the nation's history.[24] With the peacetime draft and a large standing military during the Cold War, the percentage of men and women with some military experience remained high throughout the period. Given that the draft conscripted men from all classes and geographic areas of America, veterans were also broadly representative of America as a whole. Department of Defense surveys show that, for the 1950s at least, enlistees in the armed forces reported the biggest influence on their decision to volunteer came from friends or family with military experience, not the media. Media did not gain dominant influence until the 1960s. It is also worth noting that this personal influence is not necessarily militaristic. Although some members of the military no doubt re-entered civilian life with a militarist outlook, many other veterans did not. Indeed, many disliked military service very much. These veterans were also much less likely to take presentations of the military in popular culture seriously and shared their skepticism with friends and family.

During the second half of the 1960s, popular culture increasingly divided into separate interpretations of war. One thread showed war, particularly World War II, as a fun action-adventure. A second thread had a clearly pro-military, pro-war interpretation. The third thread was an anti-war, anti-authoritarian backlash against the war in Southeast Asia. Unlike the World War II era, Hollywood did not produce films geared toward national unity or providing explanation or support to the Vietnam War effort. Similarly, entertainment television programming largely avoided setting shows in Southeast Asia. It is the comic books that had the most consistent coverage of the Vietnam War. And even pro-war comics sometimes demonstrated the frustration of American troops fighting a guerrilla war so far from home. Not even military recruiting advertising wholeheartedly embraced images of combat for its campaigns. War became such a controversial topic that both television and Hollywood studios avoided producing military stories until after 1970.

As Beth Bailey explains, "In the years following World War II a large standing peacetime military had been justified — against national tradition and inclination — by the threat of the Soviet Union and communist expansion."[25] Though American society certainly militarized in many respects during the first two decades of the Cold War, Americans did not define the changes in their society or themselves as militarism. They continued to identify themselves as fundamentally anti-militaristic, a perception reflected in much of the popular culture of this period. It is useful to explore this earlier era of militarization in order to understand its evolution in American culture since the 1980s.

1

POSTWAR TRIBUTES,
1945–1950

Taking a swig of grappa (an Italian moonshine) the haggard, unshaven captain glances back down at the paper on the table. He is writing letters to the families of the fallen in a candle-lit cave down the mountainside from Monte Cassino in Italy. Captain Walker looks up at war correspondent Ernie Pyle sitting across the table from him and confides, "The new kids that come up, that's what gets to you... Some of them have just got a little fuzz on their faces. They don't know what it's about. Scared to death. You know, Ernie. I know it ain't my fault that they get killed, but it makes me feel like a murderer." This scene from the movie *The Story of G.I. Joe* (1945) becomes even more heartbreaking for the audience when, at the end of the picture, Captain Walker himself becomes yet another casualty of war. Burgess Meredith, playing the part of Ernie Pyle, intones over the closing, "For those beneath the wooden crosses, there is nothing we can do, except perhaps to pause and murmur, 'Thanks, pal, thanks.'"[1]

American culture during the postwar era exhibited both militarist and anti-militarist sentiments. Even as Congress approved a peacetime draft and increased the manpower of the postwar armed forces, most Americans continued to believe themselves and their country to be anti-militarist. In accordance with this perception, military recruiting advertising often emphasized characteristics or conditions of military service that paralleled civilian life. In popular culture, Americans did not glorify or romanticize war, but they did highly praise soldiers and their sacrifices. The emphasis on the citizen-solider became a key venue by which Americans continued to believe themselves anti-militarist even when supporting more militaristic defense policies.

Postwar Definition of Militarism

National polls, contemporary observers, and Department of Defense surveys reveal the complexity of Americans' thoughts and attitudes toward the military, which point both to a growing militarization of and continued anti-militarism in American society. Americans of the post–World War II era understood militarism in reference to the authoritarian regimes the nation had fought against in World War II. Americans believed that militarist nations deployed their armies aggressively to expand power and that the military became the models for these societies.[2] Right after World War II, Americans routinely referenced the "aggressive military regime" or aggressive war waged by Japan and Germany.[3] One editorialist warned that "preparation for war as the chief instrument of foreign policy" would lead the United States straight into militarism.[4]

References such as these continued into the 1950s. One American reporter described the army of Nazi Germany as "a power unto itself" and as a "state within a state" existing outside of constitutional and civilian authority.[5] Further, this German army imposed its values of obedience, duty, and collective sacrifice on German society. The German army popularized the idea that war was "the source of the noblest virtues"[6] or "the most ennobling of man's endeavors."[7] Americans associated regimentation of society with militarism and worried that it could undermine democracy.[8] Other references to militarism correlate it with "unthinking obedience."[9] To protect against such militarism Americans believed that "civilian control of the armed forces is essential to the survival of any democratic government."[10] Americans, therefore, understood militarism or a militarist state to include the aggressive use of a military force; the military's possession of power outside of civilian authority or constitutional limits; and the military's imposition upon society of regimentation and values that would undermine democracy.

Citizen-soldiers fit nicely into American perceptions of anti-militarism, but regulars did not. Some editorials staunchly opposed the regular military having any influence after World War II. As one stated, "Congress cannot ... continue to regard the armed forces as the mere private preserve of West Point and Annapolis graduates."[11] Indeed, Congress and institutions of higher education both supported the Reserve Officers Training Corps (ROTC) program specifically to "civilianize" the military by promoting officers trained at civilian universities rather than the service academies.[12]

An End to War Films

As World War II drew to a close, filmmakers sought to get closer to the misery of the combat experience, though they still faced considerable restraints on language and visual effects imposed by an industry production code. Their efforts created films which were unsentimental about the war, but quite sentimental toward the men who fought in it. As historian Peter Kindsvatter explains, the returning World War II veteran thought that "because his country had sent him to war, he believed that he deserved recognition for his sacrifices and accomplishments," which is what many of these films did.[13] Many movies focused on the infantry, which was "the most *un*romantic kind of soldiering," according to one veteran.[14] These stories portrayed the muddy, gritty, everyday details of war. *The Story of G.I. Joe* and *A Walk in the Sun* presented anti-militaristic versions of World War II by focusing on citizen-soldiers, volunteerism, individualism, and the unromantic aspects of war.

During the war years, the typical depiction of G.I.s showed them as regular men who just wanted to survive the war and go home. War correspondent Ernie Pyle's influential newspaper columns, written from the infantryman's perspective, created the image of a downtrodden, enduring, and suffering combat soldier.[15] Independent producer Lester Cowan approached the War Department about making a film based on Pyle's columns, which became *The Story of G.I. Joe* (1945).[16] In it, a company of soldiers slog its way first through North Africa and then through Italy, patrolling, assaulting enemy positions, and just waiting for the next engagement. Pyle (Burgess Meredith) remarks that infantry "lives miserably and dies miserably." Given the amount of soaking rain the men endure, the constant shelling from German positions on Monte Cassino, and the psychological trauma of battle, the audience must wonder how anyone survived it in the film or in real life. Indeed, Sergeant Steve Warnicki does have a mental breakdown in the film when he finally gets to hear the sound of his baby son's voice on a phonograph record. War is not ennobling; it takes a severe psychological toll. The men fight out of a sense of duty, not because of love of war.[17]

Focusing on the plight of the men rather than the war, Thomas Pryor, a film critic for the *New York Times*, praised *The Story of G.I. Joe* as a "richly deserved tribute to the infantry soldier."[18] He believed the film captured the struggles of the "tired, desperate" soldiers fighting for democracy.[19] The film so moved Pryor that he went to see it a second time and wrote a second review of it. This time, he emphasized that there were no heroics or romanticism of war in the film. He explains, "The desperateness of warfare is all too evident in the vacant faces of the men as they stagger down from the lines in ankle-deep mud," and concluded that *The Story of G.I. Joe* was "cinema at its adult best."[20] Pryor does not believe that the film romanticizes war or creates false heroics. By including these observations, Pryor is also articulating an anti-militarist belief that war is not about glory or glorification of combat.

The film critic for *Time* magazine, a generally politically conservative periodical, claimed that Pyle and the other war reporters guaranteed the film's accuracy. The result, the reviewer determined, was "far & away the least glamorous war picture ever made."[21] Again, the perception here was that the film did not glorify war. If Pyle and other war correspondents' support was not enough, General Dwight D. Eisenhower, Supreme Allied Commander, declared it "the greatest war picture ever seen."[22] When the film was screened for audiences of soldiers in Italy, a *New York Times* correspondent reported that the soldiers praised its authenticity.[23]

Similarly, the novel and film *A Walk in the Sun* presents an unglamorous vision of war. Author Harry Brown had served as a staff sergeant for the London edition of *Yank* magazine during the war. Although missing combat experience himself, he wrote a novel based on stories from the combat veterans in the field.[24] *A Walk in the Sun* dramatizes the experiences of a platoon in the 45th Division from their landing at Salerno through a single day's six-mile advance to a German-held farmhouse. The story begins with death as the neophyte lieutenant receives mortal injuries from a shell explosion on the landing craft. The soldiers do not panic or rush to his rescue, however. Instead, they coolly ruminate on the randomness of death and their inability to control the war. Much of the dialogue reflects a deep fatalism and cynicism. One soldier says, "Everything is simple in the army: you live or you die." They question the significance of the medals

War correspondent Ernie Pyle (left) and actor Burgess Meredith (right), who plays Pyle in the movie, stand together on the set of the United Artists film *The Story of G.I. Joe* (1945) on December 31, 1944. The motion picture is based on Pyle's reporting the war from the perspective of the enlisted infantryman, what one veteran called the most unromantic kind of soldiering. *The Story of G.I. Joe* is one of the first tribute films released after the end of the war (photograph by Bob Landry; Time & Life Pictures/Getty Images).

they might win. When Private Friedman asks Private Rivera if he thinks he will be promoted to corporal, Rivera responds, "I just want to live long enough to make civilian." The desire to return to civilian life is a common anti-militarist theme in World War II films. The men do not want to be in the service. They are only there because they have to be.[25] War is a necessity, not an event for glory or adventure. Home, peace, civilian life — these are all presented as better than the military and certainly better than the experiences of war.

A Walk in the Sun won critical praise from *New York Times* film critic Bosley Crowther. He believed the film was "unquestionably one of the fine, sincere pictures about the war."[26] The film reviewer for *Time* magazine agreed that it had "excitement and some feeling of reality," but concluded that the film "never succeeds in being much more than a chamber-music arrangement of *All Quiet on the Western Front.*"[27] *All Quiet on the Western Front* (1930), also directed by Lewis Milestone, depicts the tragedy and waste of human life during World War I. It cautions against the romantic attractions of war by showing a group of young German soldiers become disillusioned with war. They are killed, one after the other.[28] Given that Milestone directed the antimilitary classic, this reviewer contrasted *A Walk in the Sun* with the earlier film's interpretation of war. Both films are similar in message.

Though *They Were Expendable* (1945) openly praises the navy regulars who were on duty at the time of the Japanese attack on the U.S.-held Philippine Islands, it, too, shows the sacrifices and suffering inherent in war. Working closely with the armed forces or serving within them often inspired writers and filmmakers to find ways to thank the men for their service. For instance, the movie's director, John Ford, had served in the U.S. Navy as a combat filmmaker. Other veterans included the screenwriter, Frank Wead, and one of the film's stars, Robert Montgomery. The origins of the film lay with John Ford, who met and served with Montgomery and John Bulkeley while filming the Normandy landings. His admiration for war heroes prompted Ford to make a film about John Bulkeley's PT boats serving General Douglas MacArthur in the Philippines during the opening campaigns of World War II. Although the story is set at the beginning of the war, Garry Wills argues that this film was Ford's farewell to the war, which "had been an exciting and fulfilling time for him."[29] War, however, does not appear so exciting in the movie.

As with many young men at the beginning of war, the sailors in *They Were Expendable* have romantic notions about the glory and excitement of war and cannot wait to get in the fight. They feel bitterly disappointed when they are relegated to messenger duty instead of combat duty. John Wayne's character, Rusty Ryan, agitates for a transfer to a destroyer rather than be stuck on the PT boats. When the PT boats do get their chance to go on a combat mission, Ryan conceals a serious wound in order to fight with his unit. The first taste of combat proves to be a bitter one, however. The crews return to their berths in a somber mood, all enthusiasm gone, as one boat has been sunk and some sailors died on the mission. The initial eagerness to go into battle fades, and it is replaced with a more sober realism of the loss and death that comes with combat.[30]

Traditional gender roles specifically give war as the domain of men and the home as the domain of women. This dichotomy plays throughout *They Were Expendable* as well, with a clear message that women do not belong in war zones. Donna Reed plays Second Lieutenant Sandy Davyss, who stays on Corregidor to care for the wounded even as the Japanese approach. Despite her skill as a nurse, Rusty reveals his disdain for women in the service with his comment that women are "uglied up in those potato bags" of uniforms. All the servicemen at the field hospital want to give the nurses "something to remind them they're women," so they throw a dance for them. All the nurses wear civilian dresses to the event instead of uniforms. The women disappear from the story soon after, and the film refocuses on the men starting the hard slog that will, eventually, win back Corregidor.[31]

Once again *New York Times* reviewer Crowther praised the men in the film. *They Were Expendable* conveyed the "gallantry and daring" of the sailors, he stated.[32] Crowther admired the filmmaker's respect for men doing their jobs for no other reason than from a sense of duty. He lamented the film had not been released during the war years when audiences would have been more receptive to it.[33] The *Time* magazine critic concluded that the film had "achieved a feeling of reality rare in war films" but that it was "long and late" in coming.[34] Each critic focused on praising the men, not the glory of war. Still, *They Were Expendable*, along with *The Story of G.I. Joe* and *A Walk in the Sun*, all performed poorly at the box office. Movie audiences were quite sick of war by that time. Hollywood executives believed that war films had run their course, and studios dramatically reduced the production of combat films.[35] First and foremost, Hollywood made movies to make money, and there was no money in war films in 1945.

Demobilization

World War II required more manpower — 16 million — than ever before in the nation's history. The government used the draft to meet its manpower needs. Though the draft is generally considered militaristic, as a democracy properly uses volunteers, Americans did not perceive that the World War II draft had made the nation militaristic or totalitarian like wartime Germany or Japan.[36] As one editorialist explained, "The common soldier ... even in time of war is a citizen of a democracy."[37] General of the Army George C. Marshall declared that "we have produced a democratic army, one composed of self-respecting soldiers whose spirit has not been crushed."[38] War Department Research Branch surveys bear out Marshall's observation. They demonstrated no "deep-seated sea change in basic interests or personality" of American soldiers returning from the war.[39]

Indeed, the citizen-soldiers themselves proved quite anti-militarist in their beliefs. One survey, conducted in January 1943, asked soldiers if they were in favor of the idea that "after the war the soldiers should take over the country and run it." Only 6 percent were strongly in favor of the idea with an additional 16 percent thinking "it might be a good idea." Some 27 percent believed it was a bad idea and 41 percent stated they were strongly against it.[40] At the end of World War II, other War Department surveys indicated that soldiers rejected militarism. When asked if they would like "to see that the U.S. is so strong that no nations would dare attack us," only 24 percent of soldiers favored that postwar aim. The most popular response, at 42 percent, was a statement supporting nations organizing to prevent wars.[41] Citizen-soldiers had not embraced the military as a result of the war, and the martial experience had not fundamentally altered their democratic belief system.

In true anti-militarist fashion, backed by long-standing American traditions, public opinion, and the desires of the troops themselves, the armed forces demobilized rapidly at the end of the war. Families of American servicemen wanted their loved ones back home as soon as World War II ended. As Lori Lyn Bogle explains, "A highly effective letter writing campaign, promoted by more than two hundred 'Bring Back Daddy' clubs, featuring pictures of GIs' children and an avalanche of baby shoes, convinced many politicians to support accelerated demobilization despite security needs to the contrary."[42] With the war over, servicemen believed it was time to put the war behind them and return to civilian life. The troops themselves wanted out of the service. "The only really great war industry in action today," wrote one contemporary observer, "is that of the enlisted men dreaming up schemes to get out of the Army and Navy in a hurry."[43]

Like their sisters who worked in the war industries, women who served their country in one of the military services were expected to return to the domestic sphere at war's end. The armed forces thanked their women for their service and sent them messages that it was time to return home. In the Army Air Forces film production "Salute To the Ladies," which highlights the work of Flight Nurses, Air Women Army Corps, Women's Air Force Service Pilots, and female civilians, the narrator intones, "Our women are once more free to follow their peaceful pursuits."[44] He reflects that "these women have the unforgettable memory of what it means to fight a modern war. They want no more of it. They want no more interference with the daily pursuits of life."[45] In other words, wartime roles were an aberration, and it was time for women to return to the home, where they belonged. Indeed, it was time for the whole nation to return to their "daily pursuits," not just the women of the armed forces. From this perspective, war is the aberration and peace is the norm for Americans.

When the pace of demobilization slowed in order to maintain manpower levels for occupation duty, American troops publicly demonstrated in January 1946 to quicken the pace of discharges.[46] From a high point of 12 million in 1945, demobilization had reduced troop levels to 1.6 million by June 1947 when demobilization concluded.[47] Americans reasserted the traditional relationship between society and the military, where the citizen-soldiers return home and the professional services draw down significantly for peace.

"We Are Anti-Militarist in Outlook"

When volunteer enlistments did not provide adequate manpower to meet postwar needs, Congress renewed the draft in 1945 and 1946.[48] According to surveys, more than 60 percent of Americans approved the peacetime draft extension, a seemingly marked shift toward militarism.[49] Popular magazines, such as *Life*, supported the peacetime draft to maintain a credible force against the Soviet Union and maintain the nation's prestige.[50] *Life* was part of the publishing empire of Henry Luce, who usually supported Republican policies and politicians and who wanted *Life* to "become a chronicle of the West's (and America's) march to greatness."[51] Already some Americans, such as Luce, were judging the nation's prestige through the militaristic measure of military prowess instead of other measures like economics, education, or science. Nevertheless, supporting the draft did not necessarily mean that Americans consciously embraced militarism. Coming out of World War II, Americans accepted the idea of serving one's nation as a civic duty, but they did not consider this service as necessarily leading to militarism in America. As one editorialist explained, "It is not true, as some pacifists maintain, that the mere possession of a great military establishment, or even universal military service, necessarily places a nation at the mercy of an army caste or leads to aggressive war."[52] Indeed, Americans "do not seek for ourselves one inch of territory in any place in the world."[53] As long as the manpower was not used toward aggressive or imperialistic purposes, it did not fit most Americans' definition of militarism. Of course, what might be considered aggressive or imperialistic might look different to people outside of the United States than to citizens inside of it.

With the wartime alliance with the Soviet Union deteriorating and Americans more supportive of an active foreign policy for the country, most Americans accepted the necessity of a postwar military establishment larger than the prewar one. In a 1946 poll, interviewers asked Americans how large they believed the peacetime Army and Navy should be five years in the future. The respondents cited an average number of one million personnel for each service. This number proved far lower than the size of the eight million-strong Army or the three million-strong Navy during World War II, but it was also significantly higher than the pre-war numbers cited in the survey: 190,000 in the pre-war Army and 140,000 in the pre-war Navy. In the same poll, 80 percent of Americans indicated that they would be willing to have a son join the service for a year and a half to support a military establishment of that size.[54] Nonetheless, postwar military officials perceived widespread indifference among the American people concerning the military and American involvement in international affairs. In addressing the New York National Guard, Brigadier General Ames T. Brown mentioned the "apathy since the war concerning the need for armed forces."[55] Although polls showed support for more militaristic policies, the military did not perceive open public support.

Based on the premise that there might not be enough time to mobilize large numbers of citizens for the next war, President Harry Truman, military planners, and Congress wrestled with the notion of Universal Military Training for the nation's young men.[56] Universal Military Training, or UMT, was meant to produce a ready reserve force of citizen-soldiers rather than large regular force. As the House Post-War Military Policy Committee asserted, "It is traditional in the United States that in time of peace our regular or standing armed forces are reduced to a minimum; that in time of emergency our able-bodied citizens of military age join with the regular forces in bearing arms in the preservation of the national security. This tradition should be maintained and preserved."[57] The House Committee reaffirmed the anti-standing military tradition long held in the United States by stating the nation cannot rely solely upon a standing army for national security. Such a large force would be too expensive, and Americans simply would not choose to join the regulars in sufficient numbers during peacetime. Finally, a large standing force "would be repugnant to the American people."[58] The committee favored peacetime military training with no actual military obligation to serve.

Nonetheless, some anxiety about militarism accompanied the idea of UMT. A Gallup poll taken in November 1945 asked the public, "Do you think that giving military training in this country will result in a group being formed of military men who will try to have too much power?" When this survey was taken, 21 percent of the respondents feared the military would take too much power, while 62 percent of them did not.[59] The fact that the armed forces in

World War II remained democratic might have mitigated against suspicion of peacetime training or the rise of power-hungry professionals. There were relatively few regular soldiers around, and some of these were among the most respected public figures of the time, such as Dwight D. Eisenhower. One commentator described Eisenhower as having combined "brilliance on the battlefield with true compassion and a repugnance for war which does credit to his qualities of heart and mind."[60] It is the repugnance for war which made regulars like Eisenhower safe for a democratic nation.

Nevertheless, 21 percent of the respondents worried about the military gaining too much power, and this anxiety did not completely subside. Opposition to Universal Military Training came from both the political left and right. The liberal opinion magazine *New Republic* firmly opposed the proposal. The editors likened Universal Military Training to "rearmament and militarization." Further, the editorialists worried that it would move the United States "toward a police state"; finally, they cautioned that "preparation for war leads to war."[61] Staunch liberal and former vice-president Henry Wallace denounced universal military service as "more dangerous to American democracy than the [House] Un-American Activities Committee, with all its threats to our civil liberties" because it "could be the entering wedge to military fascism in the U.S."[62] Wallace disliked the militaristic aspects of the armed forces, including their "authoritarian practices and emphasis on unquestioning obedience."[63] Most liberal-leaning Christian churches opposed military influence in citizens' lives, though evangelical churches supported the draft to fight communism.[64] Opposition to UMT came from conservatives as well. Speaking from the political right, Republican Senator Robert Taft complained, "Military training by conscription means the complete regimentation of the individual" among other evils.[65]

General George Marshall addressed concerns about militarism by stating, "To those who fear the Army might militarize our young men and indoctrinate them with dangerous conceptions.... I submit the evidence of our present armies.... Their minds have not be warped — quite the contrary."[66] Marshall, who had supported Universal Military Training as early as 1919, argued that "it would be the most democratic expression of our national life."[67] He followed this argument with an invocation to George Washington, who supported such military training for the new nation.[68] While the American Legion and other similar groups supported Universal Military Training, the major labor unions and other civic organizations opposed it. Ultimately, Congress failed to adopt Universal Military Training thanks to the effective opposition lobbying effort orchestrated by labor, clergy, and academic organizations.[69]

With the failure of UMT, the armed forces depended on volunteers to fill manpower needs. Unfortunately for defense planners, the nation's veterans and its young men did not flock to the flag to volunteer for military service. Even though Truman and the Congress had allowed the draft to expire in 1947, too few volunteers forced lawmakers to reinstate conscription in 1948.[70] Since the Army had the greatest manpower needs, most draftees became soldiers. Many American men simply did not want to join the Army when they had other — civilian — options.

In 1948, public opinion researcher Albert Somit observed, "Most Americans would agree that as a people we are anti-militarist in outlook. We have never favored a large peacetime army, we have expressed a dislike of war as an instrument of national policy."[71] Another editorialist echoed the sentiment: "As a nation we have sought to avoid war, to find alternatives to war, and to create conditions which make war unnecessary."[72] Clearly, anti-militarism affected postwar defense policies and remained a core identity for many Americans.

General George C. Marshall served as U.S. Army Chief of Staff during World War II, and later as Secretary of State and Secretary of Defense during the administration of President Harry Truman. A highly respected officer, Marshall supported Universal Military Training (UMT) against critics who argued it would militarize American society. The critics proved more persuasive as Congress failed to pass UMT. Marshall is pictured here, circa 1944 (Library of Congress).

"The War Is Over, Derry"

Returning home from World War II was not without difficulties for many veterans. One of the greatest anxieties of both veterans and civilians after World War II was the potential return of the Great Depression. In a June 1945 poll, 56 percent of soldiers indicated they expected a depression to return after the war. Only 29 percent thought a depression would not come back.[73]

Some of the postwar Hollywood films captured this anxiety. In one of the late scenes in *The Story of G.I. Joe*, Private Dondaro, with a hard expression on his face and a menacing tone in his voice, demands that Ernie Pyle help him find a job at the end of the war. Ernie has nothing to say in response.

The Best Years of Our Lives (1946) also captures postwar fears as it highlights the difficulties faced by three returning World War II veterans as they readjust to their civilian lives. The film addresses unemployment, alcoholism, and family readjustment issues. The goal of these men is to shed their military identities and resume their civilian lives, but it is not easy for them. The three veterans in the story continue to meet up with each other to maintain their comfort zone when reintegrating into civilian life becomes difficult. They use each other as mental and emotional "crutches."[74]

Of the three men, Army Air Forces Captain Fred Derry (Dana Andrews) has the most volatile transition to the civilian world. Prior to the war, he had been a soda jerk in a local drugstore, but had found prestige and respect as a bombardier. The film plays on the veterans' fears of joblessness and loss of standing in postwar society when Fred can find no employment except for his old job. It soon becomes clear that Fred's snappy military uniform had been the only thing that attracted his young wife, Marie (Virginia Mayo). During his absence, she had worked at a night club, and there is an implication that she had been unfaithful. A soda jerk's low pay cannot fund Marie's expensive tastes, and she divorces him. After an altercation with a customer at the drugstore, Fred loses even this paltry job. His redemption comes from the new postwar world of the suburb. Fred lands a job building prefabricated homes made from scrapped bombers, which restores his sense of self-worth. It also means dismantling the weapons of war and his wartime identity for the new postwar civilian world of the suburbs.

The sailor, Homer Parrish (Harold Russell), has a hard transition because of his wartime injuries. Metal hooks replaced the hands he lost when his ship sank in the Pacific. Once home, however, Homer has trouble accepting assistance from his family. He acts out his frustrations by becoming violent at times and pushes away his hometown sweetheart, Wilma (Cathy O'Donnell). When his father helps Homer take off his harness at night, Homer reflects that at that point each day he is completely dependent on others. He wonders if a "real" man could be so vulnerable. Only after Wilma sees his disability and her love remains steadfast does Homer begin to accept himself, his manhood, her love, and the possibility of a life together with her. He successfully makes the transition to civilian life at the end of the film when he marries Wilma to begin their new postwar life together.

Army sergeant Al Stephenson (Fredric March) returns home to a family that grew up in his absence, and he struggles with alcoholism in his readjust-

Sergeant Al Stephenson (Fredric March, center) returns home to wife of 20 years Milly (Myrna Loy, left), and his grown-up daughter Peggy (Teresa Wright, right). Like many veterans, Al copes with the changes in his life and the stresses of re-integrating into civilian society. The other servicemen featured in the movie deal with divorce, joblessness, and adjustments to amputations. *The Best Years of Our Lives* (RKO, 1946) (RKO Radio Pictures/Archive Photos/Getty Images).

ment to civilian life. He meets his wife of 20 years, Milly (Myrna Loy), and his two grown children (Teresa Wright and Michael Hall), and he can hardly believe the changes in their lives. The maid had walked off years ago for a defense job, his daughter studied "home economics" and worked at the hospital, and his son learned about atomic weapons in high school. While Al struggles with drinking too much, his biggest adjustment comes when he goes back to his banking job. He finds the transition from killing Japanese to making money difficult. Al helps a former Seabee secure a loan at the bank even though the ex-serviceman has no collateral. Al's boss makes it clear that he should no longer extend the bank's credit to such a risk. Al fumes at the injustice and lectures his banker colleagues that they must gamble on the future of the country: the former servicemen. These former citizen-soldiers know what it takes to survive, succeed, and prosper in the civilian world because they had survived the war. The war had not made them a liability society, as some feared. They could, indeed, become an integral part of the new postwar economy as citizens.

In the end, each veteran makes a successful adjustment to civilian life, which offers a message of hope for postwar audiences. The war had not fundamentally changed American society, according to this interpretation. Both critics and audiences enjoyed the film. *The Best Years of Our Lives* became a box-office hit and netted seven Oscars from the industry, including Best Picture, Best Screenplay, and Best Actor (March).[75] Additionally, the film came at the height of Hollywood movie attendance, so its popularity meant that record numbers of Americans saw it.[76]

"The Most Democratic Organization in the World"

Postwar recruiters tried several tactics, both militaristic and anti-militaristic, to fill the ranks with volunteers. One tactic was to play off of veterans' postwar anxieties, making the military appear more dependable than the uncertainty of civilian life. A Navy handbook, styled in comic book format, exemplified the way the military services framed their advertising to play off of working-class concerns in particular. "The Fable of Whyte Hatt, Civilian" focuses on the fears of losing prestige and of not having a place in civilian society. Seaman Hatt envisions a postwar life as a junior executive, living in a plush apartment in the big city. The fable debunks each of his assumptions about civilian life. Hatt discovers first that clothing and drugstore items are much more expensive in the civilian world than in the Navy. Thinking that he has been cheated in some way, he declares to the clerk in language uncharacteristic of either sailors or the working class, "It is fortunate, Peter, that you are an old friend of mine, or I should have to treat you as a common profiteer and deal harshly with you."[77] His attempts at securing a luxury apartment prove futile, and he settles for a rundown place with a lumpy bed.

Hatt's employment prospects also prove disappointing, as he can only find an assembly-line manufacturing job with little hope for promotion. He feels cheated once again when taxes, dues, and insurance deduct too much from his paycheck. His economical diet — a peanut butter and jelly sandwich — makes him nostalgic for Navy chow. Hatt daydreams about his shipmates and liberties taken in New York, San Francisco, and Hong Kong, and he promptly decides to reenlist. The recruiting pitch closes with a moral, just like at the end of children's fables: "The grass always *looks* greener on the other side of the fence!"[78] Recruiters painted a rosy picture of Navy service in which a working-class fellow could live a middle-class life. The advertise-

He is thinking of his shipmates, Jughead and Butch, of the
swell bull sessions, of liberties in Brooklyn, liberties in Frisco,
liberties in Hong Kong. He is thinking of how the bay at Rio
had looked the night they dropped their hook near Sugar Loaf.

He thinks of what his division officer says about his making
a rate pretty soon if he sticks around. A 3rd class gets about 60
bucks every two weeks, all spending stuff. And no landlady, no
doctors, no deductions.

On this page of a post-war recruiting pamphlet, released between 1945 and 1947, Seaman Whyte Hatt daydreams nostalgically about the good life he used to have in the Navy, as opposed to his high-priced, dead-end existence as a civilian. Recruiting advertisements like this one often played off of fears, such as joblessness or the draft, and showed how the military could get someone ahead in life (National Archives and Records Administration).

ment, however, left out the danger, discipline, regimentation, and other drawbacks to military life.

Some themes were overtly militaristic, playing up the presumed prestige of military service. These advertisements tapped into the camaraderie that servicemen had developed during the war and suggested that these friendships would continue and new ones would form. Those men who responded to the call of duty would be assured honor, respect, and the admiration of the American people.[79] These advertisements were not nearly persuasive enough to garner sufficient volunteers to stave off the draft.

An emphasis on technology and national security was one of the more militaristic themes in the advertising. The Navy considered itself "a vast technical and mechanical organization — one of the greatest in the world" and assured Americans that it would continue to use its expertise to protect and secure the country.[80] The Army emphasized its technical prowess, reminding Americans of its role in developing radar, electronics, aviation, and other advances. It also happens that these same advancements benefited the American public.[81] So, even in the area of technology and national security, there was a connection with the civilian world.

Along with these more militaristic themes, the Navy presented itself as a democratic institution rather than the rigid, regimented hierarchy that it actually was. "Strange as it may seem," one brochure boasted, the Navy "is the most democratic organization in the world, where your success as an individual is entirely dependent on your ability."[82] It reflects the individualism and meritocracy Americans associated with their country. The Navy was trying to counter images of rigidity and regimentation and replace them with images of independent action and accountability.[83] In other words, it assured the public that the military was democratic.

To their credit, the armed forces did make some reforms to improve service life, such as basing promotions on merit rather than seniority and overhauling the military justice system.[84] A Gallup poll revealed that 72 percent of Americans and 78 percent of World War II veterans supported reforms aimed at democratizing the armed forces through equalizing food, clubs, and social privileges for enlisted men and officers.[85] As the Army continued to rely on draftees, the men who served in this "new" Army were considered "citizen-soldiers." As New York Times correspondent Russell Porter explained, "The 'new' Army is not satisfied with mere unthinking obedience; it wants willing and intelligent cooperation from the new citizen-soldier."[86] Again, the Army wanted to assure the public, too, that it was a democratic institution.

Even with these changes and assurances, many World War II veterans refused to reenlist. When asked before the war ended, a mere 3 percent of soldiers had given any indication that they wanted a career in the military. The War Department's Research Branch found in survey after survey that the men wanted to return to civilian life.[87] When asked by Gallup pollsters after the war if they would return to their branch of service if pay increased significantly, 74 percent of veterans declined. "Whyte Hatt" notwithstanding, more than a paycheck would be needed to entice veterans back into uniform. Interviewers also asked veterans what they had liked about their wartime service, and 47 percent indicated some combination of experience, education, training, and discipline. The things veterans disliked included the regimentation and discipline, the most militarist aspects of service life.[88] As most World War II veterans were citizens turned soldiers, it is unsurprising that so many chose to return to civilian life. Given centuries of an anti-standing military tradition and a culture based on individualism, it is also predictable that many of them disapproved of the rigidity of military life.

Postwar Military Policy

Postwar legislation significantly altered the organization of the armed forces. The National Security Act of 1947 and its 1949 amendments restructured the military establishment. Congress separated the air branch from the Army, creating an independent Air Force, and they codified the service roles and missions, thus guaranteeing the existence of the Marine Corps. Congress further created a secretary of defense, a single Department of Defense, and a chairman of the Joint Chiefs of Staff. On July 26, 1948, President Truman signed an executive order establishing "equality of treatment and opportunity for all persons in the armed services without regard to race, color, religion, or national origin."[89] Not until the Korean War, however, did the military services truly integrate their forces.

Few young men willingly chose military service over civilian life. Enlistments remained low until a new selective service law went into effect in the summer of 1948. Males between 19 and 26 years of age were eligible for the draft, although the legislation exempted veterans, reservists, and national guardsmen. It had a sunset provision to expire in 1950. Polls indicate the majority of Americans supported the new draft law.[90] Prior to the new policy, enlistments per month ranged between 4,000 and 10,000. After the legislation, the numbers shot up to 20,000 per month, with three-quarters of the recruits being first-time enlistees.[91] Selective Service draft calls provided the incentive for young men to volunteer for the service branch of their choice. Few willingly chose to volunteer otherwise. While the draft plugged holes primarily in the Army's manpower needs, induction calls remained fairly low due to Truman's austere defense budgets. Such a small percentage of men were selected each month that the Army suspended draft calls in early 1949.

Another question about manpower loomed during the postwar era: should women continue to serve in the armed forces? Despite the widespread idealization that a woman's natural place is in the home, most civilian Americans at the time accepted that women could serve in the armed forces. In 1947, a Gallup poll indicated that 53 percent of Americans, both men and women, approved of females serving in the armed forces. Still, 35 percent opposed the idea.[92] Although many men in the military disliked the idea of women serving, key military figures supported a permanent position for them, including Chief of Staff Omar Bradley and his predecessor, Dwight Eisenhower.[93] In explaining his own change in attitude, Eisenhower remembered that he had been "'horror struck' at the thought of women serving in the Army" at the beginning of World War II, but concluded that, in the end, their contributions had proved vital.[94] He added that in the next war "women would have to be drafted as well as the men."[95] Military planners and most Americans believed that the next war would likely be a full-scale war with the Soviet Union. In an age of total war with the nation's very survival at stake, all sectors of society — including women — would be called upon to serve.

In 1947, the Army-Navy Nurse Act authorized permanent places for female nurses in those services. In 1948, Truman signed into law the Women's Armed Services Act, which established permanent regular duty roles for women. By 1949, women could join line components in the Army, Navy, Air Force, and Marines; the Nurse Corps in the Army, Navy, and Air Force; and women's medical specialist corps in the Army and the Air Force.[96] Many of the wartime jobs remained open to women in the peacetime armed forces, but women were prohibited from combat and restricted in their authority over men.[97] In addition, the laws imposed a 2-percent ceiling for women's strength among regular ranks so that women would not rush to join the military services. Policymakers did not fully understand the social and cultural pressures for women to wed and raise families because women did not dash off to join the armed forces. None of the services or the Organized Reserves reached the numbers to fill that modest 2 percent of manpower, not even during the Korean War. Women barely constituted one percent of the armed forces' total manpower.[98]

"Double Duty Americans"

Advertising and public relations became areas for increased military presence in American life. The armed forces plastered the print media and the airwaves with ads in a massive recruiting campaign. Over 11,000 periodicals nationwide contributed free advertising space. Widely circulated national magazines, such as *Collier's*, *Life*, and the *Saturday Evening Post*, donated free full-page advertising for military recruiting aimed at the middle class. Periodicals such as *Popular Science* and *Varsity* targeted high school graduates.[99]

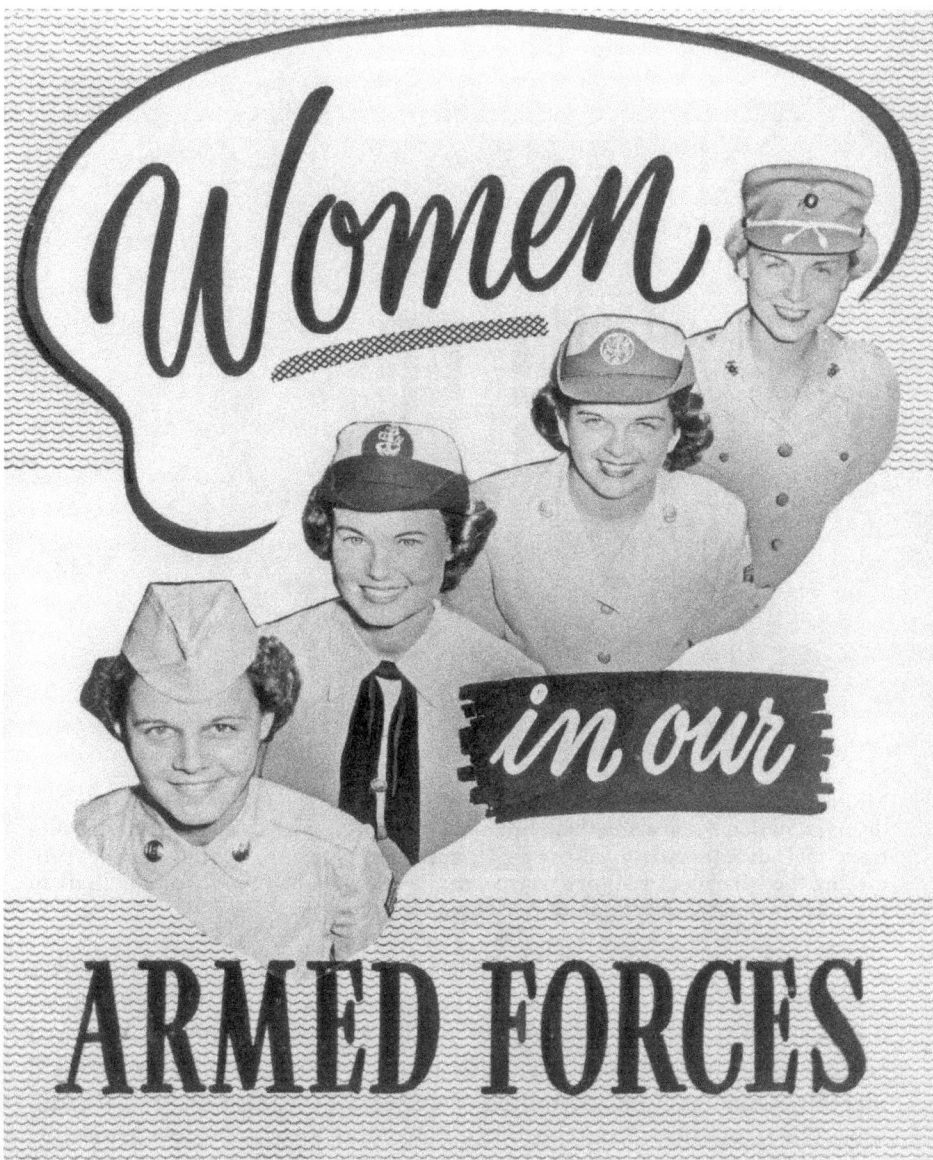

In 1948, President Harry Truman signed into law the Women's Armed Services Act, which established a permanent place for women in the active duty force, though the number of women in the services was capped at 2 percent. This July 1951 advertisement showcases each of the women's services. From left to right: Women's Army Corps (WAC) Corporal Suzanne McKeffer, Women Accepted for Emergency Volunteer Service (WAVES) Navy Chief Virginia A.E. Jackson, Women's Air Force (WAF) Sergeant Dorothea Wunderlich, and Marine Private First Class Evelyn Crumlish. Despite advertisements such as this one, none of the armed services were able to recruit enough women to meet the 2 percent ceiling (FPG Archive Collection/Getty Images).

Military recruiting drives included advertisements through radio, posters, window displays, national magazines, and billboards such as this 1950 billboard advertising travel and adventure in the U.S. Army. Despite these peacetime recruiting drives promoting the benefits of military service, the Army often had to rely on the draft to maintain manpower levels (Hulton Archive/Getty Images).

The Advertising Council provided posters, bus cards, and window displays as well as advertising spots for recruiting messages on top-rated radio shows broadcast on 900 radio stations nationwide. The Army and Air Force hired an advertising agency to manage their paid advertising for newspapers and magazines, and as funds permitted, the agency purchased additional radio time. The Navy and Marine Corps continued to rely exclusively on free public service airtime, though they also retained an advertising agency to coordinate their advertising efforts.[100] The military services recorded their bands to play on radio and later television, and stars sometimes donated their time to plug recruiting drives.[101]

In order to extend their reach further, the military services contacted national organizations such as the Knights of Columbus, the Veterans of Foreign Wars, the Sons and Daughters of the American Revolution, the American Legion, Kiwanis, Lions, and others to advocate military service in local communities. Local recruiting efforts included band performances, displays in high schools, and exhibitions at state and county fairs.[102] Public relations activities assisted recruiting efforts by raising the profile of the services. For instance, the Navy sponsored model airplane building competitions. The Department of Defense created a program that invited Boy Scouts to camp at various military bases.[103] The Marine Corps Reserves began the "Toys for Tots" program to collect Christmas gifts for poor children.[104] All of this amounted to significant advertising and public awareness for the armed forces and a much more visible role for the military in American life. Scholars assert these developments point to the militarization of American society. When one looks closely at the images contained in these advertisements, however, it is clear that the armed forces were downplaying combat, regimentation, and other aspects of military service that were unlike civilian life and playing up those aspects of military service that parallel the civilian world.

Advertising targeted middle-class parents and their young adult children to persuade them that military jobs and careers were appropriate. In a traditionally anti-militarist society, it was not a given that military service was an acceptable job. Advertising attempted to project an image of the military as composed of good, dependable, democratic citizens.[105] Although promoting military service, advertisers toned down references to combat to focus more on qualities related to leadership, management, or the corporate workplace, which made the military look more like a regular civilian career. In other words, the military services made themselves appear more civilian and, therefore, more appropriate for a democracy.

One recruiting tactic recast the military services as another arm of corporate America. A Navy advertisement frankly stated, "The World is Your Office" and illustrated the idea quite literally: it pictured a sailor sitting at a desk perched on top of the planet earth. It called for volunteers for the Navy's "world-wide offices" to take "white collar jobs ... where you can serve yourself and your country."[106] Air Force advertising started to refer to the sky as its "office."[107] An Army recruiting advertisement pictured a hand pinning a gold bar on a newly minted second lieutenant. The text read in part, "And now he's an executive in the nation's most important business."[108] The overall effect of this rhetoric made the military "seem more corporate, more American, more familiar," according to one historian.[109] Instead of making distinctions of how different military life was from the civilian world, these advertisements portrayed the military as akin to a regular, civilian career.

Although the Army continued to depict soldiers in combat, it softened the images from the war years. One advertisement called for men who were managers and who could "bring out the best in every blessed man under him."[110] He would be a teacher and a guidance counselor, listening "with his heart to some young fellow's personal problems."[111] An ad that pictured non-commissioned officers in combat fatigues, practicing marksmanship, was coupled with a caption that read, "Today's non-commissioned and commissioned officers must have leadership ability, specialized knowledge, and human understanding of men."[112] This created a new image for the Army. These men were physically and mentally combat ready, but they were also leaders with sensitivities to the human needs of soldiers, qualities appropriate for civilian life and for soldiers in an anti-militaristic democracy.

Where the Army focused on people, the Air Force and Navy focused far more on impersonal technology and used more militaristic language.[113] One Air Force ad pictured a sleek, stylized plane over a background of advanced mathematic equations. The text indicated that the "long, mysterious-looking equations" constituted the principles of jet propulsion, a "force that is opening the battle of the century."[114] Indeed, women had to compete with technology for their men's attention. A recruiting film suggested that an airman's girlfriend would have to wait because "he's got a date with a lady at Williams Air Force Base in Arizona. She's pretty, single engined, and one of the fastest things in the sky! She's the F-51."[115] How could a mere girl compete against the beauty and power of a F-51 Mustang? The Air Force was also ready to challenge nature itself, preparing to break through the sound barrier as well as overcoming rain, snow, and fog.[116]

The Navy had traditionally been the high-tech military branch, so the service did not take the Air Force's challenge lightly. It advertised its position on the vanguard of science and technology. The Navy claimed to have more aircraft models that operated in more diverse conditions than the Air Force. Unlike the newly independent air arm, the Navy had a long tradition of pioneering in aviation. The naval service boasted that it put the first plane across the Atlantic Ocean, first landed aircraft on ships, and pioneered the catapult for launching aircraft.[117] Indeed, Navy and Air Force officials viciously competed with one another over the defense budget, particularly between the Air Force's B-36 bomber program and the Navy's "super carriers." When the secretary of defense canceled the production of the Navy's aircraft carrier USS *United States*, high-ranking naval officers leaked documents critical of the Air Force's B-36 program and appealed directly to the public in articles in such popular magazines as the *Saturday Evening Post*. This "revolt of the admirals" led to a Congressional inquiry, and several officers had their careers ended as a result of the incidents.[118]

America's reserve forces, the National Guard and the Organized Reserve demonstrated the most self-conscious anti-militarism of the armed forces. They defined the serviceman's image to suit their needs, showing the history, loyalty, and effectiveness of citizen-soldiers. Guard advertising built up an image of a citizen-soldier who was supremely loyal, dedicated, and physically and mentally robust. The National Guard tied together the frontier past and modern-day imagery. In one ad, a coonskin-capped frontier fighter with Bowie knife and musket stands next to a uniformed present-day Guardsman with rifle. This "New National Guard" constituted "modern minutemen" who were made "of the same stuff as their famous forebears" and were "ready on instant notice to leap to the defense of home and country."[119] Like the Army's "modern minutemen," the men of the Air Force Reserve would be ready to defend the nation "at a moment's notice."[120] Army Organized Reserve advertising referred to its soldiers as "Double-Duty" Americans, ones who would make "a personal contribution to our nation's strength" through reserve activity.[121] Both Air Force and Navy reserve branches referred to their citizen-soldiers as "weekend warriors."[122] National Guardsmen and Reservists could defend their country as well as live in the civilian world. Though none of these recruiting materials specifically mentions the draft, the "guard did appeal to young men to serve with buddies or neighbors, with the implication clearly being that they would not have to serve with strange draftees in far away places for two years," explains William Donnelly.[123]

"Breaks Its Promises"

No matter how well the recruiters advertised military life as good as or better than civilian life, enlistees and draftees continued to recognize a distinct difference between the two—and much preferred civilian life. One survey compiled data on one-year enlistees in the Marine Corps in 1948 and 1949 and measured perceptions between military and civilian life. When asked how they first became interested in the Marine Corps, the men indicated by a wide margin that friends and acquaintances had the most influence on their decision to enlist. About a quarter of the men stated that recruiting posters, radio, or newspapers first attracted them to the Corps. Although movie attendance was high, the young men did not credit films as a significant influence on their decisions to join.[124]

The marines in this survey had just begun their service, so they had not yet experienced much of military life. Their reasons for enlisting, however, were fresh in their minds. Most of the recruits had enlisted in the Marine Corps for "education, the desire to learn a trade, and the opportunity for self-improvement," mostly skills transferable to a civilian career.[125] Some acknowledged that they felt pressured by the draft. The questionnaire included "self-discipline, self-improvement, and the challenge of Marine Corps life" in the same category, which indicates that some men might have been attracted by the demanding and elite image of the Marine Corps.[126] Becoming a Marine, however, did not translate into becoming a combatant for these young men. When asked what jobs they most wanted, enlistees indicated motor transport, aviation, engineering, and communications, not infantry, which was the core identity of the Marines. They did not want staff work, either.[127] Each of the desired occupations included a technical skill that could be translated later into a civilian job, and each of these occupation specialties were among the least martial jobs in the service.

A follow-up questionnaire of the enlistees conducted a year later determined that one year's experience in the Marine Corps negatively affected their attitudes. The results of the second survey proved so drastically different from the initial questionnaire that researchers thought that the initial survey might have been skewed. At the beginning of their enlistment, 21 percent of the recruits had indicated they would reenlist, but a year later only 1 percent wanted to follow through. In terms of comparing military and civilian life, the recruits now clearly favored the latter. For instance, in the first survey, 81 percent believed the military provided better job security than civilian employment. This percentage dropped to 48 percent a year later, with a corresponding increase in those believing civilian jobs offered more security. The researchers observed a similar shift in every comparison between perceptions of military and civilian life. A majority of the enlistees did not think that the Corps utilized their skills or knowledge, took their preferences or past experiences into consideration, or educated and trained them adequately.[128] Additionally, they "believed that they were performing more than their share of menial or undesirable jobs."[129] As a result, the enlistees thought that they had not been given an opportunity to prove themselves.[130] Clearly, these young men neither believed they had benefited from their experiences nor had they been enamored of life in the Marine Corps.

Army enlistees similarly found civilian life preferable to a military existence. In one survey, the most common motivation to leave the Army was a desire to pursue further education in civilian life. Others wanted to escape the rigidity and discipline, which they perceived as constraining their personal freedom or as interfering with family life. Some soldiers became bitter toward the Army, believing that it "breaks its promises," probably a reference to unfulfilled guarantees made by recruiters.[131] Others simply found their job assignments unsatisfactory. All was not lost for the Army, however. Some soldiers and officers truly enjoyed Army life. Others found the retirement benefits, job security, and financial rewards superior to what they believed they could find in the civilian world.[132] In the end, the majority of servicemen preferred life in the civilian world and preferred the individualism of civilian life over the regimentation of military life.

Despite the heavy emphasis on advertising, it did not appear to have much effect on the target audience, at least according to one Air Force survey. The responses indicate that the most influential source for prompting a young man to enlist was recruiters (65 percent), followed by friends in the Air Force (41 percent), and Air Force veterans (33 percent). Recruiting advertising had much less of an influence on enlistment. When asked directly if magazines, radio, newspapers "had the most to do with getting you enlisted," the airmen rated each around 1 to 2 percent.[133]

While the advertising might not have prompted an enlistment, most of the airmen remembered getting a favorable impression of the Air Force from these sources. Majorities of the enlistees remembered seeing or hearing recruiting advertising and recalled that recruiting posters, magazine ads, and radio spots gave them a sympathetic view of the air service. Although the airmen stated that friends and Air Force veterans influenced their decision to enlist, only 65 percent said that talking to friends in the service gave them a favorable impression of the Air Force. Talking to veterans specifically proved a positive influence for 53 percent of the servicemen.[134] Servicemen and veterans no doubt gave a more realistic appraisal of service life, both good and bad, than the recruiters did. It is impossible to measure how many young men spoke with active duty servicemen or veterans and did not enlist, however. The servicemen and veterans may have turned off as many or more young men than actually enlisted. Volunteer enlistments were simply unpopular with young men, and those who did enlist strongly preferred their civilian lives. These reactions are expected from a society steeped in anti-militarism.

Not Yet a Good War

One characteristic of militarism is the glorification of war as exciting, ennobling, or redemptive. During World War II, most soldiers in the conflict believed that the war was necessary, but they harbored no enthusiasm for war itself.[135] A distinct interpretation of World War II as a "good war"—a war seen in sentimental or romantic terms—only began to emerge in the late 1940s. At the conclusion of World War II, war correspondent Edward R. Murrow perceived from his fellow Americans that "seldom, if ever, has a war ended leaving the victors with such a sense of uncertainty and fear, with such a realization that the future is obscure and that survival is not assured."[136] In the same vein, Pulitzer-prize winning military correspondent Hanson Baldwin thought the Allies had lost the peace with the onset of the Cold War.

In *Great Mistakes of the War*, written in 1949 in the wake of the Communist triumph in China, Baldwin asserted that President Franklin D. Roosevelt's insistence upon unconditional surrender in World War II proved a fatal mistake. For Germany, unconditional surrender "discouraged opposition to Hitler, probably lengthened the war, cost us lives, and helped lead to the present abortive peace."[137] Further, he believed that the Normandy invasion was shortsighted, as "it would have been to the interest of Britain, the United States, and the world to have allowed — and indeed, to have encouraged — the world's two great dictatorships to fight each other to a frazzle."[138] Not only would this have weakened both the Soviets and the Nazis, but it could have created a secure peace and propelled "the democracies in supreme power in the world, instead of elevating one totalitarianism at the expense of another."[139] Other mistakes caused the loss of Central and Eastern Europe to the Soviets. In the Pacific theater, unconditional surrender proved just as fatal in delaying the Japanese surrender. He states unequivocally that the United States lost its moral leadership by dropping the atomic bombs on Hiroshima and Nagasaki.[140] He closed his book with a warning against militarism: "The German mistake was to think that a military success would solve political problems."[141] For Baldwin, the United States had not achieved a lasting victory in the war. It was not a "good war."

These critical comments about what World War II had accomplished (or failed to accomplish) were not confined to a small number of journalists or opinion makers. In September 1947, the Gallup organization asked Americans, "Do you think it was a mistake for the United States to enter World War II?"[142] Although the majority, 66 percent, supported America's participation in the war, 24 percent of the respondents believed the war had been a mistake. When questioned further, those who did not approve America's entry into the war explained, "We should stay out of other countries' affairs."[143] Some believed that "war is too expensive for our economy," while others concluded, "America got nothing out of the war and is not better off."[144] Some of these comments suggest a postwar retreat into isolationist thought. Concerns about the economic situation make sense in light of the pre-war depression and 1947 recession. Not knowing what the respondents expected in terms of the country being "better off" after the war, it is hard to decipher the meaning of the final statement. Nevertheless, it is clear that these Americans did not perceive World War II in a favorable light.

Even those Americans who supported the country's entry into the war did not express this approval in positive terms. Some respondents justified the war by the practical notion of defending the country after the Japanese attack on Pearl Harbor. Others suggested that "we would probably have been dragged in ultimately anyhow."[145] American culture had not yet developed an idealized version of World War II, and many Americans had not yet perceived many economic, financial, or other benefits in the early postwar years.

When interviewers asked Americans in 1947 whether "the war has generally made your life better or worse," 48 percent of veterans and 35 percent of nonveterans answered that it had made their lives worse. Only 24 and 9 percent, respectively, thought their lives had changed for the better.[146] None of these comments suggests a romantic or glorified perception of World War II.

By the end of the decade, however, Hollywood and television studios began producing more sentimental tributes to World War II servicemen. These stories presented the citizen-soldier in a heroic light and increasingly interpreted the war in triumphant, "good war" terms. Gerald Linderman argues that civilians largely created the morally righteous interpretation of World War II and that veterans conformed to this framework. He asserts that civilian assumptions that war was an exciting, affirmative experience helped bring a more celebratory interpretation to war stories.[147] Still, World War II veterans directly influenced these interpretations and the images of servicemen, war, and the armed forces as authors, screenwriters, directors, and producers of film and television programming.

One of the first popular tributes to World War II servicemen came from the former Supreme Allied Commander and one of the most well-regarded and popular World War II officers, Dwight Eisenhower. He stated his appreciation and gratitude for the servicemen's sacrifices in his memoir, *Crusade in Europe*. Television producers adapted the book into a 26-part documentary broadcast in 1949.[148] Featuring combat footage, the show highlighted the skill, bravery, heroism and actions of the American military in the European theater of operations. It won critical approval, and, although it had a relatively small television audience, it was one of the top-rated programs for the summer.[149]

Another tribute film, *Battleground* (1949), modeled a story that became a standard for American war films: outnumbered and outgunned American citizen-soldiers overcome the odds with their bravery, cleverness, and ingenuity. *Battleground* reenacts a particular historical event, the German encirclement of the 101st Airborne Division at Bastogne during the Battle of the Bulge. The film's producer, Dore Schary, worried that Americans would slip into the same disillusionment that the nation experienced after World War I. As a result, he specifically chose a dramatic event that justified the war's cause and sacrifices.[150] By centering on a heroic stand, the setting already frames the story with significance and meaning. Robert Pirosh wrote the film's Academy Award–winning screenplay, and the story held personal meaning for him. Pirosh had been a master sergeant in the 320th Regiment, 35th Infantry Division, one of the units that had helped relieve the beleaguered 101st Airborne Division. He lifted some elements of the story directly from the diary he kept during the war.[151] As it was shown in *All Quiet on the Western Front*, Pirosh could have depicted a disillusioned version of war, one that reflected the horror of combat. Instead, Pirosh conveyed pride in the men rather than the senselessness of their deaths.

Pirosh's story begins with the arrival of freshly minted replacements, eager to join the glorious "Screaming Eagles." One of them proudly displays his newly sewn patch, saying, "You know who you are when you wear this." Wearing the patch makes him feel special, part of something larger than himself. Unfortunately, Private Layton (Marshall Thompson) is in for a rude awakening when he finally meets the men in his unit. They do not welcome him with open arms. Camaraderie is shared only by the combat veterans, and they do not readily accept replacements because they will probably be killed. To his horror and dismay, Layton's buddy, who was assigned to a different company in the same battalion, is killed by a random German shell in their first engagement. No one in the company had even bothered to learn his friend's name. Layton is so troubled by this oversight, he makes sure someone in his squad at least knows his name.[152]

The clean encampment of the opening scenes quickly gives way to the wintry, rugged Ardennes Forest. Soldiers dig in foxholes, shiver in the cold, and endure German shelling. The filmmakers made sure to include moments of levity, too, such as when a young Mexican soldier, Private Rodriguez (Ricardo Montalban), jumps and plays in the newly fallen snow because he had never seen snow growing up in Los Angeles. As expected in war films about citizen-soldiers, there is a quip or two about returning to the civilian world. Holley (Van Johnson) refers to himself as "P.F.C: Praying for Civilian" rather than its usual meaning, private first class.[153]

Being cut off from American reinforcements and supplies challenges the men's endurance. When Private Holley runs away, other soldiers follow him, turning an act of cowardice — or survival — into a flanking maneuver that results in the capture of several German soldiers. Just as the men prepare to face a German assault with little ammunition and no fuel for the tanks, the sunshine breaks through the fog. Airplanes drop badly needed supplies, reinvigorating the men and boosting their morale. Now armed and ready, the Americans fend off the German attack. After the battle, the tired, dirty, unshaven soldiers pull themselves together to march off of the front line smartly, singing a Jody cadence to show off to the troops coming to relieve them.[154] They have faced the worst that the weather and the enemy could throw at them, and they not only survived but triumphed. It was a version of the war unlike the one Hanson Baldwin wrote and published the same year.

Battleground received mixed reviews from film critics. *New York Times* film reviewer Bosley Crowther praised *Battleground* for capturing what he considered the misery, agony, grief, and humor of American soldiers without the clichés found in previous war films. He appreciated the ways the filmmakers recreated the "feel" of war. Crowther criticized one point, however, which was the most militaristic aspect of the film: "There's a trace of heroics in that final, swinging march of the battle veterans out of Bastogne that smacks of chauvinist pride. And warfare at times seems as gallant and as glorious as it is dirty in this film."[155] After the seriousness of *The Story of G.I. Joe* and *A Walk in the Sun*, *Battleground* did have a more triumphant presentation. The *Time* magazine film critic thought *Battleground* "is littered with humor, characters and incidents made familiar by every war story since *What Price Glory*" in 1926.[156] Compared to the other contemporary films like *Task Force* and *Command Decision*, however, he concluded that *Battleground* "stacks up well."[157] The film's focus on citizen-soldiers keeps it in the anti-militarist framework but with a more triumphant tone than the late–1945 films.

World War II veterans paid tribute to the air service with *Twelve O'Clock High* (1949), which is an honest depiction of the pressures and stresses combat has on leadership. The Air Force screens the film for training purposes today because it conveys authentic leadership issues, realistic characters, and the very real stresses of combat.[158] The movie was based on a novel of the same name, which was rooted loosely in real events. This film also benefited from the insights and experiences of World War II veterans, as the screenplay author, Beirne Lay, Jr., had been a bomb group commander during the war and served in the Air Force Reserve after the war.[159] While bomber crews had safe rear areas to eat, sleep, and train for the next mission, they faced considerable danger in the air. In 1943, the U.S. Eighth Air Force took monthly losses ranging from 20 to 38 percent. Statistically, a man had a better chance of surviving in the Pacific theater of operations against the Japanese than flying in a bomber over Europe in 1943.[160]

One of the key lessons of World War II is that men can only endure combat for so long before breaking down.[161] At the beginning of the story, the men of the 918th Bomber Group stationed in England are mentally distressed and physically exhausted from back-to-back daylight bombing missions over Germany. The group commander, Colonel Keith Davenport (Gary Merrill), is on the verge of a mental breakdown. He complains bitterly that his men are nothing but numbers to top brass. His friend Brigadier General Frank Savage (Gregory Peck) cautions him against identifying so closely with his men. When Davenport refuses to remove a navigator who had made a mistake on a mission, he is relieved and Savage is given command of the group. Savage intends to push the men to their "maximum effort."[162]

The methods that Savage employs to build up battle skills are militaristic, focusing on strong discipline, obedience, and regimentation. At the first briefing, Savage advises the aircrews to consider themselves already dead. As the crews begin an intensive training regimen, Savage cancels all leave and passes and shuts down the bar to focus the men on their training. He accuses Lieutenant Colonel Ben Gately (Hugh Marlowe) of cowardice and places him in charge of the unit's losers, collected in a plane dubbed the "Leper Colony." Savage's men resent him for the severe discipline.[163]

Along with imposing strict regulations, Savage attempts to reinstate the men's pride in themselves and in their performance. He challenges the men to stop feeling sorry for themselves. Out on a mission, Savage ignores a recall order and continues on to bomb the target. Although his superior reprimands him for insubordination, the action allows the men to demonstrate their skills, which raises morale. They lose no planes, and as a reward, Savage reopens the bar. Gately learns his lessons too well, flying with a painful fractured spine for three missions. Savage's expectation of excellence motivates Gately to push through the pain to fulfill his duty.[164]

Before long, however, Savage becomes burned out as well, just like Davenport earlier in the movie. He takes the losses of the planes and their crews personally. The stress finally catches up with him, making him physically unable to pull himself into the plane. Although Savage has created a combat effective unit, it is clear that "maximum effort" has cost him deeply. In this film, war was not ennobling, but mentally, emotionally, and physically exhausting.[165]

At the time of the film's release, reviewers focused more on the militaristic aspects of *Twelve O'Clock High* and considered it a militaristic interpretation of war. *Time* magazine enthusiastically declared it "the freshest and most convincing movie of the current cycle about World War II."[166] Crowther called it a "powerful and absorbing war picture."[167] He believed that it was nostalgic because audiences were not yet ready for a film that "would deflate war."[168] Although the movie depicts the stresses of combat on aircrews and their leaders, Crowther did not consider this "deflating" war. He also pointed out one of the most militaristic statements of the film: "The conclusion is that rigid discipline brings out the best that is in men."[169] Crowther might also have mentioned the power of shame in motivating the men as well. The film reviewer for *The New Republic* found much more disturbing material in *Twelve O'Clock High*. The reviewer described it as "melo-sentimental" and warned potential viewers that the movie was "designed to sell us something ... perhaps that war is a noble pursuit."[170] Nonetheless, the film won enough critical praise that it was nominated for Best Picture, and Gregory Peck was nominated for an Academy Award for Best Actor. Dean Jagger won an Oscar for his supporting role as Major Stovall.

A third film released at the end of the decade, *Sands of Iwo Jima* (1949), presents both militarist and anti-militarist elements in American culture. Sergeant Stryker (John Wayne) is exactly the kind of tough, combat-experienced infantryman who can prepare replacements for the realities of battle. He stresses obedience and discipline in training. He pushes his men physically, hitting one man in the face with a rifle butt to impress upon him the need to learn how to defend himself correctly. Stryker snaps, "You gotta learn right and you gotta learn fast. And any man that doesn't want to cooperate, I'll make him wish he had never been born."[171]

Scholars assert that Wayne's portrayal of Sergeant Stryker is supposed to model the ideal Marine Corps' warrior image.[172] This idealization comes from Stryker's heroic battlefield action. While the green troops panic under Japanese shelling, Stryker calmly lights up a cigarette. He even offers a drag from the cigarette to calm the nerves of the captain. Stryker exudes coolness under fire. The men are finally ordered to move off the beach to take out a Japanese bunker. As American machine guns and flamethrowers open up against the bunker, the enemy picks off the demolitions crew one by one. In a demonstration of individual heroism, Stryker runs out under fire, grabs the charges, and tosses in the explosives to kill the Japanese.

Although a skilled combatant, Stryker possesses serious personal flaws. He has been demoted in rank and struggles with a drinking problem. Stryker's devotion to the Corps consumed him so much that his wife took his son and left him, and the same commitment prevents him from leaving the Corps to regain his family. Ultimately, loyalty to the Corps proved more important to him.[173]

While Stryker is the most militaristic character, Peter Conway (John Agar) is the anti-militaristic one. He is defiant, individualistic, and a reluctant warrior. Though he volunteers for the Marines out of family tradition, he has no intention of following the path of his career-marine father (whom Stryker admires very much). Much of the movie's plot is taken with Conway meeting a girl, falling in love, and marrying her. He learns out in the field that he will be a father, and therefore has an even stronger incentive to survive the war. As reluctant as he is, Conway does learn the skills necessary to survive combat. Tellingly, Stryker dies at the end of the film, not Conway. Film historian Jeanine Basinger argues that this ending is purposely constructed for peacetime audiences. Men like Stryker are needed for war, but not for peace. Stryker's death and the film's subplots figuring around family allow people to leave the war behind them. She also believes the subtext of the film "speaks against war and against Sgt. Stryker."[174] Indeed, it is the anti-militarist who survives and, presumably, reunites with his wife and child to live happily ever after.

Whether for its militaristic aspects, anti-militaristic themes, or both, audiences flocked to see *Sands of Iwo Jima*, placing it at number eight in box-office returns for 1950.[175] *New York Times* reviewer Thomas Pryor praised the film for its "savage realism," which he thought "reflects the true glory of the

Marine Corps's contribution to victory in the Pacific."[176] Here, war is being perceived as more glorious than with the earlier films. Although he appreciated how the movie honored the Marine Corps, he found fault with its many clichés, such as the men's personal problems, which distracted from the overall honesty of the story. He cited John Wayne's performance as the key that held the movie together.[177] The *Time* magazine reviewer agreed, praising Wayne's portrayal, but nonetheless concluded that "the plot has no more freshness or emotional tug than a military manual, and it is peopled by a movie-hardened cast of characters who have served too many hitches on Hollywood's back-lot battlefields."[178] Wayne's performance received a professional nod as well when he received an Oscar nomination for his role as Sergeant Stryker.

Some World War II veterans reacted harshly to the movie. William Manchester, a journalist and biographer, and another marine friend saw the film at the theater and laughed so much that management asked them to leave.[179] No doubt other World War II vets reacted as Manchester and his friend, and others presumably attended screenings that propelled the movie into the list of top-ten films of the year. In either case, veterans in the audience could discern reality from the Hollywood storytelling and likely complained about the fake elements to friends and family.

Over time, *Sands of Iwo Jima* became an icon in American culture. Audiences chose to focus on the positive, heroic aspects of the story and to ignore what did not fit, such as Stryker's alcoholism. The cultural significance of this film also underscores a growing generational divide between those who experienced or lived during the war years and those who grew up during the baby boom and after. The children of the World War II generation experienced such war films quite differently from their parents. Children and teenagers took the film's content more at face value than with critical eyes.

Many World War II veterans did not confide their war experiences to their families. It is not possible to measure accurately how many veterans kept their war experiences to themselves, but anecdotal evidence suggests it was fairly common. One wife of a World War II veteran explained, "You could never get the father of my four children to talk about the war. It was like we put blinders on the past.... That's the way we lived in suburbia, raising our children, not telling them about war. I don't think it was just [us]. It was everybody."[180] If veterans shared their experiences, they often recounted funny episodes rather than the horrors.[181]

When fathers did not talk about the war, their children turned to films, television, comics, and toys to learn about it. Based on his childhood experience, Tom Englehardt observes that the children of his generation understood that popular culture, and war films in particular, glorified World War II "as *the* American war."[182] He recalls watching war films as a child and asserts that "pride in on-screen western and war culture was any boy's inheritance."[183] Thanks to censorship of language and violence, as well as the deliberately favorable presentation of many World War II films, children did not see, hear, learn, or play an accurate portrayal of war. Children reenacted what adults allowed them to know about war and what they saw in popular culture. As a result, children played what Frank Wetta and Stephen Curley call "*image of war*," in which children "imitate actors imitating soldiers."[184] Furthermore, children picked up the triumphant tone and positive attitude of these films. Vietnam veteran Ron Kovic recalls going to see the *Sands of Iwo Jima* at the theater, humming the Marine Corps hymn along with the soundtrack and thinking about the heroism of John Wayne and the men on Iwo Jima.[185] Similarly, Philip Caputo describes how he envisioned himself as John Wayne, charging up a hill and "coming home a suntanned warrior with medals on my chest."[186] With these images in his head, Caputo says he was already sold on the idea of enlisting in the Marine Corps before the recruiters began their sales pitch.[187] It was the younger generation that was touched by the militaristic elements of the war films much more than the adults or veterans in the audience.

Conclusion

Unlike the young Kovics and Caputos in the audience, most Americans did not perceive World War II in overtly militaristic terms. Americans were very proud of the servicemen, particularly volunteer citizen-soldiers, as films from *The Story of G.I. Joe* to *Battleground* attest. Americans did not believe that the war had changed the veterans who fought in it, or the home front. Few Americans wanted to serve in the postwar armed forces. Recruiting advertisements often had to make the military seem much more like civilian life than it was, to the bitter disappointment of some of those who did enlist. Volunteers never filled out manpower needs, and Congress turned to the peacetime draft to fill billets. The draft proved preferable to Universal Military Training, which opponents suggested would actually militarize society. The surprise conflict in the Korean peninsula reinforced the anti-militarist views of war and even darker views of World War II.

2

THE DARK SIDE OF WAR, 1950–1959

King Company, which had been ordered to take and hold Pork Chop Hill, had been taking heavy casualties. When Love Company finally arrived on King Company's open flank, only 12 haggard survivors of Love Company were left. Lieutenant Joe Clemons, King Company's commanding officer, gently tells them to get into position. Clemons is desperate for relief, supplies, reinforcements, or just about anything Division can send. Nothing arrives. He sends messengers back. Still nothing comes. Out of 100 men, King Company has only 35 soldiers left in the fight. Finally, George Company comes up the hill. Clemons greets the company commander, Lieutenant Russel, who also happened to be his brother-in-law, with enthusiasm. Russel tells Clemons his orders were to help "mop up" the victory. Clemons responds in disbelief: "That's crazy! We're holding on by our teeth!" Russel explains that in the rear, "They think the fight is won." Still, with George Company in the fight, there is still a chance to hold Pork Chop Hill. Then Colonel Davis orders George Company's withdrawal three hours hence. When the photographer from Division shows up, Clemons sends him back with a stark message: "We must have help or we can't hold the hill."[1]

Even though Division finally sends relief to King Company, just as the survivors were about to be overrun by the Chinese, *Pork Chop Hill* (1959) did not share in the triumph of contemporary World War II films. Hollywood generally did not present the Korean War with jingoistic zeal. Instead, more ambiguous interpretations of the conflict appeared in cinema, including those which were anti-war. In some comic-book renderings, American soldiers proved flawed, scared, and even cowardly. The Korean War coincided with dark, unsentimental versions of World War II as well. While many of the books upon which these films were based pre-dated the Korean War, the anti-war and anti-militarist sentiments of the World War II stories fit into a society casting a critical and often negative eye toward the conflict on the Korean peninsula. Militarist themes tied to the Korean War are found predominantly in recruiting advertising, which equated manhood with combat. Advertisements did not induce enough volunteers to serve, so the Pentagon relied on the draft and the unpopular recall of World War II veterans to fill manpower needs. Much of the anti-militarism of the 1950s and early 1960s centered upon dark, ambiguous, and even anti-war themes about Korea and World War II.

Crossing the 38th Parallel

During the early morning hours of June 25, 1950, ten divisions of the North Korean army crossed the 38th parallel into South Korea, overwhelming the lightly armed South Korean forces posted at the border. Although American air and naval forces made contact against the North Koreans, they did not halt the advance. The first American ground troops arrived in Korea from Japan. Unready for immediate commitment against a skilled opponent, American units suffered a number of humiliating defeats as they conducted a delaying action down the peninsula until forming a last-ditch perimeter around the port of Pusan in August 1950.[2]

By the second week of the war, Americans at home began seeing pictures of defeated soldiers in the media. *Life* magazine, which normally did not support the Truman administration, supported the Korean War.[3] The magazine editors published photographs of exhausted, dirty, and unshaven soldiers sleeping on the rocky side of the road during their retreat south.[4] With its emphasis on human-interest stories, *Life* would, unintentionally, reveal the darker side of war even as the magazine kept a respectful and positive attitude toward the armed forces. Both the Congress and media editorials initially supported the Korean intervention, though that support began to wane as the war extended past 1951.[5]

Initially, the military did not censor media reports from the Korean War, but theater commander, General Douglas MacArthur, instituted censorship in December 1950 after several articles appeared critical of the war, of the political corruption of the South Korean regime, and of the suffering of the troops. Correspondents could no longer report on troop movements or military actions without approval. Additionally, the "military regulations stressed security and forbade mention of Allied airpower, effect of enemy fire, criticism of Allied conduct, or derogatory remarks about the U.N. troops and their commanders."[6] Censorship, however, could not hide the disappointments in fighting the war.

Korean War Mobilization

Although the armed forces grew to 3.7 million servicemen at the high point of the Korean mobilization, the war did not have the same influence as did World War II. American society did not endure the same level of economic mobilization, material shortages, or personal sacrifices. Indeed, this lack of full-scale mobilization became a source of criticism for the Truman administration. Henry Luce's *Time* magazine complained that, "more than a year after the Korean War began, six months after the President proclaimed a national emergency, there is no trace of stern austerity ... instead of becoming a garrison state, the U.S. ... never had it so good."[7] The editors wanted a World War II–like mobilization for the Korean War because they worried that the Soviet Union might make a move in Europe while America was tied down in Asia.

Troop mobilization for the Korean War also caused controversy. Starting in June 1950, the Department of Defense called up reservists and national guardsmen, many of whom were World War II veterans. Activating World War II veterans proved unpopular with family members and employers, who complained that veterans should not be called up before draftees. Furthermore, farmers, students, and married men without children were eligible for a draft deferment, but veterans in these same categories were not deferred.[8] A Gallup poll taken in January 1951 showed that many Americans also questioned the recall of veterans. Some 40 percent of respondents indicated that World War II veterans who had served less than a year in the previous war should not be activated for Korean service. Although a similar number believed that the veterans should be activated, some qualified their opinion by stating that only veterans who were single or had not seen active duty previously should serve again. Others qualified their statements by saying that the World War II veterans should serve only if badly needed.[9] Young men with college deferments during the Korean War looked askance at military service. In one study, sociologists reported that "83 percent of students can be described as having negative attitudes toward serving, with 12 percent positive and 5 percent indifferent."[10]

Increased draft calls for the war caused "voluntary" enlistments of a different kind. When young men received their draft notices, many of them promptly volunteered into the branch in which they wanted to serve rather than let the government decide for them.[11] In the first year of the war, the Army recalled 173,496 individual reservists, activated another 34,225 reservists already serving in units, federalized 95,000 national guardsmen, and conscripted 550,397 new soldiers.[12]

Unlike in World War II, women did not join the armed forces in large numbers during the Korean War even though President Truman personally launched the recruiting campaign for them. Enlistments surged at the beginning of the conflict, but both male and female volunteers dropped significantly as the war became more unpopular. In spite of encouraging patriotic zeal with recruiting slogans such as, "Share the Service for Freedom" and "America's Finest Women Stand Beside Her Finest Men," women did not flock to the recruiting stations. Instead, the Department of Defense recalled female reservists to meet personnel needs. In addition to those who activated voluntarily, 175 Women's Army Corps officers were involuntarily recalled from reserve status to active duty. In this respect, women were treated equally with veteran male servicemen involuntarily recalled for duty in the war. Overall, the draft provided sufficient numbers of men to compensate for smaller-than-expected numbers of servicewomen.[13] While the military expected 72,000 enlistments starting in September 1951, by March 1952 only 8,532 women had volunteered. These recruits brought total numbers of women in the armed forces to 48,000.[14]

Despite women's lack of enthusiasm for military service, the idea that women as well as men should participate during wartime was remarkably widespread. A Gallup poll taken in March 1951 indicated that 48 percent of Americans approved the idea of drafting women for typing and clerical work in the armed forces. Some 44 percent of the poll group opposed the scheme, though the question does not ask them if they approved of volunteer service. Broken down by gender, 51 percent of women accepted such a measure, though only 46 percent of men did so.[15] Mildred McAfee Horton, the World War II chief of the Navy's women's service, publicly endorsed the draft for women, arguing that women should accept "not only the rights but the obligations of citizenship."[16] It is striking that so many, both women and men, sanctioned compulsory service for women in the armed forces. Although the domestic ideal of a permanent stay-at-home wife and mother existed in American consciousness, women's World War II service remained recent enough to expect women to contribute to the war effort, if needed. It also suggests the acceptance of the militarist policy of conscription as a way to meet manpower needs for modern wars.

The Korean War permanently changed the military manpower system. After Truman declared a national emergency in December 1950, Congress authorized a long-term defense build-up outlined in National Security Council Memorandum 68, which significantly increased defense appropriations and grew the armed forces from 1.4 million to 3.4 million. As a result of the uneven mobilization, and the many complaints Congress received about it, the legislature reformed the system in the Armed Forces Reserve Act of 1952. It created three categories of reservists: a Ready Reserve, consisting of units and reservists designated for first recall; a Standby Reserve with fewer obligations; and a Retired Reserve for servicemen who volunteered to serve. Congress set the numbers of Ready Reservists the president could call-up involuntarily, and Standby Reservists could only be recalled if the Ready Reserve could not meet the manpower needs of the situation.[17] Even with the Cold War build-up, Truman — and President Eisenhower after him — relied on part-time citizen-soldiers as an integral part of national defense in lieu of an even larger active duty force.

"The Mark of a Man"

Some of the most militarist images associated with the Korean War appeared in recruiting advertising. Research indicated that the existence of the draft misled some Americans into believing the armed forces no longer accepted volunteers. In an effort to increase voluntary enlistments across the services, the National Advertising Council sponsored a recruiting campaign in March and April 1951.[18] Although the National Guard emphasized volunteering on the theme, "Go With the Men You Know," the reality often proved the opposite as some mobilized Guard units were used to fill manpower for other units.[19]

Combat featured as a key theme in Army recruiting. One Army advertisement pictures a combat soldier with his pack and rifle. With the cry, "All Right, Let's Go!" a squad leader calls volunteers to his side. The poster makes clear that only he — the soldier who has seen combat —"has earned the right to say it" by proving himself in battle.[20] It reflected militarism by uplifting a combat soldier above all others.

While this was not the first time the notions of manhood and combat have been connected, it proved one of the most strident and militaristic themes in Korean War recruiting. The Army inaugurated a new campaign slogan during the Korean War: "The Mark of a Man," which was visually symbolized by the Army's combat uniform. Each poster in this series featured a branch of the Army in a combat situation. For instance, one poster shows a combat soldier standing in front of his Jeep, while men work on a tank in the background. As the tanks warm up in the gray of dawn, "American soldiers are once again proving that the battle-worn combat dress of the United States Army is the mark of a *man*."[21]

A Navy poster displayed a different twist on the idea of manhood and duty. To emphasize the need for experience, one recruiting pamphlet shows a cartoon drawing of a toddler in a sailor's uniform playing with a bucket and toy shovel in the sand. It challenges the men "to get into real action — instead of some routine job in this country that Rosie the Riveter could do."[22]

ACTION PACKED

For a man in his thirties, his forties, or even his early fifties, the Seabees offer the chance to get into real action — instead of some routine job in this country that Rosie the Riveter could do.

_from far away places, cocoanuts I will send

The Seabees fight as well as build, and in the early days of an amphibious attack, there's plenty of fighting. The Seabees have to be ready at any time to drop their construction tools and grab their guns to defend against enemy counter attack. Sure, their main job may be to build advance bases, but they are very much a part of the Navy. And the Navy is quite a fighting machine.

3

The military services used several themes in its recruiting, including the idea that military service makes men. This pamphlet advertising the Navy's construction battalions — or Sea Bees — stresses the manliness of military service. Women can do the civilian industrial work at home. Note the reference to "Rosie the Riveter," the World War II–era character created to urge women to work in war production (National Archives and Records Administration).

It is accompanied by a cartoon drawing of an older, heavy-set, muscled woman wearing coveralls and heels and holding a wrench. This resurrects not only Rosie the Riveter, and the role women played working in the defense industries during World War II, but depicts her war work as an un-manly alternative to serving one's country in uniform.[23] Clearly, the message here is that the "manly" thing to do is to serve in the military.

The Marine Corps incorporated into their recruiting advertising combat imagery and pride in the long history of their service, demonstrating that combat in the Korean War is a natural extension of the Marine Corps' glorious history from World War II. One poster illustrates a Marine wearing combat fatigues with a knife strapped on his back, signaling a forward advance.[24] Recruiters reissued a 1945 poster showing marines in combat in Bougainville during World War II.[25] Another poster portrays a contemporary Marine holding an M-1 rifle at the "present arms" position. A background drawing depicts the Marines raising the flag on Mount Suribachi on Iwo Jima during World War II.[26]

In response to the atheism of communist ideology, recruiters militarized Christianity. One poster reveals a Marine in his dress-blue uniform standing in a chapel with a stained-glass window depicting Jesus Christ in the background. Another poster proclaims, "For God and Country," and pictures a Marine in combat uniform kneeling in prayer, leaning against his rifle.[27] A Navy poster pictures a sailor standing in a chapel with stained-glass windows featuring a cross in the background.[28]

A Limited War

In September 1950, American and United Nations forces began an offensive, which included the amphibious landing of marines at Inchon and the Eighth Army breakout from Pusan. As American and United Nations troops successfully pushed North Korean forces back towards the Yalu River at the Chinese border, President Truman forbade American forces from crossing the border into China. Truman wanted only South Korean troops to operate near the Chinese border of Manchuria in order to prevent the Chinese from entering the conflict. Truman deliberately chose to fight a limited war in Korea in order to provide forces for the defense of Western Europe, a decision supported by the Joint Chiefs of Staff but opposed by the theater commander, General Douglas MacArthur. While Truman did not want to extend the war to China, he did want to reunite the Korean peninsula, which he authorized on September 11, 1950. Americans supported Truman's war aim and anticipated a decisive ending to the conflict.[29]

This 1950 Army photograph shows a Third Army Division patrol pinned down by Chinese Communist fire from the hills. The soldiers are attempting to rescue the convey under attack in Northeast Korea. Chinese troops first crossed into Korea in October 1950. President Truman decided not to widen the war into China, making this one of the Cold War's limited wars (New York World-Telegram and Sun Newspaper Collection/Library of Congress).

Unfortunately for the United States and the other United Nations forces fighting in Korea, China intervened in the war. Around 120,000 Chinese troops crossed the Yalu River on October 19, 1950, a move for which MacArthur and too many of his subordinate commanders were unprepared to challenge effectively. By November, the Chinese had 380,000 troops deployed in Korea. Chinese forces fought American and United Nations units back toward the 38th parallel. By December, Truman had revised his war aims to drop the unification of the Korean Peninsula. From this point, the Americans fought to preserve South Korea and to avoid a larger war with China. Additionally, Truman limited the number of troops serving in Korea to one field army of six divisions so that American military forces could focus on the defense of the continental U.S. and Western Europe.[30]

In a challenge to American civilian leadership, American servicemen openly revealed their dissatisfaction toward the limited war to the media. *Life* magazine highlighted the bravery and heroism of American soldiers and marines while also exposing the servicemen's annoyance with the limits placed on their ability to fight. The magazine featured Army Major Carroll Cooper, who led a 360-man task force near the Yalu River. He and his men were cold, exhausted, and frustrated. After a three-day chase, the enemy escaped into Manchuria. Cooper remarked disgustedly, "To fight a war in these parts, you need a squad of lawyers traveling right with the infantry."[31] Photographs of Major Cooper, men digging foxholes with pick axes in the frozen earth, and soldiers firing a machine gun which was "always in danger of freezing" accompanied the story.[32] Similarly, Air Force Lieutenant Russell Brown, the first pilot to engage and shoot down the new Russian MiG-15 jet aircraft, expressed his dissatisfaction as well. Across the border, Brown observed MiG-15s "just playing around, doing barrel rolls and loops. It's some crazy war, I thought, when those bastards can practice stunt flying right in front of you. But we had strict orders not to cross that river boundary."[33] The MiGs had no such prohibitions, and Brown engaged the enemy fighters when they crossed the Yalu, shooting one down. As had happened to the ground troops, however, the enemy crossed back into Manchuria to escape American forces. Henry Luce, the publisher of *Life*, strongly urged the Truman administration to bring in the Nationalist Chinese and re-open the Chinese civil war on the mainland. Stories such as these criticized Truman's limited war policies. In January 1951, *Life* editors explicitly urged the country to engage in an open war with China.[34]

Americans increasingly became disenchanted with the war in Korea as the communist forces regained momentum. The 1950 Christmas edition of *Life* magazine depicted the shock and dismay of the American retreat. For the cover, the editors chose a picture of a Marine, bundled in winter gear, with a look of exhaustion on his face. The caption read, "This is the face of a man who eats frozen rations in the snow and who may be interrupted at any moment to run, to fight or to die."[35] The accompanying photo essay shot by David Douglas Duncan captured the resignation and exhaustion of American troops. Men trudge along frozen, snowy roads. One photo shows captured troops walking behind a truck carrying the dead. The legs of the fallen troops hung over the side. The caption explained, "The living walk and the dead ride. Those killed were brought down out of the hills to be buried in a hastily made cemetery near the port."[36] Tired Marines catch a nap whenever and wherever they could find a moment's peace. Duncan snapped one photo of a Marine dozing at the wheel of his Jeep "while his pet Korean puppy whines in his ear."[37]

In January 1951, a 500,000-strong communist force pushed American troops below the 38th parallel and recaptured the South Korean capital of

Soldiers from the Third Battalion, 34th Infantry Regiment, 35th Infantry Division take cover behind rocks to shield themselves from exploding mortar shells in central Korea in April 1951. By this time, American support for the war had declined with increasing numbers believing U.S. involvement in the war was a mistake (photograph by the U.S. Army Signal Corps, Library of Congress).

Seoul.[38] American public support for the war plummeted. According to a Gallup poll taken the first week of January 1951, 66 percent of those polled believed the United States should pull out of Korea. Almost half of those surveyed thought America had made a mistake in defending South Korea.[39] Opposition to the war continued, with 56 percent of respondents reporting that Korea was a "useless war" by October 1951.[40] Among male college students in 1952, the majority "report that they very often (26 percent) or sometimes (36 percent) 'feel that the war in Korean is not worth fighting.'"[41]

Life magazine continued its sympathetic coverage of the armed forces, despite the flagging public support for the Korean War. It featured a special report on "How to Make Marines?" A correspondent and photographer followed the training of a new platoon of recruits by a drill instructor, Staff Sergeant William S. Trope, described as "an omnipotent compound of God, Satan, and the Marine Corps."[42] Although the authors described the process with phrases such as "browbeat," "uncompromising discipline," and "rough and abusing," they believed the end was certainly worth the militaristic means to get there. The process was "essential" in creating "a fighting machine," and the authors believed that men who met the challenge to become marines had the toughness and discipline to survive the battlefield. With a war in Korea, comments from Sergeant Trope, such as "pray to God some guy doesn't get killed because of your foolishness," appeared ever more necessary. [43] The article ended by noting that the Marines' combat record proved the validity of the training.[44]

After the tumultuous first year of combat, the fighting in Korea settled into a pattern of fairly static lines punctuated by patrols, artillery barrages, and limited attacks. The Eighth Army defended the line during two years of armistice negotiations.[45] Though the fighting settled into a predictable pattern, other events brought additional controversy to the war in Korea.

MacArthur's Removal

Although the Truman administration made it clear that the war in Korea would be limited to the peninsula, MacArthur made public statements that in effect contradicted the administration's policy. Some commentators on the political left criticized MacArthur's behavior in light of traditional anti-militarism: the civilian control of the military enshrined in the Constitution. An editorial in the *New Republic* asserted, "General MacArthur seems not to be aware who is President of the United States" and added that "his attitude constitutes an amazing degree of insubordination toward his Commander-in-Chief in wartime."[46] In another opinion piece, the editors affirmed, "Americans further fear and resent the efforts of generals to usurp the authority of the elected representatives of the people. They believe, as General Eisenhower declared in 1948, that 'nothing in the international or domestic situation especially qualifies for the most important office in the world than a man whose adult years have been spent in the country's military forces.'"[47] Harold Ickes, the former secretary of the interior to President Franklin D. Roosevelt, added, "Nor should a general play politics or try to usurp from the President the conduct of foreign affairs ... reckless Republicans demanded that the President, not a Republican, strip himself of his Constitutional power to conduct foreign affairs in favor of MacArthur, a self-conscious Republican."[48] He warned that MacArthur was inching the United Nations into a wider war, one for which Ickes did not believe needed to be fought. He worried that MacArthur and his allies would continue "thrusting knives into the United States Constitution."[49]

Republican Congressman Joseph W. Martin, Jr., representing Massachusetts, brought MacArthur fully into partisan politics. Knowing that MacArthur and Truman disagreed on the issue of a wider war in Asia, the Congressman solicited MacArthur's comments on a speech Martin made concerning opening a "second front" in China using Nationalist troops from Formosa (also known as Taiwan). Martin read MacArthur's response into the *Congressional Record* on April 5, 1951.[50] In the letter, MacArthur explained his perception, not shared by Truman, that Asia "was the central theater for the struggle against Communism," and a loss there meant "the fall of Europe is inevitable."[51] In a line that would become infamous, MacArthur declared, "There is no substitute for victory."[52]

By the time MacArthur's letter reached Congress, Truman decided he had to be relieved of command. Although Secretary of Defense George Marshall and Chair of the Joint Chiefs of Staff Omar Bradley initially wanted to reprimand MacArthur rather than remove him, they eventually came to the conclusion that it was a "matter of civilian control and the defense of the president's constitutional powers as commander-in-chief."[53] Truman made the same case to the American people when he announced MacArthur's relief: MacArthur had undermined civilian control of the military.

Much of the American press, particularly Republican-leaning media organizations such as the Luce, Hearst, and Scripps-Howard press denounced Truman's decision.[54] Luce wrote an editorial in *Life* in which he claimed MacArthur "was ousted for no petty reason but because he chose to challenge the whole drift of events and the dominant attitudes of the Government of the United States and of the United Nations."[55] As one of the general's staunch admirers, Luce believed he would help bring the nation back from "the passive, helpless and hopeless position" Truman's policies had created.[56]

More left-leaning editorial opinion supported Truman's decision to remove MacArthur. Editors from the *New Republic* stated that "MacArthur was not a mere soldier taking orders, as he tried to picture himself. He was the head of an open conspiracy against the policy of the government he was sworn to serve."[57] Even with much of the media opposing Truman on the issue, the editors of the *New Republic* had faith in the American people and their anti-militarist tradition. They asserted, "The common sense of the American people will doubtless reject the undemocratic philosophy of militarism for which he stands when it is nakedly presented to them."[58] Having long warned readers about MacArthur, Harold Ickes added, "MacArthur's insubordination, his unrebuked defiance of his Commander-in-Chief, his unrequited defiance of all military traditions, his open attempt to make a mock of civic as well as military virtue, is a bad example for troops and civilians alike."[59]

Henry Luce (left), publisher of *Time* and *Life* magazines, long supported General Douglas MacArthur (right). Luce wrote an editorial defending MacArthur when President Truman removed him from command for insubordination in Korea. Luce, a fellow Republican, had hoped that MacArthur would run for president in 1952. When MacArthur wrote his memoirs, Luce published them in serial format in *Life* magazine. Luce is shown with MacArthur in 1963, publicizing the memoirs (New York World-Telegram photograph, Library of Congress).

MacArthur returned to the United States amid cheering crowds and ticker-tape parades in his honor. Naturally, he denied the charges laid against him by the Truman administration. He accused the Truman administration of refusing to allow him "reasonable" use of the air and sea power at his disposal. Starting on May 3, 1951, and continuing through June 27, Congress held hearings on MacArthur's removal and the administration's policies in the Far East.[60] The *New Republic*'s editors denounced MacArthur's Congressional testimony as "unprincipled, arrogant, and reckless."[61] While Republicans called many anti-administration witnesses to testify, the administration called General Marshall to their defense "to checkmate the iconic MacArthur with the iconic Marshall."[62] Marshall symbolized the loyal servant to the nation as the top military commander during World War II, as secretary of state, and now as secretary of defense. He represented the opposite of MacArthur.

The Truman administration arranged for a confidential study of the media reaction to the MacArthur affair. The survey indicated that 80 percent of the people interviewed supported Truman's reasons for dismissing MacArthur. However, more than a third of them also believed that Truman had displayed "personal malice" in the dismissal.[63] After the Congressional hearings, MacArthur went on a speaking tour and then faded into retirement in New York. To Henry Luce's disappointment, MacArthur did not become a serious candidate for the 1952 presidential nomination.[64] Republicans did not rally around MacArthur for president.

"What's Wrong with the Regulars?"

With the ongoing war in Korea and the continued anxiety about war with the Soviet Union in Europe, even left-leaning opinion supported heightened military strength. Commenting on the state of the union in January 1951, *New Republic* editors argued that "our military task is to strengthen ourselves and our allies for the long pull."[65] They wanted to bolster America's reserve forces for possible mass mobilization and to stockpile equipment for a war in Europe. While the position of the *New Republic* appears militaristic in the sense of building up American military forces and weapons for a future unspecified war, it stood in contrast to what the political right wanted. The editors explained, "We support this plan as *against the hysterical cries for unlimited forces now*" from the political right.[66] The Korean War permanently changed the set point for what Americans, from both left and right, accepted as normal. As sociologists noted in 1953, "In a nation such as the United States, which has had a long tradition of non-militaristic thinking ... it appears more and more likely that for the foreseeable future even non-militaristic nations will follow strongly military policies."[67] This trend toward militarization was clearly an aberration for the U.S. in this view, but it appeared necessary—and was accepted by most Americans—during the Cold War. Still, Americans did not display much zeal for the Cold War's first "hot war" in Korea.

Neither the American people nor the troops demonstrated enthusiasm for the Korean War. Already the conflict in Korea was becoming a "forgotten war." The Army attempted to publicize its role and raise its prestige, but those efforts did not prove fruitful. Most coverage of the war did not make front-page news.[68] Through 1952, between 43 and 51 percent of Americans believed that entering the war in Korea had been a mistake. In 1953, right before the armistice, 58 percent of Americans believed the war had not been worth fighting.[69]

On July 27, 1953, the United Nations Command signed an armistice with Communist China and North Korea. The end of the conflict signified neither a clear victory nor a clear defeat. The ambiguity of the cessation of hostilities was seen in the reporting of the final days of conflict, which dwelled on set-backs and disappointments. Tearing at Americans' heartstrings, *Life* magazine published a photo essay on the last combat death in the war. A 22-year-old marine corporal had been wounded by a Chinese mortar on the last night of fighting. Although Navy doctors worked to save his life, he died seven hours before the armistice came into effect.[70] Right after the armistice, Americans reporting that the war had not been worth fighting topped at 62 percent, higher even than the anti-war sentiment against Vietnam in 1969 when 58 percent of Americans thought entry into the war had been a mistake.[71]

Some retrospectives on the Korean War blamed civilian policy rather than the armed forces for the outcome. Luce's magazines criticized the Truman administration's conduct of the war. A *Life* editorial referred to the conflict as "the first war the U.S. did not win," but did not blame the military for the failure.[72] It suggested that American forces had had the firepower and had "come dangerously close to victory."[73] Although the war had shining moments—the Air Force's prowess in the air and the Inchon landing, for example—the editors stated that Americans would find no pride, joy, or celebration in the truce with Korea. The war burdened American families, interrupted the careers of young men, derailed the careers of good American generals, and involuntarily recalled thousands of World War II veterans who had already contributed to the last war. The editors observed, "The shares of war are never just — which is one reason Americans hate war."[74] Even a magazine that supported the war and wanted a wider war with China acknowledged "the war itself will be long remembered for its cruelty, horror, pity, frustrations and desperate bravery."[75] Instead, the Korean War would be overshadowed by the decisive World War II and become the nation's "forgotten war."

Another critique came from the prominent military correspondent Hanson Baldwin, who wrote a piece in 1953 he titled, "What's Wrong with the Regulars?" In it, he reveals many of his own militarist biases and the anti-militarism of the American people. Baldwin characterized the public's very anti-militarist attitude toward the military as "one of slightly patronizing contempt."[76] He noted the exodus of officers and men from services and detected poor leadership and low morale in all of the services except the Marine Corps. Baldwin conceived military service as "the submergence of self in a common effort toward a common good, a band-of-brother social consciousness, reasonable security and civilian respect, and work of varied interest."[77] Though Baldwin, a veteran of the Navy, believed military service was a higher calling than a mere job and certainly should have been more prestigious than a civilian career, he appeared out of touch with the majority of Americans who were not charmed by military life and did not choose to make it a career. He felt disheartened that the day's youth appeared reluctant to join the military. Baldwin himself might have been wearing the rose-colored glasses of nostalgia in this article, as the American military had never actually lived up to the romantic picture he painted of it.

Baldwin thought that young men perceived the once-proud Army infantry as "a service to be avoided like the plague; the doughboy is just 'bullet bait.'"[78] Given that the infantry had borne the brunt of the fighting in Korea, it should not have been surprising to him that young men were not clamoring to get in the branch. Even the Air Force discovered, according to Baldwin, that "many boys would rather sit in a rocker on the front porch than in a pilot-ejection seat in the 'wild blue yonder.'"[79] He quoted one admiral as admitting, "The Navy's not a profession any more — it's a job. We're getting too many officers who just want the money who want to escape the Army."[80] This is one of the most revealing comments about American attitudes toward the peacetime draft. Most servicemen who were either drafted or enlisted to avoid the draft did not intend the military to be their career. For higher ranking officers who came up through the all-volunteer force in the pre–World War II era, this reality proved a bit of a shock. These young men did not have the same affection for the military as those who chose it as a career. Once again, this attitude is in line with a society that had a long cultural animosity toward standing military forces.

Baldwin found plenty of groups to take responsibility for this unsatisfactory outlook. He acknowledged that in an economic boom (as the country was experiencing at that time), plenty of opportunities existed outside the military. Baldwin nevertheless considered the "psychological changes in the American character" as key to the problem.[81] He suggested that American youth "wants security more than adventure," which he blamed on the materialism of American culture and overprotective mothers.[82] Other contemporary critics also accused overindulgent mothers of raising effeminate sons.[83] Additionally, Baldwin blamed poor leadership from labor leaders and politicians.

Given Baldwin's militarist sentiments, it is unsurprising that he also criticized the anti-militarism of the American people for what he considered the sorry state of affairs for the nation's armed forces. He reproached public opinion for pushing a "democratic army" and the services for caving into this pressure, for he believed that it had undermined discipline and changed the "military nature" of the system itself.[84] These "democratic" changes included racial integration, inclusion of women, merit-based promotion, and a revamping of the military legal system. Yet it is precisely these characteristics that differentiated the military of a democracy from the militarism of a World War II–era German or Japanese militaries, the very criteria by which Americans of the 1950s judged militarism.

Although Baldwin had not detected low morale in the Marine Corps, this service arm also experienced dissatisfaction among the ranks. A 1952 internal Marine Corps survey of enlisted men and officers in the electronics field revealed a high level of discontent among servicemen, with around 65 percent indicating that they would not reenlist. The top three reasons for their discontent included a desire to return to civilian education, conflicts with marriage or family life, or a simple dislike for military life.[85] Most servicemen realized that they preferred the freedom, opportunities, and flexibility of civilian life.

Another prominent military commentator of the day, retired Brigadier General S. L. A. Marshall, also analyzed the end of the Korean War, criticizing the Truman administration for failing to mobilize fully or to act more vigorously. Marshall had served as the chief historian for the European Theater of Operations in World War II, and briefly served again as an analyst for the Eighth Army during the first Chinese offensive of the Korean War. Marshall noted the support President Truman received for his quick response to the North Korean attack and criticized the administration for failing to mobilize fully either the reserve forces or the nation's industrial capacity. He found the original assumptions of the war planners wanting as the "gook" army of North Korea proved more resilient than expected. Marshall believed that stronger and more numerous American forces could have turned the tide. "But no such argumentation was ever requested," Marshall lamented, "and no one arose to ask why not."[86] This limited war "confused the American public and, in confusing it, dulled its memory."[87]

Though Marshall found many additional mistakes made by the Administration and by military officials, he worried mostly that America might abandon Korea as "a strategically profitless area for the United States."[88] He believed this conclusion demonstrates the same short-sightedness that condemned the war effort. He asserted that "the retention of a strong American garrison in Korea ... might well mean the saving of Southeast Asia and even help to cool off Red China."[89] Marshall concluded, "Quite a few things enter into the prevention of world war and the preserving of peace. It's infinitely helpful when the strong power acts both willing and resolute."[90] The fact that Marshall believed that acting forcefully against communist powers would prevent another world war shows how militarization was creeping into the culture.

Nevertheless, the anti-militarist rhetoric continued to flourish. In December 1952, Lieutenant General Willis D. Crittenberger, addressing National Guardsmen at the end of his own active-duty career in the regulars, reminded them that the militia tradition "of the citizen soldier is the historical basis of our military system" and that "a change in that system would weaken the nation and destroy our way of life."[91] Granted, the lieutenant general was addressing a room of citizen-soldiers, but he also knew the idea would resonate.

"A Time to Die!"

Comic books offered dark and ambiguous representations of the Korean War. Comic books proved a popular pastime during the 1940s and 1950s, reaching an audience of millions. According to the Army newspaper *Yank*, comic books outsold *Saturday Evening Post* and *Reader's Digest* at Army post exchanges. In 1945, the Market Research Company of America gauged nation-wide readership of comic books at 70 million, which included both genders and an age range of six to 30.[92] Although exact numbers are not available for the Korean War, comic-book sales remained high and it is likely that readership continued to range in the millions, particularly among children and teenagers.

Comics during the Korean War did not mince words or situations— men died, many times in cruel, violent, and painful ways. For instance, the cover artwork from a *Battle* comic titled "A Time to Die!" depicts a wounded soldier firing his rifle with its bayonet fixed at a sword-wielding, pistol-firing enemy. In the foreground is an empty helmet cut open by shrapnel. A dead man's hand is curled-up and twisted under barbed wire. Artist Paul Reinman drew the comic's frames with dark colors and shadows, creating a gloomy atmosphere. The soldiers are tired and unshaven. When a sergeant tells a new recruit to keep his head down, the kid accuses the others in the squad of being "yeller." The sergeant snaps back, "We need live soldiers ... not dead heroes!" an antidote to any militaristic dreams of glory or romance that the soldier might have had for this war.[93] The comic portrays battle wounds in graphic detail. When an enemy soldier crawls into a cave, he is "holding in his guts." The young soldier, trapped in the same cave, listens to the enemy's "bubbling breathing" as he slowly dies.[94] Thinking that it could be him "dying like an animal," the young soldier questions "all the grandstandin' an' bein' a hero" notions that he had held.[95] When the soldier rejoins his unit the next day, the romance of war has left him permanently.

Korean War comics present morally ambiguous scenarios. In one story, a soldier and his buddies are listening from their trench for their pal Manny out on patrol. The scene is barren and desolate, with leafless tree trunks, artillery shell holes filled with water, and mud everywhere. The ragged, unshaven soldiers peer out, looking for their friend. They hear the rat-a-tat-tat of machine gun fire, followed by moaning. Al is convinced it is Manny, but Hank says with a fierce, half-crazed look, "It's a Commie trick ... one of them doin' that moanin' to sucker you out there so they can blast you!"[96] Regardless, Al rises up out of the trench to rescue Manny and is instantly killed by the enemy machine gun. The men hear laughing — it had been a trick. Later, a lieutenant calls Hank and a few more men out for a scouting mission, leaving one soldier alone in the trench. Again, the machine gun opens up and the soldier hears moaning. The soldier's eyes open wide and a look of horror crosses it. Sweat pours off his brow, and he closes his eyes tightly and plugs his ears. The moans grow weaker throughout the night until dawn approaches. The last frame depicts the soldier, hands over his face, tears streaming down his cheeks, unable to move.[97] Had he made a mistake? Had a soldier died because he made the wrong decision? This story does not sanitize war for young consumption.

Some adults attacked the comics for their anti-militaristic sentiments. The Cincinnati Committee on the Evaluation of Comic Books criticized stories that portrayed hopelessness in the Korean War. The members of this committee believed that the negative connotations in stories such as these discouraged youth from enlisting in the military. Instead, this committee supported stories which trivialized the violence.[98] They supported romantic, glorified images of war — in other words, more militaristic images.

"Where Do We Get Such Men?"

War films reflected the unpopularity of the Korean War. While the Hollywood Production Code limited the range and realism of the war movies, filmmakers nonetheless presented cynicism, resentment, weak leadership, and the troops questioning whether Americans should fight in the war. Like the comic books, the men in Korean War films face ambiguous and complex moral and ethical situations.[99] While films depicted troops in both World War II and Korean War as suffering, the sacrifices of the World War II soldiers ultimately contributed to a great victory. The same suffering and sacrifices of men in Korea did not lead to the same satisfying victory, so Korean War films retain a darker, more ambivalent connotation.

Race featured in Korean War films because communist propaganda often raised the race issue to undermine the United States in world opinion.[100] For example, the main protagonist in the film *The Steel Helmet* (1951)[101] is Sergeant Zack (Gene Evans), a racist white soldier. He accepts a black medic, Corporal Thompson (James Edwards), once Zack learns he fought in the 16th Infantry in World War II as Zack had, and both were "retreads"— World War II veterans called back to serve in Korea.[102] In this case, shared combat experience bridged the racial divide. A communist North Korean major attempts to convince Corporal Thompson and a Japanese-American soldier, Sergeant Tanaka (Richard Loo), that they should not fight for America because of the racism there. Civil rights activists probably did not care for Thompson's accommodationist answer: "One hundred years ago, I couldn't even ride on a bus. At least now I can sit in the back. There are some things you just can't rush, buster."[103] Thompson and Tanaka reject the offer to betray their country and continue to fight.

Zack, Thompson, and the others are protecting an observation post (OP) in a Buddhist temple. Zack did not really care for the mission, but agreed to stay with a unit in which he was not attached in order to help an inexperienced lieutenant survive. Members of the squad are picked off by an enemy sniper before a full assault is made by the North Korean "hordes." Desperately outnumbered, the small group manages to hold off the enemy with machine guns and bazookas. Only four survive the attack. Exhausted and hungry, the survivors are ordered to abandon the OP when a new patrol arrives. Looking around at the chaos and bedraggled condition of the soldiers, the patrol's junior officer asks, "What kind of outfit is this?" Zack replies, "The infantry." Director Samuel Fuller concluded the film with the ominous words, "There is no end to this story."[104] Another patrol, another OP, and another attack were just around the corner.

Instead of the somber mood of the film, critics focused on the aspect of race in the movie. *New York Times* film critic Bosley Crowther appreciated the subplot, noting in his review that the director "has staged an elementary demonstration of democratic principle" through the African-American and JapaneseAmerican characters.[105] Fuller, a World War II veteran who served in the First Infantry Division (the "Big Red One"), directed another Korean War film, *Fixed Bayonets!* (1951), about a platoon left behind to protect American rear lines.[106]

Some Korean War films are anti-war, while retaining a sympathetic view of the armed forces. *The Bridges at Toko-Ri* (1955) exemplifies this distinction. *The Bridges at Toko-Ri* had a long public history before making it to the silver screen, and a similar story is featured in the film *Men of the Fighting Lady* (1954). Both movies were based on the work of James Michener, who traveled on board the aircraft carrier USS *Essex* in May 1952. He interviewed pilots who were flying missions into North Korean territory and published an article about it in the *Saturday Evening Post*, wrote a fictionalized book of the experiences, and published a condensed form of the book in *Life* magazine. Michener believed that the public had forgotten the contributions of the men fighting in Korea and failed to recognize their heroism. His observations of the dangers that Navy pilots faced, such as flying off of carrier decks into heavy enemy anti-aircraft fire, crashing into near-freezing ocean waters, and landing again on moving and swaying carrier decks, impressed him greatly.[107]

Michener's stories thrust the Navy, and specifically carrier aviation, into popular culture as no other media outlet had done during the Korean War. Between the magazine articles, book, and film, Americans had a wide range of exposure to the story. Publicity did not mean automatic acceptance of the author's interpretation, though. *Life*'s readers' reactions to Michener's story varied from appreciation to disgust. Joan Young Bayly from Pasadena, California, responded, "If every so-called American would read Michener's novel the apathy which so many have concerning the Korean War might soon be turned into empathy."[108] Richard J. Cusack from New York reacted differently, complaining, "Michener's one-dimensional tear-jerker has as much depth as a windshield wiper and, if we consider the war itself, even less scope."[109]

As a film, *The Bridges at Toko-Ri* is anti-war because the main character, Lieutenant Harry Brubaker (William Holden), questions the reasons America is fighting and complains that he has already served his time in World War II. He rejects Admiral Tarrant's (Fredric March) attempts to get him to stay in the Navy for a career. He is a lawyer from Denver and wants to get back to his family and his practice. The story also imparts a sobering ending for the main character. After completing a harrowing mission, Brubaker is shot down in North Korean territory. Two helicopter crewmen who had come to rescue Brubaker are also shot down. As they are fighting for survival in the muddy trenches, Brubaker concludes that the reason men fight is simply because they are there. Brubaker and his two rescuers are all killed on the ground. Although it was a "good" mission, which destroyed the main and secondary targets, Admiral Tarrant takes Brubaker's death to heart. He wonders aloud, "Where do we get such men?"[110] Tarrant praises Brubaker for his sacrifice, but it must be kept in mind that although Brubaker completed his mission, it was more out of a sense of duty than to any commitment to the cause.

Audiences accepted the anti-war Korean War film. *The Bridges at Toko-Ri* proved a box-office success, listing in the top 20 highest grossing films of the year.[111] *New York Times* film critic Bosley Crowther named the film one of the ten best motion pictures of 1955.[112] The *Time* critic declared it "one of the best of all the many Hollywood pictures about the Korean War," and added that he liked the movie more than the novel.[113] The reviewer focused

Naval aviator Lieutenant Harry Brubaker (William Holden) dodges enemy fire in *The Bridges at Toko-Ri* (Paramount Pictures, 1955). Brubaker has just been shot down in North Korean territory and has taken refuge in a muddy trench. Rather than being heroically rescued in the film, Brubaker and two helicopter crewmen are unceremoniously shot by enemy soldiers. These deaths, coming after the completion of a successful mission, served no larger purpose and help give the film an anti-war message (photograph by John Swope; Time & Life Images/Getty Images).

his critique on the film's end and Brubaker's question, "Why did it have to be me?" The response is existential: "because you're here."[114] He concludes that the answer "is surely a poor one to die on — though just as surely many a man has had to die on it for want of a better reason in his heart."[115]

Pork Chop Hill (1959) presents another anti-war statement. It was directed by the anti-militarist Lewis Milestone, who had previously directed *All Quiet on the Western Front* and *A Walk in the Sun*. The film was based on a book of the same name by S. L. A. Marshall, which was based on research he conducted in Korea. In the book and the movie, Lieutenant Joe Clemons (Gregory Peck) leads King Company to retake Pork Chop Hill during armistice negotiations between the Americans and the Communists at Panmunjom, Korea. The anti-militarism of the draftees is clear when they are initially skeptical of Lieutenant Clemons, a regular, as he probably only knows how to bury them according to regulation. As a result of the point system of rotation adopted for the Korean War, the men count carefully the points they have accumulated on the front so they can rotate out. One soldier badgers Clemons and Lieutenant Ohashi (George Shibata) constantly because battalion has, in his calculation, miscounted his points. He believes he has earned enough to leave the front lines, but he is forced to go on this mission anyway.[116]

Like Brubaker in *The Bridges at Toko-Ri*, the soldiers openly question whether the sacrifices they are making have merit. They realize that they are expendable and that the hill is a minor piece of terrain and a mere bargaining chip in a war that will not end with the enemy's surrender. Unwavering devotion to one another comes through as they continue to fight even as their numbers dwindle. The soldiers themselves give Pork Chop Hill meaning because so many of them spilled blood there. They fought for one another, not for the cause of the war itself.

While soldiers exhibit courage and skill, the film stresses the Army's indecisiveness, poor communication, and unnecessary misunderstandings. Clemons cannot reliably communicate with headquarters behind him or even with the other platoons. As a result of poor communication, some back in headquarters believe that the battle is a low-level "mopping up" operation, as is evidenced by the arrival of a public-relations officer to photograph the victory. In addition to misunderstanding the nature of the battle, no one in division headquarters is sure of the status of the terrain. Should they reinforce it or let it fall? While the decision is kicked up ever higher in the chain of command, Clemons's troops are not reinforced or resupplied. Reinforcements do not come until the company is all but decimated. Of course, actual combat operations rarely run smoothly or flawlessly. Nevertheless, the film underscores the reality that soldiers are expendable and subject to forces completely outside their control.

The one exception to the heroism of the troops is the overt depiction of cowardice in one of the film's two featured black soldiers, Franklin (Woody Strode). The other African-American character, a sergeant, tells the cowardly, Franklin, "I have a special interest in everything you do."[117] That is, Franklin's poor conduct might tarnish all black soldiers. Nevertheless, Franklin determines that "I ain't gonna die for Korea" and attempts to fake injury to get out of the fight.[118] When this fails, he holds Clemons at gunpoint. In a dramatic scene, Clemons appeals to Franklin's sense of duty and connection with the other soldiers to convince him to return to the lines. In the end, Franklin fights with the others.

The Department of the Army assisted in the creation of *Pork Chop Hill*, and Army officials were pleased with the presentation of soldiers faithfully remaining at their posts. The soldiers did not break and run. While there were no rumors of "bug out" at Pork Chop Hill, it was a criticism that had haunted the Army since the first Chinese offensive in 1950.[119]

Film reviews focused on the anti-militarist aspects of *Pork Chop Hill*. While the critic for *Time* lamented that the audience did not get to know the soldiers, he commended the film for "not sentimentaliz[ing] or patronize[ing] its heroes."[120] This film had not glorified war, and like *The Story of G.I. Joe*, it paid tribute to the men who served. The critic liked how the filmmakers were "determined to proclaim the dignity of the individual at the moment, in the heat of battle, when it seems to matter least."[121] Stanley Kauffmann, reviewing the movie for *The New Republic*, remarked, "war continues to be hell in films" praising director Lewis Milestone for making combat "hard and dirty — not a collection of carefully planted explosions on a studio back lot" as many low-budget war films had done.[122] Crowther praised the film for its gritty and honest depiction of battle as well as the emotional drama of men realizing their fight might be needless and futile.[123] Audiences attended the anti-militarist *Pork Chop Hill* as it rated as one of the top films of 1959.[124]

"I'm a Private No-Class Dogface"

The Korean War coincided with — and perhaps opened the door to — films with darker interpretations of World War II. Many of these films are based on novels written by World War II veterans, and it is possible that these less favorable images would have appeared regardless of the Korean War. The controversy and ambiguity of the Korean War certainly created an opportunity for darker presentations and interpretations of war to reach the silver screen and be well received by American audiences. The stories develop characters and themes that do not glorify or romanticize military service or combat.

Lewis Milestone's World War II Marine Corps movie *Halls of Montezuma* (1950) came out in theaters just as the Korean War began. Although the film was conceived and created before the Korean War started, critics nonetheless compared it to the conflict Americans then faced. Even the film's dialog had an eerie resonance with the contemporary war. At the end of the movie, one Marine moralizes, "We are part of the world ... if any part suffers, we all suffer."[125] The film follows a small unit of marines on an amphibious landing on a nameless Pacific island during World War II. Lieutenant Anderson (Richard Widmark) faces the stresses of command and his fear of the assault, which manifests itself as "psychological" migraine headaches. In trying to relieve the strain, he becomes addicted to painkillers. The men struggle to take Japanese prisoners to interrogate them for information instead of killing them.

The *New York Times* film critic was struck by the timeliness of the film, which brought his attention to the suffering of the combat troops fighting in Korea. Indeed, Crowther found the tragedy, despair, and agony in the story to be rather sobering "no matter how heroic the men appear."[126] The men are disciplined and courageous, and it is a testament to "the eternal glory of the United States Marines."[127] Crowther does not appear to use "glory" in a militaristic sense, but in the sense of a job well done. He means to pay tribute to the men, not to romanticize them.

Similarly, Robert Hatch, a film reviewer for the *New Republic*, favorably placed the *Halls of Montezuma* in a larger context, noting that it was released at "an awkward moment." [128] He characterized war films as belonging to one of three categories: "pacifist demonstrations of the horror of war, vainglorious toasts to military prowess, or romantic entertainments akin to the Westerns and crook dramas."[129] He believes the film fit comfortably within the themes Milestone previously explored in *All Quiet on the Western Front* and *A Walk in the Sun*. Hatch believed that the film "documents honestly and honorably the physical and mental torments of war," which fall into the first category.[130] But then he admits the film is more complicated than that: it "seems to say that war is unendurable and we must get ready for more of it; that no one should be asked to bear such degrading torment, and that it is an experience no one should miss."[131] Hatch concludes that however baffling the theme is, it is also "an accurate reflecting of a good many public and private minds today."[132] Comments like these show how militarism and anti-militarism can overlap: war is horrible, but it should not be missed.

World War II veteran James Jones illustrates the pre–World War II regular Army with its strengths and its flaws in his novel, *From Here to Eternity*. Jones's main theme revolves around the struggle of individuality against the conformity of society, in this case personified by the U.S. Army. Along with other World War II veteran novelists such as Norman Mailer, Jones portrays enlisted soldiers as anti-authoritarian and resentful of the military caste system, while officers appear incompetent and careerist. Additionally, servicemen are generally pictured as consumed with pleasures of the flesh, including drunkenness, fornication, and other vices.[133] While neither Jones nor Mailer can be taken as an inclusive interpretation of the military from the perspective of all soldiers, their stories were read by many, and watched by more when they were turned into movies.

In order to obtain Army cooperation, the filmmakers eliminated much of the novel's objectionable material, such as the nudity, prostitution, foul language, and other details. Some modifications to the script were undoubtedly necessary as it is difficult to imagine a film that contained all of the novel's improprieties passing the scrutiny of the Production Code. Although much of the material from the novel was toned down for the film, it is also worth noting that the Army would have preferred that Hollywood not produce the film at all. Given the choice to influence the script by cooperating or not

Robert E. Lee Prewitt (Montgomery Clift, left) talks to his friend Angelo Maggio (Frank Sinatra, right) in *From Here to Eternity* (Columbia Pictures, 1953). After getting into trouble, Maggio is placed in the stockade, where he is abused by a warden. Maggio escapes from the stockade, but dies from his injuries. Prewitt confronts the warden and kills him in a knife fight, which eventually leads to his downfall. U.S. Army officials did not approve of the images of the service portrayed in this film (photograph by John Kobal Foundation, Hulton Archive/Getty Images).

having any say at all, the Army did provide some assistance to the film, such as allowing the crew to film Schofield Barracks in Hawaii.[134] Even with the changes, the finished product failed to meet the Army's standards for its self-image. It also proved a popular picture with critics and audiences. It won eight Oscars, including Best Picture, and earned good box office returns.

Set in Hawaii just prior to the 1941 attack on Pearl Harbor, each character in *From Here to Eternity* (1953) exhibits some negative quality, attitude, or behavior. Private Prewitt (Montgomery Clift) has recently transferred from a bugle company into the infantry, protesting the favoritism that placed a friend of the commander in his position in the band. Unfortunately, he would find the situation little better in his new outfit. The company commander, Captain Holmes (Philip Ober), insists that he fight on their boxing team. When Prewitt refuses, Holms orders the "treatment," a series of harassments, threats, cleaning detail, and other unpopular duties to break his defiance. He nevertheless refuses to capitulate to Holmes's demands, maintaining his autonomy and individuality.[135]

On top of enduring the "treatment," Prewitt pursues a club girl in the movie (a prostitute in the novel) named Lorene (Donna Reed). Unfortunately for Prewitt, she refuses to be the wife of a soldier, dreaming of escaping her low-class life for middle-class respectability. Prewitt, by his own description, is only a "private no-class dogface."[136] Jones clearly reinforces the impression that the regulars do not have a good reputation, and even a low-class girl like Lorene does not want to be tied to them.

Jones writes Sergeant "Fatso" Judson (Ernest Borgnine) as a truly sadistic character. Not only does Judson threaten and bully fellow soldiers in public, he uses his post as warden of the stockade to abuse prisoners. In the film, Judson repeatedly assaults Prewitt's friend, Angelo (Frank Sinatra), which leads to Angelo's death from the injuries he sustained. Prewitt goes after Judson, killing him in a knife fight. Although Judson's death might feel satisfying to the audience as just punishment, the killing ultimately brings down Prewitt as well. Hurt in the knife fight, Prewitt abandons his unit and convalesces with his girlfriend. When the Japanese attack Pearl Harbor, Prewitt attempts to return to his unit but is shot as an intruder.[137] Although he is devoted to serving his country, this quality does not save his life in the end.

First Sergeant Warden (Burt Lancaster) and Captain Holmes's wife, Karen (Deborah Kerr), act in ways that cast a negative light on the Army. Warden is the chief non-commissioned officer (NCO) under Captain Holmes, the man who truly runs the outfit when Holmes is out on the town with his girlfriends. Warden and Karen start an affair, but Karen will not leave her husband for a mere NCO. She presses Warden to go to officer candidate school. Warden has no desire to be an officer, afraid that he will turn into someone like Holmes. Faced with the choice, he remains an NCO, even though he knows he will lose Karen.[138]

Unlike the novel, there is some resolution at the film's end that leaves the audience with the impression that the Army is not all bad. Before his death, Prewitt explains to Lorene that he loves the Army and feels he belongs there, no matter how badly he has been treated by other soldiers. He actually likes his outfit, in spite of "the treatment." While Holmes is promoted in the book, in the film an inspector general investigation into his poor treatment of Prewitt results in his removal from command.[139] In the movie, a general lectures Holmes by saying, "The first thing I learned in the Army is that an officer takes care of his men. It seems to be the first thing you forgot."[140] The new company commander, Captain Ross, assures his soldiers, "No man will earn his stripes [promotions] through boxing."[141] When the Japanese attack, Warden successfully organizes the men to fight back. From this point forward, the problems of a peacetime Army slip away under the exigencies of war.

Since the film From Here to Eternity transformed the institutional problems of the World War II-era Army into individual acts of deviance, the film could not affect the audience with the same impact as the novel. Despite the changes, New York Times film critic A. H. Weiler approved the film's fidelity to the novel, complimenting its "scope, power and impact."[142] Life magazine's film critic was also impressed by the movie's adherence to the "hate and love for the U.S. Army" by keeping the "most of the rough characters and mayhem."[143] The Time reviewer emphasized the anti-militarism of the film by concluding, "It says that many Americans, in a way that is often confused and sometimes forgotten, care deeply, care to the quick about a man's right to 'go his own way,' though all the world and the times be contrary."[144]

Although From Here to Eternity had not portrayed all the negativity of the novel, some people left the theater with an unfavorable opinion of the service, just as Army officials had feared. For many adults in the audience, the immoral behavior confirmed their (probably) previously held conceptions that the regulars commonly acted in those ways. Several objected to the drunkenness of the men. Others commented on the cruelty, unfairness, and "the way they treated the non-commissioned officers."[145] Another feared the harmful influence of motion pictures, suggesting, "One can pick up bad habits from shows like that."[146] One respondent held a positive view of the Army and so denounced the behavior in the film as "unmilitary."[147]

Male teenagers reacted to the movie much as the adults did. Some male teenaged respondents objected to the cruelty, brutality, and unfair treatment toward the soldiers in the film. Understanding that it was a fictional story, another teen said, "Even if you didn't believe it, it kind of scared you" in

Pictured from left to right are Ensign Willie Keith (Robert Francis), Lieutenant Tom Keefer (Fred MacMurray), Lieutenant Commander Philip Queeg (Humphrey Bogart), and Lieutenant Steve Maryk (Van Johnson) on the deck of the ship during a typhoon in *The Caine Mutiny* (Columbia Pictures, 1954). When Queeg freezes during this storm, Maryk relieves him of command, an action for which he was court-martialed and acquitted. As U.S. Navy officials feared, audiences strongly disliked Queeg's character in the film (photograph by Loomis Dean, Time & Life Pictures/Getty Images).

reference to Sergeant Judson's sadistic behavior.[148] Another young man listed the things he disliked in the film, including: "fighting, sorrow, everything ugly. The fight to be an individual is a complete loss."[149] This last comment contains a key component of American anti-militarism: the focus on individualism. Others pointed out the stupidity, poor attitudes, and indiscipline of the men.[150]

The Navy reacted to the film *The Caine Mutiny* (1954) in much the same way that the Army approached *From Here to Eternity*. *The Caine Mutiny* was based on the Pulitzer Prize-winning novel of the same name by World War II veteran Herman Wouk, and it was adapted for the stage before it became a motion picture.[151] The story focuses on an unstable captain and a disloyal crew and is a somewhat confusing mixture of militarist and anti-militarist themes. Navy officials objected to the word "mutiny" in the title and the portrayal of the captain and refused to allow its limited cooperation acknowledged on screen.[152]

The story is set on a minesweeper during World War II, part of "the junkyard Navy" that was "designed by geniuses to be run by idiots."[153] The "good" captain in this story is De Vriess (Tom Tully), the one who does not insist on strict discipline and is more in line with the notion of American anti-militarist individuality. The "bad" captain is Queeg (Humphrey Bogart), the by-the-book career Navy man who replaces De Vriess. Queeg insists on such details as tucking in shirttails, shaving, and maintaining regulation haircuts. As Christian Appy observes:

> Where De Vriess was slack on military formality, Queeg is obsessed by it. Where De Vriess gave single-minded attention to big assignments, Queeg botches every one through cowardice, incompetence, or distraction. Where De Vriess' authority was backed by strength and skill, Queeg's tyranny grows out of weakness and insecurity. Queeg is nervous, compulsive, arbitrary and increasingly paranoid.[154]

For example, when Queeg finds a man with his shirttails hanging out, he reprimands the junior officers. While distracted by this infraction, he allows the ship to turn too far, cutting its own tow line. Instead of accepting responsibility, Queeg excuses himself by saying it was a faulty tow line. Queeg continues to make mistakes that he rationalizes away or blames on others, all the while coming down hard on the minor infractions of the crew and officers.

Meanwhile, Lieutenant Tom Keefer (Fred MacMurray) pushes the executive officer, Lieutenant Steve Maryk (Van Johnson), to commit mutiny. When Queeg freezes in a typhoon, Maryk takes the fateful step to relieve the captain of command. The other officers support him, but it is the executive officer who faces a court martial for his actions. Keefer proves a coward on the stand, refusing to admit any complicity in the events. Nonetheless, the jury acquits Maryk at his trial. Afterwards, Maryk's legal counsel, Lieutenant Greenwald (Jose Ferrer), denounces the officers for ruining the career of a man who had been defending the country long before any of the younger men had served in the Navy. He accuses the officers of disloyalty, as Queeg had asked them specifically for their support. Keefer, Greenwald says, should have been the one on trial. The order and hierarchy of the system should have been maintained and as first officer, Maryk should have been acting in accord with that system and helping Queeg be a competent commander, not letting him fail. Greenwald's position is militaristic in the unthinking and uncritical support of military authority, no matter how incompetent or dangerous. He would rather uphold the system and the hierarchy than have officers act on their individual initiative.

Simply because the film offered a militaristic interpretation does not mean the audience accepted it at face value. As the Navy feared, *The Caine Mutiny* elicited unfavorable audience responses toward the service. Male teenagers thought that Queeg's character was deeply flawed and unstable.[155] Adults similarly found the captain's character faulty. One respondent referred to "the selfishness and unreasonable attitude of the captain who set himself up as a little god."[156] Another stated that this film confirmed his previously held low estimation of some naval officers. He commented on "the possibility for such a man to be in such a responsible position. I know this happens."[157] This comment might have come from a veteran or a citizen highly critical of the military. It shows that movies cannot easily overturn personal experience or deep-seated notions. These responses also undercut the argument that this film favored the Navy and that any movie featuring the military must be pro-military.[158]

Mister Roberts (1955) presents an anti-militarist interpretation of World War II that questions the notion of heroism in combat. Written by World War II veteran Thomas Heggen in 1946 as a serial for *Atlantic Monthly*, *Mister Roberts* became a long-running Broadway Stage production before filmmakers adopted it for the silver screen. Heggen based the story on his own wartime experiences.[159] John Ford, the Navy veteran and director of *They Were Expendable*, jumped on the project. The story is set on a World War II cargo ship operating in the rear areas of the Pacific. Lieutenant Roberts (Henry Fonda), the executive officer, has been trying to get off the cargo ship and into the "real" war for some time. Captain Morton (James Cagney) refuses to approve the transfer because Roberts keeps the best record in the Navy for resupplying ships. Morton is the worst example of a commander: arrogant, manipulative, distant from the men, and wedded to appearances. He uses his rank to improve his own self-image and lord his authority over the men, as he had once been a busboy taking orders from everyone else. Roberts is an example of the best kind of officer: professional yet flexible, sympathetic toward the crew, and willing to sacrifice his own chances of transfer in order to get the men some desperately needed liberty. He looks out for the men under his command, which earns him their loyalty and respect.[160]

The story demonstrates disillusionment with notions of heroism. The ship's doctor attempts to dissuade Roberts from wanting to get into the shooting war. Doc also suggests that heroism is about opportunity rather than virtue. "It's a reflex," Doc explains, "I think that seventy-five out of a hundred young males have that reflex," even the cowardly Ensign Pulver (Jack Lemmon), too afraid even to be seen by the captain, much less confront him.[161] Nonetheless, the crew manages to wrangle Roberts the transfer he always wanted, but at a high cost. They learn through a letter that a Japanese kamikaze plane crashed into the wardroom of Roberts' ship, killing him as he sat drinking coffee. His death was meaningless because it was not tied to any military action. The film suggests that seeing the "real" war had not been worth Roberts's life. The only good consequence of Roberts' death was that it inspired his replacement, Ensign Pulver, to stand up to Captain Morton.

In an interesting historical twist, the actor who played Lt. Roberts in both the theater production and the movie, Henry Fonda, had a similar naval career to the fictional character. Fonda had a staff position in the navy in Washington, D.C. and attempted to get a transfer to combat service. When he was transferred to the staff of Vice Admiral John H. Hoover in the Pacific, Fonda missed two kamikaze attacks on the destroyer *Curtis*.[162] Like other World War II stories, *Mister Roberts* rested on actual military experience, both the good and the bad. Jack Lemmon won an Oscar for his supporting role as Ensign Pulver, and the film was nominated for Best Picture. The film was

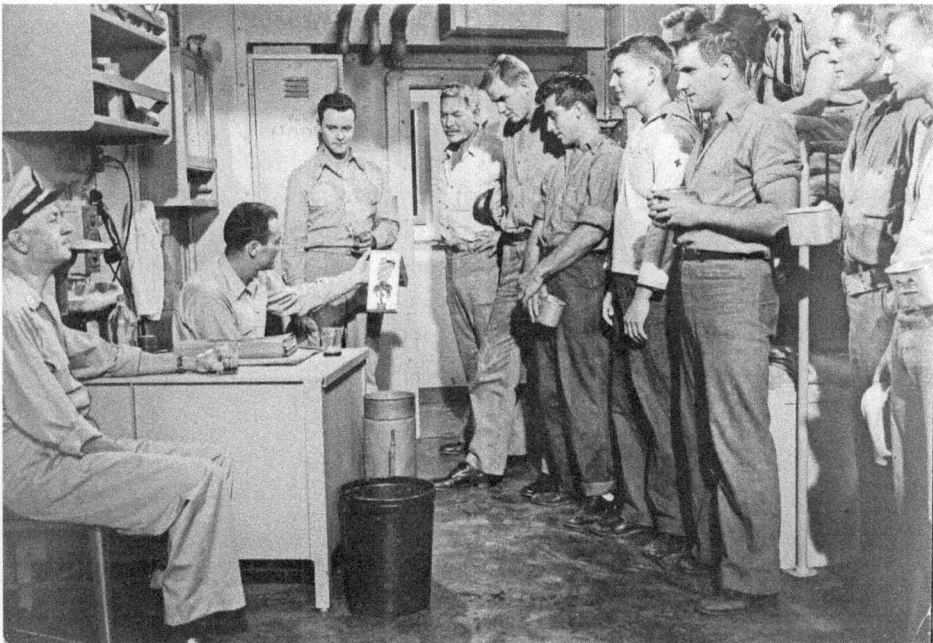

Pictured left to right are Doc (William Powell), Lieutenant Roberts (Henry Fonda, seated), Ensign Pulver (Jack Lemmon), and the ship's crew in *Mister Roberts* (Warner Bros., 1955). In this scene, the crew present Roberts with the Order of the Palm award for standing up to Captain Morton (James Cagney, not pictured). The crew went behind Morton's back to secure Roberts his highly desired transfer into the "real war." Unfortunately, Roberts does not die a hero's death, but died pointlessly in a Japanese kamikaze attack while drinking coffee (Warner Bros./Hulton Archive/Getty Images).

hailed by both critics and moviegoers. Crowther chose *Mister Roberts* as one of the ten best films of 1955.[163] A movie audience survey of 15 million people elected *Mister Roberts* as the best film out of 20 nominations.[164] It also heralded a new wave of humorous World War II movies, including *South Pacific* (1958), *Operation Petticoat* (1959), and *Wackiest Ship in the Army* (1960). Rather than glorifying heroism or creating a romantic interpretation of war, these movies showed that it was acceptable to *laugh* at World War II.

Responses of male teenagers and adults toward *Mister Roberts* proved mixed. Some teenagers cited as favorable "Roberts' devotion to his men" and a generally decent attitude of the enlisted sailors.[165] Others believed the officers and enlisted, except Roberts, were "a low type" who "were not sincere about their jobs, were not efficient," much in line with traditional stereotypes of the regulars, though not the image of the citizen-soldiers who would have manned most World War II ships.[166] The captain was mean, strict, unfair, and had a "warped personality."[167] The drunkenness and rough characterization of sailors on liberty did not agree with one teenager's upbringing.[168]

Adults praised Roberts's behavior as well, commenting on his decency, selflessness, and thoughtfulness. They came down much harder on Morton's character, objecting to his strictness, selfishness, and ruthlessness. Some did not like the way the captain treated the men and disliked the manner in which he was trying to get his promotion. Another did not care for the "picking up girls in every port" characterization of the men.[169] Unsurprisingly, audiences liked the good characteristics of Roberts and denounced the petty tyranny of Morton. No doubt some believed there were more Mortons in the Navy than men like Roberts, confirming previously held stereotypes. Others could connect with the anti-militaristic Roberts.

Conclusion

Although later referenced as "the forgotten war," the Korean War left its mark on America. It was a war that ended without a clear victory or defeat for the United States, a conclusion that stood in stark contrast to World War II, which would be known for a decisive victory. Many representations of the Korean War in popular culture reflected the unpopularity of the conflict in Asia. American servicemen, including World War II veterans, had been involuntarily recalled for duty in Korea, a move that did not prove popular with the public or with the servicemen themselves. An attempt to recruit women volunteers fizzled. While the darker images of World War II might also have appeared with or without the Korean War, it is clear that the Korean conflict set a tone that complemented the less romantic interpretations of the Second World War.

Parallel interpretations of the Korean War and World War II, seen in the next chapter, celebrates American glory and technological strength and is closely connected to the rising militarism in American culture. Just as anti-militarist themes and stories in media and popular culture also contained an element of militarism, so too do the militarist-dominated images contain elements of anti-militarism. Both themes continue to run through American culture.

3

THE NEW LOOK,
1951–1959

Since Master Sergeant Ernest G. Bilko has the Army motor pool at Ft. Baxter, Kansas, running so smoothly, he has too much time on his hands. So the chaplain convinces post commander Colonel Hall to give Bilko a training unit as a challenge. Hall strides over to the map of the post and explains, pointing emphatically, that he has moved buildings and blocked off streets so that no rookie, even by chance, could run into Bilko. Hall relents under the chaplain's urging, and the new soldiers report to Bilko. As soon as he realizes the new men have money from home, Bilko invents a "welcome rookies dance" to get his hands on it. Although Private Higgins, one of the new recruits, reminds the master sergeant that the rookies have to study in the evening, the others are not so fastidious.[1]

Under guidance from the chaplain, Higgins collects all the men's extra money and hands it to Bilko to keep in trust. At first, Bilko is thrilled that he has a new gambling fund to win back some of the money he had just lost in a poker game. When he learns that the chaplain had told Higgins to trust him, however, Bilko's conscience kicks in. He vows not to spend the recruits' money gambling, but to avoid temptation he attempts to keep it out of sight. First, Bilko hides the money under his pillow. Then he tries securing it in a book, in a safe under the bed, and in his jacket pocket. Finally, Bilko hands the money back to Higgins and tells him not to press is luck. Ernest returns to bed and falls asleep with a clear conscience.[2] Bilko, the main character in *The Phil Silvers Show*, is a product of a democracy unenamored with the military. Americans enjoyed newspaper comics like *Beetle Bailey* and *Sad Sack* and television shows like *The Phil Silvers Show*, which lampooned the regulars.

While interpretations of a "good" Korean War existed in popular culture during the 1950s, the war fairly quickly became the "forgotten" war. World

War II looked so much more victorious, decisive, and, well, "good" in comparison. The elevation of World War II in popular culture coincided with President Eisenhower's New Look national security policy, which militarized the defense establishment by increasing American military strength and building up the nation's nuclear arsenal. It also had an anti-militarist component to it: the New Look relied heavily on citizen-soldiers for manpower in order to keep the federal budget under control. Americans favored military preparedness for the Cold War, but according to survey data they also harbored negative attitudes toward the armed forces, especially male teenagers toward the draft. Even with the peacetime draft, the military services invested heavily in recruiting but did not necessarily meet their manpower goals. Eisenhower helped militarize society, but Americans did not accept this militarization unless packaged with traditional anti-militarist sentiments and language.

The "Good" Korean War

While one image of the Korean War was dark and even anti-war, the other one centered on glory and technological strength. Due to the expense of portraying aircraft and Navy ships, movie studios often approached the Air Force and Navy for assistance. As a result, these military services were able to exert influence on the scripts, which led to more heroic and favorable impressions of them.[3] Although films such as *Bridges at Toko-Ri* were able to present dark themes, many films of the Air Force and Navy did little more than glorify the services.

A model example of the "good" Korean War film is *Battle Hymn* (1957), which offers a morally righteous interpretation of American action and behavior in Korea.[4] It is based on the best-selling autobiography of Air Force Lieutenant Colonel Dean Hess (played by star Rock Hudson), who flew in the war as a fighter pilot, trained South Korean pilots, and saved the lives of hundreds of Korean orphans.[5] Hess feeds orphans, houses and supplies them in a Buddhist temple, and then, almost miraculously, manages to evacuate them ahead of a North Korean offensive.

The only moral ambiguity in this film is whether Hess, who became a Protestant Christian preacher after fighting in World War II, could bring himself to kill the enemy in the Korean War. In the previous war, Hess had accidentally killed some children when a bomb from his plane released at the wrong moment. He had been wracked with guilt about it ever since. It is a South Korean pilot with a similarly tragic experience who finally eases Hess' suffering by telling his colleague, "We have to trust Him, sir." In fact, nearly every major Korean character in the film is Christian, and at the end of the film, Hess opens a Christian orphanage on an island off the Korean coast.[6] Like the war's recruiting advertising, the film set the religious Americans—and in this case also the Christian South Koreans—apart from the "godless" communist enemy. The *Time* film critic excoriated *Battle Hymn* for picturing "the Korean war as a sort of Sunday-school outing at which some of the boys got a little out of hand," adding that, by the end of the film, "The sugar count of this picture is so dangerously high that theater managers might be well advised to offer insulin shots in the lobby."[7] Apparently audiences were in the mood for sugar — and Rock Hudson — because the film drew audiences, propelling it into the top 20 films of 1957.[8] For American audiences there was room for both *Bridges at Toko-Ri* and *Battle Hymn*. Unfortunately, box-office data cannot illuminate whether the same folks were watching both movies.

Comic books took up the "good" Korean War in the wake of the Comics Code. Adults had long been concerned about the content of comic books. As one parent put it, "Excessive reading of comics stunt the stature of the mind."[9] In order to provide wholesome entertainment for children and young adults, the comics industry adopted a code, which lasted from 1954 to 1980. As a result of this code, comic books sanitized the violence, the ambiguous moral dilemmas, and the dark and gloomy settings of the comics in all genres.[10] For example, the Comics Code directed that "policemen, judges, government officials, and respected institutions shall never be presented in such a way as to create disrespect for established authority," which included representations of the armed forces.[11] Unwavering obedience and respect for authority helped lead to militarized interpretations of war in the comics under the new code.

Given the new standards, war comics quickly idealized plots and characters. Appearances of the characters changed dramatically. Although some soldiers continued to sport unshaven faces, most men and officers appeared clean-shaven with crisp, clean, proper uniforms. Artists drew the frames in brighter, more colorful tones, leaving out much of the barren environment of the previous renditions. Stories all had triumphant attitudes and victorious endings. No matter the setting or the arm of service, every military character proved brave, loyal, and good-hearted and lived up to American ideals. For example, in "Man Alone," the character Bart Mase joins the Marine Corps during the Korean War. He is described as an actor who "had everything." The other Marines, who are mechanics, farmers, salesmen, and other blue-collar types, do not readily accept him at first. Mase proves himself by taking the men to distract a T-34 tank while the lieutenant creeps up on it from behind to shoot a bazooka at it.[12] Through combat, Mase thus establishes his courage and earns his place among the group. *Navy Combat* stories contained equally heroic stories for seaman and marines and were set on submarines, PT boats, destroyers, and planes.[13]

Similarly, in "Supply," also set during the Korean War, equipment from America's industrial might "made possible the fabulous amphibious landing at Inchon that was the first link in the chain of final victory." It presents the Korean War as a clear-cut victory rather than the stalemate that it was. And this victory extends into the Cold War: "No matter where it may be, in any part of the globe, whenever or wherever aggression threatens free peoples, the supplies will come through!" Any attempt to challenge freedom in another nation "strikes at the roots of our own liberty. And we will always supply the means to strike back!"[14] It is a forceful statement of America's Cold War ideology and suggests a proactive, aggressive, militarist stance. Although the goal had been to provide wholesome entertainment for children, the result may have been to enamor the younger generation with romantic and unrealistic notions of war.

The "Good" World War II

Compared to the uncertain, ambiguous, and questionable aspects of the darker Korean War, World War II appeared as a clear, unambiguous, morally righteous victory over tyranny. Filmmakers, television producers, and others turned to World War II stories rather than ones based in the indecisive Korean War.[15] Many of the World War II stories glorified the heroic exploits of citizen-soldiers, presenting a more militaristic image than the one presented in films like *The Story of G.I. Joe* or *A Walk in the Sun*.

Premiering in theaters during the Korean War, the World War II film *Flying Leathernecks* (1951) glorifies military service. The film stars John Wayne as Major Kirby, the new commander of a Marine fighter squadron in the Pacific theater. Kirby is a tough, by-the-book professional marine who disciplines his lax pilots. His executive officer describes him as "a classic commander," or rather, a militaristic one with this reference to ancient Sparta: "Come home with your shield, or on it." In this respect, the professional Kirby closely resembles the Sergeant Stryker character in *Sands of Iwo Jima* or Savage in *Twelve O'Clock High*. Kirby and his men are called to complete many hard missions, which exhaust the men and test Kirby's leadership. Although many of the pilots are lost while attempting to prove the viability of close air support, the surviving men learn the lessons they need to be successful. Overall, the film highlights the bravery and courage of marine aviators.[16]

New York Times critic Howard Thompson liked the militaristic images, describing the film as filled with "virility and battle casualties" and air sequences that were "fast, furious and picturesque."[17] The Marine Corps approved of the film for its favorable depiction of the service. With the emphasis on close air support, one of the key roles for aircraft in Korea, the film implied that the Marines continued their successes in the war they were currently fighting.[18] It burnished both the Marines' World War II history and their contemporary war fighting prowess.

Written and directed by Robert Pirosh, the film *Go for Broke!* (1951) presents the Japanese-American soldiers of the World War II-era 442d Infantry Regiment in the same heroic light as white soldiers. These Japanese-American soldiers, or Nisei, slog through mud, march constantly, and share the misery of infantry combat, just as their white counterparts do. Since they are Japanese-American, there is the added burden of fighting racism and prejudice from their white brothers-in-arms. *Go for Broke!* is very much like Pirosh's earlier movie, *Battleground.*[19]

Pirosh tells much of story through a prejudiced white lieutenant named Grayson (Van Johnson). Lieutenant Grayson arrives at Camp Shelby unhappy about his assignment, unimpressed with what he sees as lax discipline in the barracks, and uncomfortable with the foreign-sounding song and dance of the soldiers. He asks for a transfer to his old unit in the 36th "Texas" Infantry Division, but Colonel Pence (Warner Anderson) denies it. The colonel further corrects Grayson's casual reference to the soldiers as "Japs" by firmly stating that this is unacceptable and offensive language. What is acceptable at the time are the terms "Japanese-Americans," "Nisei," or "Buddha heads." Pence adds that these men are volunteers, and he expects that they should be respected as such. Here Pence references a key of traditional anti-militarism: volunteerism. The film notably does not mention that Japanese-American men were subjected to the draft and even conscripted out of the internment camps.[20]

Support for Japanese-Americans is not complete, however. Captain Solari (Dan Riss) points out that the regiment's soldiers have been checked and rechecked for loyalty. Moreover, he justifies the Japanese-American internment program, which the Nisei troops openly criticize. Why did these men volunteer for combat after they and their families were relocated? "We got to do something so we don't get a deal like that again," one explains.[21] He accepts the idea that proving oneself in combat and in defense of the nation should convince naysayers of their loyalty as citizens. Fighting is considered a duty of citizenship at this time. Though the men want to fight the Japanese, the unit is sent to Italy instead.

The Japanese-American troops display courage and competence, and Grayson learns to appreciate the combat abilities of his Nisei soldiers. Grayson defends his soldiers against the prejudice of his old platoon sergeant in the

36th Infantry Division. Even the old sergeant comes to appreciate the Japanese-American soldiers when the 442d rescues a "lost" battalion of the Texas Division, which had been cut off and surrounded by the Germans. At the end, the film reminds the audience that the 442d Infantry Regiment earned battle honors for their gallantry and esprit de corps "in the finest tradition of the armed forces."[22]

The timing of the film proved auspicious, too, as it refurbished the Japanese image at a time when Japan was an American ally against communism in Asia. Acknowledging some scenes as "hokum," the *Time* critic praised the film for its "strikingly realistic battle scenes" and "endowing [the soldiers] with a wry, grim humor that suits them both as G.I.s and a minority long since inured to getting the short end of the stick."[23]

On television, the award-winning and critically acclaimed World War II documentary *Victory at Sea* (1952–1953) extended tribute to the citizen-soldier and the interpretation of the "good" war to the newest entertainment outlet. Based on the work of historian Samuel Eliot Morison, the series recounts the U.S. Navy's role in World War II and emphasizes America's innocence and liberation of the oppressed.[24] As a tribute to the Allies who fought in the war, the documentary highlights the sacrifices of the combatants. In contrast to the stalemate in Korea, World War II stood out as a clear and focused conflict.

Militarization flows through *Victory at Sea*'s narration. With melodramatic language, the commentator evokes the power, might, and determination of American and Allied forces. For example, the Navy's submariners operate where the "threat of death hangs over" them, and they need a "stout hull and stouter hearts" to survive enemy depth charges. America's fight in the Pacific was not so much about defeating a particular enemy, but "island to island, continent to continent, the children of free peoples move the forces of tyranny from the face of the earth." *Victory at Sea* also spends more time replaying the machinery of war — ships, planes, tanks, and explosions— than depicting individual combat. The score replaces the actual sounds of battle — the propellers, explosions, and voices— with music.[25] Machinery and technology certainly evoke images of strength and power. These images might strike the audiences as particularly significant at a time when the Korean War was stuck in a stalemate.

Viewers had in mind the Cold War confrontation between the democratic United States and the communist Soviet Union when watching the documentary and some Americans reflected stridently militarist views in their comments about the series. One critic thought that Soviet Premier Nikita Khrushchev ought to watch the series in order to understand that America should not be pushed around.[26] Picking up on the strength of the armed forces, at least one teenager mentioned that the United States "really has great sea power."[27] Another teenager took away from the documentary that it was "an honor to serve your country."[28] Among adults who watched the series, one mused that it was a "good incentive for me to join [the] Navy."[29]

Other interpreters of *Victory at Sea* perceived it as less militaristic. Television critic Jack Gould praised the series for its "rare power and poetry," noting that it "is not alone history but a drama told with moving simplicity and restrained majesty."[30] Despite the emphasis on machines and technology, Gould believed *Victory at Sea* had a "sensitiveness and point of view that personalize the conflict in terms of the men who went to sea."[31] He urged viewers not to miss it. When the series was later compiled into a shorter 100-minute feature-length film, a *New York Times* critic reminded audiences that it "is both a sober and exciting tribute to determined and courageous men and a convincing casebook on the wanton waste of war."[32] The language of this review is reminiscent of *The Story of G.I. Joe*, paying tribute to the soldiers but recognizing the dark side of war as well.

Audie Murphy

To Hell and Back (1955), the film memoir of one of America's most decorated World War II veterans, Audie Murphy, serves as the exemplar of the citizen-soldier fighting the good war. Since the real Murphy took up acting at the end of the war, the veteran played himself in the film version of his memoir. At the opening of *To Hell and Back*, Murphy is presented as a good-hearted rural American boy, who takes care of his family and sets out to serve his country after the attack on Pearl Harbor. The Marine Corps rejects him, with the recruiter commenting, "We separate the men from the boys, but we like to have something to start with."[33] Murphy is similarly turned down by the Navy, when the recruiter remarks, "The Navy makes men out of boys, but you're too big a job for us."[34] With Murphy's youth and seeming weakness established, he joins the Army. His company commander in North Africa believes him ill-suited for infantry and asks him to consider a transfer. Murphy only wants a chance to prove himself in combat, reflecting the notion that combat makes a man.

Once given his chance, Murphy proves to be a selfless, humble, courageous hero. He quickly wins the affection of the men and recognition from his superiors, who eventually give him a battlefield commission. Murphy repeatedly takes on dangerous missions and disregards his own safety. He is awarded a Medal of Honor for one of these actions: Murphy calls for artillery fire on his position in order to halt a battalion-sized German advance. As he

Audie Murphy plays himself in the Universal Pictures film version of his autobiography *To Hell and Back* (Universal International Pictures, 1955). This scene recreates Murphy's Medal of Honor action where he holds off a battalion-size German advance by firing a .50 caliber machine gun from a burning tank destroyer. Many (but not all) who watched this film came away with a positive view of Murphy and the Army (photograph by Bob Landry, Time & Life Images/Getty Images).

pulls back, Murphy mounts a disabled tank destroyer and fires its .50 caliber machine gun into advancing German infantry.[35] He jumps off the vehicle just moments before it explodes. His actions force the Germans to retreat.

Scholars who point to the militarization of American culture can find an excellent example in the Army's relationship with this movie. The Army responded to the film *To Hell and Back* with a massive public-relations and recruiting campaign, eliciting the assistance of Audie Murphy, who was at the time a member of the Texas National Guard. According to recruiters, "Army recruiting work[ed] hand in glove with members of the Universal-International Picture Corp. publicity staff, with both recruiting and the movie people profiting from the association."[36] Army recruiters set up lobby displays in theaters. "Miss Texas of 1955" accompanied recruiters on a publicity tour to advertise the film. One newspaper in Texas ran an essay contest: "What Audie Murphy's

Life and Military Achievements Mean to Me." The publicity resulted in a temporary burst of enlistments in Dallas, Houston, and San Antonio into the 3d Armored Division, which recruiters dubbed "Audie Murphy platoons."[37]

Film critics had mixed responses to the film. *New York Times* film reviewer A. H. Weiler believed that previous films had better depicted the gallantry of the men, but praised Murphy for lending "stature, credibility and dignity to an autobiography that would be routine and hackneyed without him."[38] Weiler noted that Murphy still appeared to be the "shy, serious, tenderfoot rather than a titan among G.I. heroes" in the film.[39] Murphy appeared more like a citizen than a Sergeant Stryker-type character. The *Time* reviewer thought that Murphy "seems to be tooting his own tommy gun a bit too loud" by self-promotion in the movie.[40] Nonetheless, the critic found something haunting in the film, noting that from time to time viewers see "in the figure of this childlike man, the soul-chilling ghost of all the menlike children of those violent years, who hovered among battles like avenging cherubs, and knew all about death before they knew very much about life."[41] War, in his view, did not appear ennobling.

As hoped for by Army officials, *To Hell and Back* elicited many positive responses from audiences. According to one survey, many teenagers praised Murphy's courage, bravery, and heroism and the loyalty and camaraderie of the men. One teen suggested that the film "showed how tough it was, but made you feel like you wanted to be in there for your country."[42] Another young man explained that the "Army brought out his [Murphy's] character."[43] Other interviewees noted that the film glorified military service, which the interviewers interpreted as a positive comment about the film.[44] *To Hell and Back* made less of an impression on adults, but they also admired Murphy's heroism. One mentioned that Murphy appeared devoted to service, and another suggested that he "never thought of himself."[45]

Still, even with all the victory and triumph, some audience members made negative comments about the film. A few thought the soldiers were cowards. One interviewee thought all the soldiers disliked the Army, perhaps not understanding the usual G.I. gripes. Another teenager thought the film showed the suffering in war. Murphy was indeed a hero, he said, but "it's real rough."[46] Despite censored violence, one adult complained about the bloodshed. Another respondent detested the emphasis on one hero over a squad of common soldiers, remarking, "It was the story of an impossible soldier. It built up the Army as a place for all heroes and that one man can fight the war by himself."[47] For this viewer, as it probably was for other veterans, the movie did not depict the teamwork necessary to survive war. Even a movie as exciting as *To Hell and Back* could not replace veterans' authentic war experiences, and millions of veterans sat in movie audiences.

New Look

In 1953, President Dwight D. Eisenhower inaugurated a new national defense policy, dubbed the New Look, that deemphasized large standing conventional forces in favor of the deterrence offered by nuclear weapons. Nuclear weapons were also less costly to maintain than large standing forces, and Eisenhower wanted to rein in the defense budget.[48] Eisenhower thought conventional wars, such as the one recently fought in Korea, were unlikely to recur, so he cut manpower accordingly. The Army's strength fell from 1.5 million in 1953 to less than 900,000 in 1958.[49] While still huge compared with pre–Cold War peacetime force structure, this force was not as large as it could be given a permanent Cold "war" posture. At the same time that manpower for conventional forces dropped, the nuclear arsenal was increased. The Air Force built up its squadrons of strategic bombers, and the Navy developed atomic submarines and, later, nuclear-tipped missiles for launch from surface ships and submarines. When the Air Force gained control of all long-range nuclear missiles, the Army concentrated on short-ranged and tactical nuclear weapons thought to be suitable for land warfare. As a result of the New Look's emphasis on strategic nuclear air power, the United States Air Force and its Strategic Air Command rose to prominence.[50]

Most citizens preferred to rely on technology rather than a large conventional force to protect the nation. A Gallup poll taken in May 1952 indicated that many Americans supported a "small but highly skilled army, navy, and air force" in post–Korean War American defense policy.[51] This indicated both support for Eisenhower's New Look and vestiges of the long-standing American policy of maintaining small standing forces during peacetime. In contrast, a 1953 poll revealed that most Americans favored sustaining the strength of the armed forces upon a truce with Korea.[52] After the war, however, Americans returned to privileging technology over increased numbers in the ground forces.[53] Overwhelmingly, Americans believed the Air Force would be the most important service in the event of another world war.[54] They accepted Eisenhower's emphasis on technology and the prominence of air power.

Although a reliance on technology is usually associated with increased militarism, a left-leaning opinion piece explains why anti-militarist liberals might support air power. Although this comment was made during an earlier debate about the efficacy of Universal Military Training under the Truman administration, the observation is pertinent for New Look policies as well. William Walton explains, "Most liberals accept the necessity of increasing our [military] forces. They insist that our armed force be realistic, subordinate to an active peace policy and maintained with a minimum of militarization in our lives. Air power is the armed power which involves the least militarization and so is supported by liberals who oppose UMT."[55] When compared to militarizing the nation's youth in universal military service, reliance on a smaller force of air force professionals had more appeal. In this case, air power seemed the lesser of the evils. This thinking might also help explain liberal support for New Look policies under the Eisenhower administration.

Of course, not every liberal accepted the New Look and its emphasis on nuclear weapons. As the editors of the *New Republic* stated, "Our objective in wartime must be to achieve the destruction of the enemy power with the minimum loss on both sides of property and life. This purpose is wholly abandoned in a war of annihilation [with nuclear weapons]."[56] Another editorial from the same opinion journal criticized Eisenhower's "'budget-first' thinking" for making "one of the most momentous decision in history for what can only be termed trivial reasons" of reducing defense expenditures.[57] Budget austerity did not trump national security in the increasingly militarized United States.

In order to limit conventional manpower, Eisenhower had to rely on citizen-soldiers, particularly the reserve forces. In a special message to Congress, Eisenhower explained the three elements of his plan to increase reliance on the reserves:

> (1) active forces in the strength and effectiveness necessary to meet, to repel and to punish a first massive assault or to conduct a lesser operation that does not require mobilization; (2) reserves so organized and trained as units that they can be speedily mobilized to reinforce the active forces in combat or to man defense operations at home; (3) an unorganized reserve pool, adequate in training and numbers, to permit a quick general mobilization of all our military strength.[58]

Eisenhower stressed his desire for adequate training, preferably prior-service experience, and length of reserve service in his message.

Congress had its own ideas for reserve forces reform. In the Reserve Forces Act of 1955, Congress extended the draft, required a two-year active duty commitment, and offered a special program of six-months of active duty with a seven-and-a-half-year reserve obligation for high school students.[59] Eisenhower criticized Congress for reducing the overall military obligation from eight years to six and "failing to grant authority to induct [from Selective Service] into the Reserve if sufficient numbers to meet military requirements are not obtained voluntarily."[60] Even in this militarized era, Congress wanted to rely on volunteerism, not conscription, to meet manpower needs. The active duty forces were going to have to recruit volunteers, not rely on the draft to fill force structure.

With the emphasis on the reserves, the Department of Defense began a massive public relations campaign to highlight the role of and to recruit for

"YOUNG MEN 17-18½...
I'M SERVING THE *DRAFT-FREE* WAY IN THE
U.S. ARMY RESERVE

So can YOU!"

HERE'S THE PLAN TO PROTECT YOUR CIVILIAN FUTURE:

RESERVE SERVICE MEANS ONLY 6 MONTHS' ACTIVE DUTY

If you are between 17 and 18½, there's a great new way for you to serve in the Army Reserve. It's a special plan that means only six months' active duty. Then you return to civilian life, free to follow whatever plans you may have. You meet the rest of your military obligation as a civilian, participating part-time with a home unit of the Army Reserve.

GET THESE BIG ADVANTAGES:

1. Opportunity to plan and carry out your civilian future.
2. Only six months' active duty.
3. Your choice of Reserve Unit.
4. Better job prospects when you are draft-free.
5. Key leadership role in community defense.
6. Chance to finish high school.

Come on down and get all the facts from the Army Reserve Unit Advisor.

(ADDRESS HERE)

U.S. ARMY RESERVE

— IN THE INTERESTS OF MILITARY RESERVE WEEK THIS AD HAS BEEN SPONSORED BY: —

SPONSORS' NAMES AND ADDRESSES

Dancer-Fitzgerald-Sample, Inc.
U. S. Army Reserve   Job No. 8521   Size 500 lines, 7⅛" x 125 lines   Newspapers, 1956

This 1956 advertisement featuring the special program for high school students to serve six months active duty and seven-and-a-half years in the reserves stresses the civilian nature of the program. Created by Army advertising agency Dancer-Fitzgerald-Sample, Inc., it plays off fears of the draft interfering with civilian life plans. The draft was unpopular with young teenaged males, who believed it to be an onerous obligation rather than a privilege of citizenship (National Archives and Records Administration).

the reserve forces. Reserve recruiting advertising tapped into a fundamental anti-militarist sentiment: the ideal of small standing forces and reliance on citizen-soldiers. Yet the context of the situation was clearly militarist. One advertisement aimed at teenagers reminded them that the United States was under constant threat of attack and the only recourse was for the nation to be strong. Given the situation, America could choose a large, standing army, but "this would mean high taxes, a shortage of civilian labor, and would break up the whole American Way of Life!" Or, Americans could choose a large reserve force, which "interferes LEAST with our way of life."[61]

Similar exhortations reminded readers that the traditional "American Way has always been to have a small standing army backed up by trained reserves."[62] This advertisement reinforced the traditional relationship between American society and its military forces. One poster with the bold heading: "Our Town's Leading Citizen," depicted the citizen-soldier by showing a man

These two pages come from a U.S. Army Reserve recruiting pamphlet circa 1955–1956. The scenario depicted here is a surprise attack — likely nuclear in nature. The anti-militarist message is clear: keep U.S. military strength to respond to this attack in the reserve forces, not a large standing army, which is against the American way of life (National Archives and Records Administration).

literally half in a combat uniform and half in a business suit.[63] Another poster pictured a reservist in combat fatigues in the foreground. A set of buildings with doctors, scientists, factory workers, and others occupied the far-left corner of the background. A church with people streaming out of it was situated directly behind the serviceman, and a suburban neighborhood stood in the far-right corner. The poster's author urged, "Let us ALL support our U.S. Army Reserve."[64] It advertised for community members both to join a unit and to support local units. Citizen-soldiers appeared at the heart of American communities. It is also worth noting that these advertisements for the reserve forces, as well as those for the Army, reject the idea that the next war would be a nuclear war lasting only a day. The Army and the reserve forces assumed a longer war in which they would be needed.

Despite the massive recruiting campaign focused on citizen-soldiers, the reserves did not build up their numbers as anticipated. The special six-month active duty program, expected to pull in 20,000 recruits per month, attracted only 4,000 per month. In the mid–1950s the Army was the only service inducting draftees, and those numbers were low because the service had taken serious active-duty cuts under the New Look policy. With draft calls being kept to a minimum, many teenagers gambled that they would miss military service entirely if they did nothing. [65] Part of the problem was that teenagers did not understand the new reserve program, in spite of the massive public relations campaign. And for those teens who knew about it, they harbored only a "mildly favorable opinion of it." [66] Most teenagers thought that eight years in the reserves would interfere with their career plans. The majority expected to wait for the draft rather than to volunteer.[67]

Many teenagers also believed that military service constituted an onerous obligation rather than a privilege of citizenship. Few young men considered making the military their career. One survey indicated that only 8 percent of young men thought they would even enjoy military life. Another 38 percent declared that they wanted to get out of military service as soon as possible.[68] Without an immediate threat of hot war, patriotic calls to duty — even as temporary citizen-soldiers — fell flat. Self-interest trumped even citizen-soldier idealism.

Still, many young men did serve as draftees, even if they were not excited about the prospect. The most famous Cold War conscript was Elvis Presley, who quietly fulfilled his civic military duty when he was drafted in 1958. While news media reported on the short length of Elvis' new military haircut, the rock star reported to his local Memphis, Tennessee, draft board without complaint. He was inducted into the Army and served his Cold War duty overseas in Germany. Elvis served in the Army for two uneventful years, mustering out in 1960. After his military service, Elvis no longer appeared to possess the same rebelliousness and sexual mystique as he had before induction. According to some, the Army had tamed Elvis, transforming him from a rebellious youth into a responsible adult.[69] One recording engineer remembered that the Elvis who returned from Germany "just wasn't the same."[70] Some spark had gone out. Still, audiences clamored for Elvis, and his post-service debut performance with Frank Sinatra garnered a hefty 67.7 percent television audience share.[71]

"Germans with Guns Can't Be Trusted"

Given the example of Nazi Germany in World War II, Americans worried about the re-arming of West Germany in the 1950s. Commentators feared that the base of the German army would be Wehrmact veterans, suspect because of the World War II experience, and fretted about a corresponding move back to authoritarianism in that country.[72] In an aptly titled article, "Germans with Guns Can't Be Trusted," one editorialist warned that "members of the militarist, industrialist and Nazi cliques are finding their way back into places of power and influence" in West Germany.[73] Another editorialist worried that "the habits and attitudes of democracy have not yet taken root" in West Germany, so "there is reason to fear that conscription, and a standing armed force of 500,000, can provide a focal point for aggressive nationalism."[74]

Other commentators believed that a German army could succeed if given the proper oversight. One editorialist believed that a European defense community would "give German vigor a safe area in which to express itself, and enable the West to realize the military potential that lies in Germany without exposing German democracy to what it most fears, the revival of militarism."[75] Another commentator thought that an American presence would be necessary: "There is little chance that a German army, especially an independent army, can become politically 'safe' enough to take the specifically political risk of removing U.S. divisions in the foreseeable future."[76] Germany still appeared to be a militarist threat to these opinion-makers.

American commentators praised the German civilian leadership for asserting control over the military, a hallmark of American anti-militarism. In 1955, the German defense minister removed the German military director of personnel from command. As one editorialist explained, "General Mueller-Hillebrand showed his contempt for the civil power" which was "painfully reminiscent of the 'State with the State'" the German army had occupied in World War II.[77] The Germans, however, had reformed and now insisted on civilian control of the military.

"There's a Kind of War"

The perfect example of the New Look in popular culture is the film *Strategic Air Command* (1955), which looks like a public relations film for the Air Force's strategic air arm rather than Hollywood entertainment.[78] Visually, the film is filled with long, lingering shots of bombers taking off, flying, and landing. In this story, the Air Force Reserve activates professional baseball player Lieutenant Colonel "Dutch" Holland (James Stewart) for a 21-month active duty tour with the Strategic Air Command (SAC). The story has some basis in reality. Red Sox baseball player Ted Williams had been recalled to fly for the Marine Corps during the Korean War, and Stewart served as a colonel and later as a brigadier general in the actual Air Force Reserve.[79]

In the film, Dutch is a citizen-solider called for Cold War active duty. At first, he complains about this obligation and feels angry for the disruption of his major-league baseball career, much like the young men in the attitude surveys. He quickly realizes that "there is a kind of war" going on, however, and that only the Air Force can prevent an open war from starting.[80] He remains on active duty past his obligation so he can continue to protect the nation. His wife, Sally, (June Allyson) eagerly accompanies him on his tour at first, but quickly becomes angry, frustrated, and bitter about all the time he spends away from her and their newborn daughter. Eventually, Sally feels ashamed of her selfishness by putting herself before the defense of the country and apologizes to Dutch. From now on, she promises to support him and his mission. An injury to his shoulder sustained in a crash landing finally puts an end to Dutch's flying career.[81]

Strategic Air Command dazzled *New York Times* film critic Bosley Crowther, who lavished praise on this "most elaborate and impressive pictorial show of the beauty and organized power of the United States air arm."[82] He firmly approved the Air Force's contributions to the film. SAC's commander, General Curtis LeMay, offered extraordinary access to the film crews, and Air Force bands performed at the film's premiere.[83] For Crowther, the overtly positive image and message of the Air Force overcame the cinematic failures of the movie. He accepted the emphasis on professionalism and peace-time military preparedness, hallmarks of the growing militarism in American society at the time. The *Time* reviewer also picked up on the militarism of the film, but was more critical of it. He bluntly called *Strategic Air Command* "one soaring, supercolossal recruiting poster." [84] He also pointed out that "when the camera glides in for its first look at a B-47, the sound track bursts into organ peals of religious music, a strangely sacred serenade to one of the world's most powerful instruments of destruction."[85] He was clearly uncomfortable with the overt praise for weapons of war, suggesting that the process of militarization was not taken lightly by everyone.

Audiences appeared to accept and approve the militarist message and context in *Strategic Air Command*. Teenagers noted how the men "guard over the country in case of attack."[86] They also thought the film showed high morale, offered a "good impression of service life," and demonstrated that people were "happy in the Air Force," comments that surely warmed the hearts of Air Force recruiters.[87] Other teens admired the heroism and "courage under strain and pressure."[88] Adults approved of the film as well, noting the training, discipline, and high quality of the men. One respondent said, "I liked the idea that he wanted to stay out, felt his duty, and then loved it."[89] Another suggested that the Air Force provided a "good life" and approved of the "way they defended the country."[90] Even though Dutch began the film as a citizen-soldier, he became a regular in the Cold War Air Force. Audience feedback on the film supports an increased appreciation for the professionalism of the regulars and of their belief that the Air Force was indeed protecting the nation under Eisenhower's nuclear-heavy New Look policy.

New Look militarism also came across in comic books. One comic featuring the Navy took the reader on a tour through a nuclear-powered submarine and a live-fire missile demonstration. This "newest weapon in democracy's arsenal" would help the Cold War stay cold; or in other words, it would help the world avoid open war.[91] In a story about the Air Force, three unidentified aircraft are detected by distant early warning radar, and Air Force long-range interceptors shoot them down. After the successful mission, an officer at the Continental Air Defense Command headquarters remarks to a general, "This kind of Cold War gives me the shivers, General! Suppose we didn't shoot them down?" [92] The general muses, "Perhaps they'd destroy a major city as a prelude to a total war — or perhaps, if we let them pass, they'd send more at a later date! We'll never know because we'll never let them pass!" he concludes firmly.[93] Readers could rest assured that the USAF was protecting the nation. Similarly, the long-running comic strip *Steve Canyon* presented a positive message about the Air Force. Canyon was a veteran recalled for the Korean War, who, like the character Dutch in *Strategic Air Command*, decided to stay active duty for the Cold War. It inspired a short-lived television spin-off from 1958–1960.[94]

Sputnik

On October 4, 1957, the Soviets successfully launched the first artificial satellite, *Sputnik*. The United States had also been working on a project to launch a satellite, Project Vanguard, in conjunction with the International Geophysical Year. President Eisenhower had intentionally chosen to give the nation's space efforts a civilian face rather than a military one. Even though Vanguard was a Navy project, the satellite was developed for scientific purposes rather than military ones. Unfortunately for Eisenhower, the Soviets launched first. Though Eisenhower attempted to calm the public during a press conference in which he assured the American people that the satellite did not bother him, the public reacted fearfully.[95] Americans worried that the Soviets had surpassed the United States in developing military technology and that the Soviets could launch a nuclear-tipped missile at the country. It caused many Americans, particularly from the Democratic Party, to accuse the Eisenhower administration of failure to support national defense and call for even greater military preparedness for war. Some commentators fretted that the unaligned nations of the world would flock to the Soviet Union as the nation who had superior military power.[96] The failure of America's first and second attempts at launching satellites heightened the vulnerability Americans felt. The U.S. finally launched a successful satellite in January 1958, using the Army's Redstone missile.[97]

Americans adopted a militaristic way of measuring America's strength: the ability to launch intercontinental ballistic missiles rather than other economic, social, or political activities. They also assumed the rest of the world was measuring American and Soviet strength in the same way. As T. A. Heppenheimer observes, Americans perceived that "America's freedom and democracy might be fine in times of general peace, but would lose out to the discipline of a dictatorship in a crunch."[98] In the panic over *Sputnik*, Eisenhower received "demands for more spending, on space and missile research, for conventional forces, for federal aid to colleges and universities, for fallout shelters, and a myriad of other projects."[99] As a response of these proposals, Eisenhower created a president's science advisory committee and recommended the nation train more scientists and engineers, which led to the National Defense Education Act of 1958. Even Eisenhower, who had a large hand in militarizing American defense policy, worried about the pressures of continued militarization. In a cabinet meeting, Eisenhower explained, "We must remember that we are defending a way of life ... should we have to resort to anything resembling a garrison state, then all that we are striving to defend ... could disappear."[100]

The Military's Self-Image

Military television shows grew in popularity through the 1950s, encompassing anthologies, fictionalized dramas, situation comedies, and sports and quiz shows, but few series lasted long. Only the U.S. Army's show *The Big*

Picture, the situation comedy *The Phil Silvers Show*, and the anthology series *Navy Log* produced more than 100 episodes. Most military shows produced fewer than 40 episodes.[101] Despite the increased presence of the military in American life through the draft and a large active-duty military force during the 1950s, Americans did not automatically embrace the military-themed shows for their entertainment. It suggests incomplete militarization of American culture, particularly as *The Phil Silvers Show* did not glorify active-duty service; instead, it poked fun at it. Indeed, many of the most popular shows of the 1950s and 1960s had very strong anti-militarist themes. A few of these shows, however, presented the military's self-image in that the military supported them directly, and they presented positive interpretations of the armed forces.

For publicity purposes, the Army created an ongoing documentary series, *The Big Picture* (1951–71), which it provided to the networks free of charge.[102] Lieutenant Carl Bruton, a public information officer, conceptualized the idea of a television show "to tell and to show the American people just what the Army is doing to fulfill its obligations to them."[103] This idea turned into *The Big Picture*, which showed half-hour vignettes on Army history, biography, technology, and current events. It represented the official Army self-image. *The Big Picture* also served as a recruiting tool, weaving into its stories the recruiting slogan, "The Mark of a Man."[104] The shows were aimed at a civilian audience, as officers in the Command Information program learned that soldiers refused to watch Army-produced educational or information programs, even those featuring their own service.[105]

The Army created *The Big Picture* to highlight the positive aspects of the service, but some adults found fault with the Army anyway. Reacting to one episode, an adult disliked "the captain's attitude toward the cadets. Officers in service so long they think they are always right."[106] In response to other episodes, another adult described the "hoary drinking by men in uniform," and another criticized, "It just showed soldiers at their worst — drinking." [107] One more person complained about how "the fellows fooled around." [108] Others disliked instances of immaturity, sloppiness, incompetence, griping, and a hard life.[109] These comments reveal that these viewers held the traditional American stereotype of active duty soldiers, certainly not a vision of the brave, selfless soldiers preferred by the Army. Despite an attempt by the Army to sway public opinion, some Americans stubbornly retained a long-standing American anti-militarism.

Much later, in 1969, *The Big Picture* attracted the negative attention of Senator J. William Fulbright (D-AK), chair of the Senate Foreign Relations Committee. Fulbright criticized the series for creating segments on the Vietnam conflict and conducting public relations "with little public or congressional knowledge or interference."[110] After this unwelcome criticism, the show wrapped two years later.

The Navy also advertised its service on television through the anthology series *Navy Log* (1955–58). It received the full cooperation of the Department of Defense and the Department of the Navy and presented positive images of the sea service.[111] For example, one episode highlights the military values of bravery, sacrifice, and dedication to duty as well as prowess under difficult combat conditions. It features the training and performance of an underwater reconnaissance team who disabled Japanese underwater obstacles for beach landings during World War II. These men were the predecessors of the Navy SEALs (Sea, Air, and Land commandoes). The story includes drama and conflict, such as when the men lose faith in their lieutenant when they believe he cowardly left a man behind to die. The lieutenant regains their trust when he spearheads a mission to rescue the wounded man on the beach.[112]

Navy Log episodes also showcase the Navy's role in the Cold War. In the "Incident at Formosa," a Navy plane heads off a Chinese attack on the island now known as Taiwan. The boredom of routine is revealed in this episode, as the pilots and radar operators complain of flying the same patrol repeatedly. Nevertheless, the men perform their duty. On the night of December 7, 1950, a Navy plane over the straits picks up ships on radar. With visibility down to 50 feet or less, the observation plane flies low to confirm the radar contact. The crew observes the Chinese fleet turning around. The narrator reveals that the Chinese had turned around because the Navy plane detected them before their fleet reached the halfway mark. After that point, they would have fought their way to Formosa. This single Navy observation plane has apparently prevented an invasion. Like the Strategic Air Command, the Navy remained constantly vigilant to prevent war.[113] The writers of this particular episode certainly took some dramatic license in making their point, as the People's Republic of China did not try to invade Formosa in 1950.

Navy Log tried to show the naval service as family-friendly as well. Navy wife Sandy Lucas, in the last month of her pregnancy, must move herself and her household from Norfolk, Virginia, to San Diego, California. Initially, Sally is presented as anti-military. She declares that she does not want to be a Navy wife and wishes her husband were a civilian electrician. Sally further reveals that she did not want to become pregnant at all. If it were up to her, Sally pronounced, they would not have a baby until her husband earned the rank of admiral! Sally is juxtaposed with the ideal Navy wife, Marge. She comes to travel with Sally on the cross-country train ride. Marge tells Sally that the 12 years that she and her husband have been in the Navy have been the best of her life. Marge is happy, optimistic, strong, and enthusiastic about the trip. The rest of the episode charts Sally's transformation and acceptance of Navy life.[114]

When Sally's baby is born prematurely on the train and requires a blood transfusion, Navy personnel scramble to get the blood on a plane in Cleveland to fly to a Marine airbase in the Mojave Desert. From there, it is taken by helicopter out to the train, which has stopped in the middle of the New Mexico desert. In just over two hours, Sally's baby receives the life-saving blood transfusion. Sally marvels that the Navy is doing all of this for her baby. The doctor tells her that she is a Navy wife and they take care of their own. Sally finally realizes that she is not alone. The whole U.S. Navy is with her.[115] Indeed, the Navy becomes a caring, family-friendly institution, one that welcomes and protects its new members. It is shown as an ideal environment for rearing white, middle-class families, even if reality proved much different.

Audiences perceived favorable impressions of the Navy from watching *Navy Log*. One teenaged male viewer thought that the series helped "to show the Navy as a good builder of men."[116] Another one noted the number of heroes who had served in the Navy. A different teen thought the series "shows you that it's tough, but it makes you admire them."[117] Adult viewers responded warmly to the care and assistance that the Navy provided their servicemen and their families.[118]

In an effort to show the United States Military Academy as a way to build character and values, the Army supported the anthology series, *West Point Story* (1956–1958). The series reinforced military values of duty, honor, and country. It also showed how West Point cadets were transformed from civilian boys to honorable military men. The series received support from the Department of Defense, the Department of the Army, and the Corps of Cadets. Army recruiters hoped the television series would attract the interest of teenagers and adults.[119]

An episode that clearly demonstrates traditional Army values is "The Harder Right," about West Point's honor code. In 1951, the academy had gone through a scandal when 90 cadets had been expelled for cheating on exams. The event received much publicity, and most Americans knew about the dismissals.[120] In this television episode, a fictional cadet named Leo catches a friend cheating on an exam. Leo is torn about whether he should turn in his friend to the honor committee because his friend could be dismissed from the Academy. In the end, Leo concludes that without honor, the moral foundation of West Point would weaken. After visiting the chapel and reciting the Cadet Prayer, which includes the words "choose the harder right instead of the easier wrong," Leo reports the infraction. His friend admits to cheating, resigns from West Point, and comes to understand the meaning of honor. Although the former cadet has lost his opportunity at West Point, he hopes the lesson will make him a better civilian.[121] This episode is a morality tale meant to emphasize the Army's high standards— higher, presumably, than civilian standards. Placing the military above the civilian is militaristic, though the show did not necessarily show the cadets as such.

Bilko's Bombers

Other military television series reflected anti-militarist themes. The navy comedy-drama set in a hospital, *Hennesey* (1959 –1962), focused more on the human side of the story than the military one and presented some clearly anti-militarist sentiments. It starred Jackie Cooper as "Chick" Hennesey, a newly minted doctor stationed at the naval base in San Diego. His commanding officer, Captain (later Admiral) Schafer (Roscoe Karns) is an old-school curmudgeon, who nevertheless has a soft spot. Hennesey's assistant is an attractive nurse, Martha Hale (Abby Dalton), who becomes his romantic interest and his wife by the end of the series.[122]

In "Remember Pearl Harbor," Hennesey and Hale both arrive in Hawaii, which had just been admitted to the Union the previous year. At the time, the memorial for the USS *Arizona* was being constructed. Hennesey and Hale sail out to the memorial to lay a wreath in remembrance there. Patriotic spirit arises when the scene flashes back to documentary footage of the ship's destruction, followed by a view of the American flag snapping in the wind. This could lead to a very militarist interpretation, but instead the two characters reflect on why wars exist. Hennesey says he does not know why, but suggests that perhaps greed for power, money, or territory fuel them. He then adds, "We have to improve people instead of weapons."[123] Taps plays over the end credits. Instead of presenting anger toward the Japanese or references to the noble victory of the war, the memorial scene is somber and the character's attitudes reflect an anti-militarist aversion to war.

Given the focus on medicine, Hennessey is often shown helping seamen, whether freeing a sailor's mangled arm from a piece of machinery or carrying a wounded marine from a training exercise on his shoulders, rather than fighting in combat. More than once Hennessey mentions to Nurse Hale that it is a wonderful feeling saving a man's life. He also mentions how "the Navy exits to help others."[124] Not exactly. The Navy exists to provide for the common defense of the nation. Nonetheless, Navy recruiters liked the show because it provided believable characters and settings. They thought that *Hennesey* was good for Navy public relations.[125] Critics thought well of the show, too. It won Emmy awards for lead actor and supporting actress for the 1961– 1962 season, and another for lead actor the following year.[126]

The most striking example of anti-militarism during the Eisenhower era is *The Phil Silvers Show* (1955–1959), which lampooned much of contemporary active duty military life. Comedian Phil Silvers played Army Master Sergeant Ernest Bilko, a career regular and a con artist running schemes out of fictitious Fort Baxter, Kansas.[127] Professor J. Fred MacDonald argues that *The Phil Silvers Show* fit into the soft-handed propaganda of the 1950s. He asserts that Bilko never rejected the military. Instead, it was "well understood that at heart they [Bilko and his sidekicks] were loyal to their country if not to military decorum."[128] Equating loyalty with propaganda is a questionable premise for MacDonald to make. Is every American who is loyal to the country engaging in propaganda? It appears that only an anti-military stance would be considered non-propagandistic by MacDonald. He also states that the characters chafed against class and rank but were unable or unwilling to change the system.[129] Of course, to challenge overtly the military hierarchy would lead to dishonorable dismissal from the service or worse: a court-martial conviction and prison time. MacDonald further describes *The Phil Silvers Show* as part of the "nice guy" style, which presented the military as "a bunch of regular guys" instead of "a powerful institution with its own direction and self-interest."[130] The harmless images of Sergeant Bilko and his enlisted men apparently swayed audiences away from recognizing they were receiving propagandistic messages. MacDonald perceives *The Phil Silvers Show* and other military-themed programs as pro-military propaganda.[131]

More accurately, much of the comedy in *The Phil Silvers Show* reflects implicit anti-militarism. The series pokes fun at military discipline and regimentation, and it does not glorify the military. Instead of the selfless service and discipline promoted in *The West Point Story* and other Army public-relations materials, Bilko sought to work the system for his own benefit. At 0600, for example, the bugler broadcasts a phonograph recording of reveille and crawls back into bed. Bilko's soldiers are not the quickest, the brightest, or the most physically fit men. Coming back to the barracks from playing baseball, he complains that his men —"Bilko's Bombers"— lost the game 24 to 0, and they had stopped at the fifth inning. He quips that the soldiers should be known as "Bilko's misguided missiles" because they had lost to the Women's Army Corps' typists. These men cannot possibly be ideal soldiers if women can beat them in baseball.[132]

The Phil Silvers Show undermines military authority by showing Bilko exploiting his authority with the soldiers and having lower-ranking personnel regularly outsmart officers. Bilko shamelessly touts his authority to wrangle money from his soldiers. In an attempt to get the men to buy tickets for the football pool, he strikes a serious pose and explains, "When the United States Army put these stripes on my sleeves, they also put something on my shoul-

Pictured from left to right are Corporal Rocco Barbella (Harvey Lembeck), Master Sergeant Ernest G. Bilko (Phil Silvers), and Corporal Steve Henshaw (Allan Melvin) on the set of *The Phil Silvers Show* in 1954. Bilko, with his sidekicks Barbella and Henshaw, was forever scheming how to win money from the soldiers and non-commissioned officers at fictitious Fort Baxter, Kansas. The show routinely poked fun at U.S. Army regulars (CBS Photo Archive/Getty Images).

ders: responsibility." He adds with a mischievous smile, "Your morale is my biggest responsibility."[133] Realizing that he lost the previous night's poker game, the men scatter before Bilko can lay his hands on their money. Military authority is further undermined by the fact that Bilko himself is the real power around post, not commander Colonel Hall (Paul Ford).

Soldiers on the show fall far short of exhibiting the "noblest virtues" of society. In one episode, Bilko's none-too-smart cousin, Swifty (Dick Van Dyke), joins the Army and arrives at Fort Baxter. Bilko quickly realizes that his cousin is too naïve to survive in the Army. Even Private Doberman (Maurice Gosfield), not the brightest bulb himself, manages to sell Swifty his own rifle, claiming that the Army only gives them out for free during war time! Bilko decides he will protect his cousin by making him an officer, clearly a position in which he could do little harm. After all, Bilko tells Swifty, "You don't have to think. You are going to be an officer."[134] Colonel Hall fears that this is one of Bilko's schemes to spread his control of the camp from the enlisted men into the officer corps. Bilko almost has Hall convinced to send Swifty to Officer Candidate School, until Swifty tells Hall that he wants to be an officer so he can ride a big white horse and wear shiny medals.[135]

Audience response to *The Phil Silvers Show* suggests that Americans did not perceive the show as pro-military, as MacDonald posits. Of course, Mac-Donald argues that Americans were unwittingly propagandized by these shows and, therefore, did not realize it was happening. Still, one would expect Americans to have a positive reaction to the series if they were being persuaded to accept the military. Unsurprisingly, U.S. Army personnel did not think *The Phil Silvers Show* reflected well on the service. One officer described Bilko as "a four-flusher, a sharpie, a cad who exploits an oafish colonel and an element of tramps, no-goods, and semi-criminals doing nothing all day long."[136] Confirming this officer's fears, one teenager in a survey thought the series showed "typical life in the Army," but it is impossible to measure how widespread this view may have been.[137]

Civilian adults and teenagers perceived both positive and negative elements in *The Phil Silvers Show*. Some comments indicate that adults thought the show was fun, amusing, and fairly harmless. One woman said that the "comedy situations are a real parody of Army life — even my husband laughs," [138] which might reveal more about her husband's personality or *his* experiences in the military than *The Phil Silvers Show*. Other male teenage audience members found the series funny and thought it showed good, clean fun. Various adults and teens disapproved of the gambling and the constant schemes to get the soldiers' money. In reference to the pilot episode, one adult said he did not like "Phil Silvers as an officer taking advantage of new recruits."[139] Some criticism probably came from adult men who had some military experience. They complained that "the Army isn't anything like that" and "it's not military and it's propaganda that is unbelievable." [140] A teen disliked the soldiers' laziness, while another thought the show "puts Army life in a bad light."[141] *The Phil Silvers Show* did not appeal to those interested in images of an efficient, well-disciplined army, but rather to those who did not take it too seriously.

Given the popularity of the show, many Americans must have accepted the less serious, and anti-militaristic, view. In 1955, *The Phil Silvers Show* won Emmy awards for Best Comedy Series, Best Actor, Best Comedian, Best

Comedy Writing, Best Producer, and Best Director. It won three Emmys in each of the following years through 1959.[142]

"Hurry Up and Wait!"

Military comic strips often demonstrated anti-militarism through their parodying of military values, attitudes, and behaviors. Both the *Beetle Bailey* and *Sad Sack* comics display this anti-militarism by spoofing active-duty Army life. Sad Sack and Beetle Bailey both entered the comic-book arena in the early 1950s, though neither character served in the Korean War. Although attempting to lampoon the Army in a more lighthearted way, William Savage argues that they nevertheless were "political in nature, denigrating the military without a corresponding pitch for the war effort" in Korea.[143]

Mort Walker, who had been drafted for World War II service in the Army in 1943, created "Spider" Bailey in 1950 as a college student. The comic gained a wide audience when the character accidentally joined the Army. Walker describes his main character as "the embodiment of everybody's resistance to authority — all the rules and regulations you've got to follow. He deals with it in his own way. And in a way, it's sort of what I did when I was in the Army. I just oftentimes did what I wanted to do."[144] Beetle Bailey and Sad Sack are stand-ins for America's boys-next-door, muddling through the boredom and drudgery of the Army just as America's citizen-soldiers performed their duties when called to serve. The material in these comics resonated in a society with millions of citizen-soldier veterans, just like Mort Walker. In 1954, there were 20 million veterans in a population of just over 163 million Americans, one of the highest percentages of veterans in the nation's history.[145]

Army life is not romanticized in these comics. One 1954 *Beetle Bailey* comic shows just what enlisted men would miss: cars, steaks, money, a soft bed, and a sexy woman, of course. In exchange, the military let the soldier "see the world." To illustrate exactly how much the soldiers actually saw the world, Walker sketched a group of soldiers with their noses buried in the comic books they are reading while their troop transport sails by spectacular foreign scenery.[146] In another story, Sergeant Snorkel orders Beetle and Killer to dig a two-foot ditch around the mess hall and Bammy and Zero to fill it in again. He adds as he walks away, "It's vital military work, so get hot on it!"[147]

The comics undermine military authority as well. In "Caught on Guard," Beetle is on guard duty when he reports seeing Snorkel sail by. The officer of the guard misinterprets the message to mean that Beetle saw a submarine snorkel rather than Sergeant Snorkel in his sailboat. Going up the chain of command, one snorkel turns into a fleet of flotillas or packs of submarines, and the chief of national defense mobilizes to respond to the attack. Once the truth is discovered, everyone blames the man below him in rank until Beetle is left standing. He replies that he was only reporting what he saw, and the men start blaming their commanding officers until the chief of national defense is left standing.[148] This also struck a chord with current and former enlisted men, who might have questioned not just the abilities of an officer now and again, but his integrity as well.

Even WACs occasionally joined the spoofing in *Beetle Bailey*, though the strip did not feature a major recurring female character in uniform until the 1990s. WACs in *Beetle Bailey* appeared either as buxom and shapely or as older and heavyset. In one comic published in April 1950, a young, slim, buxom WAC private comes into the office with a rifle over her shoulder. The WAC staff sergeant, a very heavyset older woman, comments, "Pvt. Blips, you're taking this lady-soldier business too seriously. You don't need to carry a rifle in the office." [149] The next frame shows a very eager male lieutenant colonel twisting his moustache in anticipation. In a sing-song voice he says, "Miss Blips! I'm ready to give you some dictation." [150] Private Blips dutifully walks over to his office with pad and pencil — and her rifle — ready. As realization settles in, the WAC staff sergeant murmurs "oh..." as Blips strides past, facing a combat of a different sort.[151]

Walker aimed *Beetle Bailey* at civilian audiences, but the military periodical *Stars and Stripes* also published the comic. Some of the strips offended military personnel, who believed the irreverence lowered troop morale. One officer referred to the comic as "a disgusting, unfunny satire of an army that never existed."[152] Indeed, one 1954 comic's irreverence for military authority

This 1955 *Beetle Bailey* comic strip shows both types of WACs depicted in the series: a young, buxom servicewoman and an older, heavyset one. Creator Mort Walker, a veteran himself, regularly spoofed active duty army life in his light-hearted comic aimed at civilian audiences. Army officials did not always approve of the content, and the military periodical *Stars and Stripes* even dropped the strip temporarily (Beetle Bailey © 1955 King Features Syndicate).

sparked the military newspaper *Stars and Stripes* to drop the comic. Beetle's foot locker was so stuffed that it would not close in time for inspection. Sgt. Snorkel jumps on it to make it close. Beetle warns him, "Watch it! My tube of shaving cream is on top." Too late. The shaving cream squirts out right into the captain's face as he comes in for inspection. Beetle remarks, "At least you can't see his face!"[153] Once *Stars and Stripes* cancelled the strip, civilian newspapers "ridiculed [the action] as an example of the military being unable to laugh at itself."[154] Indeed, much in the comics would be familiar to someone who had served. In the wake of this publicity, *Stars and Stripes* and additional civilian newspapers picked up the comic.[155]

Fellow comic-strip author George Baker was drafted in the World War II Army just as Mort Walker had been. He created the character Sad Sack for the Army wartime publication *Yank.* Baker intentionally drew a character in line with America's draftees rather than the soldiers who appeared in propaganda images. Just like the citizen-soldiers of the war, Sad Sack endured Army life so he could return home after the war. Baker resurrected the comic in the 1950s.[156]

As with *Beetle Bailey*, *Sad Sack* undermines military authority, questions military values, and presents an unglorified view of Army life. In one story, Sad Sack describes the qualifications of an officer. He begins by saying that an officer's ratings are based on the best jokes told at the officer's club. Mixing drinks, dancing, ordering "vintage wine in a French restaurant" and playing cards, golf, and tennis are the other qualifications of an officer. Each one of these characteristics describes a socialite rather than a soldier. Monster says to Sad Sack, "I thought officers were trained for wars." He replies, "But there aren't any wars right now! They've got to do something to kill time!"[157] These comments reveal the tensions inherent in a peacetime standing army. What does the military do when there is no war? This comic suggests that, at least for officers, it turns into a social club. This sentiment significantly differs from the watchful vigilance portrayed in the film *Strategic Air Command* or *Navy Log* television series. There is no glory or brave heroics in the drudgery of peacetime duty, either. Sarge orders Sad Sack on a 20-mile hike. By the end, all Sad Sack can think about is crawling into his bunk.[158]

Red-headed Private Sadie Sack starred as the main WAC character in the series, who found life in the Army just as dreadful as Sad Sack often did. In one story, Sadie finds herself pulling kitchen duty under the loud-talking, and aptly named, Gertie Gallstone. Slicing vegetables for stew for 2,000 WACs, Sadie watches first potatoes, carrots, and beans, then tomatoes, cabbage, dishwater, tulip bulbs, wax, spaghetti, and floor sweepings all drop into the stew pot. When Sadie's ring comes off her finger and falls into the stew, she takes off her shoes and stockings to wade in and find it. When the WACs ate the stew for dinner later, Sadie listens to the praise emanating from the mess hall. Despite hearing, "This is the best I've ever had," Sadie crawls into bed, feeling a bit sick to her stomach, knowing what actually went into that supper.[159]

As with *Beetle Bailey*, some Army officers did not appreciate the humor in *Sad Sack*. Lieutenant General John R. Hodge suggested that *Sad Sack* merely perpetuated negative stereotypes about the Army, such as "the dictatorial First Sergeant, the perpetual KP [kitchen patrol], fatigue, the guardhouse, etc." [160] He also thought it would give "the impression that the Army will take anything and is a refuge for the bum who can get nothing else to do."[161] It certainly could cause a reader to question the official line on Army life. What Hodge failed to realize was that *Sad Sack* was meant to appeal to audiences in a democracy, who applauded individualism and autonomy, and not the militarist ideals of a well-regulated, disciplined professional military force.

"Choice, Not Chance"

Officers and recruiters increasingly came to view recruiting as an aspect of commercial marketing. The commanding general of the Fleet Marine Force Pacific described recruiting in his command as "a sales program in which we offer military careers as our product. Our 'buyers' are young men who have been conditioned, good or bad, to make the best possible bargain when they 'buy' i.e., reenlist. We offer incentives, a bonus and options to assist this 'sales' program."[162]

Marine Corps advertising highlighted the militarist values of honor, spirit, pride, valor, and elitism. Each of the posters simply showed a disembodied head wearing a different-style cap: dress white, garrison green, or khaki.[163] Marine Corps-recruiting themes at the end of the decade pushed the idea that the Corps developed leaders, with a series of posters that included such slogans as, "A Leader Among Men," a "Portrait of a Leader," and "A Leading Lady" for the Women Marines.[164]

Air Force and Navy advertising added a new emphasis on space technology. After the 1957 launch of Soviet satellite *Sputnik*, the Air Force claimed a place on the vanguard of the "Age of Space." Recruiting advertising suggested: "A Bright Future Becomes Real Where the Age of Space is Real" in the Air Force. This and other posters pictured supersonic jets and ballistic missiles.[165] The Air Force also assisted in the production of the short-lived science-fiction television series *Men into Space* (1959–1960), about futuristic Air Force space exploration. The Navy touted space, too. One poster boasted the Navy's "Space Age Leadership" through naval aviation. Like the Air Force advertising, the poster shows both jets and missiles in the picture.[166] Even hobbies were militarized during the Cold War. Advertising targeted hobbyists who built model rockets, asking them to "make your hobby your career" in the military.[167]

The Army's advertising agency believed that their target audience did not respond to calls of patriotism or service to one's country, but rather operated on a "what's in it for me?" mentality. Advertisers assumed the attitude "is a natural tendency, stimulated by a rising economy since World War II and the heritage of a *non-militaristic democracy*."[168] The Army coupled the "what's in for me" attitude with fears of the draft in the "Choice, Not Chance" slogan.[169] A recruiting poster pictured a helicopter mechanic and instructor working on the rotor with the words, "Choose it yourself before enlistment!"[170] With draftees providing manpower for infantry slots in the active-duty army, the Army wanted regular enlistments, which were longer than the draftee obligations, to fill out the technical military occupation specialties. Given that more intensive and expensive training was involved in technical specialties, it made sense for the Army to want those positions to go to longer-serving volunteers. Army recruiters placed many of these ads in periodicals such as *Popular Science* to attract young men into the technical fields.

The Navy also picked up the same theme of "choice." One of its recruiting posters showed a high school student surrounded by the insignia for aviation, medical, electronics, and nucleonics fields. The poster suggested, "Choose Your Field.... Then Enlist."[171] For both the Army and the Navy, choice pointed to American individualism rather than the chance of the government making decisions for a person. It was a theme very much in line with traditional American anti-militarism.

In 1957, Cabell Phillips, a correspondent for *Harper's Magazine*, recognized the inherent anti-militarism of the nation's draft-aged young men. He observed that recruiting advertising targeted "a young but relatively sophisticated audience which feels little romantic enchantment about wars or about the men who fight them. It does not bang the drums of patriotism nor stir up the glandular juices in fear or anger toward a foreign foe."[172] Despite the repeated favorable messages in film, comics, and television, and recruiting advertising, Phillips perceived that these young men harbored no romantic notions of military service. Without a hot war, Phillips recognized that the military turned to a different set of appeals to recruit. In addition to such inducements as education, travel, adventure, the "flattery of a uniform," and "the prestige of the particular service he chooses," young men could choose to "Be a Leader of Men" with the Marines Corps or have "a career and yet a way of life, filled with honor, tradition, and personal rewards" in the Navy.[173] Indeed, a volunteer could "tailor his military service to his personal preference and needs."[174] These young men valued their choices and their individualism.

Despite the massive publicity and various sales incentives, recruiting sufficient numbers continued to be problematic at the end of the decade. Reenlistment of trained personnel in the technical fields was especially difficult, as most of these skills were in demand in the civilian world. As one Navy officer noted, "The more complex the training, the poorer the retention" for the service.[175] In advertising military service as a stepping stone into a civilian career, recruiters had created the framework for young men to perceive the military not as a career, but as a temporary job. Given this mental framework, it is unsurprising that retention of skilled technicians proved difficult. Whatever incentives the armed forces offered servicemen to reenlist apparently did not outweigh the pull of a civilian career for most of them. With the work of soldiers transforming from combat skills to more technical ones, soldiers had more marketable skills in the workforce.[176]

"You're More Than a Woman"

With the active-duty forces open to women during peacetime, each of the branches duly sought to recruit women to fill them. Women recruiters did not always receive a warm welcome in recruiting offices. The director of the recruiting division for the Marine Corps had to send instructions to all recruiting stations that Women Marine recruiters should not be used as clerical staff. Some women recruiters had difficulty obtaining funds and assistance to publicize their programs, and some men questioned the suitability of women Marines traveling alone. The director instructed male recruiters to give Women Marines all due assistance and assured them that the women could travel without escort.[177] The Navy also had problems with recruiters. In some cases, male recruiters turned away potential female recruits, telling them that women did not belong in the Navy.[178]

Advertisers attempted to show that women in uniform shared certain military qualities with men, namely sacrifice, loyalty, and service to country. In addition, recruiting emphasized pride, prestige, and elitism. For example, the Marine Corps poster entitled "Serve" portrays a pretty, slim woman marine in dress-blue uniform, standing next to a suitcase.[179] One Navy poster proclaims, "Serve with Pride and Patriotism." It pictures enlisted and officer WAVES in dress uniforms and a Navy nurse in white nursing uniform.[180] In direct contradiction to the attitude of male sailors, the Navy advertised for its women: "Respected as an Officer, Honored as a Navy Nurse." This poster shows a WAVES officer in dress uniform, placing a nurse's cap on a younger Navy woman.[181] A Navy career woman would serve proudly, devote herself to the Navy and to the United States, consider it a privilege to belong to the

Navy, and wear her uniform with honor. She would assist the WAVES in "upholding the freedom of the seas for all nations," doing everything from photography to directing planes in a control tower.[182] Even though WAVES could not sail except on transports, women performed "the same duties as Navy men."[183] Although ceilings existed for women to advance, recruiting pamphlets suggested that women "receive equal occupational advantages to those enjoyed by Navy men."[184] Coupled with pay and benefits, Navy women could be entirely self-supporting and attain "a comfortable and more than adequate standard of living."[185] Though it advertised an independent life for women at a time when young women were expected to marry and start a family, it only hinted at the coming "second wave" of feminism.

In terms of overall numbers of personnel, women Marines could afford to be the most exclusive of the service branches, though that did not guarantee the most prestige in the public's eyes. Marine Corps recruiters did not prove subtle in their advertising. One poster proudly boasts "Elite," and pictures the head of a woman Marine wearing her dress-uniform cap.[186] As with her male counterparts, an entire set of posters features women Marines in their dress-blue uniforms.[187] Options for women Marines expanded in the early 1950s, allowing them to serve in Hawaii for the first time since World War II.[188] Opening this exotic locale might attract attention from women seeking travel opportunities. Just as posters for men showcased the pride, tradition, and prestige of the service through the dress uniform, so too did these women share in the pride, tradition, and prestige of their particular service.

Most recruiting materials designed for women, however, downplayed the masculine aspects of military service. They guaranteed that women would retain their femininity in the military, emphasized the social opportunities, and accentuated the comfortable living and recreational standards. In order to soften the masculine attributes of their service and entice more women to join, Marine Corps recruiters sent their advertising materials to female high school graduates in pink envelopes.[189]

Annual training for female Army Reservists was not advertised as a test of stamina as it was for men. Instead, field training combines "the best of outdoor living with city conveniences, in an atmosphere of great American tradition."[190] Going to summer camp is marketed as a vacation with sports, swimming, and other recreational programs that "parallel those found at popular resorts." [191] Women can also enjoy catching a film at the post movie theater and attending social events at the service clubs. Lest the women worry about their spiritual development, they "have plenty of opportunity to attend church."[192] There are also formal aspects of military training, such as learning Army traditions, regulations, and courtesy. Women may also experience "that most inspiring of all military formations— a Retreat ceremony."[193] Taken at face value, the literature portrays reservist summer camp as a patriotic resort vacation. Women could retain their femininity by maintaining physical and social standards but also experience some aspects of traditionally male service to country.

To assure women that they would not become unfeminine, Navy advertisers mentioned that Navy women "keep up with the latest fashions" and are allowed to wear their civilian attire off duty.[194] Many bases provide beauty parlors for their women. Not only do Navy accommodations prove to be clean and spotless, quarters are "spacious, airy, homelike, and equipped with modern conveniences throughout." [195] After a delicious meal, women can enjoy the recreational facilities "attractively furnished with writing tables, books, radios, and other comforts" or catch a movie, play tennis, or enjoy a host of other activities.[196] Navy women date, just like their civilian counterparts, and make lasting friendships. A woman's health is expertly looked after by trained medical personnel, and her spirit guided by the Navy Chaplain Corps.[197] Alongside classes, drills, and inspection, Reserve Officer Candidates can enjoy sailing, concerts, theater, and a cruise on a destroyer escort.[198]

With the huge popularity of comic books among young people, the Navy adopted the format for recruiting enlisted women with *Judy Joins the Waves*. Clearly aimed at the teenaged high school girl, the story features Judy Watson, a high school graduate who cannot attend college and realize her dream of travel and a journalism career. By chance, a high school classmate who had enlisted in the Navy gives her a WAVES booklet. Judy recognizes this as an opportunity and convinces her parents to consent to her enlistment.[199]

At basic training, Judy meets a snobbish rival, Sheila. Nicknamed "Park Avenue," Sheila is a rich socialite who has joined the WAVES out of boredom. Why she enlisted rather than applying for officer training is not adequately explained, but it sets up tension throughout the story when Judy is selected for leadership roles instead of Sheila. With the teenage target audience in mind, the story also contains a romantic sub-plot, with Judy and Sheila vying for the affections of the same corpsman. The drama between Sheila and Judy comes to a happy resolution upon their first assignment as petty officers on the West Coast. Judy, a journalist, and Sheila, a photographer, accompany a VIP to an offshore island prior to a firing exercise there. Sheila falls and injures herself, but Judy finds her minutes before the shelling starts. Sheila apologizes to Judy, promises to set the record straight with the corpsman, and the two women sing a WAVES song together. [200] As unrealistic as the ending is, for high school girls longing for travel, adventure, education, career, camaraderie, and love, this story has it all! As *Judy Joins the WAVES* circulated during the Korean War, recruiters subsequently had to be reminded "to keep in proper perspective the elements of glamour, uniforms, and adventure."[201]

Judy Joins the WAVES, issued in July 1951, is a Navy recruiting advertisement in the popular comic book format aimed at high school girls. It has travel, adventure, camaraderie, career prospects, and a love interest (National Archives and Records Administration).

Not only would the military not take away women's femininity, the popular film *Operation Petticoat* (1959) even suggested that women would make the military more feminine.[202] Some of the film's plot is based on actual World War II events. American submarines had been called to evacuate American personnel from Corregidor shortly before it capitulated to the Japanese. The *Spearfish* rescued 12 Army nurses and a Navy officer's wife. Another submarine, the *Seadragon*, sailed from the Philippines after a Japanese attack. Because they had not finished repairs, it sailed with a pinkish tinge to it, an event exaggerated in the film.[203]

In *Operation Petticoat*, the submarine *Sea Tiger* picks up five stranded Army nurses. Almost immediately, Lieutenant Barbara Duran (Dina Merrill) falls in love with Lieutenant Nick Holden (Tony Curtis), who does not bother to mention that he is already engaged to another woman back home. Confiding in her commanding officer, Major Edna Haywood (Virginia Gregg), Barbara says, "I've been turning corners for 24 years. I think I've finally turned the right one." The 38-year-old Haywood retorts, "I may not be able to make to the next corner!" but advises Barbara to take things slow.[204] After some humorous mix-ups, love prevails.

Similarly, Lieutenant Delores Crandall (Joan O'Brien), a buxom brunette who inadvertently causes havoc wherever she goes—finds love, marriage, and family with the submarine's commander, Matt Sherman (Cary Grant). The moment she steps onboard, Delores catches her high-heeled shoe in the deck plating. On climbing down the ladder into the sub, she hits the collision alarm. Crandall tries Sherman's patience throughout the film, but her mishaps prove endearing to him in the end.[205]

Operation Petticoat garnered laughs from placing women in a man's world and showing how women were out of place on a submarine and in combat. For example, Crandall accidentally pushes a firing mechanism early so that a torpedo hits a truck on the beach instead of sinking a Japanese oil tanker. The boat turns into a floating maternity ward when two women from a nearby island give birth onboard. Seaman Fox (Tony Pastor, Jr.)—a young male character—experiences sympathetic labor pains. When an American destroyer fires on the *Sea Tiger*, they send up debris to trick the ship into thinking the submarine sank. The destroyer does not cease firing until Crandall's full-figure bra appears. After all, "The Japanese have nothing like this!" The *Sea Tiger* is saved "by the grace of a woman's brassiere."[206]

Time magazine's film critic did not approve of the comedic aspects of the film, grumbling that it "treats World War II as a big, noisy joke."[207] While the reviewer did not like the film, he did detect the anti-militarism in it. Referring to Nick Holden, the critic remarks that his " 'scrounging,' i.e., stealing vast quantities of naval stores in a manner apparently intended to suggest that he is a true-blue, anti-authoritarian American boy"[208] (even though Commander Sherman actually encouraged Holden in the story). Distaste for the film aside, it is significant that the critic is defining "true blue" American as an anti-authoritarian.

Even with the outrageous plot, the Department of Defense and Department of the Navy cooperated with the production of *Operation Petticoat*. Navy recruiters liked the film for providing an upbeat attitude for audiences and tied in their recruiting with the movie. Navy recruiters were instructed to set up materials in the lobbies of theaters so they could take advantage of the people coming out of the film in "a receptive Navy mood."[209]

In spite of vigorous recruiting efforts such as these, military women still had to fight for a good reputation in American society. Despite efforts to recruit only morally upstanding women, a bad reputation continued to haunt female service members.[210] When Marilyn Monroe posed with four servicewomen from the Army, Navy, Air Force, and Marine Corps, an Army recruiting officer worried about the impact of having Marilyn's image of sexuality tarnish the women. He "tried to 'kill' this shot of Marilyn" so, "naturally, the picture was then widely reprinted," reported the *Saturday Evening Post*.[211] The magazine published the photograph for the enjoyment of its readers, though surely some in the Department of Defense cringed at what officials considered negative publicity. Male teenagers might not have thought so badly of it, though.

When Captain Winifred Quick took over as chief of Naval Personnel for Women, she perceived that the problems facing her consisted of "poor quality in recruiting for both officers and enlisted women, impediments to career development, inadequate housing and recreation, low morale, poor self-image, and negative public attitudes."[212] Perceptions of low morale and poor-quality recruits extended throughout the entire Navy. Quick believed that the public felt apathy toward the military in general.[213]

Women in the services perceived negative attitudes toward themselves from both inside and outside the military. Although most women indicated that the enlisted and commissioned men with whom they worked directly harbored a favorable outlook toward them, women reported mostly adverse or mixed attitudes from servicemen in general. Women also perceived the attitudes of civilian men as mostly unfavorable or mixed at best.[214] Women in the services believed that civilian women their own age had a positive view of them, while "other," presumably older, women did not.[215]

A survey of teenaged civilian females reveals that not all attitudes were negative, particularly for the target audience. Fully 87 percent of the teenagers believed that the armed forces really needed women. When asked to express "ways in which the military service does women good," the most frequent response was "character building and discipline," which was not a theme regularly emphasized in recruiting advertising for women.[216] Rather, these are the themes emphasized in male-recruiting pitches. Other factors mentioned included "opportunities for travel and work," "getting along with other people," and "increasing feelings of patriotism."[217] The female teenagers' response to male-recruiting themes anticipates the "second wave" of feminism that emerged in the 1960s and 1970s.[218]

The teenagers were also asked about "ways in which military service does women harm," which measured stereotypes and imagery not created by the military services themselves.[219] About one-third of the teenagers responded that military service "hardens them, causes them to become immoral, lose their femininity, and have degrading associations."[220] Others suggested that military life attracted the "escapist" type. These answers are harsh charges and reflect some deep animosity toward the military service of women. They also echo the slander campaign of World War II. In keeping with the social and cultural ideals of marriage, the females also mentioned that military life was incompatible with married life.[221]

The survey charted the strength of the teenagers' desire to join the military. Only 6 percent of the females considered joining the military for a career, though 45 percent thought about joining short-term. Nearly half refused to consider joining one of the women's services at all. The survey further asked them to rate their preferences. The WAVES proved the most popular with 40 percent of the pool choosing it, while the WAF came in second with 33 percent. Only 3 percent chose the WAC or Women Marines as their preference. A full 73 percent of the teenagers indicated they would like to be a commissioned officer if they joined the military.[222]

Once women took the step to join one of the services, the Department of Defense wanted to ascertain what prompted them to enlist. One January 1952 Department of Defense survey questioned enlistees in the Women's Air Force. Like their male counterparts, these women were influenced more through personal contacts, especially recruiters, than the media. The enlistees indicated that posters influenced them more than advertisements in magazines, newspapers, radio, or television in getting them to talk to a recruiter. The survey reveals that half of the women enlisted in the WAF "to receive an education, training, or job experience." [223] These women chose the Air Force rather than the Army because the women perceived the Air Force had a better reputation, higher standards, and more attractive uniforms.[224]

Women who joined the Women's Army Corps also indicated that personal contacts had a greater influence on their choice to enlist than media sources. Like the women who joined the Air Force, women who joined the Army came for the educational, training, or job experiences offered by the service. Patriotism was a stronger motivator for women to join the Army, with one in five mentioning it as a significant factor. These women preferred the Army because of shorter enlistment periods, because they failed to qualify for the WAF, or because they were looking for better opportunities.[225]

When enlisted women in the four services were surveyed in 1953 about their attitudes, the only recruiting theme for which the vast majority said had been fulfilled was the chance to "meet new people and make new friends." Half of respondents reported that women who joined "for security" did receive food, clothing, and medical care to their satisfaction. Those who wanted "excitement and adventure" tended to be disappointed, as did those who wanted to travel or joined for a particular kind of job. Servicewomen felt ambivalent about whether they were doing something "useful or necessary for their country," whether they were truly improving themselves, or whether they received useful job experience or training. Nonetheless, 57 percent of women from all the services reported they "have had a square deal in most ways."[226] This leaves 43 percent of women unhappy or discontented with their military service in some way. When broken down by service, differences among the armed forces become apparent. Women in the Navy and Air Force had the most positive outlook on their experiences, while Women Marines felt the most dissatisfied. Women in the Army, however, were most likely to think they would make the military a career.[227] The survey does not illuminate specifically why more career women chose the Army, but if they sought the largest community of like-minded women, they would be drawn to the WAC.

In comparison, a 1952 internal Marine Corps survey revealed a high level of discontent among servicemen, with around 65 percent of marines planning to leave the service. As with some of the women, many servicemen found that military life did not live up to expectations. Men indicated that the top reasons for leaving were a desire to continue an education, the conflicts with marriage and family life, and a dislike for military life itself. Men as well as women highly regarded marriage and family. For those men staying in the service, they enjoyed their work or had an affinity for military life.[228] Other surveys indicated additional reasons that influenced marines' decision to leave, including dissatisfaction with the promotion system, perceived loss of prestige, lack of good leadership, and an inability to change job assignments.[229] Women, too, found it difficult to be assigned to a specific job. These surveys indicate a higher level of discontent in the Corps than the service admitted publicly. For marines as well as the other armed forces, a majority of both young men and women perceived military service as a temporary part of their life, not their career.

Once again, contemporary observers pointed to the continuing anti-militarist perceptions among the public. In 1956, Dr. Eli Ginzberg reported to the Defense Advisory Committee on Women in the Services that the problems with recruiting women stemmed primarily from an American culture that did not accept military service overall as part of the national life, much less as appropriate employment for women. He commented that the problem "may have more to do with uniforms than with women."[230]

"No One Is Really Watching"

In order to determine the military's place in society, the Department of Defense contracted with the Gallup organization in 1955 to conduct a survey of males between 16 and 20 years of age and civilian adults. From a list of 19 professions provided by the interviewers, teenage males ranked officers fourth, tied with a college professor. Enlisted men, on the other hand, ranked 14th among teenagers. One-quarter of the teenagers thought that enlisted men remained in the military because they were "either unable or unwilling to make a civilian living," suggesting that only low-quality men pursued enlistment.[231] Adults rated officers seventh and enlisted men 16th on the list of professions. The interviewers noted that the more educated adults tended to rate military careers lower than less educated ones. At the same time, half of the adults indicated that they would be pleased if a son were to make the military a career, suggesting that the career was acceptable, if not the highest preferred. Some of the adults commented that military service was "a good, honest job," that "he would be serving his country," and that military life offered "discipline and character development."[232] About half of the adults stated that they would be pleased if a daughter married a career serviceman, particularly if he was an officer. One-fifth indicated they would be displeased.[233]

While the high listing of officers suggests the growing militarism of American society, a contemporary observer, Morris Janowitz, interpreted the survey results to mean that the American public did not regard the professional armed forces as highly prestigious. In his view, there had been no change from the "traditional negativism and opposition to governmental authority which has so deeply characterized American history."[234] Other contemporary observers at *Life* magazine also detected poor attitudes. When *Life* correspondents visited an Army basic-training class in 1955, they noted that "civilians seem indifferent or sometimes hostile to soldiers. The draftees get the general feeling that no one is really watching."[235] Granted, President Eisenhower's New Look policies weighed heavily on the Army, but this still indicates the soldiers felt Americans' ambivalence toward the actual military services.

This *Life* cover story on a "Draftee in a Peacetime Army" followed one recruit, Private Tedford, as he and others explored "the painful mysteries of KP and close-order drill."[236] The article highlighted the tensions the Army had in defining a role for itself in the Cold War, when most Americans believed the next war would be an air war and include nuclear weapons. The recruits asked themselves, "What do they want with the M-1 when they got the A-bomb?"[237] The training continued to emphasize the basics of ground combat, with the course culminating in a two-week bivouac in the foothills of the Rockies.[238]

Compared to the recruits in *Life*'s 1951 article on making marines, the peacetime Army recruits had a much easier time of basic training. Where the Marines faced harsh punishments for failing to meet standards, the *Life* photographer snapped a shot of Tedford yawning during a lecture. Where the article on the Marines indicated no life outside of boot camp, this article showed Tedford on pass in Denver, and with a date. Indeed, these are pictures of regular young men doing regular civilian activities, which are representations more appropriate for peacetime and for citizen-soldiers.[239] At the end of his training Tedford told the reporters that he "liked the Army no better but he had to admit his grudging admiration for it," noting that "the discipline is good for you."[240]

A separate poll conducted in 1956 by the advertising agency Dancer-Fitzgerald-Sample, Incorporated, recorded negative responses about the Army from their sample of young men aged 17 through 23. Nearly 40 percent of their sample made an unfavorable comment about the Army. One-quarter of the respondents indicated that the Army "stinks," "is the worst," or "this is the lousiest."[241] According to this survey, 43 percent of the young men associated physical discomfort with Army life, particularly regarding training and living conditions. The next most frequent response, at 12 percent, was "loss of individual freedom and discipline,"[242] two qualities most at odds with an anti-militaristic democracy. Praise in popular culture still did not translate to high regard for the real-life Army.

It is important to remember, too, that just because someone served in the military did not make that person necessarily sympathetic to it. For example, one veteran admitted, "I hated military life, I detested discipline, and above all I was angry with myself for adapting so easily and comfortably to militarism, discipline, and vegetablism."[243] After his discharge, however, this man "avoided all attempts to glorify the 'good old Army days.'"[244] No doubt this veteran was not alone in his attitude.

Conclusion

Throughout the 1950s, the dual strands of American militarism and anti-militarism continued to thread their way through American culture. With a

Cold War defense posture resting on a large standing military, the Eisenhower administration kept the peacetime draft and relied on reserve forces to round out the defense structure. The teenagers who were subjected to the draft believed it to be an onerous obligation, not a privilege. While the military became a larger part of American life during the 1950s, it did not necessarily mean it was popular. Trying to recruit women into the services proved even more difficult than enlisting men despite rigorous efforts to feminize military life. Even with the military's advertising and public relations, Americans stubbornly held on to their negative stereotypes of active-duty military service.

Although many films and television shows were based on the military, many of the most popular cultural outlets spoofed military service, such as *The Phil Silvers Show* and *Beetle Bailey*. No doubt the vast numbers of veterans in the audiences found something that resonated with their own experiences in these anti-militarist comedies. Militarism appeared strongest in images related to the Air Force, particularly with its nuclear bombers. Films like *Strategic Air Command* showed the public that the Air Force was prepared for war and defending the nation from surprise attack. The Navy, too, tied its contemporary imagery to technology and the image of constant vigilance in the Cold War.

Reliance on technology and on nuclear weapons for defense also created a climate of fear in the United States. Several books and films in the early 1960s reflected the fear of an accidental nuclear war and of the professional military forces (particularly the Air Force) acting on their own. At the same time, praise for the citizen-soldier continued in popular culture as the Korean War truly became forgotten and World War II became the standard military fare on the small and the silver screens.

4

CITIZEN-SOLDIERS AND CIVILIAN CONTROL, 1959–1964

James Garner, playing U.S. naval Lieutenant Commander Charles Madison stationed in England during World War II, declared: "War isn't hell at all. It's man at his best; the highest morality he's capable of."[1] He explains that war itself is not the problem, but how humans perceive the morality of it. Madison clarifies, "Wars are always fought for the best of reasons: for liberation or manifest destiny. Always against tyranny and always in the interest of humanity."[2] By this time, however, the audience knew Madison was no militarist. His monologue continued, pointing out that the so-called virtuous Second World War had already killed ten million people. He remarked sarcastically that in the "next war its seems we'll have to destroy all of man in order to preserve his damn dignity."[3] So long as people associate war with virtue, wars will continue to be fought, Madison mused. His solution is simple: "Through cowardice, we shall be saved!"[4]

This scene from the 1964 film *The Americanization of Emily* presents a stridently anti-militarist interpretation of World War II, going further in criticizing war than many anti-militarist films, comics, and television shows of the previous decade. As with the 1950s, the decade of the 1960s offered conflicting views of World War II: some anti-militarist, some militarist. Military recruiting advertising continued to focus on technical skills transferable to civilian careers, rather than the fighting skills of the combat arms. On the silver screen, unglorified versions of World War II, such as *Hell Is for Heroes*, proved popular with critics and audiences alike. More militaristic interpretations of World War II appeared in some 1960s films, such as *The Longest Day*, which romanticized the war and its fighters. Interestingly, film critics found a romanticized World War II distasteful, which suggests that the "good war" version of the conflict still did not immediately resonate with many adult Americans.

Television comedies such as *McHale's Navy* carried the torch of anti-militarist comedy from *The Phil Silvers Show*. Television combat dramas offered sophisticated stories about human suffering in war. While many of the themes of these combat dramas were anti-militarist in nature, some militarist themes proved popular as well, especially the idea that military sacrifice is redemptive.

One of the most significant events of the early 1960s was the Cuban Missile Crisis. A series of best-selling anti-nuclear, anti-technology books and popular films soon followed. Given the importance of the Air Force in America's nuclear defense, it is not surprising that this service was the focus of the anti-nuclear scare. An anti-militarist distrust of military professionals resurfaced during this period, though conservative commentators believed that the military was safe enough under civilian control. The scare of imminent nuclear war between the U.S. and the Soviet Union deeply influenced American popular culture in both subtle and not-so-subtle ways.

"Until Called to Defend His Nation"

Although the 1960s-era peacetime standing military force was the largest in American history, it was also increasingly what contemporary sociologists termed "civilianized." That is, an ever-decreasing percentage of billets in the services were dedicated to combat. Following World War II, there was an increase in the number of technical and non-combat military occupational specialties. Many of these non-combat tasks were menial in nature, such as having soldiers mow post lawns, paint buildings, and perform KP duties. For those soldiers trained in a technical skill, the military had a hard time holding onto them. In 1962, before the conflict in Vietnam, only 26 percent of all first-time enlistees chose to reenlist, preferring to transfer their technical training to a civilian career.[5]

Recruiting images and themes in the first half of the 1960s differed little from those of the previous decade. Almost all advertisements focused on technical training as those who enlisted served a longer term of service than the two-year draftee. It was a better investment for the military services to hold on to an expensively trained serviceman longer than the draftee.

Even during the continuing peacetime draft, U.S. Army advertising stressed the idea of choice. Army recruiters published a series of ads focusing on vocational training for technical skills, such as those needed for construction and telephone technician work.[6] Other advertisements continued to emphasize the theme of manhood. Increasingly, the Army focused on technology, too, even linking manhood and new technology. One ad boasted, "The whole Army is like a huge, well-oiled engine — with men and machines closely interlocked. It takes men to fit into this kind of picture."[7] Just like its sister services, the Army stood ready to fight the next war, even if it was a nuclear war. A joint advertisement for the regular Army, Army Reserve, and Army National Guard pictured the face of a determined looking soldier ; behind him was nuclear-tipped missiles ready to launch.[8]

The Air Force and the Navy took advantage of the newest technological triumphs of the space age. The Navy linked its aviation branch with space-age technology.[9] Similarly, the Air Force encouraged interested candidates to "join the aerospace team."[10] Although these two services touted their space-age technology, President Eisenhower had placed the manned space program in the hands of a civilian agency, the National Aeronautics and Space Administration (NASA), rather than place it in military hands. President John F. Kennedy also charged NASA with his 1961 challenge to land a man on the moon by the end of the decade. Though the astronauts were all drawn from the military services, both Eisenhower and Kennedy wanted a civilian face for the U.S. space program.[11]

While all of the armed forces urged military preparedness, the Marine Corps emphasized it more than the others. One of its key recruiting themes was the idea that "as Marines, we are dedicated to the principle that the best guarantee of peace is preparedness."[12] The Corps stressed that its mission was "to be ready!"[13]

Most mainstream recruiting advertising targeted the high-school-aged and young adults, so various surveys were conducted to measure the attitudes from these groups toward the military. A 1963 *Scholastic Magazine* survey of high school boys determined that 25 percent of them would prefer to be drafted into the Army, followed with a tie between the Navy and Air Force at 19.4 percent. The Marine Corps followed at 12.6 percent. Most surveys did not include the Coast Guard, but this one did. It trailed the other services with only 8.2 percent of the boys' preference. As a career option, though, the boys favored the Air Force at 25 percent, with 18 percent choosing the Navy. The majority of the teenagers, however, did not have a stated preference, suggesting that the high school students either had not thought about career possibilities yet, or simply did not consider the military to be a career option for them.[14] It is interesting to note that the pro-military *Life* magazine assumed that young Americans in this age group did not want to go into the service. In one article, James Mills observed, "Most soldiers, both in war and peace, spend a good part of their military careers wishing they were out. Those young men who profess to like the service life are exceptions."[15]

While high school students may not predict exactly how they would act, the Department of Defense was quite interested in what motivated those who actually volunteered for service. Surveys conducted in 1964 for those in the armed forces indicated that upwards of 70 percent of those who joined an Army Reserve or National Guard unit did so to avoid the draft. Over 75 percent of naval reservists joined as a response to the draft, as did 80 percent of all Air Force reservists. Of course, the draft affected active-duty volunteerism. According to the Air Force, 43 percent of their enlisted men and 39 percent of their officers volunteered to avoid being drafted.[16] While the draft weighed heavily on the minds of the nation's young men, the government did not have particularly high draft calls during peacetime. As the Baby Boom generation came of age, 17 million young men were in the draft pool. Draft calls of 16,000 per month affected a very small percentage of them.[17]

In 1964, Secretary of Defense Robert McNamara proposed reforms for the nation's reserve forces. When Jack Raymonds reported the news item for the *New York Times*, he immediately placed the reserves in the context of America's anti-militarist tradition. He explained, "For the Reserve forces, which are intended as a backup to the regular military forces, have an emotional as well as strategic place in American life. They bear out the tradition of the 'citizen soldier,' the 'minuteman,' who sticks to his hearth until called to defend his nation."[18] He reminded his readers that the Founders placed their trust in citizen militias rather than professional standing armies. These militias were today's National Guard units.[19] McNamara proposed to merge all of the federal reserve forces with the national guards, creating a pool of reservists from which to draw manpower.[20] While the National Guard Bureau tepidly supported the plan, the Army Reserve and Reserve Officer's Association lobbied hard against it. Opponents of the merger swayed Congress, which killed the notion in the Defense Appropriations Act of 1966.[21] America's citizen-soldiers would retain their distinct identities, especially important for some National Guard units which traced their lineages back to the Colonial era.

Women in the Military

Despite the militarist policies of Cold War America that enlarged the armed forces and adopted peacetime conscription for men, women's military service had not changed much since the 1940s. Women who volunteered for military service in the 1960s agreed to the same basic stipulations as those women who entered service in the 1940s. They worked in medical or clerical fields, they remained childless if staying for a career, and they accepted restrictions on their advancement and eligibility for combat duty. Women's occupations within the military only began to open later in the decade.[22] Militarism affected women in uniform the least, as the services continued to focus on a feminine version of military duty for them.

Just like ads for men, the Marine Corps emphasized the most militarist themes in its women's recruiting advertising, which continued to promote the pride, prestige, and elite nature of its women's service. One poster shows an attractive woman Marine in dress uniform with the Marine Corps flag in the background. The word "Pride" is in bold letters above her and the slogan "Be a Marine Officer" is printed below.[23] Another one pictures two smiling women Marines examining the insignia on their dress-blue uniforms, this poster bearing the words "Be a Woman Marine."[24] These women exhibit the same institutional pride as corresponding images of male marines.

The Women's Army Corps continued to emphasize the respectability of its members into the 1960s. The Army sustained the higher intelligence and moral standards for women's entry into the service than it required for men. Army officials justified the qualifications to ensure the moral, mental, and physical character of its female members. They self-consciously attempted to create an "impeccable public image" of women in the Army.[25] Much of this effort stemmed from a desire to counteract the persistent negative perceptions among the public about women's service in the military.

In an attempt to emphasize the feminine aspects of military duty, Air Force and Navy recruiting advertising increasingly focused on physical beauty. According to WAF director Jeanne Holm, the Air Force Chief of Staff instructed its Recruiting Service to find more attractive women. Potential recruits were required to pose for four photographs because "physical appearance became the chief criterion in the selection process."[26] In January 1961, the Navy's Captain Quick changed the regulation to allow for longer hairstyles. She forbade short, "mannish" haircuts in favor of more attractive, longer styles. Quick also worked to lower the weight requirement for women personnel by ten pounds.[27] She assigned recruiters based on their looks. She made sure "we assigned the most attractive, articulate, and motivated women officers and enlisted petty officers for recruiting duty."[28] Given that recruiting duty counted toward women's promotions like sea duty counted for male service members, Navy women advanced according to their good looks, at least in part. Quick also pushed for a new, more attractive uniform for her women. This new uniform style won accolades from the fashion magazine *Women's Wear*, which congratulated the Navy for choosing a design that balanced imagination, tradition, and femininity. In fact, the dress-mess uniforms included an optional tiara.[29] Since tiaras are about as unmilitary as one can get, women's uniforms were certainly less martial than corresponding men's uniforms.

Even stressing the unmilitary aspects of enlistment, the women's military services had serious retention problems. An Army study determined that part of the problem was that restrictions were placed on women's military occupation specialties. Although 181 fields were nominally open to women, most Army women fell into only 94 of them. Supervisory roles proved even more limited. Although women technically qualified for ten management fields, they only served in the medical and administrative ones.[30] Navy women suffered similar restrictions. In 1962, 90 percent of the Navy's enlisted women worked in administrative, clerical, or nursing slots. Additionally, women could not reach general rank by law until 1967, which suggested that perceptions of women's leadership qualities were also questioned, despite what recruiting advertising published.[31] These restrictions discouraged advancement and retention, though many women still chose military service as a temporary occupation. The message in society for women was clear: military service was not for women, even under the pressure of the Cold War.

In its 1962 research for women's motivations for joining the Army's Nurse Corps, the Army's advertising agency learned that recruits continued to place family and marriage before a career in the Army. They joined only for the short-term and out of immediate financial need. They were not motivated by patriotism, adventure, travel, or long-term financial or career security. The advertising agency also confirmed the continued poor public reputation of women in uniform. Accusations that the women were immoral, "loose," or "easy" persisted into the early 1960s despite the services' best efforts to counteract it. Young women also worried that females who joined the military were unfeminine, unattractive, or unable to do something better. The advertisers additionally concluded that "the glamour of the other services, their more exciting 'images,' and the superiority of their uniforms may affect young women."[32] So the Air Force and Navy's emphasis on looks had paid off for them in attracting young women's preferences.

For career women already in the Nurses' Corps, they wanted professional advancement, status, and responsibilities. The benefits, education, and early retirement attracted these women to military service. Patriotism and a desire to serve their country motivated some of these women as well. They generally had a favorable view of the Army, particularly the social life, officer clubs, and the status of being officers.[33] Indeed, it was one career that could afford women some prestige within the institution at a time when there were still few corresponding civilian careers for women to choose. It is perhaps ironic that the military, still bound to have no more than 2 percent of its personnel as women, actually offered better advancement for them than in many civilian careers.

In 1963, *Scholastic Magazine* surveyed high school girls' attitudes toward the armed forces. About 36 percent of the girls reported that they would consider a career in the military, which suggested that recruiters had successfully gained the attention of their target audience. Of the girls who would consider serving, 41 percent each chose the Air Force and the Navy as their first choice. The Army trailed at 18 percent, confirming the Army advertiser's conclusion that the other services proved more attractive to young women. None selected the Marine Corps as their first choice.[34] In reality, few women chose military service, either as a temporary job or as a career until after the end of the draft and creation of the All Volunteer Force. In the early 1960s, the military was still a socially inappropriate job or career for women.

A *"Smashing Fight"*

In 1960s popular culture, more militaristic interpretations of World War II appeared, which romanticized the war and its fighters. An example of this interpretation is *The Longest Day* (1962), which recreated the Allied landing at Normandy. It is a celebration of the soldier — whether American, British or French — and how these allies unified for victory. Given the Cold War context of the film, this same message urged the North Atlantic Treaty Organization (NATO) powers to unify against the common communist threat.

Based on the best-selling book by Cornelius Ryan, *The Longest Day*'s production team employed 37 military advisors, used genuine equipment and supplies, found authentic-looking locations to shoot, and borrowed actual soldiers as extras from the U.S., Britain, and France.[35] In exchange for such cooperation, each contributing nation had the opportunity to screen the movie and censor unwanted material.[36] The film was produced by Darryl F. Zanuck, a documentary filmmaker for the Army Signal Corps in World War II. His proud service is reflected in the positive interpretation of the military in the film. The cast featured 42 stars, including John Wayne, Robert Mitchum, and Henry Fonda. Zanuck also sought young actors (Robert Wagner, Sal Mineo, Paul Anka, and Fabian) who could attract a young audience to see the film. The film's producers did not assume young people would pay to see a movie about a war that "occurred before they were born."[37] It is interesting that in an era that other scholars consider militarized, the filmmakers worried about attracting a young moviegoing audience; it was not a given that a young audience would want to see this movie.

Overall, the theme of *The Longest Day* is a great Allied victory made possible by the selflessness and sacrifice of the Allied partners. As American forces prepare for the upcoming landings, Lieutenant Colonel Benjamin Vandervoort (Wayne), a battalion commander in the 82d Airborne Division, mentions that the Americans are newcomers to the war on the continent. The British have been fighting for five years. In this context, the Americans' attitude of "itching to go" is dwarfed by the long commitment already borne by the British. Americans are but one player in the grand struggle against fascism — just as the Western allies had to be unified in the fight against communism.[38]

The dangers of hindsight in the script are apparent here, as all the soldiers reflect gravely on the significance of the day. Although soldiers would have known it was an important event at the time, the melodrama in the film promotes a glorified and lofty place for D-Day in the memory of World War II. It is presented as *the* defining moment of the war, at least from the American perspective. Although there are some horrific moments, as when the paratroopers fall into burning buildings and are shot in the trees, the violence of the day is overshadowed by the glorification of the great victory. It is a story that rallies the goodwill of the audience and takes them to a time that is heroic and victorious. It also purposefully reinforces that America did not win the war alone, though Soviet participation in the war is absent, given the Cold War context.

With an ensemble cast, authentic equipment and locations, state-of-the art special effects, and an appealing patriotic story, *The Longest Day* proved successful at the box office.[39] As historian Stephen Ambrose noted, "The film reinforces a patriotic theme: the triumph of democracy over dictatorship."[40] It was the anti-militaristic democracies that vanquished the militarist dictators. The filmmakers made sure to burnish the images of the valiant democratic soldiers in the movie.

Ambrose observed a number of historical inaccuracies in the film. One error that posed a problem for the heroic images of American soldiers concerns the landings of the Higgins boats on the beach. As Ambrose explained,

> In the movie, they [the soldiers] leap into the water, rush through the waves, dash across the beach, throw themselves behind the sea wall and start firing at the enemy. In reality, they plunged in over their heads, inflated their life jackets, struggled to shore, hid behind beach obstacles, crawled forward to the sea wall and threw themselves down, exhausted.[41]

In sanitizing the beach landings, the filmmakers of *The Longest Day* contributed to the glorification of the war and its fighters.

Even though *The Longest Day* presented an interpretation of World War II more like *To Hell and Back* than to *A Walk in the Sun*, New York Times film critic Bosley Crowther perceived the film as showing the horror of war, not its glory. He praised the depictions of hardship and violence and the courage and sacrifice of the participants. He employed colorful language to describe aspects of the film, referring to "the immensity and sweep of the great battle" and "the thunder of the first landing craft."[42] For Crowther, the danger, action,

Brigadier General Coda (Robert Mitchum, far left), Captain Frank (Ray Danton, second on left), and other American soldiers land on Omaha Beach in Normandy, France, on June 6, 1944, in *The Longest Day* (20th Century–Fox, 1962). The film glorifies the significance of the landing — and the unity of the Allies — without showing the horrors of that day that cost more than 10,000 Allied casualties (killed, wounded, and missing in action) (Keystone-France/Gamma-Keystone/Getty Images).

and glory came in the battles the heroes experienced. He concluded that the film showed that "war is hell and that D-Day was a gallant, costly triumph for the Allied forces, not for any one man."[43] He finished by writing that no other film had done "any more any better or leaving one feeling any more exposed to the horror of war than this one does."[44]

The film reviewer for *Time* had a very different reaction. Although the critic admits the film is riveting, there are many flaws in the dialogue, direction, and effects. For example, "The mighty invasion fleet looks like a silly flotilla of peanut shells in a puddle."[45] More damning is the film's interpretation of war in this critic's view: "It is fundamentally false to the spirit of events. Most of the time, Zanuck shamelessly sugars his bullets— men die by the thousands, but not one living wound, not one believable drop of blood is seen on screen."[46] Such filmmaking is not only an "insult [to] the intelligence" of the audience, but "sometimes insult[s] the dead."[47] A second blurb on the film in *Time* magazine proved even more blunt: "It is basically an episodic documentary that sometimes has the bad taste to say: war is swell."[48] These reviewers found the romantic version of World War II distasteful, suggesting that the "good war" version of the conflict did not immediately resonate with all Americans.

A darker interpretation of the World War II soldier came out the same year as *The Longest Day*. Robert Pirosh, the former World War II infantryman who created *Battleground* and *Go for Broke!*, wrote *Hell Is for Heroes* (1962).[49] The main protagonist in the film is John Reese (Steve McQueen), a soldier who had been busted down from master sergeant to buck private. Reese is an anti-social loner with an attitude, who is purposely rude to the other soldiers. There is little sense of camaraderie between Reese and the other men, though he does have a relationship with Sergeant Pike (Fess Parker), with whom he served in North Africa. Reese openly threatens a Polish displaced person who wants to join the fight, warning him that if "you show up on the line, I'll blow your head off."[50] He never integrates with the other soldiers to be part of the group, unlike the international teamwork repeatedly emphasized in *The Longest Day*.

Although Reese is assuredly a good fighter, he does not submit readily to military authority. He openly disregards the rules by going into town for alcohol, which is strictly off-limits. Reese acts on his own on the front lines, too. Reese has an idea to sneak up on the German pill box under the cover of darkness and destroy it with demolitions. Sergeant Larkin (Harry Guardino), who as Corporal Henshaw (James Coburn) explains, was "trained to follow orders," will not give permission for the attack without consulting his superior, Sergeant Pike. When Larkin returns to the squad to find that Henshaw left the men to get demolitions from a nearby supply dump, he loses his temper with Reese: "You are going to follow orders. My orders!" he demands. A moment later, a German shell kills Larkin.[51]

Without Larkin opposing him, Reese leads the mission to throw a satchel charge into the German pill box pinning them down. On the treacherous journey, crawling through a German minefield, two more men of the squad are killed. When Reese returns to American lines, Sergeant Pike asks him if the decision to make the attack was the right one. With a haunted look in his eyes, Reese replies, "How the hell do I know?" Captain Loomis (Joseph Hoover) also finds Reese and chews him out for the action and for disobeying his superior's decision not to go after the target. Privates take orders; they don't give them.[52]

Perhaps out of a sense of guilt, or perhaps to redeem himself, Reese takes it upon himself to throw the satchel charge into the pill box during the company's attack the following morning. Reese pitches the explosives into the German pill box at the same moment a bullet catches him in the chest. To add insult to injury, the Germans toss the explosives out. With his remaining strength, Reese grabs the charge and rolls into the front of the pill box as it explodes, which kills him and the Germans inside. The film ends with Reese's death, although the larger battle still raged. There is not much glory in this film, though one could argue that Reese's attempt to redeem himself through military sacrifice is militaristic. On the other hand, Reese's open disregard for military authority is quite anti-militaristic. As one scholar notes, the central theme of the film is that young men are in war to die,[53] hardly a romantic or militaristic notion.

The other soldiers of the squad are more reminiscent of Sergeant Bilko and Ensign Parker than the heroes of *The Longest Day*. Private J.J. Corby (Bobby Darin) is a looter, taking pens, watches, and a silver punchbowl and cup service, among other treasures. He proves a competent soldier on the line, but he is clearly looking forward to life as a civilian again — and making a buck or two in the process. Private James E. Driscoll (Bob Newhart) bumbles his way into the squad. A trained typist, he is driving around in a Jeep trying to find division headquarters. Unable to read the map he has, Driscoll is about 20 to 30 miles away from where he needs to be. The squad commandeers the jeep, which Corporal Henshaw cleverly (if unbelievably) tinkers with to make it sound like a tank. Driscoll, meanwhile, tries to fool the Germans, who are eavesdropping on their command post, that their numbers are greater than they are. He pretends to be "Lieutenant" Driscoll, the company morale officer, talking about the movie he has been showing the men and other disinformational chit-chat. Although Driscoll's character is being employed for comic relief, he, too, proves himself a decent combat soldier by the end of the film.[54]

Given Reese's anti-social attitude and his death at the end, the movie could have been received poorly by critics. But *New York Times* film reviewer Eugene Archer accepted the conflicts in McQueen's character. Describing Reese as "surly and unpredictable, a dangerous misfit," Archer acknowledges that at the moment when decisive action had to be taken, it was the anti-social Reese who took command rather than the other soldiers.[55] Overall, Archer gave the film a favorable review, suggesting the continued acceptance of less romantic versions of World War II.

Flexible Response and the Cuban Missile Crisis

In the presidential election of 1960, with Republican Vice-President Richard M. Nixon running against Democratic Senator John F. Kennedy, public estimates of Soviet nuclear strength favored the Soviets over the Americans at a ratio of 3 to 1 or 2 to 1, depending on the source. A *Life* missile "scorecard" cited that the Soviet Union had ten intercontinental ballistic missiles (ICBMs) in 1960 to the American ICBM count of three (in reality, the Soviets had four missiles). Moreover, *Life* reported that the gap was predicted to widen in the coming years, with the Soviets having between 400–500 ICMBs by 1963 and the U.S. having merely 200–250.[56] *Life* editorials accused the Eisenhower administration of short changing the defense budget and urged him to "close the missile" gap, safeguard the Air Force's Strategic Air Command, and perhaps even raise taxes to secure an adequate defense budget.[57] Senator Kennedy ran his presidential campaign, in part, on this (mis)perceived missile "gap." In reality, the "gap" was actually in America's favor. In 1962, the U.S. had 17 missiles for every Soviet missile.[58]

Influenced by Army General Maxwell Taylor's book *The Uncertain Trumpet* (1960) and Robert Osgood's *Limited War* (1957) extolling the benefits of limited war rather than the massive retaliation of Eisenhower's New Look defense policy, Kennedy adopted a new "Flexible Response" strategy. Instead of simply relying on the nuclear deterrent, Flexible Response depended on non-nuclear conventional forces and limited nuclear war to respond to various levels of communist military threats short of nuclear annihilation.[59] The shift to Flexible Response did not signal a decrease in the militarization of American defense policy, however. The Kennedy and subsequent Lyndon B. Johnson administrations expanded America's nuclear capabilities as well as conventional forces and increased the size of the standing active-duty force.[60] Congress supported this enhancement of military preparedness.[61]

In response to the Soviet construction of the Berlin Wall in 1961, Kennedy temporarily called to active duty 148,000 reservists and national guardsmen.[62] Since the majority of the mobilized reservists never served overseas during the crisis, some of them questioned the disruption the mobilization caused for them and their families. According to military correspondent Hanson Baldwin, a "small but significant minority of mobilized Reservists and National Guardsmen" reacted with "bitterness, resentment, and frustration" to the call-up.[63] This attitude was not the reaction of militarized soldiers wanting to fight communists over the Berlin Wall. It was the response of civilians not wanting the disruption in their lives unless it was a true emergency. Nonetheless, many Americans supported a tough stance against the Soviet Union on the Berlin issue. As Don Ross, a correspondent for the New York *Herald Tribune* stated about the citizens of a small New York town: "They are determined, even the little old ladies rocking on the porches, that you [the Soviets] shan't have it [Berlin]."[64] Yet, while Americans liked to talk tough, few of them followed the talk by volunteering for service in the armed forces.

After the failed Bay of Pigs invasion of Cuba in April 1961, Fidel Castro allowed the Soviet Union to build a nuclear missile base on the island, a mere 90 miles away from the shores of Florida. In October 1962, an American U-2 spy plane discovered the construction of the missile base in Cuba. According to historian John Lewis Gaddis, unknown to Kennedy and his advisors there were already 158 nuclear weapons on the island, with at least 42 able to reach American shores.[65] After consulting with national security advisors and the Pentagon, Kennedy chose to enact a naval "quarantine" to prevent Soviet ships from delivering missiles to Cuba, as a blockade was an act of war in international law. October 22 began one of the most anxious weeks in world history when Kennedy addressed the American people about the missiles and the quarantine. Soviet premier Nikita Khrushchev publicly denounced the "quarantine," but he ultimately ordered his ships to observe it. As David Welch explains, "Neither Kennedy nor Khrushchev wanted to risk nuclear war over the issue, and both became increasingly concerned that an accident or inadvertent military action might trigger escalation."[66]

Khrushchev sent two messages to Kennedy to resolve the situation. Kennedy agreed to pledge publicly not to invade Cuba and secretly acquiesced to remove American intermediate-ranged ballistic missiles from Turkey. In return, Khrushchev removed the missiles from Cuba. At the time that many Americans scrambled to build nuclear bomb shelters in the their backyards, relations between the U.S. and the Soviet Union actually stabilized with the installation of a "hot line" between Washington and Moscow and the following year's Limited Test Ban Treaty.[67] Nevertheless, the scare of imminent nuclear war between the U.S. and the Soviet Union deeply influenced American popular culture.

Television Combat Dramas

By the beginning of the 1960s, nearly 90 percent of homes had one television set, and Americans watched around five hours of programming per day.[68] During this time, the networks populated their offerings with many shows set in combat or featuring military characters.[69] Only a few of them proved enduringly popular with viewers, including *Combat!*, *McHale's Navy*, *Gomer Pyle U.S.M.C.*, and *Hogan's Heroes*.[70] Only one of these shows was a drama; the others were comedies. It appears that audiences preferred to laugh at the military.

Many of the military shows on television were set during World War II. Given the Cuban Missile Crisis and civil rights-related violence, broadcasting a "good" version of World War II might be comforting for American audiences. *Combat!* Executive Producer Selig Seligman described his show as "a searching in our history for the ideals and heroism that can sustain the American people in a troubled time."[71] Producers from *Combat!* and *Hogan's Heroes* admitted that setting their stories in World War II avoided controversy. *Combat!*'s producer Richard Caffey said that World War II was "a classic period," and *Hogan's Heroes* producer Ed Feldman explained, "It makes for blacks and whites,"[72] not the indecision of Korea or the unpredictability of the Cold War.

Television military dramas introduced a new generation to the citizen-soldier imagery depicted in the films *Battleground* and *The Story of G.I. Joe*. Robert Pirosh, who had just written *Hell Is for Heroes*, created the television series *Combat!* (1962–1967). Pirosh developed the show based on his wartime diary, the same source as his material for *Battleground*. Like the film, the television series drew inspiration from Pirosh's personal experience with combat infantry and presented stories from the perspective of a common soldier. *Combat!* attempted to create a sense of realism, so producers sent the actors to a week-long "boot camp" held at an army post to learn how to portray authentic soldiers. In addition, the show used World War II combat footage. Department of Defense policy at the time extended footage, equipment, and advice to television productions which provided a favorable image of the Army. *Combat!* also retained an Army advisor.[73] One of the show's producers, Richard Caffey, explained the Army's cooperation: "The Army feels it's good for them that it presents a good image to youth," he said, adding, "They like the way we depict war."[74] At the height of its popularity in the 1964–1965 television season, *Combat!* ranked number ten in ratings, which points to a wide viewing audience who presumably liked the show's interpretation of World War II.[75] It also received good ratings from TV critics. *Time* magazine's reviewer described it as having "some of the dusty menace of *A Walk in the Sun*," and concluded it was a good show.[76] It is interesting to note the reviewer likened *Combat!* to *A Walk in the Sun*, a decidedly unromantic version of World War II rather than a more romantic version like *To Hell and Back* or *The Longest Day*.

In the show, Lieutenant Gil Hanley (Rick Jason), who received a battlefield commission like Audie Murphy, and Sergeant Chip Saunders (Vic Morrow) lead their fellow citizen-soldiers across the European Theater of Operations during World War II. Enlisted men Kirby, Littlejohn, Braddock, Nelson, Doc, and Caje were the old hands in Saunders' squad. The men share fierce camaraderie with each other. As Hanley explains, "The first time someone shoots at you, you don't have a command, you have a family."[77]

One episode distinctly shows the superiority of American citizen-soldiers against the militaristic (if humanized) Germans. In "The Enemy," a German officer has booby-trapped a French town. It is a battle of wills, deceit, and cleverness, with Hanley forcing the German to reveal the traps, and the German attempting to trap Hanley in them. The German shows disdain for Hanley and the entire U.S. Army, which is filled with civilians with merely six months' training. He openly wonders how the Americans have managed to last this long in the war. This German is a professional who spent years preparing for war. Hanley nonetheless outsmarts the German — the scrappy citizen-soldier beating the cool professional.[78]

Combat! also expresses the human cost of war, which shows how tough it was for the citizen-soldiers. In the episode "The First Day" four new replacements join the platoon: Loomis, McBride, Tate, and Tobin. Commenting on the youth of the new soldiers, Kirby quips, "We better win this war soon. We're running out of men." Saunders takes a squad with the replacements on a mission. Tate hides his fear behind a tough, know-it-all façade. When the squad encounters a German half-track, however, Tate panics. As he runs away, the Germans shoot him in the back. Saunders snaps at the other replacements, "He made a wrong move and now he's dead. That's all the speech you get." Not long afterwards, Loomis is seriously wounded, which in turn causes Tobin to have a complete breakdown. Down to his last replacement, Saunders rallies McBride, and the two advance to take out the rest of a German patrol. When the men are back from the mission, Doc muses: "Four bright, shiny new replacements. One dead, one wounded, one cracked up, and one you can't tell the difference from the rest of us."[79]

A few episodes show anti-militarist and anti-war themes, such as the meaninglessness of sacrifice. In "Cat and Mouse," Hanley orders Saunders and his exhausted men out on a mission just after a grueling patrol on which snipers and landmines had killed five men. Saunders is put with Jenkins, a regular, who complains about "soft" volunteers who are to blame for the war taking so long. (Of course, the reality is that most World War II soldiers were draftees, not volunteers.) Later, Saunders learns that Jenkins had been demoted from lieutenant to sergeant after two of his soldiers died from heat exhaustion after a forced march. Simply being a regular did not mean a soldier was more competent than a citizen-soldier.[80]

After being captured by Germans, Jenkins sacrifices his life so that Saunders can take information regarding an impending German attack to headquarters. When Saunders returns to American lines, he learns that the Americans had broken the German code earlier in the day and already knew about the enemy plans. The idea that Jenkins's death had not contributed to the American defense hits Saunders hard. He questions how higher headquarters could value the lives of soldiers so little. Most episodes, however, do not reflect this bleak attitude toward war or the meaningless of the squad's actions. Many times the information the characters gather does help prevent

Lieutenant Hanley (Rick Jason, left) and Sergeant Saunders (Vic Morrow) in the pilot episode of the TV series *Combat!* (1962–1967). Hanley and Saunders lead fellow citizen-soldiers across Europe after the D-Day landing. The show has many anti-militarist themes, especially ones about the superiority of citizen-soldiers over regulars (ABC Photo Archives/Disney ABC Television Group/Getty Images).

the Allies from incurring casualties. While the war is tough physically and mentally on the men, it is worth it in the end.[81] Overall, *Combat!* is not militarist. With the focus on citizen-soldiers' superiority to regulars and the repeated message that war was not ennobling, the series does not fit the American definition of militarism.

While *Combat!* proved to be the most enduring of the television dramas, other shows presented a tough but good war with citizen-soldiers as the heroes. *The Gallant Men* (1962–1963) attempted to closely model the film *The Story of G.I. Joe* in plot and setting. The central character, war correspondent Conley Wright (Robert McQueeney), performs the same function of Ernie Pyle in the earlier film. In addition, Wright's character often talks with the commander before he makes a decision and plays the peacemaker by explaining the captain's decisions to the soldiers or the soldiers' actions to the local population. In the pilot episode, Captain Benedict (William Reynolds) is a young, green commander unsure of his abilities and afraid to lose the men under his command. He becomes a more confident leader in subsequent episodes. First Sergeant McKenna (Richard X. Slattery) is the tough, disciplined old hand, a regular who had been in the Army prior to World War II. He offers both leadership and stability to the unit. Italian-speaking Private D'Angelo (Eddie Fontaine) is hot-headed and prone to gambling and romancing the ladies. Lieutenant Kimbro (Robert Ridgely) and Privates Hanson and Lucavich (Robert Gothie and Roland La Starza) round out the cast of citizen-soldiers. Both anti-militarist and militarist themes are present in the show. Although *The Gallant Men* received good reviews from television critics, it fell flat with audiences.[82]

As with *Combat!*, *The Gallant Men* deals with the human costs of war, showing how tough the experience had been. In "The Warriors," Conley, D'Angelo, and Gibson run into a British officer, Blagdon, and a Canadian officer, Wells, on the road. German shells begin landing around the men, wounding Gibson. They find refuge in a nearby shack where they meet a group of American soldiers who have been separated from their units. It does not take long before D'Angelo and Conley suspect that all of their companions are deserters. Blagdon is fighting an internal battle: he is consumed with self-doubt, believing that another commander would have lost fewer men in battle. Conley sagely advises Blagdon that no man can fight two wars at one time, one with the Germans and one with himself. Wells maintains that he is no warrior, but a lover, a civilian, a philosopher. Before long, the Germans discover the men's hiding place. Despite down playing his martial characteristics, Wells dies fighting the Germans in hand-to-hand combat. His sacrifice saves the others. The message in this episode is that military qualities such as courage and sacrifice are meaningful and desirable. Even citizens can find them within themselves as Wells did.[83]

A militaristic theme in *The Gallant Men* is that sacrifice is inherently redemptive. A replacement soldier, Draper, initially appears as a cold, emotionally detached sniper who deliberately distances himself from the other soldiers in the unit. When Benedict orders Draper to kill a German sniper, he bursts into the home of Signora Cirasella, who is praying over the coffin of her dead husband. He yells at her, "Do you think if there were a God, he would allow something as ugly as war?" He calls God a "cruel deity," and sarcastically remarks, "Thank the Lord for thy bounties" as "that is the fourth man I've killed today." Conley explains to Signora Cirasella that Draper shuts out emotion because he is too sensitive for war. Draper begins to break out of his shell when he teaches the local children geography. This allows him to reconnect to his humanity and his old life as a teacher in the civilian world. In order to make up for his poor behavior, Draper volunteers to assault a German mortar crew that is harassing the town. He kills a machine gun crew and two of the mortar crew before a German soldier shoots him. Draper lunges at the German with a grenade in his hand, blowing up both of them off-screen. Signora Cirasella and other villagers come to see Draper as a hero for his self-sacrifice.[84]

Redemptive sacrifice in war is also a theme in the air-combat drama, *Twelve O'Clock High* (1964–1967). The series also places more emphasis on technology, discipline, and teamwork, on the surface placing it closer to the militaristic interpretation of war. However, both teamwork and discipline were necessary for basic survival in the World War II strategic bombing campaign, and the show emphasized the pressures, stresses, and human cost of war. It does not glory in the adventure of war, only in a job well done. Ultimately, *Twelve O'Clock High* does not appear overly militaristic.

The television show picked up the same setting and characters as the 1949 film: the 918th Bombardment Group in the American Eighth Air Force stationed in England during World War II. Brigadier General Frank Savage appears again as the Group's commanding officer, while the character Major Harvey Stovall reprises his role of executive officer. Sergeant Komansky is the only regular character who is not an officer. Savage's character dies at the beginning of the second season, making way for the rise of Colonel Joe Gallagher into his leadership position. Most *Twelve O'Clock High* episodes interweave sophisticated themes, such as the pressures of war, battle fatigue, responsibility, leadership, sacrifice, and teamwork. Although Savage and other regular characters exhibit the best military qualities, they also struggle with personal demons. While some of the regular cast members are long-service professionals, the men they lead are America's citizen-soldiers. (The roles this time around are portrayed by Robert Lansing as Savage, Frank Overton as Stovall, Chris Robinson as Komansky, and Paul Burke as Gallagher.)

Twelve O'Clock High shows the militaristic theme of redemption through military sacrifice. Savage's mentor, Colonel Hartley, arrives at the Group headquarters. While reminiscing about old times, Hartley complains about being stuck behind a desk. Savage arranges to get Hartley back up in the air. Hartley cannot pass up a chance at heroics, however, and takes the bomber down to strafe a German patrol boat after a failed bombing run. The waist gunner observes, "He still thinks it's the old days." Upon returning, Hartley "flat hats" the airfield, a World War I–era victory flyover. Savage reprimands him but allows Hartley to remain flying. Unfortunately, Hartley continues to disobey orders, peeling out of formation to attack German fighters on the next mission and lying about it afterward. On a mission to destroy a German ammo dump, Savage aborts the operation when the target is too well protected by anti-aircraft fire. Hartley decides to trade his life for the target. He disobeys orders and takes in his plane. After the co-pilot is killed by flak, Hartley orders the rest of the crew to bail out. He slams his bomber straight into the ammo, bursting into flames and becoming an instant hero. Savage is heartbroken by the loss of his mentor, even though Hartley was too independent to fly in formation, follow orders, and maintain discipline. Hartley sacrificed himself rather than adapt to the new war and its necessity for teamwork and discipline.[85]

In "The Sound of a Distant Thunder," Savage pushes citizen-soldier Lieutenant Lathrop to consider a career in the Army Air Forces after the war. Under continuous pressure from Savage, Lathrop goes to a pub, gets drunk, and starts complaining to the waitress, "In Tennessee, nobody bothers you and tries to make you into something you're not." Clearly, he does not want to become a military professional. When Lathrop comes in late the next morning, Savage reprimands him for acting like a lowly private just off the boat instead of a responsible officer. Deciding that he wants a family, Lathrop steals a Jeep in order to propose to the waitress he had seen the night before at the pub. Unfortunately for him, she dies in an air raid that evening. After seeing the effects of the German bombs, Lathrop no longer wants to be a part of the war. He asks Savage, "How many people do I have to kill before I can wear a star?" Surprised, Savage replies, "Is that all a star means to you, Andy? Killing?" Savage explains that it takes men to take responsibility and make tough decisions. Savage does not like or revel in war — he is not a self-aware militarist. He nevertheless has faith in the bombers and believes the bombing can end the war. In the end, Lathrop comes to understand the importance of his duty and continues to serve, a militaristic version of the citizen-soldier.[86]

The episode "The Hot Shot" illustrates concretely the virtues of teamwork over the pitfalls of individualism. After one mission, a P-51 fighter commander, Colonel Troper, is furious with Gallagher because one of his planes crashed from friendly-fire. Angrily, he accuses Gallagher of deliberately targeting the P-51 and tells a reporter that he will not fly with Gallagher again. When General Britt orders Gallagher and Troper to work together to write the procedures for long-range fighter escort, Gallagher insists that the P-51 pilots do things by the book, instilling discipline and raising the ire of the pilots. Although he is quick to criticize the bomber gunners, Troper misidentifies his own P-51 profile twice in the flash cards the bomber crews use to identify enemy aircraft. Troper's bad attitude gets worse, and he starts to get drunk and act out. After he is grounded, the P-51 pilots rally around Gallagher. Troper kids his men about needing him up there to get more Nazi kills, but the pilots tell him their mission is to protect the bombers, not to dogfight with the enemy. The P-51 pilots learned to work as a team with Gallagher, and they feel pride in accomplishing their mission.[87] While disciplined aircrews who followed orders and stayed in formation were key to the effectiveness of the air campaign in World War II, it is worth noting that privileging these traits contrasts sharply with the initiative and inventiveness that are key to the image of the citizen-soldier.

While the vast majority of military popular culture focused on World War II, one drama was set in the contemporary 1960s. The Lieutenant (1963–1964) was created by Gene Roddenberry, who later produced Star Trek. Both shows feature anti-militarist themes and characters. Star Trek's Captain Kirk almost always used fighting as a last resort in resolving conflicts. In the case of The Lieutenant, the main character, marine officer Lieutenant William Rice (Gary Lockwood), is a regular stationed at Camp Pendleton who has to struggle with contemporary issues like the Vietnam War and racism in the ranks.

In the episode "To Kill a Man," which aired on April 18, 1964, before the Gulf of Tonkin incident or the arrival for American ground combat troops, Lieutenant Rice and a few other Americans are taking new radio equipment to Hanang, Vietnam. He boards a helicopter and watches the villages, river, boats, and a rice paddies pass below him. During the flight, the helicopter starts taking fire from the ground. An African-American non-commissioned officer attempts to fix an oil leak from a bullet that hit them, but the chopper is forced to land anyway. Armed with rifles, the passengers set up a perimeter with shifts for guard duty. This is Rice's first time in action, so his nerves keep him from falling asleep. A South Vietnamese officer reassures him by saying that it is okay to miss a night's rest on one's first day in combat; it is not a poor reflection on Rice's bravery. The two discuss liberty, freedom, the Constitution, and the Bill of Rights. The Vietnamese officer says he wants to be his country's Benjamin Franklin, Thomas Jefferson, George Washington, or Nathan Hale.[88]

Not long after being grounded, the small encampment comes under attack. In the fray, six Americans are killed. Rice survives the attack, but is wounded. He wanders into the jungle, where a Vietnamese woman finds him and tends to his wound. He feels guilty both for killing and for being unable to save the lives of the other Americans. The South Vietnamese officer, who turns out to be a communist, finds Rice in the village. The communist claims to be the equivalent of the American patriots and revolutionaries and quotes the Declaration of Independence. Rice retorts that the government is by the consent of the people, not by communist dictate. After giving him an opportunity to drop his weapon and surrender, Rice is forced to kill the Vietnamese officer. Although the episode supports America's role in Vietnam, it also suggests that war was not glorious. The whole experience leaves Rice troubled, and he feels remorse about killing. He did not accept easily the taking of another life.[89] It reflects an anti-militaristic attitude.

The Lieutenant also confronted the contemporary issue of race relations in the service. African-American Private Cameron attacks a racist white Corporal Devlin for calling him a "black monkey." Lieutenant Rice, a white officer, believes it is his duty to try to reach the two men and help them resolve their differences. He forces them to work together constantly in the field and pairs them up for a rock-climbing exercise. The two men resent the lieutenant's efforts and remain obstinate. Cameron refuses to go into the same tent with Devlin when it is raining. Rice's commanding officer counsels him that he can try to get the two to work together, but he probably cannot change their attitudes. Cameron's girlfriend, Norma (Nichelle Nichols, the future Lieutenant Uhura on *Star Trek*), tells Rice flatly that he does not truly understand African-American issues and that he cannot make peace between Cameron and Devlin just because he wants to do so.[90]

Cameron is convinced the world has not changed for the better. He carries a large chip on his shoulder and accuses an African-American lieutenant and non-commissioned officer of being "Uncle Toms." When confronted by Rice, however, Cameron admits that no one calls him a "nigger" in the Corps. There is a single lighthearted moment at the end of the episode when Devlin offers Cameron blackface paint for night operations. This hopeful ending suggests that the ice may be breaking between the two men.[91] Unfortunately, the show was not renewed for subsequent seasons, indicating that audiences were not ready to address such deep and complicated contemporary issues, at least not in entertainment television.

Comics Under the Code

In the continuing wake of the Comics Code, comic books showered praise on the sacrifices made by American servicemen during World War II. Like their counterparts in the movies and on television, the stories often acknowledged the hardships of war in order to show how American servicemen overcame the great odds against them. One story from *Battlefield Action* recounts Army attacks on the German Siegfried Line near the end of the war. Even with victory clearly in sight, and with the knowledge of hindsight, the author describes "the tired, grimy G.I.'s ... pitiful in comparison with the Nazi's, well-fed and protected by their thick gray walls." Yet the American soldiers "went at their hopeless task with a will!" Even with victory around the corner, the war is still hopeless for these soldiers. Under murderous fire from the Germans, one company loses their captain, lieutenant, and master sergeant, leaving a corporal in command. With the heavy burden of command weighing unexpectedly on his shoulders, this young man rises to the occasion, earning a battlefield commission to first lieutenant at the end of the day.[92]

Similar stories abound for the war in the Pacific theater. For example, the campaign on Guadalcanal was an "island of death" according to one comic-book author. He outlined the tens of thousands of casualties, where "the dead lay in piles the size of hills." The horror of the campaign shows just how tough it was for American Marines.[93] Another story suggests that "war in all its horror makes every man a hero." This particular comic emphasizes the camaraderie and self-sacrifice of the Marines. At the end, one Marine takes a bullet in his back trying to carry a fellow Marine to safety.[94] War is tough, but American servicemen are brave, dedicated, and self-sacrificing.

"Germans in Arms Again"

In the mid–1950s, when West Germany began to rearm, editorialists on the political left warned about the dangers of placing weapons back in the hands of militarists. By 1960, West Germany had reconstituted its military and was ready to become part of NATO. Notably, the Republican-friendly *Life* magazine went to great lengths to assure its readers that the new German army was not militarist, suggesting that fears of German militarism lingered in the American consciousness.

A *Life* editorialist explained to readers that the new German army has been built with several "safeguards to insure against German aggression," such as the stipulation that the Germans can only fight under NATO orders.[95] Furthermore, their "commanders, from sergeant major to general, have been drilled in the principles of democratic leadership."[96] As a result, the "new West German military establishment is not militaristic in the old Prussian sense."[97] In order to protect against the emergence of a professional military elite, the German army limited the service of draftees. The *Life* article also noted that the German defense minister was "a firm believer in civilian control of the military."[98] By assuring the public that the German army was not aggressive, that no military elite would form, and that it was firmly under civilian control, the authors touched on nearly all facets of the American definition of militarism, which included the aggressive use of a military force; the military's possession of power outside of civilian authority or constitutional limits; a national emphasis on maintaining military preparedness during peacetime; and the military's imposition upon society of regimentation or values that could undermine democracy. Even if Americans did not see the rising militarism in their own culture, they were still looking for it as a danger from the outside.

"This Is Going to be a Lousy War"

Comedies like *McHale's Navy* continued the implicit anti-militarist sentiments prevalent in *The Phil Silvers Show*, *Beetle Bailey*, and *Sad Sack*. *McHale's Navy* (1962–1966) privileges civilian attitudes over military ones, while still showing that citizen-soldiers can fight and defend the nation. Indeed, Charles Moskos finds the characters in *McHale's Navy* part of a long-standing comedic tradition that makes American servicemen appear non-militaristic.[99] The show inverts traditional military values to create an irreverent (and humorous) World War II story.[100] Lieutenant Commander Quinton McHale (Ernest Borgnine) commands a PT boat in the South Pacific. His commanding officer is Captain Binghamton (Joe Flynn), who ran a yacht club before the war. Although it never reached top-ten status, *McHale's Navy* ranked closely behind the top-rated shows.[101]

McHale and his men prove capable and patriotic when called upon, but they would much rather spend their time on something other than war. McHale and his men are not terribly concerned with the rule-bound Navy, and McHale allows his men to have fun in their down time. McHale permits the men to lounge around and does not enforce uniform discipline. McHale is also lax with Navy schedules and regulations. In the pilot episode, McHale tells his new executive officer, Ensign Parker (Tim Conway), to leave them alone until brunch at 1000. The men have a still for alcohol, and the sign on their island announces, "McHale's Island: All armed forces personnel keep off — girls come on in."[102]

Binghamton is also a citizen-soldier, but he makes up for lack of talent by embracing the Navy's rules and appearances. In the pilot episode, Binghamton gives Ensign Parker one week to straighten out the crew or receive the worst transfer in naval history. When McHale learns of this threat, he sympathizes with Parker enough to order his men to "try the Navy" for one week to help Parker. The men march, hang correct signage, and wear proper uniforms. Binghamton reluctantly allows Parker to stay as McHale's executive officer.[103]

McHale's Navy repeatedly presented the message that the citizen-sailors with their civilian clothes and attitudes were the effective combatants, not the ones who followed Navy regimentation. Although he excels at following

Lieutenant Commander Quinton McHale (Ernest Borgnine, left) pulls bungling Ensign Parker (Tim Conway, right), out of harm's way on the television show *McHale's Navy* (1962–1966). The series repeatedly showed the competence of the rule-bending, individualistic PT boat crew and the incompetence of the rule-bound Parker and Captain Binghamton (Joe Flynn, not pictured) (ABC Photo Archives/Disney ABC Television Group/Getty Images).

regulations, Binghamton proves inept when it comes to actual combat. In "The Captain's Mission," Binghamton boasts at the officers' club that he sank half the "Nips" in the area. His companions, two officers on combat duty tours, make fun of him for fighting the war behind his desk. Binghamton feels self-conscious about missing combat duty, so he decides to take McHale's boat for a mission. McHale's crew devises a fake operation so that Binghamton can have a war story and they can send him back to the office as a war hero. Unfortunately, Binghamton bungles the mission and accidentally launches a depth charge on an island. Then they encounter a real Japanese boat. Binghamton fires the torpedo prematurely, and it hits a truck on a nearby island (much like a plot element in the film *Operation Petticoat*). Nevertheless, Binghamton has his war story, which he inflates considerably to brag to the other officers at the club.[104]

Competent citizen-soldiers were not confined to men in the South Pacific. Edward J. Montagne, the creator of *McHale's Navy*, also produced *Broadside* (1964–1965).[105] Like its predecessor, *Broadside* is set on a South Pacific island, and it utilizes many of the same silly, slapstick comedy routines. Base Commander Rogers Adrian (Edward Andrews) has a good deal going for him: gourmet food, luxury items, and no threat of going out for wartime sea duty. If the new unit of WAVES proves they can replace the male motor pool, more men would be cleared for combat duty. In nearly every episode, Adrian schemes to get the women off his island, and each time the women, led by Lieutenant junior grade Anne Morgan (Kathleen Nolan), outsmart him.

The WAVES are portrayed as strong, clever, and competent as well as stereotypically feminine. During the pilot episode, "Don't Make Waves," Adrian orders the women to repair marine invasion vehicles for which he knows there are no spare parts. Machinist Mate Molly McGuire breaks into tears as she says, "We have just begun to fight," juxtaposing feminine crying with a traditional male battle cry. Despite her tears, Molly insists, "We're just as much Navy as any other man." The WAVES employ their feminine wiles to accomplish this "man's" job. Morgan sets up a scavenger hunt for the men on the island. For every part they find, they receive a kiss from one of the women. The next day, as an admiral arrives for inspection, the WAVES drive out the marine invasion vehicles in their clean, khaki uniforms. The admiral notices that a garter belt is being used for a fan belt, and finds the solution brilliant. It is a perfect example of American anti-militarist ingenuity. He tells Commander Adrian, "This is the kind of American know-how that is going to win the war." Beaming at the WAVES, the admiral adds, "I think they are going to be with us for a long time." Adrian responds glumly, "This is going to be a lousy war."[106] The women prove their worth to the war effort, despite Adrian's scheming. The show did not last long, though. It faced stiff competition from *The Ed Sullivan Show*, one of the longest-running television series.[107] Maybe television audiences were not quite ready for such feisty military women yet, either.

"It's the Virtue of War That's the Fraud"

As noted earlier, one of the most stridently anti-militarist films of the decade is *The Americanization of Emily* (1964). The story is set in London in May 1944. James Garner, himself an infantry veteran of the Korean War, plays American Lieutenant Commander Madison, the personal attendant to Admiral Jessup (Melvin Douglas). Madison embraces personal consumption and immediate gratification. His job is to keep the admiral well clothed, fed, and admired. As such, Madison runs a black market out of his suite, bribes the supply officers, and runs a female escort service for officers.[108]

Emily (Julie Andrews) is an enlisted British servicewoman who harbors deep cynicism for the Americans. She tells Madison with disgust, "You Americans are really enjoying this war, aren't you?" She denounces Madison's glib attitude and side business by saying, "I think it profane you enjoy this war." While Madison and Emily might have mutual contempt for each other at first, they eventually fall in love and fall in bed. In what would be a scandal in previous war films, Emily worries at one point that she does not get pregnant. Emily is attracted to Madison because he is a coward and is not likely to run off and get killed. Madison described himself as "yellow through and through," and Emily approves by affirming, "That's your most attractive feature."[109]

The Americanization of Emily subverts the heroic, good war interpretation of World War II shown in *The Longest Day*. In a state of delusion from the pressures of war and an obsession with the Navy's rivalry with the Army, Admiral Jessup announces that he wants the first death on Omaha Beach to be a sailor, not a soldier. Instead of dismissing the lunacy of the suggestion, Lieutenant Commander Bus Cummings (James Coburn) becomes obsessed with making it happen. He determines that Madison will be part of a filming crew to capture the image of the first sailor killed on Omaha Beach. Madison flatly refuses to endanger his life for this absurdity, but Cummings forces him to go. In a scene that completely undercuts the heroic image of America's soldiers bravely facing deadly fire on Omaha Beach, Cummings pushes Madison onto the beach at gun point. He starts shooting at Madison, who runs toward the beach in terror. When the Germans start firing, it appears that Madison dies, fulfilling the admiral's wish.[110]

Madison's picture is plastered on the front page of *Life*, making him a

Lieutenant Commander Charles Madison (James Garner, left) is chased at gunpoint onto the beach at Normandy on D-Day by Lieutenant Commander Bud Cummings (James Coburn) in *The Americanization of Emily* (MGM, 1964). Admiral Jessup (Melvyn Douglas, not pictured) had a mental breakdown and insisted that the first man to die in the invasion must be a sailor rather than a soldier. Cummings tries to make it happen by forcing Madison onto the beach against his will. The scene under-cuts the heroic images of the soldiers landing at D-Day, such as in *The Longest Day* (1962). When Madison later turns up with the wounded survivors, Cummings complains he is a live coward rather than a dead hero (photograph by Don Cravens, Time & Life Images/Getty Images).

hero for being the first dead man in the Normandy landing. At this point, the admiral regains his lucidity and learns of Madison's death. Jessup is shocked that anyone would follow his orders when he was clearly mentally distressed. The men who made Madison into a supposedly dead hero for dying have a problem when he returns to London along with the wounded. Cummings complains that instead of a dead hero they have a live coward. Nevertheless, for public-relations purposes, the Navy intends to award Madison with the Navy Cross. Madison wants everyone to know the truth. He explains, "I want people to know I'm a coward." Emily disagrees. She reminds him of his earlier declaration that "it's the virtue of war that's the fraud, not war itself."[111]

While scholars assert that this film is anti-war,[112] more to the point, it attacked the glorification of war and the romance of heroic virtue and courage. Madison firmly blames wives and mothers for taking part in this fraud by glorifying the bravery and heroism of their husbands and sons, which just encourages more men to go off to war. While Crowther of the *New York Times* admired the pacifism of the film, it did not do well at the box office.[113] Perhaps it was not time for such sentiments to resonate with an audience that had not experienced open war since 1953. *The Americanization of Emily* might have garnered a more enthusiastic anti-war audience base had it been made a few years later at the height of the opposition to the Vietnam War.

Anti-Nuclear Films

Eisenhower's New Look emphasis on nuclear weapons, the threat of annihilating war with the Soviet Union, and the enlarged post–Korean War permanent military establishment prompted a backlash of anti-nuclear, anti-technology films. While the existence of atomic bombs had already affected the culture, including a spate of science-fiction movies about radiation-induced monsters like giant ants in *Them!* (1954), a number of new films graced the silver screen starting in 1959.[114] *On the Beach* (1959) appeared as a cautionary tale of the dangers of military technology, as it confronts issues of radioactive fallout after a nuclear war. After an unexplained nuclear exchange which killed most of the world's population, an American submarine crew finds temporary refuge in the last radiation-free place: Australia. People in Australia are waiting for an irradiated cloud to reach the continent that will end all life on earth. Although the setting is bleak and survival hopeless, the characters in the film end their lives with dignity intact. The captain, Commander Towers (Gregory Peck), is a model officer who remains loyal and devoted to his now-dead wife and children. When the crew picks up a signal from California, Towers leads his sailors back into the radiation to see if someone might be alive. He orders one last dive at the end of the film, so that the crew could perish together as a family. The film ends on a somber note as the Americans dive away and the remaining Australians take poison before they die of radiation.[115]

New York Times' Bosley Crowther praised *On the Beach*. He found in it a message that "life is a beautiful treasure and man should do all he can to save it from annihilation, while there is still time."[116] Although the film portrays Captain Towers as a role model for a calm, dignified naval officer, it does not blame the Navy or the United States for the nuclear war. Still, the U.S. Navy provided little assistance to *On the Beach*, believing that public support for nuclear weapons should not be undermined. *On the Beach* allowed the filmmakers to explore the horrors of war without impugning the military services themselves.[117]

Other critics did not like the film, with the *Time* movie reviewer declaring "the picture actually manages for most of its length to make the most dangerous conceivable situation in human history seem rather silly and science-fictional."[118] The critic for *The New Republic*, Stanley Kauffmann, dismissed the artistic merits of the dialogue and direction but conceded, "The book has frightened hundreds of thousands, the film will frighten millions—in a good cause ... probably the most urgent in history."[119]

In the wake of the Cuban Missile Crisis, it is unsurprising that a new wave of anti-nuclear films reached the silver screen: *Fail-Safe*, *Dr. Strangelove*, and *Seven Days in May* all in 1964. Before becoming motion pictures, both *Fail-Safe* and *Seven Days in May* were best-selling novels in 1962.[120] Michael Sherry dismisses these films as simply expressing liberal filmmakers' perceptions of the dangers of the political right, which he claims did not influence the center in American politics.[121] Yet the reason a right-wing military coup d'état appeared so unlikely was the place of civilian control of the military in American culture. Civilian control of the military was an anti-militarist policy that had been a fixture in American culture since before the Constitution. It was perhaps one of the most ingrained and persistent aspects of anti-militarism in American culture.

The most extreme anti-militarist commentary on nuclear weapons and military power comes in a satirical comedy, *Dr. Strangelove, or: How I Stopped Worrying and Learned to Love the Bomb*. Each of the military characters in this film presents an exaggerated caricature very unflattering toward professional officers. The aptly named General Jack Ripper (Sterling Hayden), on his own authority as an Air Force wing commander, orders his bombers into the Soviet Union for a nuclear attack. Ripper acts on his own because he believes that military officers know better than civilians how best to employ the nuclear arsenal. He explains, "Today, war is too important to be left to politi-

Royal Air Force Group Captain Mandrake (Peter Sellers, left) and United States Air Force General Jack Ripper (Sterling Hayden, right), in a scene from *Dr. Strangelove, or: How I Learned to Stop Worrying and Love the Bomb* (Columbia Pictures, 1964). Ripper had ordered a nuclear attack on the Soviet Union out of a paranoid fear (promulgated by the real-life extreme right wing John Birch Society) that there was a communist conspiracy "to impurify all of our precious bodily fluids." Mandrake failed to convince Ripper to recall the bombers (Michael Ochs Archives/Getty Images).

cians. They have neither the time, the training, nor the inclination for strategic thought." This is a clear case of a professional military officer subverting the Constitutional authority of the president because he believes that the military, and himself in particular, is better suited than civilian authorities to make decisions about war and peace. Even more disturbing, Ripper orders the attack out of a paranoid fear (promulgated by the real-life extreme right wing John Birch Society) that there was a communist conspiracy "to impurify all of our precious bodily fluids." After Army paratroopers fight their way onto the base, Ripper commits suicide rather than face the consequences of his actions.[122]

When the president (Peter Sellers) confirms with General Buck Turgidson (George C. Scott) that only he should have the authority to order such an attack, the general responds, "Although I hate to judge before all the facts are in, it's beginning to look like General Ripper exceeded his authority." Turgidson believes that they should take the opportunity to broaden the nuclear war with callous disregard for the consequences. He pleads with the president, "Mr. President, I'm not saying we wouldn't get our hair mussed. But I do say no more than ten to twenty million killed, tops." He adds, "Depending on the breaks." He cannot help but cheer that his bombers made it through Soviet defenses, even though the disaster could be averted if the Soviets destroyed them. Other military characters are similarly colorful. The only sympathetic military officer is Royal Air Force Group Captain Mandrake (also Sellers), who tries to reason with Ripper to have the bombers recalled before Ripper kills himself.[123] The overall effect of the caricatures, the absurd plot, and the death of the planet from the Soviet doomsday machine at the end, is to erode confidence in military technology and the wisdom of allowing military commanders access to power.

Crowther referred to *Dr. Strangelove* as both "the most shattering sick joke I've ever come across" and "one of the cleverest and most incisive satiric thrusts at the awkwardness of the military."[124] Tom Prideaux of *Life* believed that *Dr. Strangelove* was overblown, as all satires are, but it also was "doing its duty" for peace by mocking war.[125] Similarly, Loudon Wainwright, also writing in *Life,* declared the film "a brilliant and edifying, even a moral, movie."[126] The *Time* film critic praised it as "an outrageously brilliant satire — the most original American comedy in years and at the same time a supersonic thriller that should have audiences chomping at their fingernails right down to the funny bone."[127] None of these reviewers objected to the central message of the film. Critics of *Dr. Strangelove* attacked the film as "defeatist," "destructive of morale," and "anti–American" among other epithets.[128]

Editorial comments from regular audience members, though often biased strongly for or against a given topic, offer some insights into how the average American might have reacted to *Dr. Strangelove.* Florence Allence of Washington, D.C., sympathized with the message of the film, stating, "[Director Stanley] Kubrick uses exaggeration to warn of the danger of the nuclear arms race. In an age when scientists are regarded as supermen, Kubrick tells us they are human, too."[129] Others, like John E. Mullins of St. Louis, remarked, "There was little laughing at *Dr. Strangelove* in the theater when I attended," and denounced the film as being in poor taste.[130] Emily Kennedy of Huntley, Illinois, related that most of the satire went over the heads of the audiences in her Midwest home: "When the general outlined the Commie plot against his body fluids, there was nothing but a respectful silence in that theater. I had the distinct impression that the audience thought it was learning something new about fluoridation. The average American is simply not tuned in for satire."[131] Whether the audience agreed with the central message of the film, hated the movie, or reacted as one of these audience members described, *Dr. Strangelove* broke box-office records.[132]

Another anti-nuclear film, *Fail-Safe,* tested the resolve of military personnel and the faith the Air Force placed in its technology. *Fail-Safe* spins a tale of a computer malfunction at SAC Headquarters, which sends a bomber group orders to bomb Moscow with nuclear weapons. At the same time, Soviet radio jamming technology prevents SAC Headquarters from contacting the planes and rescinding the orders. General Bogan (Frank Overton), SAC commander, had been trumpeting the Air Force's technology to skeptical civilians before the malfunction occurred. The filmmakers stress the Air Force's confidence in its technology, while the Bogan in the novel is more uncertain about it. Bogan squirms when the president (Henry Fonda) confronts him about the failures, but realizes that his own bombers must be brought down to avoid nuclear war. He cooperates with the Soviets to shoot down the bombers and remains loyal to his oath to protect and defend the Constitution.[133]

In contrast, Bogan's subordinate, Colonel Cascio (Fritz Weaver), is a pure militarist. He is convinced that the whole situation is a plot by the Soviets to launch an attack on the United States. Cascio is paranoid that the politicians "will sell them out," and urges General Bogan to use his position to start a war with the Soviets. When Bogan declares this reasoning treasonous, Cascio pushes him aside, and attempts to take over SAC. Security forcefully escorts Cascio out of the room. Instead of condemning him, Bogun is sympathetic and apologizes for his behavior. He explains, "Anyone could crack under the strain. He was a good soldier." Cascio certainly was not a "good soldier." He did not follow his orders, nor did he remain loyal, dutiful, or committed to civilian control of the military. Cascio proved too inflexible and narrow-minded to see the "big picture" as Bogun does.[134]

Unfortunately, the bomber group commander, Colonel Jack Grady (Ed Binns), proves as inflexible in his thinking as Cascio. In the story, SAC procedure stipulates that the bombers do not respond to voice commands after a designated length of time. The Soviets used a new technology, unknown to SAC, to jam the radio signals to the bombers. When the Soviets finally lifted the jamming, the American president tries to persuade Grady to return to base. "I can no longer receive tactical orders by voice," Grady responds. When the president persists, Grady angrily shouts, "What you're telling me I've been specifically ordered not to do!" Despite the pleas from the president, Grady cuts the radio so he does not have to listen. SAC next tries to reason with Colonel Grady by bringing his wife to the radio. Helen Grady (Janet Ward) tells her husband, "It's not a trick. You must turn back." He ignores her. Helen becomes increasingly desperate: "There's no war! We're fine! Answer me, please!" Once again, Grady cuts off the radio. He blindly follows procedure rather than using his critical-thinking skills to question whether an attack had actually happened. It is the opposite of the individualism and initiative usually displayed by America's citizen-soldiers. Because Grady did exactly as he was trained to do, the story's authors showed that rigid professionalism is potentially dangerous. Given that the actual SAC emphasized just such rigidity in its training and procedures, the film might not have been too far off in that critique of the Air Force.[135]

Brigadier General Warren Black (Dan O'Herlihy) represents the most liberal military character. He and the president have been friends since boyhood, so he implicitly trusts the decisions of his commander-in-chief. Throughout the film, Black argues with Professor Groeteschele (Walter Matthau), who is the civilian war "hawk" to Black's peace "dove." Black alone worries that the technical systems they have set up are beyond human control. The president orders Black to drop nuclear bombs on New York City to prove to the Soviets that the attack on Moscow was an accident. Black becomes the very thing he feared: the destroyer. Since the bomb not only destroyed New York City, but Black's own family and the first lady, Black commits suicide at the end.[136] It is a bleak ending.

Fail-Safe received cautious praise from Crowther. He described the film as "a valid shocker that induces the viewer to think."[137] The *Time* film critic disagreed, stating that "*Fail Safe* too often makes a serious subject soggy" given that in the last half of the movie "the illusion of reality slowly collapses into a steaming mess of socio-political platitudes."[138] *Life* magazine's Richard Oulahan did not believe "anything could become quite so botched up as it in *Fail Safe*" with respect to the nation's nuclear system. He worried that "the picture is so stylishly produced, so well acted and so loaded with suspense that millions of movie-goers will probably all believe it could happen this way."[139] Oulahan, like Emily Kennedy, did not give audiences much credit for thinking critically about what they were seeing on the silver screen. For these two, audiences were passively accepting the superficial action of the doomsday films. Stanley Kauffmann of the *New Republic* believes that the real theme of this film, and of *Dr. Strangelove,* ought to be that "men are in control: of increasingly large mechanisms without correspondingly developed judgment and morality."[140] In this view, the indictment was not on the technology, but the failure of leaders to deal with its moral and ethical implications.

The Air Force wanted to rebut the serious accusations against SAC made in *Fail-Safe* and *Dr. Strangelove.* The service developed a documentary, *SAC Command Post,* which "depicts the Command's nuclear forces, ground and airborne alert operations, and the decision-making system that controlled those forces."[141] Strangely, the Air Force never released the film to the public. Historian Dr. William Burr hypothesizes that the film's message was not consistent with President Lyndon Johnson's attempts to ease tensions with the

Soviet Union. He also points out that the documentary actually dodges one of the most serious accusations *Dr. Strangelove* made about command and control: "Unmentioned is the program initiated during the Eisenhower administration to predelegate presidential nuclear use decisions in the event of emergency conditions ... it was one of the most sensitive official secrets of the Cold War."[142] Unfortunately for the Air Force, its public image took another hit with another best-selling story: *Seven Days in May*.

This notable film deals seriously with the inherent dangers of a professional military in a democracy. *Seven Days in May* (1964) casts doubt on the commitment of professional military officers to democracy. Rod Serling, a World War II veteran, wrote the film script.[143] Air Force General Scott (Burt Lancaster), the chairman of the Joint Chiefs of Staff, is portrayed as a dynamic, controversial, and popular military leader. He is a true war hero with a Medal of Honor. When the President Jordan Lyman (Fredric March) negotiates a treaty with the Soviet Union to disarm their nuclear arsenals, Scott publicly criticizes the decision. He spearheads a plot of the Joint Chiefs of Staff, minus the Chief of Naval Operations, to take over the government from what they perceive as a weak and liberal president who is endangering national security. Scott believes himself wiser and more competent than his civilian commander-in-chief.[144]

Marine Corps Colonel "Jiggs" Casey (Kirk Douglas) is the hero of the film because he remains loyal to the legitimate government and to the Constitution. "As a military officer, I steer clear of politics," he explains, exemplifying the apolitical military officer appropriate for a democracy. Casey takes his suspicions of Scott's intentions to the president and works to stop the plot with the aid of his Army buddy, Colonel Henderson (Andrew Duggan), and the president's close friend, Senator Clark (Edmond O'Brien). When Casey is asked to spy on Scott and to obtain incriminating letters of his sexual indiscretion, Casey finds the assignment distasteful and "dirty." He felt that an officer, and a Marine, does not do such things, though in this case, the survival of democracy was at stake. Casey acquires the letters, but President Lyman does not need to use them. With a confession in hand from the commander of the Sixth Fleet, Lyman secures the resignation of the chiefs of staff from the Army and Air Force.[145]

At the end of the film, President Lyman addresses the American people. He begins by acknowledging that rumors have been spreading about how the nation had lost its greatness or no longer has the capacity to fight for freedom in the world. Lyman dismisses the negativity as slander and emphasizes that the country is strong. Through this strength, the nation can be patient and be a leader in making peace. He concludes, "We will remain strong and proud, peaceful and patient, and we will see a day when on this earth all men will walk out of the long tunnels of tyranny into the bright sunshine of freedom."[146] Anti-militarism won out against the misguided militarist conspiracy thanks to Casey's devotion to the Constitution, which led him to bring the conspiracy to the attention of the president. A central message of the film is that the country need not go to war in order to win the Cold War.

Crowther did not care for the subject matter of the film, but felt encouraged by the ending. He praised the movie for its "solid base of respect for democracy and the capacities of freedom-loving men."[147] The *Time* reviewer had no such laudatory comments for the film. The critic described *Seven Days in May* as "more far-fetched than a campaign promise" and denounced "some of the dialog in the final reels" as having been "cribbed from a prep school essay on 'What Democracy Means to Me.'"[148] For this critic, anxiety about militarism was unfounded. Nevertheless, the themes struck a chord with American audiences and the film earned good box-office returns.[149] Edmond O'Brien earned an Oscar nomination for Best Supporting Actor.

General Scott Redux

While the film critics might not have believed there was much credibility in *Seven Days in May*, an editorial in the *New Republic* invoked the story as a cautionary tale for present-day political maneuvering by the Air Force. In the 1964 presidential campaign, conservative Republican Barry Goldwater challenged incumbent President Johnson. The editorialist Raymond Senter worried that the Air Force might rally its men to "elect a President who is believed to be more tractable to the Air Force's demands— obviously Senator Barry Goldwater, a major general in the Air Force Reserve who has long been its outspoken and uncritical supporter on the Hill."[150] He cites public statements by the Air Force Association critical of the nuclear test ban treaty and various articles in the *Air Force* magazine warning "of dire consequences unless more funds are given to the Air Force."[151] The effect, Senter concludes, is open defiance of the commander-in-chief. While the charge might not meet the technical definition of insubordination, his examples certainly evoke a spirit of trying to influence public opinion in favor of the Air Force and contrary to the policies of the civilian administration. Though Senter acknowledges no "'putsch' is in the offing," he is clearly concerned about the parallels between *Seven Days in May* the Air Force's foray into politics.[152]

Even before *Seven Days in May*, conservative general officers had given cause to question their conduct. Previously, the Army's Troop Information and Education program "Pro-Blue" had raised liberal suspicions of militarism in the professional military ranks. Major General Edwin A. Walker, commander of the 24th Infantry Division stationed in West Germany, directed the creation of a troop information program designated "Pro-Blue," which stressed anti-communism, citizenship, support of NATO, and conservative politics.[153] The officers in charge of the program publicized it beyond the division, however, extending the indoctrination to the soldiers' "families, dependents, and local German friends and acquaintances."[154] In April 1961, the magazine *Overseas Weekly* denounced the inappropriateness of the Pro-Blue program and questioned the intentions of Major General Walker. Specifically, *Overseas Weekly* charged the general with promoting ultra–conservative politics, particularly of the John Birch Society, and revealed that Walker had accused former First Lady Eleanor Roosevelt and President Harry Truman of being communist sympathizers, among other notable Americans. The Kennedy Administration moved quickly to relieve Walker from command.[155]

Testifying before a Congressional subcommittee about Pro-Blue, Walker confirmed many anti–militarist fears by condemning civilian control of the military and accusing Democratic officials of communism.[156] Given the popularity of the story, it is not surprising that one of Kennedy's aides likened Walker to General Scott in *Seven Days in May*. Historian Christopher DeRosa believes that Walker also inspired the character of General Ripper in *Dr. Strangelove*. DeRosa observes that "Ripper's ranting about communist infiltration of the water supply (in order to sap Americans' precious bodily fluids) recalled Walker's association with the John Birch Society" which made similar warnings.[157]

Interestingly, some of Walker's defenders supported him from an anti-militarist position. *Life* magazine, for instance, denounced those who made the Walker affair into "a campaign to picture all U.S. military men as political jugheads or dangerous firebrands."[158] The *Life* editors believed the military was completely trustworthy because of civilian control of the military, the cornerstone of American anti-militarism. They argued, "West Point and Annapolis graduates have had ... a sounder education in American political principles than most college graduates, especially in the absolute primacy of political over military authority."[159] The editors conclude that continuing the current policies of prohibiting "partisan stands on U.S. domestic affairs or [advocating] policies in conflict with the government's" is sufficient for a military already firmly under civilian control.[160]

The political left, however, worried about military "indoctrination" of the public. Writing in the *New Republic*, Frederic W. Collins warned that "the top brass at the Pentagon has assigned to itself the task of educating civilians in what they should think about the Cold War combat against Communism."[161] He pointed to the Pentagon's mass of publications, the material's emphasis that American civilian leaders were losing the Cold War, and the message that civilians "must fully engage themselves" in "a total non-military war."[162] Collins cites as an example a presentation by retired Rear Admiral Chester Ward who not only criticized the president of the United States, but also appeared to advocate preventive war. Another source Collins presents is an Army handout that listed, among other points, "Identify public officials and policies displaying 'softness' toward Communism."[162] Collins was concerned that such "intrusion in civilian education assists in the undermining of civilian leadership, including the Presidency, and specifically in that leadership's question for a decent peace."[163] Not only did the military equate compromise and negotiation with appeasement, Collins cautioned, they might "create circumstances in which a frustrated public could one day wish to turn to the military for *their* answer to the Cold War."[164] He recommended that civilian authorities needed to reassert solid civilian control of the military.[165] While Collins only represented a segment of liberal opinion on the subject, he clearly worried that the military was gaining too much influence over the public and that this would one day lead to a coup d'état. His statement embodied a persistent anti-militarist fear of military power.

Another anti-militarist warning came in response to the upsurge in popularity of war toys and games for children. Trendy games included *Risk*; a Milton-Bradley game named *Stratego*, in which assassination is a key move; and *Tactics II*, in which players unleash thermonuclear war on one another. A series of games focused on World War II, including a spin-off game based on the television series *Combat!* and other games based on the German "Afrika Corps" and the Battle of Stalingrad. Editorialist William Honan warned that the officer corps of the British and Germans had looked at the map of Europe as a game board in 1914, but "by August 1914, the military gamesters of the world were no longer content with make-believe."[166] Although Honan does not state it explicitly, he clearly implies that playing these war games will make children more militaristic and more inclined to wage war.

Cartoonist Bill Mauldin of World War II "Willie and Joe" fame also weighed in on the issue. In a political cartoon, he sketched a dime-store window display which advertises: "Kiddies! Small nations! Be the first in you bloc to have your very own Thermo Jr. H-Bomb. High yield! Low cost! Complete — ready to assemble. Available soon!" Grown men in uniform and in Asian-inspired clothing stared wonderingly at the display.[167]

Conclusion

American military policy in the early 1960s became more militarist as a response to the shift to Flexible Response and the crises in Berlin and Cuba early in the Kennedy administration. Eisenhower had chosen deterrence with nuclear weapons as a way to keep the defense budget in check, but under Kennedy and Johnson the military budget grew, both nuclear and conventional forces expanded, and the United States armed forces increased readiness. As the country was militarizing in these ways, some high-ranking military officers pushed strong anti-communist and far right-wing politics from positions of authority in the military hierarchy. While liberals denounced the "indoctrination" of the military and civilians through such propaganda programs, commentators on the right responded that the military remained firmly under civilian control.

In popular culture, more militarist interpretations of World War II appeared in films like *The Longest Day* and comic books. Some television dramas included militaristic stories of redemption through military sacrifice in *The Gallant Men* and *Twelve O'Clock High*. The film *Hell Is for Heroes* featured the redemptive military sacrifice, though it did not necessarily have an overall militarist interpretation of World War II.

While military dramas mixed militarist and anti-militarist themes, the military comedies *McHale's Navy* and *Broadside* presented implicit anti-militarist messages, which poked fun at the professional military and its rules, discipline, and regimentation. Other areas of popular culture proved more stridently anti-militarist, such as *The Americanization of Emily* with its message that the glorification of war is the problem, not the reality that war is sometimes necessary.

While the threat of nuclear annihilation created anti-nuclear reactions among Americans, these fears were heightened by the Cuban Missile Crisis, which prompted a series of anti-nuclear books and films, including *Fail-Safe* and *Dr. Strangelove*. Fear of nuclear war, coupled with the decade-long rise in the power of the Air Force, prompted anti-militarists to focus on the Air Force as the service most likely to fall to militarism. Given the actual militarist public statements of Major General Walker and Rear Admiral Ward, the attempted military coup d'état featured in *Seven Days in May* did not appear so far-fetched, though most film critics believed it was. While the Cuban Missile Crisis had more to do with the anti-militarism in films like *Dr. Strangelove*, these movies foreshadow the anti-war, anti-authoritarian backlash against the war in Vietnam. While a few areas of popular culture, like comic books, offered stridently pro-war interpretations of the war, militarism faded under the shadow of the growing anti-war theme in the second half of the decade.

5

THE VIETNAM ERA, 1965–1970

"We're wet, bug-bit, tired, and sick ... sick of Viet Nam, sick of an enemy who won't stand up and fight. Sick of dying in Viet Cong tunnels, endless swamps, and impenetrable jungles," complains an American soldier. An army platoon is crossing a rice paddy, where the Viet-Cong (VC) have set a trap. A VC fighter emerges from the water, half-naked, with a machete in his hand. Lieutenant Kramer whacks the VC in the head with the butt of his rifle. After the firefight, the dirty and unshaven Kramer remarks to a medic, "Nine casualties? That's too high a price to pay for a stinkin' rice paddy." Most of the soldiers killed were brand-new replacements who had not known what to look for in the paddy. It placed more strain on the experienced soldiers, who "got to keep on fighting no matter how badly we need a rest." Kramer muses, "Why couldn't I fight in a nice, simple war?"[1]

This scene comes from a pro-war Charlton Comics book, *Army War Heroes*, in 1968. Unlike the World War II era, Hollywood did not produce films geared toward national unity or providing explanation or support of the war effort. Similarly, entertainment television programming largely avoided setting shows in Southeast Asia. Even recruiting advertising for the armed forces largely avoided mention of combat in Vietnam. It is the comic books that had the most consistent coverage of the Vietnam War. And even pro-war comics sometimes demonstrated the frustration of U.S. troops fighting a guerrilla war so far from home. As the U.S. commitment to Vietnam increased — and with it the number of young men conscripted by the draft — an anti-militarist backlash against the draft came from both the political left and right.

Popular culture fractured into separate interpretations of war during the second half of the 1960s. One thread depicted war, particularly World War II, as an exciting action-adventure. Some of these stories featured citizen-soldiers, others had anti-heroes in them. These films were geared toward a young, male teenaged audience rather than the veterans or adults who lived through the war. A second thread was clearly pro-military, pro-war interpretations. The third thread was an anti-war, anti-authoritarian backlash against the war in Southeast Asia. Particular movies, television shows, or comics did not always fit neatly into one of these threads. Nonetheless, by the end of the decade, anti-militarist sentiments dominated popular culture and would do so into the 1970s.

The Adventure of World War II

Spy stories became increasingly popular during the second half of the 1960s, and this fascination with intelligence and spying influenced World War II stories. Cold War spy stories, such as *The Man from U.N.C.L.E.* (1964–1968), *The Girl from U.N.C.L.E.* (1966–1967), *Get Smart* (1965–1970), *I Spy* (1965–1968), and *Mission Impossible* (1966–1971), proved popular with American television audiences, while the James Bond spy stories became popular on the silver screen.[2] Plot elements from these series spilled over into other series, including the military shows.[3]

Some World War II television depictions intentionally blurred the history of the war for entertainment or commercial purposes. Network executives instructed producers to avoid using real names, such as Charles de Gaulle and Adolf Hitler, so that the young audience would not get confused. Executives also frowned upon frequent references to Germany and Italy as the enemy, given that they were current allies and markets for American television. Instead, the allies simply fought "the enemy."[4] Despite this trend on television, the characters on *Combat!*, *The Gallant Men*, *Twelve O'Clock High* and other military shows specifically refer to the German enemy, and sometimes refer to them with the deliberately disrespectful slang, "Kraut." Shows such as *The Rat Patrol* and *Hogan's Heroes* frequently referenced the Gestapo, which was the Nazi secret police. *Hogan's Heroes* often cited Adolf Hitler by name, though these last two television shows often represented the Nazis and Gestapo as inept or foolish. Contemporary audiences were not likely meant to draw parallels between the German enemy of the past and the current West German allies in the Cold War.

Hogan's Heroes (1965–1971) is set in a World War II German prisoner of war camp, not exactly the best backdrop for comedy. The show depicts war more as an adventure, not exactly ennobling, but certainly not a traumatic event depicting human suffering. As the representation of the military is respectful, war looks like fun, and the anti-militarist themes of shows like

Sergeant Schultz (John Banner, left), Colonel Hogan (Bob Crane, center), and Colonel Klink (Werner Klemperer, right) in the TV series *Hogan's Heroes* (1965–1971). Though more militaristic in its themes by depicting war as an adventure, the series still displayed anti-militarism by showing the men's desire to end the war and return to civilian life (CBS Photo Archive/Archive Photos/Getty Images).

McHale's Navy are missing, the series is overall more militaristic than previous military comedies. Like *The Longest Day*, *Hogan's Heroes* features an international effort against the German enemy. Colonel Robert Hogan (Bob Crane) is the commander, an American Army Air Forces officer. Newkirk (Richard Dawson) is a British sergeant, whose expertise runs to the shady elements such as pick-pocketing. The Frenchman, LeBeau (Robert Clary), is a tailor and a cook. African-American Staff Sergeant Kinchloe (Ivan Dixon) is the group's expert at communications, and Sergeant Carter (Larry Houis) works on demolitions. Many of the men are citizen-soldiers. In one episode, Kinchloe receives a final notification of his draft status in the POW's mail. His final Selective Service status was 4-F, which meant he did not have to serve. "Now they tell me!" Kinchloe exclaims.[5] The pilot episode included a Russian POW, though his character did not remain.[6] Apparently, the Cold War-era show was not quite ready to include *all* of America's World War II allies on its team.

Colonel Robert Hogan is disciplined, loyal to his men, dedicated to his cause, and exhibits a deep sense of duty and responsibility as well as having a quick wit, a sense of humor, and an inventive mind. Hogan's dedication to duty is tested when he is ordered home for a hero's welcome and bond-selling tour. He decides to stay with his command rather than return to the United States. Although Carter pokes fun at Hogan by saying, "He's behind the times," to which Newkirk replies, "Well, he is an officer," Hogan believes he can continue to contribute to the success of Allied operations.[7]

Hogan proves a very different character than Savage on *Twelve O'Clock High*. Savage shuts down the officer's club, pushes his men, and is not afraid to earn his men's displeasure to instill discipline in his bomber crews. Hogan is also disciplined in the sense of following orders, no matter how difficult the assignment. He expects his men to follow his orders, and no one ever questions Hogan's authority. The men look up to Hogan for leadership and guidance, and they have a warm relationship with him. The men know that Hogan would sacrifice for them, and they are loyal to him in return. It is not necessary for him to badger or deprive the men to make them better fighters. Still, there were moments in which the show displayed anti-militarism. Hogan remarked in one episode, "'Civilian.' What a beautiful word. Next to 'girls.'"[8] In another story, Hogan complains about Carter saluting him: "Do you have to act so military?"[9]

Like the bomber crews on *Twelve O'Clock High*, Hogan and his men are team players, and the show downplays typical American individualism. In one story, Hogan approaches a house with a suspected traitor in it alone, telling his men to return to camp if he is captured. LeBeau complains, "But, Colonel, we're a team!" When Hogan does not return, LeBeau and Newkirk go to rescue him.[10] In another episode, LeBeau complains about a Texan pilot whom they have rescued. Although he was shot down, the Texan cannot help but boast about his flying skills. LeBeau says sarcastically, "Hey, why don't we all go home and let him finish the war all by himself?"[11] Clearly, the international message was a positive one for Cold War relations among allies.

Although demonstrating slightly more militaristic qualities than other military series, *Hogan's Heroes* clearly differentiates the allies from the Nazis. For example, unlike the Nazis, the democratic allies follow a code of conduct. For instance, before Hogan learns that an atomic scientist wants to defect, he decides the man is too dangerous to keep alive. He attempts to bring an assassin to the camp because killing him, as Carter says, just "doesn't sound like us." They may sabotage and manipulate, but they do not murder (as a real OSS team might do). In typical comedic fashion, a bungling British Colonel Crittendon arrives as their assassin, suggesting they use everything from poison to bombs. He settles on a crossbow. Although Crittendon shows much enthusiasm for his role in the plot, even he remains uncomfortable with the idea of killing a man at close range. Fortunately, Crittendon proves inept as an assassin as in everything else he does. In the end, the scientist is able to defect.[12]

When the series first aired, there was some controversy in setting a comedy in a prisoner of war camp. Nonetheless, *Hogan's Heroes* proved popular with audiences, ranking highest among new shows in the 1965–1966 television season. Overall, it ranked ninth for the season among Nielsen scores, followed by 17th the following year. Thereafter, it remained below the top-ranking television series, but still popular enough to stay on the air until 1971.[13]

At the same time that the creators of *Hogan's Heroes* were thinking of even more fantastical ways for the prisoners of war to conduct espionage, another television show turned the North African desert into an exciting action-adventure. *The Rat Patrol* (1966–1968), set in the deserts of North Africa, pit the Allies against the German Afrika Korps, specifically an armored unit commanded by Captain Dietrich (Eric Braeden). The Rat Patrol, which consists of three Americans and one British soldier, moves independently of any recognized American or British unit. They travel around in Jeeps, armed with machine guns. Their leader is Sergeant Sam Troy (Christopher George). Private Tully Pettigrew (Justin Tarr) is the team's conman, while Private Mark Hitchcock (Lawrence P. Casey) is the youngest Patroller. Sergeant Jack Moffitt (Gary Raymond) is the British demolitions expert.[14] Its aggressiveness in tone and action is more militaristic than previous shows.

As an action-adventure story and an image of war, *The Rat Patrol* contains a great deal of shooting, fighting, chasing, and exploding. *The Rat Patrol*'s executive producer, Lee Hitch, explained that the studio purposely exaggerated the plots and action in the show. He said, "What people want to watch is action. Our philosophy is movement."[15] The action on the show achieved a level of unreality. The Rat Patrol always outsmarted, outmaneuvered, or outwitted the generally superior German enemy. While this was a common theme in shows such as *Combat!*, the level of unreality in *The Rat Patrol* approached comic-book-like action.

"The David and Goliath Raid," is typical for the show. In the opening scene, the Rat Patrol's machine guns pour bullets into a German motorcycle and sidecar. The motorcycle veers off the side of the road, throwing out the riders. One dies instantly; the other is wounded. Before the Patrol can figure out what kind of documents they have just captured from the motorcycle couriers, a German patrol leads a counterattack that blows up the only Jeep the Patrol has to escape. Troy decides to take his chances in the desert rather than surrender to the Germans, even though they have no water and no transportation. Following an Arab map that they just captured, the Patrol walks the rest of the day and night to find water, only to discover the water supply has been poisoned. By that time, the Germans have tracked them down and demand that the exhausted and dehydrated men surrender. Troy refuses. The episode gets its title from the escape scene: first, they use sunlight glinting off of a knife to get one of the Germans to look their way. The light blinds the German, just as Tully uses a slingshot to hit him in the face. The Patrol overwhelms a second German guard and steals a jeep. As soon as the other Germans notice what has happened, they scramble back inside their vehicles and give chase, opening fire on the jeep. The Patrol tosses a grenade into the oncoming group of Germans, which destroys the chasing vehicle and enables the Patrol to make the final escape, with documents intact.[16]

A contemporary reviewer of *The Rat Patrol* complained that the series deviated so far from reality that it "has degenerated into boundless gimmickry that shows nothing but contempt for the viewer's intelligence."[17] The author also mockingly observes that the "submachine guns never run out of ammunition" and denounces the absurdity of the Gestapo all wearing "their black overcoats in the desert."[18] The show's departure from reality also caused it to lose at least one international market. Only a few episodes were aired in England because of understandable complaints that the British, not the Americans, led the fight against the Germans in North Africa.[19] Certainly, this show presented an American-centric view of World War II, where Americans led most, if not all, significant aspects of the war. Both Hollywood and American television programming framed World War II stories in such a way as to have the Americans save the day, even in places where American allies deserved much credit and praise. In this way, the Americans become the only heroes of World War II. Unfortunately, this a historical trend continued for most subsequent American-made World War II films and television shows.

World War II movies in the mid–1960s began to show the same action and adventure twist of the television shows. After its support for *The Longest Day*, the Department of Defense tightened its guidelines for military assistance to the motion picture industry and restricted them further in 1964. As a result, fewer filmmakers requested military assistance after the new guidelines came into effect. When producers did choose to make war films, they were driven more by creating a profitable movie than making a film the Pentagon would approve.[20] Those profitable movies tended to look a lot more like the action-adventure of *The Rat Patrol* than the romanticism of *The Longest Day*.

Although *The Battle of the Bulge* (1965) attempted to recreate the entirety of the that operation in the same sweeping way that *The Longest Day* had for the Normandy landings, the battle action is clearly influenced by the Cold War spy-mania. The plot frequently turns on the actions of a small group of German infiltrators, who speak English, wear American uniforms, and can pass as American G.I.s. They change road signs, which causes confusion with the American withdrawal. They prevent a bridge from being destroyed so that the German tanks can advance. The German infiltrators almost secure the American fuel depot, if not for an American lieutenant who recognizes one of the infiltrators from the sign-changing incident. Though the Germans were frequently presented as being better armed than the Americans in earlier representations of the war, in this film the Germans intend to rely on advancements in technology to win the war, from updated Tiger tanks to the V-weapons and a veiled reference to a German atomic bomb.[21]

A battle of wills between an American intelligence officer, Colonel Kiley (Henry Fonda), and the German tank commander, Colonel Hessler (Robert Shaw) drives the plot of the movie. Kiley is the only American officer convinced the Germans will attack along the Ardennes, and he amasses various bits of evidence that may support that conclusion, depending on one's interpretation. Hessler ensures the infiltrators secure the bridge for his tanks to cross, convinces his superiors to allow him to push the Americans out of their positions, and personally tries to secure the American fuel depot. Only the intrepid actions of a scrappy group of Americans prevent the Germans from taking the fuel. The operations of the Battle of the Bulge are centered around the American and German tanks, rather than infantry operations.[22]

Although the Americans retreat initially, division headquarters notes that the troops are "retreating like soldiers. There is still fight in them." These soldiers, most of them citizen-soldiers, are not running out of fear or cowardice. Indeed, Sergeant Gruffy mutters to General Gray as he slips out a door, "When are they going to let us fight?"[23] This eagerness to fight differs markedly from the dirty, exhausted soldiers depicted in *The Story of G.I. Joe* or even the more triumphant *Battleground*. War is much more an adventure here, a more militaristic interpretation than these older films contain.

The *New York Times* film critic found *The Battle of the Bulge* dishonest in its rendering of the World War II military action. Crowther dismissed the personalized story, Kiley's independent actions, and "soldier-boy heroics" as merely elements in modern war films.[24] He refused to condone the "evident distortion of the material and of history to suit the giant Cinerama screen."[25] Crowther discerned a growing divide between older and younger audiences in terms of expectations and tastes. He concluded that the film would appeal to youth, who liked the "loud and flame-filled spectacles," but that adults "who have some sober, rueful sense of World War II, and also a respectful regard for the memory of the men who fought and died in the real 'bulge'" would find the film irritating.[26] Crowther had been reviewing films for the *New York Times* since World War II and consistently praised films that offered a realistic or sympathetic view of the war. *The Battle of the Bulge* may have been set in World War II, but Crowther was uncomfortable with the modern rendering of it.

Similarly, *Time* magazine's film critic despaired at the poor telling of *The Battle of the Bulge*. The reviewer pointed out an anti-militaristic aspect of the film: Henry Fonda as Major Kiley, playing "a folksy intelligence officers whose outlook remains sensible and somehow civilian. This, the film implies, puts him one up on the hardheaded military professionals."[27] Praise of citizen-soldiers trumping German professionals continued even in this more militaristic version of World War II. Whether it was the unrealistic story, the militarist interpretation, or some other factors, the film did not do well at the box office.[28]

"You Can't Kill John Wayne"

In Harm's Way (1965) presented a mid–1960s version of *From Here to Eternity* with adultery, alcoholism, and rape in the story. It is set in the Pacific theater and begins with the Japanese attack on Pearl Harbor. Director Otto Preminger did not intend to make a movie to glorify war. "I would never have done that," he explained, "because I am completely against war."[29] Despite his attitude toward war, Preminger received cooperation from the Navy to make the film, and he cast John Wayne in the lead role of captain, then rear admiral, Rockwell Torrey.[30] Although Torrey, a career regular, is a brave, dedicated sailor, he is estranged from his son, much like his character Sergeant Stryker in *Sands of Iwo Jima*. Torrey has a sexual relationship with a Navy nurse without benefit of marriage, something that was rarely seen for the heroes in war films.

Many of the regulars in the story do not acquit themselves well. Admiral Broderick (Dana Andrews)lacks strategic or tactical competence, spending more time playing croquet and worrying about institutional politics than the war. Commander Paul Eddington (Kirk Douglas) is an alcoholic and a rapist. When the nurse he raped commits suicide, Eddington tries to redeem himself by taking a plane to conduct reconnaissance straight into a Japanese naval task force. He is shot down and killed in the attempt. Torrey refuses to recommend a medal for Eddington because Torrey knew he was just trying to assuage his guilt rather than making a truly selfless act. In this case, military sacrifice was *not* presented as redemptive.[31]

The citizen-sailors in *In Harm's Way* acquit themselves better than the regulars, save for Torrey. Although he begins the film as a spoiled brat, Torrey's estranged son Jeremiah (Brandon De Wilde) ultimately chooses to do his duty and is killed in combat. Commander Egan Powell (Burgess Meredith) is a competent reserve intelligence officer. The one "bad apple" of the citizen-sailors is Commander Neal Owynn (Patrick O'Neal), who is using a cushy staff position to advance his political career.[32]

Unlike Sergeant Stryker, who died at the end of *Sands of Iwo Jima*, "You can't kill John Wayne," announced Bosley Crowther in the opening of his review for *In Harm's Way*.[33] "That's the message — the only message — that comes through loud and clear in Otto Preminger's big war film," Crowther complained.[34] He did not have much good to say about the film. Crowther referred to it as "slick and shallow" and a "cliché-crowded melodrama."[35] He disliked the "cagy politicking and professional back-stabbing among the 'brass'" as well.[36] The only character he liked was Henry Fonda's Admiral Chester Nimitz, as the only character who appears interested in the actual war.[37] As with his dismissal of *Battle of the Bulge*, he did not believe this film reflected the reality of the World War II experience.

Time magazine's reviewer proved more forgiving. Although the critic declared the film's message to be "that World War II was fought to make the world safe for wide-screen melodrama," he also described the plot as "interesting."[38] Though the reviewer disliked some of the filming techniques that made the ships look like toys, he concluded "but even toy battleships do not seriously impede the progress of a slick, fast-moving entertainment as warm with characters who seem quick-witted, courageous, and just enough larger than life to justify another skirmish in the tired old Pacific."[39] Unlike Crowther, this critic approved of the more action-adventure-oriented war films with larger-than-life characters. He appreciated the entertainment value of such a story, which livened up "the tired old Pacific," which presumably had lost the interest of movie audiences and critics alike. The reviewer framed it as entertainment, not history or a tribute to the generation who fought in the war.

The Anti-Hero

By the mid–1960s, music, television, and Hollywood began to reflect the youth counter-culture and the anti-war movement. Rock and roll had long been non-conformist, and other music genres, such as country, also incorporated mature themes more openly. On television, *The Smothers Brothers Comedy Hour* addressed the counter-culture, social protest, and the Vietnam War. Movies became increasingly popular with male teenagers, while attendance of middle-aged adults declined. Films increasingly featured non-conformists and characters not traditionally in the mainstream. Hollywood embraced youth culture and themes of personal rebellion and social alienation in such films as *Bonnie and Clyde* (1967) and *Easy Rider* (1969), among others.[40]

This increased focus in popular culture on non-conformists like gangsters, killers, and criminals, often found in Film Noir, also influenced war films. Standard plot devices were purposely turned upside-down or "inverted" against type. In some cases, the characters in these inverted films exhibit the characteristics normally associated with the enemy. Taking on the qualities of the enemy also undermined the presentation of World War II as the "good war." These "inverted" plot devices and characters had been seen before in American war films in such pictures as *Stalag 17* (1953), but the imagery became more prevalent and dominated cinema from mid–1960s through the end of the decade in such films as *The Dirty Dozen* (1967), *Devil's Brigade* (1968), *Play Dirty* (1969), and *Kelly's Heroes* (1970).[41] While the anti-authoritarian themes in these films are certainly anti-militaristic, the delight in violence and military might is decidedly militaristic.

The Dirty Dozen set the standard. The plot revolves around a highly unorthodox commando raid on a German-held French chateau the day before the allies' Normandy invasion. It begins in a military prison with the hanging of a scared young private. One of the witnesses of this hanging, Major Reisman (Lee Marvin), is unhappily "volunteered" by General Worden (Ernest Borgnine) to lead a team of a dozen Army prisoners sentenced to die by hanging or to long sentences of hard labor. Their mission is to parachute to the chateau and kill as many top German leaders as possible. General Worden admits the unusual nature of this mission by saying, "As far as I'm concerned, a soldier's job is to wear his uniform and kill the enemy." He does not like "this behind the lines nonsense."[42]

As the mission unfolds, the men of the "dirty dozen" act more like murderers than soldiers facing an enemy on the battlefield. They use deception to infiltrate the compound, dressing and acting like German soldiers. Where previous American films had presented infiltration as a deception only the enemy used, this film actively embraced unconventional tactics. The soldiers kill the majority of the Germans by pouring gasoline down the air vents for the chamber where the Germans have taken refuge. When the Americans throw grenades down to detonate the gasoline, the entire complex bursts into flames. Only one of the dozen survives the assault. Although the dead are hailed as heroes at the end of the film, film heroes had never acted in such a cutthroat manner and received praise for it. The actions of Reisman and his troops violate previously defined standards of acceptable soldierly behavior.[43]

The dozen prisoners all exhibit some anti-social behaviors and harbor bad attitudes toward authority, discipline, and the Army. The prisoners shout out "up yours" to the military police and heckle a colonel. The black character, Jefferson (Jim Brown), initially refuses the assignment, stating defiantly that fighting Germany is "their war" not his, that is, that World War II is a white man's war. Franko (John Cassavetes), in particular, is mouthy and disobedient. Major Reisman threatens him, "Either you'll march or I'll beat your brains out, understand?" Franko does not take him seriously until Reisman actually throws him down and kicks him in the face. Although Reisman's character takes after the tough, disciplinarian leaders in *Sands of Iwo Jima* and *Twelve O'Clock High*, his methods are even more unconventional. He gives the men alcohol and busses in prostitutes to celebrate the end of the men's training.[44]

Predictably, Crowther disapproved of *The Dirty Dozen* in his review of the film in the *New York Times*. He considered the film "sadistic," "silly and irresponsible," and "morbid and disgusting beyond words."[45] He disliked the blatantly fictional nature of the story, as well as the low quality of the men. The idea that criminals would be committed enough to carry out the raid was ridiculous, according to Crowther. He did not regard the prisoners as heroes in any way and accused the film of "encouraging a spirit of hooliganism that is brazenly antisocial."[46] Crowther argued that the film could have been about war's ugliness and horror had the battle scenes not been aimed at delighting and stimulating the audience.[47] Once again, the target audience for this film was male teenagers rather than adults or war veterans.

One retired Marine Corps officer, Colonel James Donovan, observed that most combat veterans and career military personnel considered most of the contemporary war fiction misleading or exaggerated. He worried that Hollywood films and other depictions of the military in popular culture gave Americans a false image about servicemen, military life, and the "bad guy" enemy.[48] Donovan's depiction of the audience's naiveté might not be exaggerated considering *Time* magazine's review of *The Dirty Dozen*. In praising the performances of the actors, the reviewer concluded that the film "proves that Hollywood does best by World War II when it does it straight."[49] The critic also deemed it "the definitive enlisted man's picture."[50] Once again, there were clear differences of opinion on what was considered a good military film. Crowther and the *Time* critic are on opposite ends of the "generation gap," and the younger end of that gap liked the more militaristic, glorified, fun, and adventure-filled version of war movies. As one letter to the editor in *Life* in 1969 explained, "I grew up on a diet of Hollywood war films. The heroism, the romance, the adventure and even the death excited my interest."[51] Unfortunately for this young man, he did not find that kind of war when he was sent to Vietnam.

"The Scourge of the West"

While the vast majority of war stories in the 1960s focused on World War II, *F Troop* (1965–1967) combined the popular Western genre with *The Phil Silvers Show* in a military farce set in the post–Civil War Western frontier. *F Troop* is openly anti-militarist because it directly parodies the professional military, as the soldiers of *F Troop* are all regulars. Captain Wilton Parmenter (Ken Berry), a bumbling, effeminate, but good-hearted man, came to command Fort Courage by accident. During the Civil War, he sneezed at just the right moment to lead an unintentional but important attack by Union forces. This earned him a field promotion to captain and the postwar command of Fort Courage. Parmenter is not a natural leader and has trouble being assertive, especially with other officers. When Major Duncan (James Gregory) comes in to take yet another capable soldier from his rolls, Parmenter attempts to enforce the regulation that "no personnel essential to the welfare of the fort can be taken until a replacement can be found." Parmenter cannot make Duncan listen to him, but his subordinates, Sergeant Morgan O'Rourke (Forrest Tucker) and Corporal Randolph Agarn (Larry Storch), sabotage Duncan's plans and successfully end the officer's raiding of Fort Courage's rolls.[52]

Post Commander Parmenter is often dominated or influenced by the women in his life. When Parmenter's mother comes to visit, he demands that she treat him as an adult, a soldier, and a leader of men. Instead, she bosses him around. She declares, "I made a general out of your father, and I will make a general out of you." O'Rourke again saves the day. Parmenter's mother finally leaves the fort in peace after her son, "The Scourge of the West," foils an "attack" by the Native Americans arranged by O'Rourke.[53] Parmenter also acts in an effeminate way when he insists the fort be cleaned and kept up properly. He makes the men scrub and clean the fort for guests, including washing the paper on the bulletin board. Major Duncan quips that Parmenter will make someone a good wife someday and remarks, "The Army is looking for men, not housekeepers."[54]

With the exception of O'Rourke, the men of *F Troop* prove inept soldiers, if well-meaning ones. O'Rourke follows in the model of Master Sergeant Bilko, a self-interested conman, who is nevertheless clever and capable. The rest of the men are not nearly as skilled or as intelligent. The post's bugler cannot play his instrument at all and requires regular encouragement from Parmenter to keep trying to play. The men cannot drill properly, and they utterly fail to pass a basic obstacle course. When the fort is attacked by actual hostile Indians, Jane, the Annie Oakley-type character, fends them off more ably than any of the soldiers.[55]

If historians are correct about the massive militarization of American culture by this time, one would expect a militarized audience to reject a military parody such as *F Troop*. Instead, it proved popular with audiences. According to the Nielsen ratings from the 1965–1966 television season, *F Troop* ranked number four among new shows for the season, and it hit the number eight slot for prime time.[56] Audiences enjoyed laughing at the military, given the popularity of shows like *The Phil Silvers Show*, *McHale's Navy*, and now *F Troop*.

"This Dirty War"

Once again as the nation went to war, Henry Luce supported the war effort. Luce's views on Vietnam aligned with the Lyndon Johnson Administration, and the president sought Luce's help to sell the war to the American people.[57] Still, the correspondents, photographers, and editorial staffs of the Luce publications did not always follow a pro-war agenda. Already in 1966, *Life* magazine began showing pictures of wounded, exhausted servicemen, much as it had done during the Korean War.[58] As author Andrew Huebner observes, "Such images were not necessarily 'antiwar'; journalists surely understood that wounds and death were part of any conflict ... but these images, like ones from Korea, reminded viewers of war's costs."[59] Nevertheless, even *Time* and *Life* could not help but acknowledge their readers' later concerns about the war.

While virtually every medium of popular culture ignored the Vietnam War, Charlton Comics, which published *Fightin' Marines*, *Army War Heroes*, *Battlefield Action*, and similar titles, embraced it. Charlton's comics endorsed anti-communism, American intervention in Vietnam, and escalation of the war. Stories framed the war in terms of absolute good and evil, in which "the United States would ultimately triumph through the nobility of its motives and the might of its military power."[60] These stories were militarist through and through. Charlton dominated the niche of pro-war comic readers, which

By LARRY BURROWS in VIETNAM

WITH A BRAVE CREW IN A DEADLY FIGHT

Vietcong zero in on
vulnerable U.S. copters

In a U.S. copter
in thick of fight—
a shouting
crew chief,
a dying pilot

APRIL 16 · 1965 · 35¢

Though Henry Luce, publisher of *Life* and *Time* magazines, supported the war in Vietnam, pictures from the war zone often depicted a more sobering reality. In this April 1965 *Life* magazine cover photograph (taken by Larry Burrows) on March 31, 1965, helicopter crew chief James C. Farley (pictured with his hand on a jammed machine gun) shouts to his crew. Wounded pilot Lieutenant James E. Magel lies dying beside him (Time & Life Pictures/Getty Images).

proved small but long-lived. The company's best-selling titles did as well as its competition's least popular comics.[61] All of the Charlton stories earned the approval of the Comics Code Authority as appropriate subject matter for young adults.

An increasing commitment of American troops to the situation in Southeast Asia attracted the attention of comic-book writers, though the outlines of the war were not yet fully understood. The United States had been involved in Vietnam during the 1950s under the Military Assistance and Advisory Group, which provided funds, equipment, and advisors to the non-communist South Vietnam. President Kennedy modestly expanded the program of military advisors, and sent American Special Forces into Vietnam in 1961.[62] In the April 1963 comic book story "Homecoming," a Latino marine is driving a jeep in Laos when he is hit by a guerrilla "Commie" sniper. A Laotian patrol assists the Marine and his captain. For the men's bravery under fire, they received a Purple Heart, a Bronze Star, and a medal from the Laotian government for their actions.[63] No Marines were actually serving in Laos at the time, so the story is completely fictional.

As American policy in Vietnam remained unknown to a majority of the public, particularly young people, the comic writers began to incorporate explanations of it into stories.[64] American support for the non-communist South Vietnamese was a frequent theme in the early war comics. In one story, an American advisor accompanies a Vietnamese unit on patrol. Told in the first-person, this soldier explains that he expected an exotic locale, but "I didn't know that I'd be riding a heavily armed helicopter, making strikes and landing deep into communist territory!" Nor did he know "how exposed and helpless a helicopter crew could be when it was coming into jungle country with the enemy waiting below!" Viet-Cong guerrillas ambush the helicopter and crew, but they fight back gallantly and escape. Grateful non-communist villagers come out to thank the troops. Back at headquarters a major explains, "You see, we're not officially fighting in this fracas! We're here in an advisory capacity and if I tried to tell the brass in the Pentagon that you fought heroically, they'd court martial us both!" Reflecting on his experience, the advisor realizes he admires the Vietnamese who are fighting the communists.[65]

In the aftermath of the presumed August 1964 attacks on the American naval ships *Maddox* and *C. Turner Joy* in the Gulf of Tokin off North Vietnam's coast, Congress authorized President Johnson to take whatever measures necessary to prevent further aggression or attacks on the United States armed forces. Though not initially taken as "a blank check" to escalate the war in Vietnam, it did serve to strengthen American resolve in the conflict. The air campaign began in February 1965 with retaliatory strikes against North Vietnamese staging areas and strongholds. It escalated in March 1965 when the United States Air Force started a continuous air bombardment dubbed "Rolling Thunder" to respond to North Vietnamese raids on American personnel stationed in South Vietnam. Expecting additional attacks on American advisors, General William Westmoreland requested and received the first ground troops in Vietnam: two Marine Corps battalions to secure the air base in Da Nang.[66]

As American involvement in Vietnam increased dramatically in and after 1965, representations of the war in comics reflected this participation as well. Charlton's representations of fighting in Vietnam contained a mixture of conventional and guerrilla elements. American characters often appear as idealized selfless heroes who help the weaker local Vietnamese population and engage an enemy who does not fight fairly. In "The Protégé," for example, the Vietnamese enemy were pictured as menacing-looking conventional enemy army with properly matching uniforms and caps. This particular story shows a wise American helping out a determined Vietnamese man. Kafoum tells Staff Sergeant Lloyd how the Viet-Cong terrorize the villages at night with guns and grenades. He says that he does not know how to fight them, and adds, "But, if I had weapons like theirs, I would fight them." Lloyd requisitions weapons and ammunition for the village and teaches them how to fight. Eventually, Kafoum leads his village and other non-communists to fight the Vietcong. Lloyd believes in him, saying, "I believe you're going to beat the commies in this dirty war!"[67]

More changes to the appearance of the enemy and the war appeared in 1966. In one story, the Viet-Cong are portrayed as black-pajama-clad fighters, who "have no fancy equipment, no rations to encumber them as they flit like skinny wraiths through the twilight world of the jungle." The Viet-Cong in this rendition are muscular, menacing men with shaved heads, wearing bandanas. The author goes on to explain that the Viet-Cong killed a loyal Vietnamese village chief, and the "people are afraid of these assassins, so they shelter the Viet Cong." This explains why otherwise loyal Vietnamese could harbor the enemy.[68]

One story in the April-May 1966 issue of *Fightin' Army*, "Fighting Air in Viet-Nam," reveals that victory may not be assured for America. The story is told in the first-person by a military advisor who did not understand why the American-trained and equipped Vietnamese kept losing to the VC. One of the problems, he learns, is that it is difficult to distinguish between the Viet-Cong and the supposedly loyal villagers. A Vietnamese lieutenant explained that the VC "have been known to smile and bow as we entered a village, and slip a grenade into a soldier's pack." One villager lures a squad into the jungle, where a VC ambush is waiting for them. The American springs into action, organizing the men and leading a counterattack. The American advisor thinks he has killed "four Hanoi terrorists," but the Vietnamese lieutenant corrected him. "We killed four local Viet Cong," he explained. As he walked out of the village, the American thought to himself, "I had the uncomfortable feeling that we hadn't won a victory at all!"[69] This story offers a realistic and accurate portrayal of the difficulty in discerning the Viet-Cong from the villagers. Although the story is still pro-war, it deviates from most Charlton comics by offering an ambiguous ending that did not conclude with a clear American victory.

While the Charlton Comics series embraced the Vietnam War, Hollywood did not.[70] John Wayne decided he wanted to make a film about the Green Berets to counter anti-war protests that were gaining momentum at the time. The first national anti-war protest in Washington, D.C., occurred in April 1965, around the time that Wayne began to pursue the film project.[71] The anti-war movement gained momentum in the following years, with large protests in New York, San Francisco, and other major cities. Anti-war protests clearly express a fundamental anti-militarist strain in American culture, though not all anti-militarists participated in the protests and some probably supported the war as necessary. Given that these protests were also denounced by many Americans denotes the militarism present in the culture as well, though again, some anti-militarists did not approve of the protests, either.[72]

Wayne directed and starred in the film *The Green Berets* (1968).[73] He chose to base the film on Army Special Forces, often referred to as "Green Berets." Though they had been established in 1952 and had first deployed in support of the Korean War, Special Forces expanded under the Kennedy administration for counterinsurgency missions in Latin America, Vietnam, and elsewhere.[74] They received more publicity and popular recognition in the 1960s than in the previous decade. Special Forces represent the highest example of skilled combatants. Green Berets acquired battle tactics as well as medical skills, the ability to speak foreign languages, and techniques for winning the "hearts and minds" of local peoples. These units became so popular that a song by Barry Saddler, a Green Beret himself, called "The Ballad of the Green Berets," topped the music charts.[75] Unlike citizen-soldiers, Green Berets were highly trained professional soldiers.

Wayne based his film on one of the best-selling Green Berets stories, a novel by Robin Moore, supposedly based on true accounts. The Pentagon, however, disliked much of the material in this book as it reflected poorly on the Army and required significant script changes before assisting with the production. Moore shows Vietnamese allies as corrupt, engaging in torture, and encouraging sexual license. He depicts Green Berets as both racist and sadistic.[76] They are "mainly soldiers of fortune from many different nations, men who enjoy their work, exulting in their skills and in the perks of the job (mainly sexual)."[77] After changes had been made to the script, the Department of Defense provided significant assistance for the film's production at Ft. Benning, Georgia. This assistance prompted harsh criticism from Senator J. William Fulbright, who disagreed with the film's politics and who accused the Pentagon of under-billing Wayne's production company for the use of Army equipment.[78]

The way these highly trained professionals are depicted in the film is militaristic. Through the opening "Ballad of the Green Berets," the audience learns that the soldiers are the best the country has to offer and that they are fearless. John Wayne plays Colonel Mike Kirby. He is an idealized commanding officer: traditional, by-the-book, stalwart, and unflinchingly courageous. His loyalty, dedication to duty, and willingness to sacrifice himself are beyond question. Master Sergeant Muldoon (Aldo Ray) is the typical crusty officer who has years of professional experience, including three tours of duty in Vietnam. His response to a question about why he spent so much time in Vietnam is, "A soldier goes where he's told to go." This sentiment is echoed by another member of the Green Berets, who volunteers for a tour in Vietnam for one reason, "I'm a soldier and that's where the action is." African-American Sergeant "Doc" McGee (Raymond St. Jacques) is the squad's medic. Petersen (Jim Hutton) is the most anti-militarist character in the group, surrounding himself with civilian creature comforts even in a forward operating base. Muldoon comments to Petersen, "Three tours of duty and you're still acting like a civilian." Muldoon was not paying Petersen a compliment.[79]

Characterizations of the soldiers in *The Green Berets* resemble comic-book characters. In both venues, the soldiers exude cool, professional competence. In the field, they remain calm and unflappable under repeated attack by the Viet-Cong. Although the Green Berets display some sadness at the loss of buddies, the most common emotional response is anger and revulsion against the VC. Like their comic-book counterparts, the Green Berets in this film are mouthpieces for the war advocates. Throughout the film the characters continuously recount the horrors and brutality of the VC, also a recurring theme in the comic-book stories. The one instance in which Muldoon loses his professional demeanor is at a briefing of "liberal" journalists at the film's opening. He becomes quite rude and shoves Soviet- and Chinese-made small arms into the correspondents' faces to show them that the VC have outside support. This characterization of the liberal journalist reverses the actual experiences of correspondents in Vietnam. Journalists generally went to Vietnam believing in the necessity of the war but returned with questions about the war and America's policy in Vietnam.[80]

The Green Berets received scathing criticism from reviewers, with the most vitriolic coming from the *New York Times* correspondent Renata Adler.[81]

Most of her criticism centered on the film's right-leaning politics in support of the Vietnam War. In terms of the images of the services and servicemen, Adler pointed out that Wayne has the Air Force mow down VC troops, who "have won fairly hand-to-hand, without apparently noticing that this is not exactly the stuff of which heroic fantasies are made."[82] Indeed, in an American World War II film, it is the scrappy Americans who are pinned down by superior German firepower and must escape through their wit and ingenuity. In this instance, the Americans were the ones with superior firepower and used it. Given that this is a "John Wayne" film, there was an expectation that he would fight honorably. On the other hand, this presentation of events fit well into many pro-war comic-book stories. Partly because of John Wayne's strong association with the traditional combat formula, many critics dismissed *The Green Berets* "as a failed throwback to another era."[83]

Nevertheless, Wayne's popularity drew Americans to the theaters, and the film proved successful at the box office. One possible explanation offered by one of Wayne's biographers was that "people who did not want to know about the actual Vietnam War could feel that the national unity and resolve of World War II might turn around this strange new conflict."[84] John Wayne embodied the classic military hero, so who better to turn the Vietnam conflict into another *Longest Day*-version of World War II? The film's success, however, did not spark Hollywood to produce further Vietnam films. Even with *The Green Berets'* pro-war interpretation, public support for the war in Vietnam continued to decline.[85]

Public Opinion

While the ground and air wars in Vietnam continued, public opposition to the war grew slowly. Most Americans supported the war at first. In February 1965, 91 percent of respondents in a Gallup poll indicated that they had heard or read about recent developments in Vietnam. Of those who indicated that they followed developments, 67 percent approved of U.S. activities in Vietnam. A full 64 percent wanted to continue present efforts rather than pull out. Of the 64 percent who supported American efforts in Vietnam, 31 percent thought the U.S. should continue operations even at the risk of nuclear war.[86] The willingness of some Americans to risk nuclear war in Vietnam suggests the extent to which militarism had influenced American society and the degree to which Americans believed in the struggle against international communism.

The war's opponents made their case in the face of these beliefs. In 1966, a *New Republic* editorial reminded its readers in very anti-militaristic language that "a responsible nation does not go to war except for compelling reasons of national survival, not in the atomic age, not ever."[87] Bill Mauldin sketched an accompanying political cartoon showing President Johnson beating his own war drum, while America's allies scattered.[88]

Over the course of the war, the Gallup organization repeatedly asked Americans, "In view of the developments since we entered fighting in Vietnam, do you think the U.S. made a mistake sending troops to fight in Vietnam?" In 1966, those Americans who approved American entry into the Vietnam War ranged from 48–52 percent. Respondents who believed U.S. involvement in Vietnam was a mistake hovered between 31–36 percent.[89] So, only half of those polled supported the war effort with around one-third of Americans already in opposition. In 1967, Gallup measured opposition to the war around 46 percent, and support falling from 50 percent to 42 percent.[90] Though anti-war sentiment was becoming more mainstream, many Americans looked down upon anti-war protesters themselves as unpatriotic and subversive.[91]

On January 30, 1968, the communist forces launched a coordinated attack on American and South Vietnamese forces, referred to as the Tet Offensive. In the media reporting of the war, the language used to describe Vietnam changed after the Tet Offensive. Before this attack, "Journalists on television in particular had described the war as 'our side' versus 'their side' and had cast it in terms of the so-called good war, World War II."[92] After the Tet Offensive, correspondents still did not question American motives, but "'our war' became 'the war,' and references to World War II faded."[93] After 1968, images of the soldier in the media became less heroic and correspondents began to frame the war as a "quagmire in process."[94] American support for the war had been steadily slipping before the January 1968 Tet Offensive, and it continued to decline through the rest of the war. In February 1968, 49 percent of the population believed U.S. entry into the war had been a mistake, while 41 continued to support it. By October, those opposing the war grew to 54 percent and those supporting it declined to 37 percent.[95]

"Civilians Have a Lot to Learn about the Military"

If *The Green Berets* stridently supported the war in Vietnam, a popular contemporary television show completely ignored it. Of the military comedies, *Gomer Pyle U.S.M.C.* (1964–1969) is the most militaristic in its open praise of military service, but it does not mention the war in Vietnam at all. *Gomer Pyle* presents military service as honorable and fulfilling. The Marines are treated respectfully in the series, with the humor originating primarily from the bungling Gomer Pyle (Jim Nabors) and the foibles of Sergeant Carter

(Frank Sutton), not from the Marine Corps itself. There are actual recruiting appeals in the show, through episodes where Carter gives the men reenlisting speeches. These appeals came as America's commitment to Vietnam continued to expand. As many affluent Americans sought exemptions, deferments, or refuge in the reserve forces, *Gomer Pyle* reinforced the values of volunteerism and citizen-soldering. Despite Carter's efforts to get Gomer out of his hair, Pyle reenlists. There are episodes where Pyle becomes the model for a recruiting poster, and another in which Gomer and Carter star in a publicity film about the Corps.[96]

Gomer Pyle began as a spin-off from *The Andy Griffith Show* when Gomer received his draft notice in the mail. In what sounds like a recruiting pitch for the U.S. armed forces, Gomer explains to Andy that every man ages 18 to 35 is expected to serve in the military, so he quite enthusiastically joins the Marine Corps. Andy does not think that naïve and simplistic Gomer has what it takes to be a Marine and gently tries to dissuade him. After all, as Andy explains, "The Marines is a very demanding outfit." They need men who are quick, alert, and tough. Gomer admits that he does not have those things right now, "But I'll meet them half-way." Gomer tells Andy that his daddy told him he would be tested one day, and Gomer chose to join the Marine Corps to be tested. In this way, the show reinforces the idea that military service builds men, which was a contemporary Marine Corps recruiting slogan.[97]

When Gomer and Andy meet Sergeant Carter for the first time, he is what has become a stereotypical drill instructor, shouting insults (appropriate for television viewers) at the recruits and explaining how hard it is to become a Marine. Carter is a crusty old sergeant with combat experience in Korea and over a decade of service. Despite his tough exterior, his ego can bruise easily. Carter's tough nature comes through during the pilot episode when the other recruits trick Gomer into wearing Carter's dress-blue uniform. Carter places a bucket over Pyle's head and orders him to sing the Marine Corps hymn. Rather than being ashamed, though, Gomer happily bursts out in song under the pail. This established the motif for the following episodes: Carter would act tough and push hard, but Pyle would bounce back from every encounter with enthusiasm and further affection for Carter.[98]

Throughout the series, Pyle repeats endlessly how much fun he has and how much he has learned in the Marine Corps. When Carter coaches Pyle to pass the test for the promotion to private first class, Pyle resists at first. He explains that Carter told them at boot camp that privates are the backbone of the Marine Corps. Gomer is happy where he is, plus he does not want folks back home to think he is getting uppity with a stripe on his sleeve. Pyle gets the promotion, but does not make corporal when Carter attempts "to do the impossible again" in a subsequent episode.[99]

Sergeant Carter (Frank Sutton, left) shouts at Gomer Pyle (Jim Nabors, right) in the television show *Gomer Pyle U.S.M.C.* (1964–1969). In this scene from the episode "PFC Gomer Pyle," Carter has to coach Pyle for his promotion from private to private first class. Gomer initially resists as he does not want to appear "uppity" with a stripe on his sleeve. *Gomer Pyle* presents military service as honorable and fulfilling with the humor originating primarily from Pyle's bungling and Carter's foibles, not from the Marine Corps itself (CBS Photo Archive/Getty Images).

"A Visit from Aunt Bee" justifies the harsher aspects of service life. When Aunt Bee (Frances Bavier) visits Gomer, she is surprised that he does not have his own room and that he is doing the housework around the barracks. In horror, Aunt Bee asks, "How long has this been going on?" Gomer answers, "About 200 years, I guess." Aunt Bee complains that with so many millions of tax dollars, they could at least spring for a maid. She insists on cleaning up, which lands Pyle in trouble with Sergeant Carter. Aunt Bee immediately chides Carter for yelling at Gomer and complains to a journalist that Pyle had to shovel sand in punishment. After a few more run-ins with Carter, Gomer tells Aunt Bee, "There are a few things about Sergeant Carter and the Marines that you need to know about," and explains to her the values of military life. Aunt Bee publicly retracts her negative complaint about the Marine Corps. She admits that she had simply been judging things from a civilian point of view, and describes what she has learned: all the shouting was helping the men become better Marines, and the punishments teach them not to do the same wrong things again. Carter is pleased with the apology, commenting, "Civilians have a lot to learn about the military." This episode justifies the seemingly negative aspects of military service by placing them in the context of improving the men and building them into good Marines.[100] The message is far more militaristic than other military comedies like *McHale's Navy* and *F Troop*.

Episodes of *Gomer Pyle* even had something to say about the role of women in the military, and in this case, it strongly presented an ideal of traditionally feminine characteristics. In one story, Corporal Carol Barnes (Carol Burnett) resembles Sergeant Carter. She yells at her women Marines, calls them knuckle-heads, and otherwise acts as a tough, insulting, hard-nosed non-commissioned officer. When male Marines ogle her women, she tells them to shove off. Gomer runs into Corporal Barnes, and she mistakes his enthusiasm for flirting with her. Since Gomer does not have an assertive bone in his body, he cannot tell her that he already has a girlfriend, Lou Ann.[101]

Finally, Gomer sits down with Carol to explain her place. He tells her that he is flattered by her attention, and that such an attractive girl should have "lots of fellers." He has one suggestion: she should allow the man to arrange the dates. The man should do the asking, the driving, and the planning. Carol admits that she comes on too strong, though this helped her earn promotions. Gomer tells Carol, "You was a lady before you was a Marine." Later, when Carol trips over a folding chair, she initially pushes away the men who rush to help her. Gomer catches her eye, and Carol pretends to faint. She acts coy, bats her eyes, and asks for some water, all the while she tells the men how happy she is to have such strong men around her. Instead of encouraging Carol to be herself, Gomer urges her to change her personality entirely.[102]

The show remained popular with audiences, earning the number ten spot in the 1965–1966 Nielsen ratings and rising to number two by the 1968–1969 season.[103] Something about Gomer's innocence, patriotism, traditional values, or the fact that it was set during peacetime while a real war waged overseas, appealed to segments of the television audience. One contemporary reviewer described Gomer Pyle as a warm, innocent, non-professional character who appealed even to those folks, like himself, who despised the military.[104] *Gomer Pyle U.S.M.C.* offered an escape from the real war by presenting a simpler television military world.

The Secret of Getting Ahead

In previous wars, military recruiting advertising reflected the combat situation, highlighted skills useful for combat, and called young men to serve their country. During the Vietnam War, military recruiting advertising generally ignored the reality of combat. Instead, advertising continued to emphasize technical training, financial stability, and other peacetime advantages of a military career.[105] Army recruiters ran print advertising in *Life*, *Newsweek*, and *Sports Illustrated* as well as targeting specific audiences in periodicals such as *Hot Rod*, *Electronics Illustrated*, *Popular Science*, and *National Future Farmer*.[106]

The military services believed that recruiting advertising influenced enlistments. The Army considered building a favorable image of the service as necessary to attract volunteers. Constructing that favorable image included advertising, salesmanship, and publicity.[107] A Navy recruitment survey conducted in September 1967 indicated to Navy recruiters that "in general, booklets and pamphlets, and recruiter visits to schools are very effective current influences on decisions to enter the Navy" and that Navy publicity ranked higher than "*all* forms of personal contacts, friends in the Service, parents, brothers and sisters, other relatives and school counselors" in the influence of young people to join the Navy.[108] This proved a significant shift from the findings of the 1955 Public Opinion Survey, which had indicated that personal contacts far outweighed any other influence.[109] If this report is accurate, it appears that media had replaced human experience in influencing young recruits by the 1960s. These young men apparently did not have contact with or were not directly influenced by the men who had previous military experience. Advertising may have been particularly important to the Army because a 1969 survey found that the Army recruiter ranked last in influence over potential recruits compared to the other services.[110]

Army advertising confronted the draft directly, but usually did not specifically address the ground war in Vietnam. According to an Army survey taken at selected Armed Forces Examining and Entrance Stations, fears of the draft motivated 42 percent of enlistees in 1964. By 1969, the draft motivated 49.7 percent of enlistments.[111] In 1965, the Army responded directly to increased anxiety about the draft. One advertisement helpfully suggested "5 things you should do about the draft." Number one on their list was "Don't panic," likely the most useful piece of information in the ad. The second item asked the potential draftee to "write down what you want from life," then "talk to people." Naturally, it suggested that the young man investigate his options by talking to his recruiter or reading a helpful Army booklet, *The Secret of Getting Ahead*.[112] Other advertisements promised that young men would get "a straight answer" from their local Army recruiter.[113]

Regular Army advertising trumpeted traditional combat attributes often without any overt references to the ground war in Vietnam. When one poster proclaims, "This is the day you learn about guts!" it does not mean proving oneself in combat. Rather, it means joining an airborne unit and learning to parachute out of planes.[114] Another ad pictures a jeep and truck in a forested area with men in combat fatigues. The setting is not Vietnam, however, and the scene does not depict combat. Instead, it features an electronics expert on a field exercise.[115]

A few ads did reference Vietnam and combat, some making the traditional connection between combat and manhood. Others focused on leadership or patriotism. In one example, four soldiers are wading across a stream. The lieutenant in front is glancing behind his shoulder and waving his arm to direct his men forward. The ad warns, "It takes mental and physical fortitude" to be successful.[116] In another poster eerily evocative of a twenty-first century Army recruiting theme, the text exhorts:

> One man.
> One man skilled and dedicated.
> One man proud and quiet.
> One man cool and resourceful.
> One man serving his country.
> One man who is his own man.
> One man is an army.[117]

The second lieutenant pictured is in combat gear with his M-16 pointed upward, finger on the trigger.[118] Images such as these did not entice volumes of young men to volunteer for overseas combat, and the Army dramatically increased monthly draft calls.

Army Reserve recruiting advertising did not deviate from its peacetime themes during the Vietnam War. Tapping into a theme of building manhood, one poster showing a picture of combat boots, states, "Reservists wear man-size," and asks, "Can you fill them?"[119] A poster that commemorates the 60th anniversary of the Army Reserve pictures a row of silhouetted rifles with bayonets fixed.[120] Though meant to supplement active duty troops during times of war, President Johnson never mobilized reserve forces on a large scale during Vietnam. Johnson believed activating the reserve forces would be too politically risky because it would alarm middle-class America and give Congress an opportunity to debate his war plans.[121]

This U.S. Army Reserve poster circa 1965 promotes a long-standing recruiting theme that military service builds men. This poster was published just as the ground war was starting in Vietnam. Much of the recruiting advertising during the war in Vietnam made no reference to the conflict in Southeast Asia, but rather stuck to traditional themes like manhood, travel, and education (U.S. Army Center of Military History).

While many men in the reserves and National Guard were disappointed that they were not activated for the Vietnam War, Johnson's decision to keep the reserve forces sidelined had a negative effect on their public images. As with previous draft authorizations, Congress included many deferments in the Selective Service Act of 1967. One of the most popular deferments sought by young men was admission into the Reserves and National Guard to avoid the draft — and a deployment to Vietnam. Throughout the Vietnam War years, the reserve forces had long waiting lines for available slots. Many Americans perceived the reserves as a "haven for draft dodgers."[122]

Unlike its previous advertising in World War II and the Korean War, the Marine Corps did not relate its recruiting advertising specifically to combat in an ongoing conflict, though it came closer than the Army to doing so. One poster shows three marines on an unidentified beach, just coming out of a landing craft.[123] Another poster portrays a Marine in a flight suit, who points to something on a map being held by a lieutenant in combat gear.[124] It references combat, if not combat in Vietnam specifically. Navy recruiting advertising focused on tradition and on technology. "Leadership Through the Years" pictures a sailor with a dress uniform cap in the foreground, while 18th, 19th, and twentieth century ships sail in the background. "Nuclear Navy" and "Fly Your Own Jet" advertises aircraft carriers and naval aviation, respectively.[125] One poster implied combat. "Action with the fleet" shows a battleship firing its guns, though there is no enemy or other identifying feature in the poster to provide context.[126] One poster themed "Travel" shows a battleship in the seas off of a rocky coast with small, Asian fishing boats in the foreground.[127] It might be Vietnam, but it might not be.

Although the Air Force participated heavily in the Vietnam War, recruiting advertising did not focus on combat. Instead, the Air Force continued to praise its technological prowess. Even when it faced enlistment shortfalls, the Air Force chose to focus on the future rather than the present. The ad "About-Face!" reaches out to former airmen to return to service either in the old job or to train for a new "space age" skill.[128] In advertising for the space age, the Air Force looked firmly into the future rather than at the war at hand.

By the mid–to late–1960s, the military services stepped up their advertising for African-American recruits. Recruiting advertising targeted African-American publications to find qualified candidates.[129] It also began showing African-Americans in mainstream recruiting advertising distributed to the general population. A Marine Corps poster, "Ask a Marine," pictures a white Marine recruiter in his dress uniform, holding open a Marine Corps brochure. He explains something to two students, one white and one black. The African-American student is standing in front of the white student, facing the recruiter.[130] In the Army poster, "Learn a skill. Make a future," recruiters tell their audience that "with your own hands, with your own God-given talents you can make a future for yourself. In the Army." The ad shows soldiers learning about a helicopter's rotor from an African-American sergeant first class. The white students are in fatigues, while the black sergeant first class is wearing his class-A uniform.[131] By having the sergeant wear a dressier uniform, he appears more professional and more of an authority figure. "Enroll in the Army" is aimed at high school graduates and advertises Army job training to fulfill one's military obligation. It pictures a classroom of male students in their class-A dress uniforms. An African American student is prominently featured in the front and center seat of the first row, while another black student sits behind him among the class of white students.[132] A Navy poster, "Bold Team," shows a close-up photograph of two sailors, one white and one black, operating some equipment on deck of a ship.[133] Some ads specifically tried to recruit black officers. One ad that appeared in the college edition of *Time* magazine shows a black second lieutenant who received his commission through Officer Candidate School. The ad explains, "Learning to be a leader was the best thing that ever happened to me."[134] Overall, the message in these advertisements is of the success of integration and of career opportunities, not combat in Vietnam.

Despite efforts to recruit African-American officers, their numbers remained low. In 1962, African-Americans constituted less than 2 percent of the officer corps. A decade later, they comprised 4 percent of Army officers, 1.7 percent of Air Force officers, 1.5 percent of Marine Corps officers, and 0.9 percent of naval officers. In 1973, a captain was the highest-ranking African-American female in the Marine Corps.[135]

War on Poverty

Concerns about the draft predate the ground war phase of the Vietnam War, usually publicized around the periodic renewals of the draft law. In 1964, Bill Mauldin sketched a cartoon of a badly vibrating desk fan with wisps of smoke emanating from the motor. He labeled the fan "1948 draft law" and showed President Johnson's hand resting on the on/off switch. An accompanying editorial urged the president to end the draft. Repeating the words of Senator Gaylord Nelson (D-WI), the future founder of Earth Day, the draft was "costly, inefficient, and unnecessary."[136] The editorialist suggested ending the draft and moving to an all-volunteer force. Reflecting the left-leaning political nature of the *New Republic*, the writer added: "The Administration talks about its war on poverty. The Department of Defense needs men to fill jobs and it is equipped to train them. Why not use it as a weapon in the poverty war?"[137] The Johnson Administration must have been on the same page as this editorialist because two years later it launched Project 100,000.

Pushed by the Johnson Administration as part of the Great Society, the Defense Department launched Project 100,000 in 1966, which allowed enlistments for recruits who could not score above the minimum on the aptitude exam. Project 100,000 increased military manpower by 350,000 with 66 percent heading to the Army and the remainder split nearly evenly between the other services. Nearly 41 percent of the recruits under Project 100,000 were African-American, and 37 percent of those recruits ended up in the combat arms. Many deployed to Vietnam.[138]

In early 1968, the Assistant Secretary of Defense directed each of the armed services to test a pilot program in Detroit, Philadelphia, and St. Louis to target "poverty sections of cities" for intensified recruitment.[139] This program specifically focused on areas that suffered unemployment or underemployment and set quotas in addition to Project 100,000. It featured an advertising push that included radio spots, television ads, recruiting posters that featured minorities, and other recruiting aids.[140] In May 1968, the program expanded to an additional 18 cities.[141]

While the rationale for the program came from the Johnson Administration's desire to eliminate poverty, the Department of the Defense was not enthusiastic about accepting manpower from the lowest categories of its aptitude tests. These men took longer to train, needed more attention from their non-commissioned officers, and required repeated reinforcement. Furthermore, the soldiers from the lowest mental category "were less likely to survive combat and more likely to endanger other members" of their unit.[142] Congress finally ended manpower quotas based on mental categories in 1971 when it appeared that the Department of Defense had lowered recruiting standards too low to meet manpower needs. Congress eliminated Project 100,000 at the same time.[143] The whole program reflected the liberal social welfare principle of using government to help the most vulnerable citizens, not a drive to militarize society. Of course, the citizens living in poverty who were recruited under this program likely wondered how much the government was trying to help them if they were being sent into harm's way in Vietnam.

Earn "a Man's Wages"

Unsurprisingly, recruiting advertising for women generally did not mention the war in Vietnam, though the first WACs arrived there in 1965. While the nation did not mobilize for the war in Southeast Asia like it had for World War II, the Army did attempt to increase the size of the Women's Army Corps by 3,596 starting in July 1967. To meet this goal, the U.S. Army's Recruiting Command assigned additional recruiters, increased advertisements for the WAC, expanded the enlistment options, and simplified the enlistment process. The Army's print media advertising included *Co-Ed, Seventeen, Teen, Time,* and *Glamour* as well as specialist periodicals such as the *American Journal of Nursing.*[144]

Like earlier recruiting campaigns, advertising for women focused mainly on the unmilitary aspects of the services. Most recruiting attempts stayed with the themes of travel, education, camaraderie, and career advancement. For example, an ad for the Army Nurse Corps Reserve shows a nurse in traditional white uniform holding up a newborn baby. The caption reads, "The little guy doesn't know it, but the lady is a Captain." The ad emphasizes extra income, education, and travel — to Oslo, Norway.[145] A booklet featuring nursing careers likewise failed to mention any possibility of active-duty deployment or assistance to soldiers then in combat. Postgraduate education, on the other hand, was a strong possibility.[146]

Camaraderie featured as an important advantage of military service. One advertisement printed in a June 1967 *TV Guide* described a WAC detachment as a college dorm where women would always have fun things to do and ready-made companions to come along. The most significant shift in this image is that the Army chose to compare military service with college life, reflecting the higher numbers of women attending college. It also appealed to consumerism by reminding the potential recruit that the money she would be saving without having to pay room and board could go toward buying herself new clothes or a new car.[147] Another ad of the same theme pictured a WAC in uniform playing an acoustic guitar and singing for a group of Army friends. It explains, "Discover a young world of people like you."[148]

Patriotism could also be fun, according to one WAC ad. It pictured a man and a woman in civilian attire happily riding horses on the beach in Cape Cod. No military uniforms, equipment, or symbols are visible. "To a girl like Joan Fifer, patriotism isn't strictly a man's province," the ad explains. Joan is proudly serving in the Women's Army Corps. "And it's not so surprising that patriotism should wear a happy face," the ad continued, "Joan hasn't had so much fun since she graduated from high school." Why? Because in the WAC she met new friends, has new surroundings, and the chance "to do something worthwhile. For herself. And for her country."[149] All of these themes are remarkably reminiscent of the 1950s advertisements which characterized military service as a patriotic vacation for women. The main difference is that the hair and clothes have been updated for the 1960s generation.

A few glimpses into the future rise of feminism could be seen in military advertising, however. With more women attending college and working outside the home, plus the momentum building in the women's movement, the Army advertised that it had a better deal for women than did the civilian world. The Women's Army Corps offered interesting work "with a lot more responsibility than you'd be likely to get anywhere else." The women would earn "a man's wages" to travel around the world, take four weeks of vacation per year, and act as leaders.[150] In this respect, the Army was targeting not the traditionally minded women who wanted to get married and raise a family but the more independent and career-minded ones influenced by the growing feminist movement.

The Navy also attempted to attract modern women. One recruiting poster pictures a woman in civilian clothing, wearing sunglasses. "If you think Rachelle DeHoff is just another good-looking, well-educated admired WAVE officer," it proclaims, "you're right."[151] Another one reveals a close up picture of a woman's face and states, "This is Linn Anderson, WAVES Officer."[152]

At the same time that the Marine Corps expanded opportunities for women, it continued to emphasize Corps tradition. A 1968 Marine Corps poster, "Share a Proud Tradition," pictured two enlisted marines, one woman and one man, saluting into the distance. Standing just behind and to the side of them is a Marine Corps color guard.[153]

Like their predecessors, Vietnam-era servicewomen were expected to maintain a feminine appearance and remain separated from the masculine aspects of military service. Somewhat in jest, General William Westmoreland, commander of the Military Assistance Command, Vietnam, requested a WAC officer and sergeant, who were not only competent in their abilities, but were also "extremely intelligent, an extrovert, and beautiful." In response, WAC director Colonel Emily Gorman noted that "brains and beauty is, of course, common in the WAC."[154]

A few recruiting ads did appeal to women's patriotism to serve for the Vietnam War. One ad targeted nurses. It showed a field with a soldier helping a wounded comrade, arm bandaged. The advertisement read, "Our fighting men deserve the finest nursing care America has to offer. And in times of conflict, American nurses have always answered the call to help heal and comfort the wounded." An appeal to "heal and comfort" fits into the most traditional feminine qualities and one of the most customary ways women have been involved in war. It also implicitly allows women to choose overseas service: it has a box where the potential recruit could check "I am a registered nurse. I am interested in serving my country where needed." "Where needed" could certainly be Southeast Asia.[155]

The military services continued to want conservative, demure images for its servicewomen. Army leadership objected when photographs of women "roughing" it in combat fatigues appeared in the newspapers.[156] The combat fatigues suggested that women were getting more masculine or closer to combat than a woman should. Of course, nurses had always been close to battle and to the wounded. Women serving in Southeast Asia also followed civilian trends, shortening the length of their skirts, wearing tank tops or halters despite regulations, and sporting very short shorts.[157] They appeared feminine, but not with the modesty that the leadership desired. A cartoon in the *Navy Times* played off the Marine Corps's slogan "The Marine Corps Builds Men" by showing a very pretty, slim, curvy, and buxom woman Marine with two men gawking, adding "...and women, too!"[158] This was not the elite and prestigious image of women Marines presented in recruiting advertising.

Opportunities for women in the armed forces expanded slightly during the 1960s. While more than half of the WACs served in administrative capacities, the Army had more than 100 military occupational specialties open to women. In 1968, however, some billets were still restricted by "the social acceptability of the job." Women who chose to reenlist in the Army did so first for assignment and travel opportunities, second for continued education, and third for promotion and job security, similar reasons women had reenlisted in earlier years.[159]

In 1967, after a seven-year-long lobbying campaign by the Defense Department Advisory Committee on Women in the Services, Congress rescinded the 2-percent ceiling on women in the armed forces and the bar against women being elevated to general officer rank.[160] The Army was the first military service to promote women to general officer rank. In May 1970, Colonel Anna Mae Hays, chief of the Army Nurse Corps, and Colonel Elizabeth P. Hoisington, director of the WAC, became the first two women brigadier generals in the Army.[161] Most changes for women, however, did not come until after the end of the draft and the rise of the All Volunteer Force in the 1970s.

"I Would Serve if I Had to, But I Wouldn't Like It"

In 1969, surveys indicated that Americans tendered an overall favorable attitude toward the military even as opposition to the war in Vietnam grew in strength. According to surveys, the public believed military service contributed to the maturity, education, responsibility, and self-confidence of the men. In terms of ranking the services, Americans preferred the Air Force, followed by the Navy. The Army ranked fourth after the Marine Corps. Unsurprisingly, the Army was the least popular service for young people under 21 years of age, the group most likely to be worried about being drafted into the war in Vietnam. Respondents ordered the Army last in the categories of:

"travel opportunities, less pride in one's branch of service, lower quality officers, fewer chances for educational advancement and/or acquiring a trade or skill, a less modern and up-to-date service, slower advancement, less adequate quarters, not as much prestige, poor quality food, harder work (except for Marines), a less glamorous life, and a greater danger to one's life."[162] Pride, prestige, glamour, and modern technology are all qualities emphasized by the Army's sister services. "Lower quality officers" reflects the common stereotype. "Greater danger to one's life" must reference the Vietnam War and acknowledge the fact that the Army simply has more soldiers overseas in harm's way than the other military services.

One of the most telling influences of the Vietnam War on American attitudes concerned veterans. Surveys indicated that while 87 percent of Army veterans believed they had achieved something worthwhile in their service, 70 percent of them would not advise others to join the Army. These veterans would direct others to serve in the Air Force or Navy. Some of this sentiment might be related to having others avoid combat duty in Vietnam. Still, it is not a good sign when veterans are advising others to avoid the Army. The surveys also revealed that younger veterans harbored less favorable views of their service than older ones. Reasons junior officers and enlisted men felt dissatisfied with the Army included low pay, family separation, frequent moves, mismanagement of skills, poor leadership, and unhappy wives.[163]

According to Army surveys, the increasing anti-war sentiments among the public were directed mostly at the top levels of command. Some studies indicated that Americans believed that the Army was "interested in maintaining the peace, not just in waging wars."[164] Others suggested that Americans feared a growing militarism. Researchers concluded "the outspoken criticism today suggests a lack of trust for 'military statesmen,' a dread that the military-industrial complex is a reality and a belief that military leaders advocate wars, or at least a theory of military victory, as solutions to political problems."[165]

Reports indicated mixed results concerning the idea of a "generation gap" with respect to attitudes toward the armed forces. According to the *National Observer*,

> Older people — with important exceptions — tend to retain full confidence in their soldiers and sailors and their generals and admirals. Younger people are more skeptical, and sometimes they are openly hostile. The draft, it would appear, has a good deal to do with the formation of young people's attitudes.[166]

Another survey done by the Army in 1970 makes the opposite conclusion. Instead, the researchers discovered that most young men favored the *status quo*, believing it was important to fight the spread of communism in Vietnam. Furthermore, the young men did not oppose the draft. Most considered military service as "an opportunity to serve the country and to prove oneself a man." Only about 20 percent of the survey sample did not support the Vietnam War and indicated that "they would serve in the military only grudgingly." Researchers cautioned that the responses could be biased. The young men favored answers written as an agreement statement rather than a disagreement, even though the statements sometimes contradicted each other. While only 13 percent indicated they would be happy to serve in the military, half of the young men selected "I'd serve" on the questionnaire. It is interesting to note that the researchers considered this the neutral answer and believed it reflected the view of military service as an obligation, not a choice. An additional 22 percent indicated that they "would serve if I had to, but I wouldn't like it." Finally, 4 percent refused to serve, checking the box stating that they would rather go to jail or leave the country. [167]

A generation gap also existed with respect to attitudes toward the Vietnam War. Youth had always been the main factor in the anti-war demonstrations, and younger Americans identified more with this group than older Americans. A 1969 survey asked, "In general, just as far as their objectives are concerned, do you sympathize with the goals of the people who are demonstrating, marching, and protesting against the war in Vietnam, or do you disagree with their goals?"[168] Unsurprisingly, 52 percent of respondents under the age of 35 supported the demonstrators, while only 28 percent of the 50 and older group did so. However, when researchers looked at the age breakdown for support of the Vietnam War in general, they found that older Americans opposed the war earlier and more consistently than younger Americans. In March 1966, for instance, only 21 percent of the 21–29 age group opposed the war, while 30 percent of those 50 and older did. In November of that year, younger American attitudes remained unchanged, while older citizens opposed the war by 36 percent. When 43 percent of the 21–29 age group opposed the war in October 1967, 53 percent of the older participants did. The gap increased in 1968. In October, 44 percent of 21–29 aged Americans opposed the war, while 64 percent of 50 and older did. The gap closed in 1969 with 58 percent of 21–29-year-olds opposing the war and 63 percent of those 50 and older agreeing. Hazel Erskine concluded, "There has never been a time when youthful doubters outnumbered older, *in response to this particular question.*"[169] Older Americans had grown up in a more anti-militarist culture than younger Americans. Younger Americans had grown up with the draft and with militarist Cold War defense policies. It seems that the older generation was more skeptical of war or what their political and military leaders said about the efficacy of war than the younger generation, which had been raised in the militarism of the Cold War and accepted that as normal.

The Debate Over the Draft

Since the inauguration of the peacetime draft in the 1940s, Americans had held two seemingly contradictory positions: they favored the anti-militarist ideal of volunteerism and supported conscription through the draft. When asked to select between these two choices, a survey indicated that Americans preferred volunteers to draftees and apparently associated the term "patriotic" with the volunteers. Researchers concluded that this association meant that "military service and patriotism are still strongly associated in people's minds."[170] This finding is consistent with images in popular culture since the 1940s that emphasized volunteerism in the armed forces, even in World War II, during which the vast majority of servicemen had been drafted. The image remained of American men volunteering for patriotic reasons, even if the reality of men's motivations to serve during the draft era did not match the popular perception.

Even though Americans had long supported a peacetime draft, it was also open to criticism. Some opponents of Selective Service focused on the system's inefficiency. One editorial claimed that "97 percent of all draftees leave the minute their hitch is up."[171] Others accused the draft of the Vietnam War as unfairly targeting poor and minority men. According to polls, confidence in local draft boards steadily eroded over the decades, from World War II to Vietnam. According to one scholar: "At the end of World War II some 79 percent of the public had agreed that local draft boards were fair. And the end of the Korean War in 1953, 60 percent had felt the same way.... In August 1966 some 49 percent said the system was fair, but 37 percent felt it was unfair."[172] The *New Republic* denounced Selective Service as openly discriminatory.[173] African-Americans in particular harbored negative views about draft boards. In 1969, surveys of black communities indicated that almost half of the African-American respondents believed Selective Service was biased against them. At the same time, reenlistments plummeted from over 60 percent in 1966 to less than 13 percent in 1970.[174]

As historian Beth Bailey points out, "The antiwar and antidraft movements were overlapping and intertwined throughout the Vietnam War, but supporters of the nation's war policy were sometimes too quick to dismiss antiwar protest as driven primarily by fear of the draft."[175] By equating antiwar protests with fear of the draft, opinion-makers and politicians concluded that eliminating the draft would decrease the antiwar protests. The head of Selective Service, Lieutenant General Lewis Hershey, increased the controversy by decreeing that all college students arrested or detained in relation to anti-war protests would immediately lose their deferred status and become immediately eligible for the draft.[176] The *New Republic* denounced the measure, point-

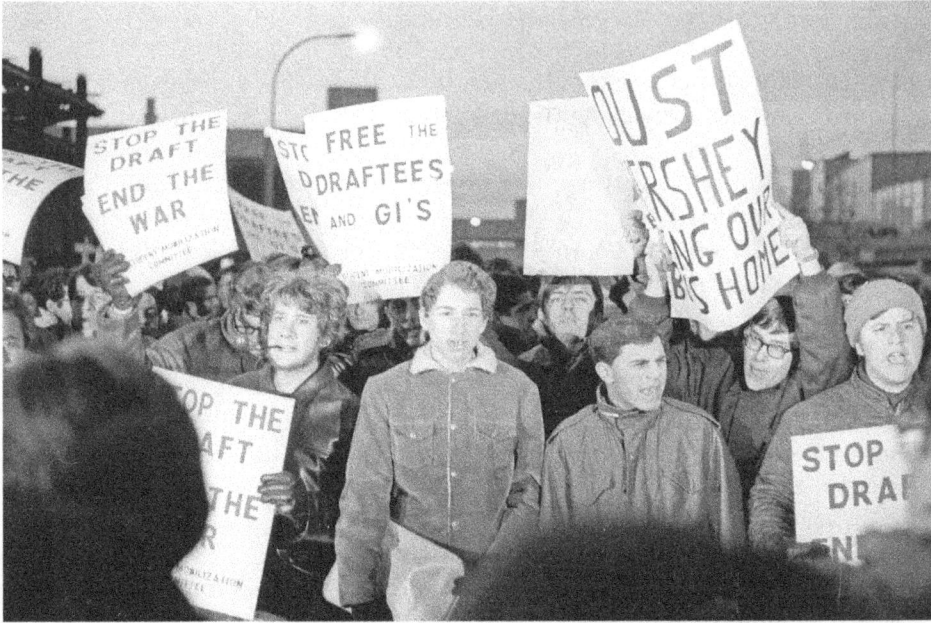

Photographer Michael Ochs snapped this picture of a group of anti-draft and anti-war student protesters in May 1965 in Washington, D.C. Note the poster demanding the removal of Lieutenant General Lewis Hershey, the head of Selective Service. Hershey increased the controversy of the draft when he decreed that any college student detained in an anti-war protest would lose his deferment status, which would make him immediately eligible to be drafted — and potentially serve in the Vietnam War (Michael Ochs Archives/Getty Images).

ing out "the draft was never intended as a form of punishment, certainly not as a club to be used against political dissent."[177] Hershey fueled the fire with his comments that "reclassification is quicker at stopping sit-ins than some indictment that takes effect six months later."[178]

In 1968, Republican presidential candidate Richard Nixon campaigned to end the draft and replace it with an All Volunteer Force (AVF). As president, Nixon used strong anti-militarist language to make his case for ending the draft. A country dedicated to liberty, justice and equality could not operate an equitable draft, Nixon claimed.[179] He argued, "The idea that a professional army of mercenaries posed a threat to the republic was equally dubious because the volunteers would be American citizens, proud to serve their flag."[180] Free market economist Milton Friedman also supported an AVF because it would "limit the military's influence on the setting of social priorities in America."[181] Political conservatives consciously chose ideals that appealed to the traditional anti-militarism of the American people.

The political left also framed their opposition to an All Volunteer Force in the language of anti-militarism. According to Blair Clark, Senator Eugene McCarthy's national campaign manager, a volunteer army was really a professional one. He feared that "a professional military force could take this country headlong down the road of endless military adventures and, finally, destroy the democratic fabric of this society."[182] Clark believed that a professional force would focus exclusively on "purely military" concerns and become "isolated from the rest of society."[183] Already, political liberals lamented the loss of civilian control of the military in the conduct of the Vietnam War, according to Clark. While Congress might be able to reign in presidential power with a smaller professional force, and thus end the tradition of undeclared wars, he also believed that "free people risks its liberties when it surrenders to professional soldiers the right and duty to protect itself."[184] Clark also pointed out that contemporary sociologists had discovered that military life was "repellant to most Americans."[185] Both sides of the debate on the draft clearly used anti-militarist ideas to make their points, recognizing, consciously or not, that Americans had an anti-militarist self-perception. According to feedback given to the President's Commission on an All-Volunteer Armed Force, better known as the Gates Commission after its chairman, Thomas Gates, objections to the volunteer force fell into five broad categories:

> (1) An all-volunteer force would be alienated from civilian society, thus undermining civilian control of the military and increasing the likelihood of a coup d'état; (2) an AVF would have a negative effect on civilian society because military service offers education and training and makes men better citizens; (3) an AVF would lead to unnecessary military involvements overseas; (4) an AVF would lower military morale and be less effective; and (5) an AVF would be less flexible and less able to meet emergencies.[186]

The Gates Commission had a hard time responding to the subjective aspects of these critiques. In the end, their final report emphasized the free market economics of the AVF and the principles of individual freedom and liberty. The draft had become a routine fixture of American life, however, and most Americans continued to support it. A majority of 62 percent of Americans supported the institution, with only 39 percent favoring the All Volunteer Force.[187]

Unsurprisingly, among young people subject to the draft a much higher number, 61 percent, supported a shift to an All Volunteer Force. Tellingly, however, the same survey conducted by the U.S. Youth Council determined that only 42 percent of the interviewees would actually volunteer for military service. President Nixon signed legislation that ended the draft and created an All Volunteer Force in 1973.[188]

As the armed forces prepared for the shift from a draft to an all-volunteer force, the Army took steps to "publicize the role of women in the Army team."[189] The service increased advertising and planned to expand the WAC by 80 percent, from 1,100 officers and 12,400 enlisted women in 1969 to 2,000 officers and 22,400 enlisted women. Opposition to the war in Vietnam among the public affected recruiting for women, all of whom were all volunteers. In 1969, enlistment in all of the women's services dropped drastically. As President Nixon pulled American troops out of Southeast Asia, potential recruits reported that they thought the military no longer needed their service. Those who did join the military cited "the chance to do something different, to learn about the world, to meet more people, and to further an education" as the reasons for enlisting. Recruiting began to recover by 1972.[190]

Anti-Military Backlash

In March 1966, mothers marched in demonstration against military toys in front of the American Toy Fair in New York City. Many of the women dressed as the British nanny Mary Poppins and carried umbrellas or wore sashes with the slogan, "Toy Fair or Warfare."[191] One of the leaders described her motivations: "Toys influence children's attitudes. Children who learned to glorify violence are much more likely to unleash it when they grow up."[192] Although widespread opposition to the Vietnam War was only starting by 1966, these women were already distressed by the popularity and availability of military-themed toys. While retailers were just capitalizing on a market, these women objected to the glorification of warfare in general. Though the women were unsuccessful in banishing military toys, anti-militarist attitudes strengthened during the decade.

By the end of the 1960s, images of war in film differed dramatically from earlier movies, partly because of significant changes in the Hollywood ratings system. A new Classification and Rating Administration replaced the old Production Code Administration in 1968. Films were no longer censored for inappropriate references to sexuality, language, and violence, but rated by the expected maturity level of the audience. This allowed more explicit references to sex, vulgar language, and gruesome violence.[193] The filmmakers for *MASH* and *Catch-22* included nudity, expletives, and graphic wounds in their movies.

Popular culture also reflected the cultural elements and antiwar sentiments of the Vietnam era. *MASH* (1970) is set during the Korean War at a mobile Army hospital, but many scholars consider the film a commentary on the forces playing out in American society and culture in the 1960s.[194]

Robert Altman, who had previously directed a number of anti-war themed episodes of the television show *Combat!*, directed *MASH*.[195] The film's protagonists, Hawkeye Pierce (Donald Sutherland), John McIntyre (Elliot Gould), and Duke Forrest (Tom Skerritt) are irreverent, loud-mouthed drunks who happen to be excellent surgeons. By contrast, both Major Frank Burns (Robert Duvall) and Major Margaret O'Houlihan (Sally Kellerman) are by-the-book, regulation Army, and, accordingly, are clearly unwanted and unwelcome by the others. Major Burns is depicted as less competent than the other surgeons, though O'Houlihan is recognized for her medical skills.[196]

The film displays no respect for rank or authority. Hawkeye, McIntyre, and Duke provoke Burns and O'Houlihan through taunting, teasing, and outright harassment. She, in turn, yells at her commanding officer, Colonel Blake (Roger Bowen), for letting Hawkeye, McIntyre, and Duke "get away with everything." As Blake himself is in bed with a nurse, O'Houlihan shouts at him, "This isn't a hospital, it's an insane asylum!" The only way for her to survive is to give up her stiffness and join the insanity. Only in surgery does any professionalism emerge, and this only with respect toward the patients themselves, not to upholding military regulations.[197]

MASH violates many previous conventions. The doctors (married or single) pursue the nurses (married or single) for sexual encounters. Duke gives a Korean boy a pornographic magazine to teach him to read, and Hawkeye and McIntyre visit prostitutes in Seoul. The doctors overtly act to undermine the war effort by giving a Korean boy drugs so that he will fail his Korean army physical. There are outright references to homosexuality and suicide as well. Although alcoholism and drunkenness have appeared in films before, such as *From Here to Eternity,* alcohol consumption runs freely among the hospital staff in this movie, as does smoking marijuana. As the story takes place in a mobile Army hospital, the film shows graphic scenes with bloody wounds, including a artery gushing a fountain of blood.[198]

MASH proved immensely popular and won critical acclaim. It garnered a Best Writing Academy Award, and the movie was nominated for Best Picture, Best Director, and Best Actress in a Supporting Role. The *Time* magazine critic put it, "Nothing is sacred because everyone is scared."[199] War is neither exciting nor ennobling in this critic's view. The reviewer added that the main characters are "the penultimate draftee, a drooping lugubrious sack of sadness who makes Beetle Bailey look like Douglas MacArthur."[200] Donald Sutherland, playing Hawkeye Pierce, had previously played the similarly anti-authoritarian Pinkley in *The Dirty Dozen* and would soon appear as Sergeant Oddball in *Kelly's Heroes.*

New York Times film critic Vincent Canby described the main characters in *MASH* as "surgeon-heroes," and considered it the second anti-war service comedy after *Dr. Strangelove*. He acknowledged that the humor was shocking and nasty, particularly in the ways the men harassed O'Houlihan. He warned against both overselling and overanalyzing the film.[201]

Film critic Richard Corliss did not like *MASH*. He objected to labeling the surgeons as "heroes," referring to them instead as "ruthless" and "bully boys."[202] He described Blake as a "benign, befuddled, absent-minded professional soldier."[203] Corliss did not consider the film anti-war or radical either, as the "heroes are experts at beating the system, not smashing the system."[204] While this critic reads the film as accepting the military as the institution, the film does not portray the Army as having any redeeming value. *MASH* is more appropriately interpreted as anti-military.

Anti-militarist, anti-authority, and anti-establishment themes are also found in the novel and the film *Catch-22* (1970).[205] Joseph Heller, a World War II Army Air Corps veteran, published the novel in 1961 about themes present in the Cold War. Although the fictional story is set in World War II, Heller explains that his themes reflect the Cold War. The distrust of the government, feelings of helplessness and victimization, and anti-war sentiment all stemmed from the Korean War and the 1950s Cold War confrontation. Still, the book became popular a decade later during the Vietnam War, when its anti-authoritarian themes found a wider audience.[206]

The film's main protagonist, a World War II bombardier Captain Yossarian (Alan Arkin), is an anti-hero. He does not want to fly anymore, convinced that he will be killed if he keeps going up. Unlike the crews on *Twelve O'Clock High*, Yossarian panics under the stress. He keeps trying to convince the doctor and the chaplain that he is crazy, and therefore, should be taken off the flight list. Unfortunately, there is a catch: he has to be crazy to keep flying, but if he asks to be grounded, that proves he is not crazy; therefore, he must keep flying. Yossarian's surest chance to get out of war is to make a deal with Colonel Cathcart (Martin Balsam) and Lieutenant Colonel Korn (Buck Henry) to pretend to be a hero. At the end, Yossarian takes his chances on the run rather than go through the charade of being a false hero.[207]

Other characters in *Catch-22* are disturbed, anti-heroic, and embody the values of personal consumption and immediate gratification. A lieutenant, Milo Minderbinder (Jon Voight), acts as an amoral, perhaps evil, version of Sergeant Bilko. Where Bilko's cons and deals were generally harmless, Milo gets his hands into the black market and prostitution, and even makes a deal with the Germans, whereby the Americans bomb their own post. Another Army airman rapes a girl and throws her out the window to her death because "I couldn't let her go around and say bad things about me, now could I?" He is never arrested for his crime, but Yossarian is arrested for being away without leave, proving that even justice is turned on its head.[208]

Catch-22 upsets classic notions of glory and heroism by awarding the men medals for flying in perfect formation. On this particular mission, Yossarian refuses to drop bombs on an Italian town of no strategic value, releasing them instead in the ocean. Since they flew in perfect formation, the men get awards for it anyway. Yossarian receives his medal buck naked, further eroding previously accepted notions of the seriousness, honor, and respect given to war.[209]

Although the *New York Times* film critic loved *Catch-22*, the film produced poor box-office returns.[210] The *Time* magazine reviewer had a theory as to why: "When the novel was published in 1961, its nonviolent stance was courageous and almost lonely. But antiwar films have become faddish lately, and *Catch-22* runs the risk, philosophically, of falling into line behind *MASH* and *How I Won the War*."[211] Given the strong anti-war sentiments of the era, *Catch-22* apparently did not stand out among its competition. Even though this film did not do well, the popularity of *MASH* suggests the era of *The Longest Day* and even *The Battle of the Bulge* was slipping away.

Old Blood and Guts

The film *Patton* (1970) can best be understood in the polarized climate of the late 1960s, as those with divergent political views interpreted the film in radically different ways. *Patton* is a character study that presents its subject, General George S. Patton, Jr., as a unique and controversial figure with both strengths and flaws. War drives and inspires Patton. In one scene, after surveying the carnage from a recent battle, he admits, "I love it. God help me, I love it so. I love it more than life." He believes that "compared to war, all other forms of human endeavor shrink to insignificance." Indeed, Patton is so martial-oriented that he believes his fellow Americans share his enthusiasm for war. He says, "All real Americans love the sting of battle." These sentiments reflect the militaristic belief that war is ennobling.[212]

Bravery and courage rank high for Patton, and he holds high standards for himself and his soldiers. Acts of bravery brought out strong emotion in Patton. He almost comes to tears pinning a Purple Heart medal to the pillow of a severely wounded soldier. He kisses the forehead of the sole remaining survivor of a tank platoon that fought the Germans in hand-to-hand combat. In order to preserve the sanctity of sacrifice, he orders that all men with self-inflicted wounds be separated from the men who earned their wounds in combat. The cowards would taint the sacred space of men who suffered for their country. As a result of the high value he places on courage, Patton refuses to acknowledge cases of combat fatigue. In one scene, Patton strikes an enlisted man for breaking down emotionally from the shelling. Patton does not believe he did anything wrong by hitting the soldier. Eisenhower upsets Patton's entire world-view when he forces Patton to apologize for it. Uncomfortable with the apology, Patton explains that he merely wanted to shame the coward to restore the man's self-respect.[213]

Patton molds his men from civilians into accomplished soldiers. He explains, "I don't want the men to love me. I want them to fight for me." He demands exacting discipline and training among his troops, ordering the doctors at the hospital to wear helmets and the cook to wear proper gear in the mess hall. Patton wants his men to fear him rather than the Germans. Behind his back, the soldiers call Patton "Old Blood and Guts." One soldier comments sarcastically, "Yeah, our blood, his guts." After Patton berates a battalion commander during a battle, a major remarks, "Colonel, there are 50,000 men on this island who would like to shoot that son of a bitch." Patton expected bravery from his men because he exhibits courage and selfless disregard for his own safety. During a German air raid, he defiantly stands in the street, shooting his ivory-handled pistol at the offending planes.[214]

Patton sought personal glory for himself. He competes with British Field Marshal Bernard Montgomery, and Patton placed his personal rivalry over that of the mission. Unlike *The Longest Day*, Patton has only contempt for allied warfare and complains about General Eisenhower capitulating to Montgomery's wishes. As a result of Patton trying to beat Montgomery to Messina, General Omar Bradley's forces are left to face stiffer German resistance. Bradley and General Lucian Truscott both plead with Patton to postpone an attack in order to relieve the pressure on their troops. Patton flatly refuses, determined to beat Montgomery to the Sicilian town. Once there, Patton's band plays louder than Montgomery's bagpipes in a contest of one-upmanship.[215]

Patton's battle scenes are infused with a tone of triumph. Patton's army races through France, and his men cheer him in the streets. He volunteers elements of his army to relieve the 101st Airborne Division, which was surrounded by Germans in Bastogne. Although his men must pull out of one fight and travel one hundred miles in the snow to engage another battle, Patton is convinced his soldiers are capable of the challenge. As he walks among his troops, Patton states, "God, I'm proud of these men." They do, indeed, relieve the troops at Bastogne the day after Christmas.[216]

It comes as a personal shock when Patton is relieved of command twice and denied a command in the Pacific at the close of hostilities in Europe. Patton fervently advocates attacking the Soviet army in Germany, though the Soviets are still allies at the time. He complains that "politicians always stop short and leave us another war to fight." The comment is also dis-

Lieutenant General George S. Patton, Jr. (George C. Scott) in a scene from *Patton* (20th Century–Fox, 1970). War drives and inspires Patton. He believes that "compared to war, all other forms of human endeavor shrink to insignificance." This sentiment reflects the militaristic belief that war is ennobling. Audiences polarized by the war in Vietnam interpreted this film very differently, either looking at Patton as a man to emulate in Vietnam or as the kind of militarist officer to reject (photograph by Michael Ochs, Michael Ochs Archives/Getty Images).

turbingly militarist, like something General Scott would say in *Seven Days in May*. In the last scene of the film, however, without a command, Patton is uncertain of his future. As Patton walks his dog in the winter snow, his voiceover intones the last words of the film, "All glory is fleeting." In real life, Patton died in an automobile accident shortly after the events depicted in the film. His personal glory of winning more battles against Japan may have been thwarted, but his legacy certainly remained and was reinforced by this film.[217]

The context of the Vietnam War allowed for alternate interpretations of *Patton*. Those who disliked or distrusted the military could look to Patton's negative qualities, while those who appreciated the military and the values that Patton embodied could focus on those aspects. Some thought a Patton-like general is what was needed to win in Vietnam.[218] Actor George C. Scott chose to accept the role of Patton because, he said, "I liked the man. He was a professional, and I admire professionalism. And for whatever else he was, good or bad, he was an individual. That's what's most important to me today, when everybody around seems to be some kind of damn ostrich."[219] Critic Vincent Canby perceived *Patton* as a reverent treatment of a general about "whom only the Establishment could become genuinely sentimental."[220] He admired that the filmmakers allowed Patton to admit that he loved war, making the film "a good deal less hypocritical than most patriotic American war movies" which pretended war was horrible but actually glorified it, in his view.[221] Had *Patton* appeared before the Vietnam War, audiences and critics might have accepted it simply as "another glorification of a great military leader and a confirmation of America's military superiority in the world."[222] Instead, the Vietnam War made the movie a lightning rod for both pro- and anti-war sentiments.

Within the context of Vietnam, many audience members perceived anti-war or anti-military themes in the film. Peter Schjeldahl, also writing in the *New York Times*, states that the only difference he detected between the massive casualties that Patton wrought on Germany and the periodic Vietnam body counts was one of style and not of nature. He believed it was dishonest to characterize Patton as an anachronism because, "Old generals don't die; they just make way for new generals."[223] Patton, in his estimation, was not the historical aberration the film makes him out to be.[224] In 1971, the anti-establishment *MASH* competed with *Patton* at the Academy Awards. Where *MASH* had been nominated for five Oscars and won one, *Patton* was nominated for ten Oscars and won seven, including Best Picture and Best Actor.

Patton's influence persisted long past the Vietnam era. The character resonates with career soldiers. Roger Spiller, at the Army's Command and General Staff College, observes,

> I have known career military officers who, in a strange sort of burlesque, seem to be acting out their impression of George C. Scott's portrayal of the lead role in *Patton*, knowing all the while that they were doing it, and knowing that others knew as well. What is stranger, the performance seemed to be regarded as an acceptable pose to strike.[225]

In November 2004 in southern Baghdad during Operation Iraqi Freedom, Private First Class Benjamin Morgan repeated to a Public Broadcasting correspondent one of the opening lines from the film *Patton*: "Now I want you to remember that no bastard ever won a war by dying for his country. He won it by making the other poor dumb bastard die for his country!"[226] Whether Morgan knew the film *Patton* well enough to quote it or whether he knew the line because it has been repeated so often, *Patton*'s militarist influence in American culture endures.

CONCLUSION

Two historians writing in the mid–1960s summarized their view of prevailing American sentiment toward citizen-soldiers. Russell Weigley explained that the supporters of the citizen-soldier, and thus supporters of the National Guard and Reserve forces, wanted "an army tied closely to the whole body of the nation" which would "respect nonmilitary national aims."[1] Those citizen-soldiers would be informed citizens who could "pass judgment on military issues."[2] Peter Karsten, in arguing for a positive historical record for America's nonprofessional soldiers, concluded that the American soldier "has never been the model military man; but, happily, neither has America ever been a model military state."[3] From the perspective of these two historians, America remained safe from unbridled militarism.

As the war in Vietnam wound down in the early 1970s, anti-militarism gained ascendency in American culture. After 1970, the number of war films and television shows featuring the military plummeted. Just as American audiences became burned out on war films in 1945, the unpopularity of Vietnam made war stories no longer commercially viable by 1970. When war reappeared on television, it was in the guise of the anti-militarist show, *MASH* (1972–1983). Hollywood resumed production of war films at the end of the decade, but they were dark stories that did not glorify war, such as *The Deer Hunter* (1978) and *Apocalypse Now* (1979). Both in film and on television, Vietnam veterans were often characterized as crazy or mentally unstable, as in the film *Taxi Driver* (1976).

When the draft ended in 1973, the Army in particular suffered a "hollow" decade. The force that returned from Vietnam "was at a low ebb of morale, discipline, and military effectiveness."[4] The Army suffered from large numbers of unauthorized absences and incomplete enlistments, racial tensions and violence within the ranks, drug problems with soldiers, and poor leadership within the ranks of junior officers and non-commissioned officers, among other challenges. Initially, the quality of recruits declined, and the military had to shift to monetary incentives to attract more desirable recruits. In order to make the All Volunteer Force work, the army had to professionalize it by shifting many of the menial tasks, like KP duty, to civilian workers. The Army avoided personnel shortages, in part, by expanding the number of blacks and women in the service. It also integrated women into the force and disbanded the separate Women's Army Corps in 1978.[5]

In the wake of the Vietnam War, Americans became aware of the limits of military power. As Bruce Shulman explains, "Foreign policy debate revolved around the slogan 'No More Vietnams'—around bitterly contested understandings of the failed war in Indochina. For many Americans, 'No More Vietnams' embodied a dovish, neoisolationist lesson."[6] For these Americans, the lessons of Vietnam suggested that the U.S. should no longer intervene in the domestic affairs of other countries, particularly in the Third World, and it should not send its young men to fight and die abroad. The more hawkish interpretation of the Vietnam War, however, came to the opposite conclusions. Instead of becoming dovish, the U.S. should continue its internationalist foreign policy. Should military force be necessary, the military ought not fight "with one hand tied behind its back" in a limited war, but have the full resources to wage a war for clear, unambiguous victory.[7]

The anti-militarism of the 1960s and 1970s created a counter-backlash toward a more open and strident militarism. According to Professor Andrew Bacevich, "The new American militarism made its appearance in reaction to the 1960s and especially to Vietnam," a transition which developed during the following decades.[8] Many groups in American society, including politicians, intellectuals, military officers, religious leaders, and creators of pop culture all "saw military power as the apparent answer to any number of problems" from the decline of "traditional" morality in the 1960s to regaining America's image and confidence after a humiliating defeat.[9] In particular, Bacevich credits President Ronald Reagan with rehabilitating the image of the military, encouraging the American people to support service members as patriots and heroes. Reagan so emphasized the military and infused the Pentagon with funding that it became the single measure of the nation's strength. Bacevich believes these changes happened so gradually that few Americans were necessarily aware of the increasing militarization in policy and culture.[10] Of course, Americans had already measured national strength by military power at least as early as the launch of the Soviet satellite *Sputnik*, which appeared to show superior Russian military capabilities and a "missile gap" in the Soviet's favor. It is true, however, that Reagan's elevation of professional soldiers differed markedly in tone from the emphasis placed on the citizen-soldier during the draft era. The citizen-soldier image emphasized individuality, scrappy inventiveness, and other democratic qualities, while

Reagan's professionals symbolized pride, loyalty, determination, and overwhelming force.

The drive to honor the military that started under Reagan has turned into a strong militarism in American culture. Some Americans now credit the military with all of the nation's freedoms. A poem by Charles M. Province epitomizes the militarism of this segment of the population:

> **It is the soldier,** not the reporter,
> Who has given us freedom of the press.
> **It is the soldier,** not the poet,
> Who has given us freedom of speech.
> **It is the soldier,** not the lawyer,
> Who has given us the right to a fair trial.
> **It is the soldier** who salutes the flag,
> Who serves under the flag and
> Whose coffin is draped by the flag
> Who allows the protester to burn the flag.

Although these words originally appeared on the Northeast Kansas Korean War Memorial, they have been appropriated for other uses.[11] The poem appears in the U.S. Army's *Transition Assistance Workbook* for soldiers returning from deployments in Iraq and Afghanistan.[12] No doubt, many of the soldiers who read the poem did not dwell on it a great deal, as it contains much they have heard several times before in recent political speeches and memorial celebrations. If the founders of the country read this poem, however, they likely would fear what has become of the anti-militarist nation they created.

While the safety of the nation rested in the hands of citizen-soldiers during the era of the peacetime draft, there is a different focus in the era of the All Volunteer Force. Instead of volunteerism reinforcing anti-militarism in American culture, the All Volunteer Force has distanced the American people from the military. As Bacevich notes, the All Volunteer Force severed the link between citizenship and military service that had existed since the end of World War II through the draft. Today, even the National Guard and reserves are near-professional forces, though they were until recently still called citizen-soldiers.[13] Currently, the Army refers to them as "warrior-citizens." Instead of being part of American society, these men and women in uniform are set apart from regular citizens, being warriors first.[14] The implication is that warriors are better than regular citizens because of their sacrifice, courage, and other attributes.

In 2008, a Gallup poll indicated that Americans respected the military the most out of a list of 16 institutions.[15] Americans today continue to embrace the idea of American exceptionalism by seeing the nation as "a benign, liberal, and progressive hegemon."[16] By believing that the American armed forces are standing up for freedom and democracy worldwide, it is easy for Americans to set themselves apart from the "bad guys" whether they be Nazis or terrorists. Despite spending more on their military than the next nine nations combined, Americans still do not consider themselves militaristic. It is often easy for politicians and pundits to play off American fears to justify continued support for an ever-growing national security apparatus.

Unsurprisingly, the new militarism appears in popular culture. Starting in the 1980s, Americans increasingly enjoyed stories where the nation's professional military might overwhelmed the enemy in spectacular displays of technology and armament. Tom Clancy popularized stories that based America's supremacy on its cutting-edge technology and highly trained professionals in novels and films such as *The Hunt for Red October* (1990). Similarly, the naval aviators in *Top Gun* (1986) spend most of the film honing their professional skills. Where the citizen-soldiers of *The Story of G.I. Joe* learned from experience, these professional aviators painstakingly perfect their skills before facing the enemy. When American F-14 Tomcats are outnumbered by enemy MiGs at the end of *Top Gun*, the Americans outfly the enemy with professional skill and even some traditional American ingenuity. More recently, television shows such as *The Unit* (2006–09) glorified the capabilities of super-secret professional covert operatives sent on missions around the world by the president's authority outside of Congressional oversight. Films like *Black Hawk Down* (2001) and *We Were Soldiers* (2002) put the fierce camaraderie of soldiers fighting for each other at the forefront, and do not even allow the political context of the conflict into the background of the story. War is presented as a noble endeavor and its soldiers as heroes. The militarist elements of these films differ from the kind of militarism present in the early Cold War. Even John Wayne's martial characters do not match the spectacular military might of a John Rambo.

The addition of realistic wounds and frequent violent death scenes in the movies and on television has not swayed Americans from supporting the military or supporting the aggressive use of military power in preventive war. American audiences have become accustomed to and desensitized to the realism of battle violence and death. While the graphic opening of the Normandy invasion in *Saving Private Ryan* (1998) caused a sensation when it first premiered, it has not disillusioned Americans from war. If anything, the gruesome scenes have reinforced the drive to pay tribute to America's veterans by showing how badly they suffered.[17]

Though no longer dominant in American culture, anti-militarist themes do persist at a very low-key level. The comedy film *Stripes* (1981) pokes fun at the military, and its characters are a band of misfits, not the brave heroes of the Reagan and post–9/11 eras. Hollywood even remade the television series

The Phil Silvers Show into the contemporary film *Sgt. Bilko* (1996), starring comedian Steve Martin as the lead character. *Beetle Bailey* celebrated its six-tieth anniversary in 2010, and still ruffles feathers. Army Vice Chief of Staff Peter Chiarelli described the comic as "occasionally inappropriate."[18] Vietnam television series *Tour of Duty* (1987–1990) and *China Beach* (1988–1991) dis-played less romanticized, more realistic views of the military and of war, much in the model of *Combat!* More recently, director James Cameron pro-duced a stridently anti-militarist film, *Avatar* (2009), which sympathizes with native aliens against the technologically superior militarized mercenaries from Earth who have come to advance the interests of a human mining com-pany. In this era of twenty-first century militarism, however, some viewers have criticized the "hidden" anti-military message in the film.[19] Americans of the twenty-first century take it for granted that the brave, technologically superior American military force is the "good guy" in the story. Anti-militarism still exists in the twenty-first century, but it is far less prevalent or accepted than it was during the 1940s, 1950s, and Vietnam era.

While this new era of militarism has its roots in earlier decades, the mil-itarization of 1945–1970 co-existed with a strong anti-militarist self-percep-tion among the population and anti-militarist images in popular culture. Though Americans supported national security, they put their trust more in citizen-soldiers (volunteers and draftees) than in the regulars. From polls to contemporary observations, Americans perceived themselves as anti-mili-taristic, particularly because the nation did not follow the path of autocratic nations like Nazi Germany, which is how they defined militarism. In their eyes, their nation did not use military power aggressively (though citizens elsewhere in the world might disagree with that statement), and the military neither usurped power from civilian authorities nor imposed military disci-pline and regimentation on society. The draftee military force of 1940–1972, plus the draft-induced "volunteers" Selective Service produced, gave millions of citizens insights into the foibles of military life and appreciation for the humor of a Beetle Bailey or a Sergeant Bilko. For many veterans, these military experiences helped deflect militarist cultural messages from them and those family and friends they influenced.

Military recruiters found that overt militarist images did not work well in recruiting volunteers. Recruiting advertising almost always focused on the education, training, and benefits that the military could offer in support of a future civilian career. Military service offered travel and adventure, too, and the chance to work on state-of-the-art technology. Only the Marine Corps consistently used more martial imagery and language in their advertising. Even in time of war, military advertising did not rely on battle imagery to find recruits. More patriotic themes did appear during times of war, but these did not dominate recruiting imagery. Recruiting for women, of course, not only shied away from any militarist language, it assured women they would retain their femininity and marriageability while in the service of their country. Military service for women, according to advertisements, was essentially a patriotic vacation.

Popular images of citizen-soldiers during the era of the draftee military convey both pro- and anti-military sentiments. Popular culture reflected both the attitudes of those who romanticized the military and combat and those who questioned those interpretations. Comedies often depicted an anti-militarist message, as the characters parodied the military. For every Sergeant Stryker, there was a Sergeant Bilko who subverted protocol, decorum, and authority. Military dramas presented citizen-soldiers like Audie Murphy and Sergeant Saunders as the equals in combat of regular soldiers. Other examples underscore the vulnerability of America's Constitution by military professionals, as in the satirical comedy *Dr. Strangelove* and the drama *Seven Days in May*. These examples confirm that anti-militarism remained a strong narrative in national culture.

On September 3, 2010, in honor of *Beetle Bailey's* 60th anniversary, newspapers printed one of the winners of the "Best of Beetle Bailey" fan favorite strips originally published in 1964. Sgt. Snorkel and Beetle are peering through binoculars from a hillside observation post. Sarge asks Beetle, "See anything?" Beetle reports, "I see happy children at play ... people of all races working together ... busy factories with no pollution...." Sarge looks over at Beetle's field glasses. "Wups," he says, "You got the rose-colored ones."[20] Though a commentary on the social, racial, and environmental issues in 1960s America, many of these themes are still relevant for Americans of the twenty-first century. Perhaps there are other things Americans can learn from this historically anti-militarist character.

CHAPTER NOTES

Introduction

1. "Battle for McHale's Island," *McHale's Navy*, aired December 20, 1962 (UCLA Film and Television Archives).

2. Alfred Vagts, *A History of Militarism: Romance and Realities of a Profession* (New York: W. W. Norton, 1937), 15. See also Volker Rolf Berghahn, *Militarism: The History of an International Debate, 1861–1979* (New York: St. Martin's, 1982); Peter H. Wilson, "Defining Military Culture," *The Journal of Military History* 72 (January 2008): 11–41.

3. Arthur A. Ekirch, Jr., "Militarism and Antimilitarism," in *The Oxford Companion to American Military History*, ed. John Whiteclay Chambers II (New York: Oxford University Press, 1999), 438. A longer introduction to the concept is in Arthur A. Ekirch, Jr., *The Civilian and the Military: A History of the American Antimilitarist Tradition* (Colorado Springs: Ralph Myles, 1972).

4. Michael S. Sherry, *In the Shadow of War: The United States Since the 1930s* (New Haven, CT: Yale University Press, 1995), xi.

5. Ekirch, "Militarism and Antimilitarism," 438.

6. Richard H. Kohn, "The Danger of Militarization in an Endless 'War' on Terrorism," *The Journal of Military History* 73 (January 2009), 186.

7. Christian G. Appy, "'We'll Follow the Old Man': The Strains of Sentimental Militarism in Popular Films of the Fifties," in *Rethinking Cold War Culture*, Peter J. Kuznick and James Gilbert, eds. (Washington, D.C.: Smithsonian Institution, 2001), 76.

8. J. Fred MacDonald, *Television and the Red Menace: The Video Road to Vietnam* (New York: Praeger, 1985); David L. Robb, *Operation Hollywood: How the Pentagon Shapes and Censor the Movies* (Amherst, NY: Prometheus, 2004); Stephen J. Whitfield, *The Culture of the Cold War*, second ed. (Baltimore: Johns Hopkins University Press, 1996).

9. Carl Boggs and Tom Pollard, *The Hollywood War Machine: U.S. Militarism and Popular Culture* (Boulder, CO: Paradigm, 2007), xi.

10. Benjamin L. Alpers, "This Is the Army: Imagining a Democratic Military in World War II," *Journal of American History* 85, no. 1 (1998), 132.

11. Melvin J. Lasky, "A New German Army: Hopes and Fears," *New York Times*, July 10, 1955, SM 7.

12. Ekirch, *The Civilian and the Military*, xv.

13. See Ricardo Herrera, "Self-Governance and the American Citizen as Soldier, 1775–1861," *The Journal of Military History* 65 (January 2001): 21–52; Ekirch, *The Civilian and the Military*; Benjamin L. Alpers, This Is the Army: Imagining a Democratic Military in World War II," *Journal of American History* 85, no. 1 (1998): 129–163.

14. For some of the most significant studies of the origins of the anti-standing military tradition, see Bernard Bailyn, *The Ideological Origins of the American Revolution* (Cambridge: MA: Belknap Press of Harvard University Press, 1967); J. G. A. Pocock, *The Machiavellian Moment: Florentine Political Thought and the Atlantic Republican Tradition* (Princeton, NJ: Princeton University Press, 1975); Lawrence Delbert Cress, *Citizens in Arms: The Army and the Militia in American Society to the War of 1812* (Chapel Hill: University of North Carolina Press, 1982); James Kirby Martin and Mark Edward Lender, *A Respectable Army: The Military Origins of the Republic, 1763–1789* (Arlington Heights, IL: H. Davidson, 1982); E. Wayne Carp, *To Starve the Army at Pleasure: Continental Army Administration and American Political Culture, 1775–1783* (Chapel Hill: University of North Carolina Press, 1984); Jack P. Green, *The American Revolution: Its Character and Limits* (New York: New York University

Press, 1987); Gordon S. Wood, *The Radicalism of the American Revolution* (New York: Vintage, 1992); Joyce Appleby, *Liberalism and Republicanism in the Historical Imagination* (Cambridge, MA: Harvard University Press, 1992); and Alan Ray Gibson, *Interpreting the Founding: Guide to the Enduring Debates Over the Origins and Foundations of the American Republic* (Lawrence: University Press of Kansas, 2006).

15. Jerry Cooper, *The Rise of the National Guard: The Evolution of the American Militia, 1865–1920* (Lincoln: University of Nebraska Press, 1997), 4.

16. Cooper, *The Rise of the National Guard*, 70, 106, 158. For a study of the nineteenth-century militia, see Marcus Cunliffe, *Soldiers and Civilians: The Martial Spirit in America, 1775–1865* (New York: Free, 1973). For an analysis of how changing concepts of nineteenth-century masculinity affected the National Guard, see Eleanor L. Hannah, *Manhood, Citizenship, and the National Guard: Illinois, 1870–1917* (Columbus: Ohio State University Press, 2007).

17. Cooper, *The Rise of the National Guard*, xiii.

18. Russell Porter, "New Army Fighter Is Citizen-Soldier," *New York Times*, November 2, 1948, 27, 32.

19. "Why the GIs Demonstrate," *New Republic*, January 21, 1946, 72; "Germany's New Army," *New York Times*, November 12, 1955; Lasky, "A New German Army: Hopes and Fears," 52; Arthur J. Olsen, "Bonn to Elevate 'Citizen-Soldier,'" *New York Times*, May 8, 1960, 15.

20. George Flynn, *The Draft, 1940–1973* (Lawrence: University Press of Kansas, 1993), 3.

21. See Michael S. Nieberg, *Making Citizen-Soldiers: ROTC and the Ideology of American Military Service* (Cambridge, MA: Harvard University Press, 2000). In *The Hollywood War Machine*, Carl Boggs and Tom Pollard argue the opposite view less convincingly: that any experience with the military automatically militarizes civilians.

22. See William H. Chafe, *The Paradox of Change: American Women in the 20th Century* (New York: Oxford University Press, 1991); Joanne Meyerowitz, *Not June Cleaver: Women and Gender in Postwar America, 1945–1960* (Philadelphia: Temple University Press, 1994); Elaine Tyler May, *Homeward Bound: American Families in the Cold War Era*. Revised and Updated ed. (New York: Basic, 1999); Susan, Douglas, *Where the Girls Are: Growing Up Female with the Mass Media* (New York: Random House, 1994); Richard M. Dalfiume, *Desegregation of the U.S. Armed Forces: Fighting on Two Fronts, 1939–1953* (Columbia: University of Missouri Press, 1969); Mary L. Dudziak, *Cold War Civil Rights: Race and the Image of American Democracy* (Princeton, NJ: Princeton University Press, 2000); Bernard C. Nalty, *Strength for the Fight: A History of Black Americans in the Military* (New York: Free, 1986); James E. Westheider, *Fighting on Two Fronts: African Americans and the Vietnam War* (New York: New York University Press, 1997).

23. Beth Bailey, *America's Army: Making the All Volunteer Force* (Cambridge, MA: The Belknap Press of Harvard University Press, 2009), 188.

24. Andrew J. Huebner, *The Warrior Image: Soldiers in American Culture from the Second World War to the Vietnam Era* (Chapel Hill: University of North Carolina Press, 2008), 132; U.S. Census Bureau, *Historical National Population Estimates*, available at http://www.census.gov/popest/archives/1990s/popclockest.txt (accessed 20 July 2010).

25. Bailey, *America's Army*, 198.

Chapter 1

1. *The Story of G.I. Joe*, directed by William Wellman (United Artists, 1945).

2. Benjamin L. Alpers, "This Is the Army: Imagining a Democratic Military in World War II," *Journal of American History* 85, no. 1 (1998), 132.

3. For an example, see "Terms for Japan," *New Republic*, July 30, 1945, 119–120.

4. Henry Wallace, "Militarization in the United States," *New Republic*, January 26, 1948, 22.

5. Melvin Lasky, "A New German Army: Hopes and Fears," *New York Times*, July 10, 1955, SM 7.

6. Ibid.

7. Michael Strake, "Atomic Attack," *New Republic*, 21 September 21, 1953, 7.

8. Alpers, "This Is the Army," 135–36; "Text of the House Post-War Military Policy Committee Report on Universal Military Training," *New York Times*, July 6, 1945; George C. Marshall, "Testimony Before the House Select Committee on Postwar Military Policy," in *The Draft and Its Enemies*, eds., John O'Sullivan and Alan M. Meckler (Urbana: University of Illinois Press, 1974), 193.

9. Porter, "New Army Fighter Is Citizen-Soldier," 32.

10. Gerald W. Johnson, "Horse Without Rider," *New Republic*, January 20, 1958, 8.

11. "Why the GIs Demonstrate," *New Republic*, January 21, 1946, 73.

12. Michael S. Neiberg, *Making Citizen-Soldiers: ROTC and the Ideology of American Military Service* (Cambridge: Harvard University Press, 2000), 3, 40.

13. Peter S. Kindsvatter, *American Soldiers: Ground Combat in the World Wars, Korea, and Vietnam* (Lawrence: University Press of Kansas, 2003), 263.

14. Samuel Hynes, *The Soldiers' Tale: Bearing Witness to Modern War* (New York: Penguin, 1997), 145. Emphasis in the original.

15. James Tobin, *Ernie Pyle's War: America's Eyewitness to World War II* (Lawrence: University Press of Kansas, 1997), 132, 242.

16. Lawrence H. Suid, *Guts & Glory: The Making of the American Military Image in Film*, revised and expanded ed. (Lexington: University Press of Kentucky, 2002), 92.

17. *The Story of G.I. Joe*, directed by William Wellman (United Artists, 1945).

18. Thomas M. Pryor, review of *The Story of G.I. Joe*, *New York Times*, October 6, 1945, 9.

19. Ibid.

20. Thomas M. Pryor, review of *The Story of G.I. Joe*, *New York Times*, October 14, 1945, X1.

21. Review of *The Story of G.I. Joe*, *Time*, July 23, 1945, 96.

22. Quoted in review of *The Story of G.I. Joe*, *Time*, July 23, 1945, 96.

23. "'G.I. Joe' Seen in Rome," *New York Times*, July 24, 1945, 26.

24. *A Walk in the Sun*, directed by Lewis Milestone (Twentieth Century–Fox, 1945); Steven Jay Rubin, *Combat Films: American Realism: 1945–1970* (Jefferson, NC: McFarland, 1981), 4–5.

25. *A Walk in the Sun*, directed by Lewis Milestone (Twentieth Century–Fox, 1945).

26. Bosley Crowther, review of *A Walk in the Sun*, *New York Times*, January 12, 1946, 10.

27. Review of *A Walk in the Sun*, *Time*, January 14, 1946, 90.

28. *All Quiet on the Western Front*, directed by Lewis Milestone (Universal Pictures, 1930).

29. Garry Wills, *John Wayne's America* (New York: Simon and Schuster, 1997), 112.

30. *They Were Expendable*, directed by John Ford (MGM, 1945).

31. Ibid.

32. Bosley Crowther, "'They Were Expendable' Seen at Capitol, Called Stirring Picture of Small but Vital Aspect of War Just Ended," *New York Times*, December 21, 1945, 25.

33. Ibid.

34. Review of *They Were Expendable*, *Time*, December 24, 1945, 98.

35. Rubin, 22; Suid, *Guts and Glory*, 97; Lawrence H. Suid, *Sailing on the Silver Screen: Hollywood and the U.S. Navy* (Annapolis, MD: Naval Institute, 1996), 81.

36. John O'Sullivan and Alan M. Meckler, eds., *The Draft and Its Enemies: A Documentary History* (Urbana: University of Illinois Press, 1974), 162.

37. "Why GIs Demonstrate," *New Republic*, January 21, 1946, 73.

38. George C. Marshall, Testimony before the House Select Committee on Postwar Military Policy, in *The Draft and Its Enemies*, John O'Sullivan and Alan M. Meckler, eds. (Urbana: University of Illinois Press, 1974), 193.

39. Samuel A. Stouffer, Arthur A. Lumsdaine, Marion Harper Lumsdaine, Robin M. Williams, Jr., M. Brewster Smoth, Irving L. Janis, Shirley A. Star, and Leonard S. Cottrell, Jr., *The American Soldier: Combat and Its Aftermath, Vol. II* (New York: John Wiley and Sons, 1949; reprint, Manhattan, KS: *Military Affairs* with permission of Princeton University Press, 1977), 610.

40. Ibid., 615.

41. Ibid., 590.

42. Lori Lyn Bogle, *The Pentagon's Battle for the American Mind: The Early Cold War* (College Station: Texas A&M University Press, 2004), 50.

43. Arthur Eaton, "Getting Out of the Army," *New Republic*, September 3, 1945, 285. See also, "Why the GIs Demonstrate," *New Republic*, January 21, 1946, 72–73.

44. Knickerbocker Productions, "To the Ladies," October 1947, Box 1, Motion Picture: Scripts, Correspondence, etc., 1947–1953: Special Film Projects 115–228, Pictorial Branch, Office of Information Services, RG 340, NARA; Letter from Howard Lesser to Joseph Yovin, 21 November 1947, Box 1, Motion Picture Scripts, Correspondence, etc., 1947–1953: Special Film Projects 115–228, Pictorial Branch, Office of Information Services, RG 340, NARA and Records Administration (hereafter NARA).

45. Knickerbocker Productions, Inc., "To the Ladies"; Mattie E. Treadwell, *The Women's Army Corps* (Washington, D.C.: GPO, 1990), 191. Women who worked in the factories during World War II were also praised for such feminine qualities as manual dexterity. See William H. Chafe, *The Paradox of Change: American Women in the 20th Century* (New York: Oxford University Press, 1991), 124.

46. R. Alton Lee, "The Army 'Mutiny' of 1946," *The Journal of American History* 53, no. 3 (1966): 555–71; United States Center of Military History, *American Military History*, Revised ed., *Army Historical Series* (Washington, D.C.: GPO, 1989), 530–31. See also John C. Sparrow, *History of Personnel Demobilization in the United States Army*, Reprint ed. (Washington, D.C.: U.S. Army Center of Military History, 1994).

47. Charles C. Moskos, Jr., *The American Enlisted Man: The Rank and File in Today's Military* (New York: Russell Sage Foundation, 1970), 2; Allan R. Millett, *The War for Korea, 1950–1951: They Came from the North* (Lawrence: University Press of Kansas, 2010), 54.

48. Flynn, 94–95; Mark R. Grandstaff, "Making the Military American: Advertising, Reform, and

the Demise of an Antistanding Military Tradition, 1945–1955," *Journal of Military History* 60, no. 2 (1996), 301.

49. George Gallup, *The Gallup Poll: Public Opinion, 1935–1937*, vol. 1, 1935–1948 (New York: Random House, 1972), 566, 575. The poll conducted from March 15–20, 1946 revealed 65 percent support for the continuation of the draft while the poll taken from April 26–May 5, 1946 indicates 63 percent approval.

50. "The Army," *Life*, April 22, 1946, 29.

51. Alan Brinkley, *The Publisher: Henry Luce and His American Century* (New York: Alfred A. Knopf, 2010), 330.

52. "What Does Mr. Truman Mean?" *New Republic*, November 5, 1945, 587.

53. Ibid.

54. Gallup, *The Gallup Poll*, vol. 1, 601. Americans were interviewed between 30 August 30 and September 4, 1946.

55. "Drum Sees Danger of New Conflict," *New York Times*, September 6, 1947, 2.

56. Russell Weigley, *History of the United States Army* (New York: The Macmillan Company, 1967), 501. Weigley proposes that the idea of universal military training gained acceptance outside the military during the 1940s and early 1950s because of its emphasis on "a citizen army attuned to democratic institutions." Universal military training did not become policy largely because most Americans and their elected officials envisioned the next war as an atomic one, fought primarily by the Air Force. A large number of trained soldiers for the Army did not appear necessary.

57. "Text of Report for Post-War Training," *New York Times*, July 6, 1945, 7.

58. Ibid.

59. "The Quarter's Polls," *The Public Opinion Quarterly* 9, no. 4 (1945–1946), 521.

60. "General Ike," *New Republic*, July 2, 1945, 5.

61. "Universal Military Training," *New Republic*, June 23, 1947, 11. See a similar editorial: Michael Straight, "Billions for Aggressive War," *New Republic*, February 2, 1948, 15–16.

62. Henry Wallace, "Universal Military Training," *New Republic*, December 1, 1947, 12.

63. Ibid. See also Henry Wallace, "Militarization in the United States," *New Republic*, January 26, 1948, 22–23.

64. Bogle, 61–63.

65. Robert Taft, Speech at Gettysburg National Cemetery, May 30, 1945 in *The Draft and Its Enemies*, 191.

66. George Marshall, "Chief of Staff Gives His Ideas of What We Require to Prevent Another Catastrophe," *New York Times*, October 10, 1945, S11.

67. Ibid.

68. Ibid.

69. Bogle, 69; Helen Guller, "UMT's Big Barrage Falls Short," *New Republic*, February 16, 1948, 6.

70. Flynn, 100.

71. Albert Somit, "The Military Hero as Presidential Candidate," *The Public Opinion Quarterly* 12, no. 2 (1948), 193.

72. Strake, "Atomic Attack," 7–8.

73. Souffer, et al., *The American Soldier, Vol. II*, 598.

74. William Wyler, *The Best Years of Our Lives* (RKO, 1946).

75. Bosley Crowther, review of *The Best Years of Our Lives*, *New York Times*, November 22, 1946, 27. It also won Best Director (William Wyler), Best Actor in a Supporting Role (Harold Russell, who also received an Honorary Oscar, probably designed to be a consolation prize because it was assumed that he would lose the bigger award; consequently, he became the *only* performer to take home two Oscars for a *single* role in one film), Best Film Editing, and Best Original Score.

76. Mitchell K. Hall, *Crossroads: American Popular Culture and the Vietnam Generation* (Lanham, MD: Rowman and Littlefield, 2005), 2. About 90 million people went to a movie each week in 1946.

77. Bureau of Naval Personnel, "The Fable of Whyte Hatt, Civilian," n.d. Box 52, Recruiting Circular Thru Recruiting-Misc., Document Collection of the Technical Library, 1942–1947, Administrative and Management Division, RG 24, NARA.

78. Ibid., Emphasis in the original.

79. Bureau of Naval Personnel, "Looking Ahead (Second)," December 29, 1945, Box 53, Recruiting Circular Thru Recruiting-Misc., Document Collection of the Technical Library, 1900–1985, Administrative and Management Division, RG 24, NARA; Bureau of Naval Personnel, "An Officer's Career in the Peacetime Navy," October 22, 1945, Box 52, Recruiting Circular Thru Recruiting-Misc., Document Collection of the Technical Library, 1900–1985, Administrative and Management Division, RG 24, NARA.

80. Bureau of Naval Personnel, "There's More Room at the Top in the U.S. Navy," n.d., Box 52, Recruiting Circular Thru Recruiting-Misc., Document Collection of the Technical Library, 1900–1985, Administrative and Management Division, RG 24, NARA.

81. United States Army, "Army Day," *Life*, April 1, 1946, 98.

82. Bureau of Naval Personnel, "An Officer's Career in the Peacetime Navy."

83. Ibid.; Bureau of Naval Personnel, "There's More Room at the Top."

84. Grandstaff, 306–07.

85. Gallup, *The Gallup Poll*, vol. 1, 574.

86. Porter, "New Army Fighter Is Citizen-Soldier," 32.

87. Souffer, et al., *The American Soldier, Vol. II*, 598.

88. Gallup, *The Gallup Poll*, vol. 1, 575–76, 600.

89. Richard M. Dalfiume, *Desegregation of the U.S. Armed Forces: Fighting on Two Fronts, 1939–1953* (Columbia: University of Missouri Press, 1969), 171. See also Bernard C. Nalty, *Strength for the Fight: A History of Black Americans in the Military* (New York: Free, 1986), 242; Sherry, 145.

90. Gallup, *The Gallup Poll*, vol. 1, 758. Americans approved the draft law by 73 percent.

91. Flynn, 118.

92. Gallup, *The Gallup Poll*, vol. 1, 667.

93. Susan H. Godson, *Serving Proudly: A History of Women in the U.S. Navy* (Annapolis, MD: Naval Institute, 2001), 115; Jeanne Holm, *Women in the Military: An Unfinished Revolution*. Revised ed. (Novato, CA: Presidio, 1992), 116–118.

94. "Forrestal Urges Corps for Women," *New York Times*, 19 February 19, 1948, 20.

95. Ibid.

96. Holm, 108–113; Bettie J. Morden, *The Women's Army Corps, 1945–1978, Army Historical Series*. (Washington, D.C.: Government Printing Office, 1990), 49–55.

97. Sherry, 150.

98. Godson, 182; Holm, 122.

99. Director of Recruiting, "What the Marine Corps Has Done and Is Doing to Recruit Women Marines," September 28, 1951, Box 141, Central Files, P14-3/1–P14-4, July 1, 1950–December 31, 1955, RG 127, NARA; Grandstaff, 302–306; Anna Rosenberg to George H. Mahon, 1951, Box 20, Formerly Classified General Correspondence, Public Information Division, Office of Information Services, RG 340, NARA; The Chief of Naval Personnel, "Naval Reserve Recruiting Publicity for Fiscal 1950," August 25, 1949, Box 502, General Correspondence, 1946–1960: P14-4/P14-(A–Q), January 1949–December 1949, Administrative and Management Division, RG 24, NARA; Arthur Hews Peterson, "An Investigation of the United States Army and United States Air Force Recruiting Organization and Program" (MS: Columbia University, 1948), 70–71.

100. Commander John P. Floyd, Memorandum to the Director of Civil Relations: Meeting of the Joint Committee on Procurement of Personnel, November 13, 1947, Box 7, Subject Files P14-4, Office of Information, RG 428, NARA; Lieutenant Colonel R. H. Hayden, Memorandum for Counsel for Bureau of Naval Personnel, June 23, 1949, Box 502, P14-4 January 1, 1952–December 1952 through P14-4/P14 (A–Q) January 1949–December 1949, General Correspondence 1946–1960, 1949–52, Administrative and Management Division, RG 24, NARA; Francis P. Matthews to Mr. John P. Davis, June 28, 1949, Box 502, P14-4 January 1, 1952–December 1952 through P14-4/P14 (A–Q) January 1949–December 1949, General Correspondence 1946–1960, 1949–52, Administrative and Management Division, RG 24, NARA.

101. Director of Recruiting, "What the Marine Corps Had Done Is Doing to Recruit Women Marines"; Grandstaff, 304–305; Peterson, 70–71; Rosenberg to Mahon, "Naval Reserve Recruiting Publicity for Fiscal 1950."

102. Grandstaff, 304–306; Peterson, 2, 30.

103. Air-Age Education Liaison Officer, "U.S. Navy's Liaison with the Schools of America and the Applicability of Some of Its Methods to the Problem of Recruiting Combat Infantrymen," March 31, 1950, Box 23, Central Subject Files, 1949–1950, Office of Information, RG 428, NARA.

104. Allan R. Millett, *Semper Fidelis: The History of the United States Marine Corps* (New York: Macmillan, 1980), 467.

105. Grandstaff, 302–306.

106. Bureau of Naval Personnel, "The World Is Your Office," n.d. Folder: Recruiting — Misc. Occupational Specialties Pamphlets, Box 53, Document Collection of the Technical Library, 1900–1985, Administrative and Management Division, RG 24, NARA.

107. Major Ernest P. Schwartz, Memorandum on Air Force Motion Picture "New Wings for Peace," June 10, 1949, Box 2, Special Film Projects 229–236, Motion Picture Scripts, Correspondence, etc., 1949–1953, Office of Information Services, Pictorial Branch, RG 340, NARA.

108. U.S. Army and U.S. Air Force Recruiting Service, "That's Your Future on His Shoulder," *Life*, October 4, 1949, 155.

109. Grandstaff, 313.

110. U.S. Army and U.S. Air Force Recruiting Service, "That's Your Future on His Shoulder," 155.

111. Ibid.

112. U.S. Army and U.S. Air Force Recruiting Service, "The Inside Story on Your New Army," *Life*, March 28, 1949, 125.

113. According to Carl Builder, each military service has a personality. The Army and Marine Corps are more people-focused, while the Navy emphasizes tradition, and the Air Force emphasizes technology. See Carl H. Builder, *The Masks of War* (Baltimore: Johns Hopkins University Press, 1989), 17–30.

114. "Handwriting on the Sonic Wall," *Saturday Evening Post*, March 20, 1949, 104.

115. Schwartz, Memo on "New Wings for Peace."

116. U.S. Army and United States Air Force Recruiting Service, "How Small Is Your World?" *Life*, September 13, 1948, 1975; United States Army and United States Air Force Recruiting Service, "They Proved Mark Twain Was Wrong," *Life*, April 25, 1949, 137.

117. Bureau of Naval Personnel, "The Navy Airman," June 15, 1948, Box 53, Document Collection of the Technical Library, 1900–1985, Administrative and Management Division, RG 24, NARA.

118. Allan R. Millett and Peter Maslowski, *For the Common Defense: A Military History of the United States of America*, revised and expanded ed. (New York: Free, 1994), 504–505.

119. "Salute the New National Guard," *Life*, April 21, 1947, 26–27.

120. A.F. Stonesifer, "Weekend Paratrooper SPF 262," November 17, 1950, Box 6, Special Film Projects 256–266, Motion Picture Scripts, Correspondence, etc., 1947–1953, Pictorial Branch, Office of Information Services, RG 340, NARA.

121. United States Army Organized Reserve Corps, "It Takes More Than Talk," *Popular Science*, July 1950, 6.

122. A. F. Stonesifer, "Weekend Paratrooper SFP 262," November 17, 1950, Box 6, Special Film Projects 256–266, Motion Picture Scripts, Correspondence, etc., 1947–1953, Pictorial Branch, Office of Information Services, RG 340, NARA; United States Naval Reserve, "Naval Reserve," February 10, 1950, Box 53, Document Collection of the Technical Library, 1900–85, Administration and Management Division, RG 24, NARA.

123. William M. Donnelly, *Under Army Orders: The Army National Guard During the Korean* War (College Station: Texas A&M University Press, 2001), 17. The "Go with the Men You Know" gained new traction during the Korean War, particularly with men who were receiving their draft notices. See Donnelly, chapter 2.

124. United States Marine Corps Headquarters Personnel Research Division, "A Comparison of the Attitudes of Two Groups of One Year Enlistees," 1949, Box 561, General Correspondence January 1939–June 1950, 1535-10 to 1535, Office of the Commandant, RG 127, NARA.

125. Ibid.

126. Ibid.

127. Ibid.

128. Those favoring civilian job security jumped from 11 percent to 44 percent. Office of the Director of Personnel in Headquarters United States Marine Corps, Procedures Analysis Office, "One Year Enlistees: Their Attitudes Upon Entering the Marine Corps; Their Attitudes After Service One Year," February 1950, Box 561, 1535-10 to 1535, Office of the Commandant, RG 127, NARA.

129. Ibid.

130. Ibid.

131. U.S. Army, "Re-enlistments: One of Your Chief Responsibilities as an Officer in the United States Army," Box 452, Decimal 341–350, Decimal File, 1949, Army Chief of Staff, RG 319, NARA.

132. Ibid.

133. Attitude Research Branch, "Sources of Information About the Air Force and Reasons for Enlistment," March 1950, Armed Forced I & E Division, Surveys on Troop Attitudes, 1942–June 1955, Assistant Secretary of Defense (Manpower, Personnel, & Reserve), RG 330, NARA.

134. Ibid. Recruiting advertising was visible: 98 percent of enlistees remembered recruiting posters, 68 percent recalled magazine ads, and 69 percent had heard radio advertisements. Television was a new technology, and only 9 percent remembered seeing an advertisement there. Airmen rated the sources of favorable impressions of the Air Force as follows: posters at 92 percent, magazine ads at 76 percent, and radio spots at 75 percent.

135. Stouffer, *The American Soldier, Vol. II*, 596–97, 643.

136. Quoted in Peter J. Kuznick and James Gilbert, "U.S. Culture and the Cold War," in *Rethinking Cold War Culture*, Peter J. Kuznick and James Gilbert, eds. (Washington, D.C.: Smithsonian Institution Press, 2001), 2.

137. Hanson W. Baldwin, *Great Mistakes of the War* (New York: Harper and Brothers, 1949; facsimile print, Ann Arbor, MI: University Microfilms International, 1978), 14.

138. Ibid., 10

139. Ibid.

140. Ibid., 90–106.

141. B. H. Liddell Hart, *The German Generals Talk* (New York: William Morrow, 1948), 194; quoted in Baldwin, *Great Mistakes of the War*, 108. The quotation is from a captured German general.

142. Gallup, *The Gallup Poll*, vol. 1, 679.

143. Ibid.

144. Ibid.

145. Ibid.

146. Stouffer, *The American Soldier, Vol. II*, 633.

147. Gerald F. Lindermann, *The World Within War: America's Combat Experience in World War II* (New York: Free, 1997), 360–61.

148. Tim Brooks and Earle Marsh, *The Complete Directory to Prime Time Network TV Shows, 1946– Present*, fourth ed. (New York: Ballantine, 1988), 174.

149. Ibid., MacDonald, *Television and the Red Menace*, 112.

150. Suid, *Guts and Glory*, 104.

151. Rubin, 24–36.

152. *Battleground*, directed by William Wellman (United Artists, 1945).

153. Ibid.

154. Ibid.

155. Bosley Crowther, review of *Battleground*, *New York Times*, November 12, 1949, 8.

156. Review of *Battleground* by William Wellman, *Time*, November 14, 1949, 105. *What Price Glory* set many standards in military film storytelling by the characters Quirt and Flagg in both peacetime and wartime settings.

157. Review of *Battleground*, *Time*, 106. *Task Force* is a documentary-style film highlighting the Navy's use of aircraft carriers in the Pacific during World War II. *Command Decision* focuses on the pressures of command during the early stages of the Army Air Force's strategic bombing campaign against Germany.

158. Suid, *Guts & Glory*, 109.

159. Ivan Butler, *The War Film* (South Brunswick, NJ: A.S. Barnes, 1974), 83; Rubin, 129.

160. Williamson Murray and Allan R. Millett, *A War to Be Won: Fighting the Second World War* (Cambridge, MA: Belknap Press of Harvard University Press, 2001), 317.

161. Ground forces could only endure about three days of continuous combat before losing effectiveness. Michael D. Doubler, *Closing with the Enemy: How GIs Fought the War in Europe, 1944–1945* (Lawrence: University Press of Kansas, 1994), 25.

162. Henry King, *Twelve O'Clock High* (USA: Twentieth Century–Fox, 1949).

163. Ibid.

164. Ibid.

165. Ibid.

166. Review of *Twelve O'Clock High*, *Time*, January 30, 1950, 84.

167. Bosley Crowther, "The War in Retrospect," *New York Times*, January 30, 1950, 73.

168. Ibid.

169. Ibid.

170. "Movies: The War Goes On," *New Republic*, January 30, 1950, 30.

171. *Sands of Iwo Jima*, directed by Allan Dwan (Republic Pictures, 1949).

172. Craig M. Cameron, *American Samurai: Myth, Imagination, and the Conduct of Battle in the First Marine Division, 1941–1951* (New York: Cambridge University Press, 1994), 261; Suid, *Guts & Glory*, 116–35.

173. *Sands of Iwo Jima*, directed by Allan Dwan (Republic Pictures, 1949).

174. Jeanine Basinger, *The World War II Combat Film: Anatomy of a Genre*, Updated ed. (Middletown, CT: Wesleyan University Press, 2003), 153–54.

175. Suid, *Guts and Glory*, 122–23.

176. Thomas M. Pryor, Review of *Sands of Iwo Jima*, *New York Times*, December 31, 1949, 9.

177. Ibid.

178. Review of *Sands of Iwo Jima*, *Time*, January 16, 1950, 86.

179. Linderman, *The World Within War*, 315.

180. Ibid., 362.

181. Ibid., 360.

182. Tom Engelhardt, *The End of Victory Culture: Cold War America and the Disillusioning of a Generation* (Amherst: University of Massachusetts Press, 1995), 73. Emphasis in the original.

183. Ibid., 52.

184. Frank J. Wetta and Stephen J. Curley, *Celluloid Wars: A Guide to Film and the American Experience of War* (New York: Greenwood, 1992), 1–2.

185. Ron Kovic, *Born on the Fourth of July* (New York: Pocket, 1976), 54–55.

186. Philip Caputo, *A Rumor of War* (New York: Ballantine, 1977), 6.

187. Ibid.

Chapter 2

1. *Pork Chop Hill*, directed by Lewis Milestone (United Artists, 1959).

2. Allan R. Millett, *The War for Korea, 1950–1951: They Came from the North* (Lawrence: University Press of Kansas, 2010), 85–231.

3. Alan Brinkley, *The Publisher: Henry Luce and His American Century* (New York: Alfred A. Knopf, 2010), 364–365.

4. "No Whistles, No Cheers, No Dancing," *Life*, August 3, 1953, 16–17. This retrospective photo essay reprints the magazine's visual coverage from the beginning of the conflict through the armistice in 1953.

5. Millett, *The War for Korea*, 120–122.

6. Elizabeth Schafer, "Press (Western) and the Korean War," in *The Korean War: An Encyclopedia*, ed. Stanley Sandler (New York: Garland, 1995), 271.

7. "Mobilization: Half Speed Ahead," *Time*, July 16, 1951. www.time.com/time/printout/0,8816,889061,00.html (accessed September 6, 2010).

8. Flynn, 115–118; Millett, *The War for Korea*, 368–371; William M. Donnelly, *Under Army Orders: The Army National Guard During the Korean War* (College Station: Texas A&M University Press, 2001), 177–181.

9. George Gallup, *The Gallup Poll*, Vol. II, 1949–1950 (New York: Random House, 1972), 965–966. According to the published responses, the interviewees or the pollsters used the term "active duty," though the respondents probably meant to characterize overseas service, as all World War II veterans had been on active duty wherever they served.

10. Edward A. Suchman, Robin M. Williams, Jr., and Rose K. Goldsen, "Student Reaction to Impending Military Service," *American Sociological Review* (June 1953), 296.

11. Flynn, 115–118, 123–126.

12. William M. Donnelly, "'The Best Army that Can Be Put in the Field in the Circumstances': The U.S. Army, July 1951–July 1953," *Journal of Military History* (July 2007), 815.

13. Godson, 182; Holm, *Women in the Military*, 152; Morden, 95–106.

14. "G.I. Urged to Accept Women in Services," *New York Times*, March 21, 1952, 46.

15. Gallup, *The Gallup Poll*, vol. II, 972.

16. "Ex-Head of Waves for Women Draft," *New York Times*, February 11, 1951, 6.

17. Millett, *The War for Korea*, 367–371.

18. D.C. Hart, Memorandum from Commandant of the Marine Corps, RE: Armed Forces Recruiting Advertising Campaign, January 30, 1951, Box 141, P 14-3/1–P14-4, July 1, 1950–December 31, 1955, Central Files, RG 127, NARA.

19. See Donnelly, *Under Army Orders*, especially chapter 8.

20. U.S. Army and U.S. Air Force Recruiting Service, "All Right ... Let's Go," *Life*, March 5, 1951, 122.

21. U.S. Army and United States Air Force Recruiting Service, "The Mark of a Man!" *Life*, April 16, 1951, 107. Italics in the original.

22. U.S. Navy Bureau of Personnel, "Who's Too Old!" June 26, 1951, Box 53, Recruiting Misc.— Recruiting Service Manual, Document Collection of the Technical Library, 1900–1985, Administration and Management Division, RG 24, NARA.

23. Ibid.

24. U.S. Marine Corps, "Wanted — Volunteers," August 4, 1950, P-101, NAVMC Series 6038, Combat Art Records, Marine Corps Historical Center.

25. Major G. Harding, United States Marine Corps, "Bougainville," June 24, 1952, NAVPERS MCNPB 6000, Combat Art Records, Marine Corps Historical Center.

26. Ibid.

27. U.S. Marine Corps, "United States Marines," September 20, 1951, NAVMC Series 6049, Combat Art Records, Marine Corps Historical Center; United States Marine Corps, "For God and Country," October 17, 1952, Combat Art Records, Marine Corps Historical Center.

28. U.S. Navy, U.S. Navy Recruiting Service, c. 1950s Navy Art — Posters, Photographic Section, Naval Historical Center. For an examination of the role of Christianity and the Chaplain's Corps in anti-communism, see Lori Lyn Bogle, *The Pentagon's Battle for the American Mind: The Early Cold War* (College Station: Texas A&M University Press, 2004).

29. Millett, *The War for Korea*, 238–239, 277, 314–315.

30. Ibid., 297, 317, 363, 393; Donnelly, "The Best Army," 816.

31. "A Small Task Force Fights and Freezes on Far North Front," *Life*, December 11, 1950, 35.

32. Ibid.

33. "U.S. Pilot Shoots Down MIG in First Fight Between Jets," *Life*, November 27, 1950, 34.

34. Brinkley, 366.

35. David Douglas Duncan, photographer, *Life*, December 25, 1950, cover, 9. See also Huebner,

Warrior Image, 121–126. He believes Duncan and other photojournalists captured the anti-war mood in their Korean War pictures.

36. Duncan, *Life,* December 25, 1950, 14.
37. Ibid.
38. Michael J. Varhola, *Fire and Ice: The Korean War, 1950–1953* (Mason City, IA: Savas, 2000), 14.
39. Gallup, *The Gallup Poll Vol. II,* 960–61. Only 25 percent indicated America should remain in Korea. A full 49 percent indicated that the U.S. had made a mistake in defending South Korea.
40. Ibid., 1019.
41. Suchman, Williams, and Goldsen, "Student Reaction to Impending Military Service," 300.
42. "How to Make Marines?" *Life,* October 8, 1951, 141.
43. Ibid., 144.
44. Ibid., 150.
45. Donnelly, "The Best Army," 817.
46. "MacArthur Tries to Make Policy," *New Republic,* September 4, 1950, 7.
47. "Truman or MacArthur — The Choice in Asia," *New Republic,* September 11, 1950, 5.
48. Harold L. Ickes, "MacArthur Talks Too Much," *New Republic,* December 11, 1950, 18.
49. Ibid.
50. Millett, *The War for Korea,* 414, 421.
51. Quoted in Millett, *The War for Korea,* 414.
52. Ibid.
53. Millett, *The War for Korea,* 421.
54. Ibid., 423, 436.
55. Quoted in Brinkley, *The Publisher,* 369.
56. Ibid.
57. "MacArthur's War Party," *New Republic,* April 23, 1951, 5.
58. Ibid.
59. Harold L. Ickes, "Nathan Hale and MacArthur," *New Republic,* May 7, 1951, 15.
60. Millett, *The War for Korea,* 435–438.
61. "War to the Death," *New Republic,* May 14, 1951, 10.
62. Millett, *The War for Korea,* 439.
63. Ibid., 424.
64. Brinkley, 370; Millett, *The War for Korea,* 441.
65. "Strength in Arms," *New Republic,* January 15, 1951, 15.
66. Ibid. The italics are mine.
67. Suchman, Williams, and Goldsen, 299.
68. Donnelly, "The Best Army," 839.
69. Hazel Erskine, "The Polls: Is War a Mistake?" *The Public Opinion Quarterly* (Spring 1970), 138.
70. "Death in the Gaze of Prayerful Men," *Life,* August 10, 1953, 24–26.
71. Erskine, 136, 138.
72. "The Cause and Cure of the Korean Truce," *Life,* July 20, 1953, 26.
73. Ibid.
74. Ibid.
75. "No Whistles, No Cheers, No Dancing," *Life,* August 3, 1953, 15.
76. Hanson W. Baldwin, "What's Wrong with the Regulars?," *Saturday Evening Post,* October 31, 1953, 20.
77. Ibid.
78. Ibid., 19–20.
79. Ibid., 19.
80. Ibid.
81. Ibid., 21.
82. Ibid.
83. William W. Savage, Jr., *Comic Books and America, 1945–1954* (Norman: University of Oklahoma Press, 1990), 52; Whitfield, *Culture,* 43.
84. Baldwin, "What's Wrong with the Regulars?," 21, 101, 107.
85. United States Marine Corps Manpower Utilization Council, "Survey of Utilization of Manpower in the Electronics Field," 1952, Box 141, July 1, 1950–December 31, 1955, P 14-3/1–P 14-4, Central Files, RG 127, NARA.
86. S. L. A. Marshall, "Our Mistakes in Korea," *The Atlantic Monthly,* September 1953. http://www.theatlantic.com (accessed January 20, 2010).
87. Ibid.
88. Ibid.
89. Ibid.
90. Ibid.

91. "Militia Plan Held Best," *New York Times*, December 6, 1952, 15.

92. Bradford W. Wright, *Comic Book Nation: The Transformation of Youth Culture in America* (Baltimore: The Johns Hopkins University Press, 2001), 57. Some 98 percent of the 6–11 age group were readers, while 80 percent of the 12–17 age group read comics. In the 18–30 age group 41 percent of men read comics and 28 percent of women did so.

93. Paul Reinman, "A Time to Die," *Battle*, May 1952. Browne Popular Culture Library, BGSU (hereafter BGSU).

94. Ibid.

95. Ibid.

96. "Don't Move!" *War Comics*, August 1952. Browne Popular Culture Library, BGSU.

97. Ibid.

98. Wright, 133–134.

99. Basinger, *The World War II Combat Film*, 161–162; Robert. J. Lentz, *Korean War Filmography* (Jefferson, NC: McFarland, 2003), 9.

100. Mary L. Dudziak, *Cold War Civil Rights: Race and the Image of American Democracy* (Princeton: Princeton University Press, 2000), 87; Sherry, 146.

101. *The Steel Helmet*, by Samuel Fuller (Lippert Pictures, Inc., 1951).

102. The 16th Infantry was a white unit until 1952. The film does not explain how a black soldier served with the unit, though it is possible that he was in one of the black platoons sent to white companies during the winter of 1944–1945 when replacements were in desperately short supply.

103. *The Steel Helmet*, directed by Samuel Fuller.

104. Ibid.

105. Bosley Crowther, "'Steel Helmet' Dealing with an American Infantry Patrol in Korea, at Loew's State," *New York Times*, January 25, 1951, 21.

106. Basinger, *World War II Combat Film*, 163.

107. James Michener, "The Bridges at Toko-Ri" *Life*, July 6, 1953, 58–87; Suid, *Sailing on the Silver Screen*, 97–99.

108. Joan Young Bayly, "Editorial," *Life*, July 27, 1953, 7.

109. Richard J. Cusack," "Editorial," *Life*, July 27, 1953, 7.

110. *The Bridges at Toko-Ri*, directed by Mark Robson (Paramount Pictures, 1955).

111. Lentz, 68.

112. Bosley Crowther, "Best Films of 1955," *New York Times*, December 25, 1955, 11.

113. Review of *The Bridges of Toko-Ri*," *Time*, January 24, 1955, www.time.com (accessed 2 October 2009).

114. Ibid.

115. Ibid.

116. *Pork Chop Hill*, directed by Lewis Milestone (United Artists, 1959).

117. Ibid.

118. Ibid.

119. Rumors that Army soldiers had broken and run, especially at the Chosin Reservoir, haunted the Army's image in the Korean War. Craig M. Cameron, *American Samurai: Myth, Imagination, and the Conduct of Battle in the First Marine Division, 1941–1951* (New York: Cambridge University Press, 1994), 236–237. Millett, *Semper Fidelis*, 498.

120. Review of *Pork Chop Hill, Time*, June 8, 1959, 91.

121. Ibid.

122. Stanley Kauffmann, "Death in Two Sizes," *New Republic*, June 15, 1959, 22.

123. Bosley Crowther, review of *Pork Chop Hill*, May 30, 1959, 9.

124. Lentz, 283–284.

125. *The Halls of Montezuma*, directed by Lewis Milestone (Twentieth Century–Fox, 1950).

126. Bosley Crowther, "'Halls of Montezuma,' Realistic Depiction of Goriness of War, Presented at Roxy Theater," *New York Times*, January 6, 1951, 9.

127. Ibid.

128. Robert Hatch, "Admirably Cast," *New Republic*, January 29, 1951, 23.

129. Ibid.

130. Ibid.

131. Ibid.

132. Ibid.

133. Moskos, 4–5.

134. Suid, *Guts and Glory*, 143–149.

135. *From Here to Eternity*, directed by Fred Zinnemann (Columbia Pictures, 1953).

136. Ibid.

137. Ibid.

138. Ibid.

139. Suid, *Guts and Glory*, 147.

140. *From Here to Eternity*, directed by Fred Zinnemann.

141. Ibid.

142. A. H. Weiler, review of *From Here to Eternity*, *New York Times*, August 6, 1953, 16.

143. "Soldier vs. System," *Life*, August 31, 1953, 81.

144. Review of *From Here to Eternity*, *Time*, August 10, 1953, 96.

145. Public Opinion Surveys, "Attitudes of Adult Civilians," 34.

146. Ibid.

147. Ibid.

148. Public Opinion Surveys, "Attitudes of 16 to 20 Year Old Males," 42.

149. Ibid.

150. Ibid.

151. Whitfield, *Culture*, 60; *The Caine Mutiny*, directed by Edward Dmytryk (Columbia Pictures, 1954).

152. Suid, *Sailing on the Silver Screen*, 120–123.

153. *The Caine Mutiny*, directed by Edward Dmytryk.

154. Christian G. Appy, "'We'll Follow the Old Man': The Strains of Sentimental Militarism in Popular Films of the Fifties," in *Rethinking Cold War Culture*, Peter J. Kuznick and James Gilbert, eds. (Washington, D.C.: Smithsonian Institution, 2001), 83.

155. Public Opinion Surveys, Inc., "Attitudes of 16 to 20 Year Old Males," 43.

156. Public Opinion Surveys, Inc., "Attitudes of Adult Civilians," 33.

157. Ibid.

158. Whitfield, *Culture*, 60–62. Whitfield argues that the film's message supports authoritarianism. Christian Appy argues that it reflects sentimental militarism by falsely presenting Queeg as the "the most dangerous leadership the military can produce." Appy, "Sentimental Popular Films," 85.

159. Philip D. Beidler, *The Good War's Greatest Hits: World War II and American Remembering* (Athens: The University of Georgia Press, 1998), 31; Christian Appy, "Sentimental Popular Films," 87.

160. *Mister Roberts*, directed by John Ford and Mervyn LeRoy (Warner Bros., 1955).

161. Ibid.

162. Beidler, 32, 38.

163. Crowther, "Best Films of 1955," 11.

164. Appy, "Sentimental Popular Films," 88.

165. Public Opinion Surveys, Inc., "Attitudes of 16 to 20 Year Old Males," 43.

166. Ibid.

167. Ibid.

168. Ibid.

169. Public Opinion Surveys, Inc., "Attitudes of Adult Civilians," 34.

Chapter 3

1. "The New Recruits," *The Phil Silvers Show*, aired September 20, 1955 (CBS and Paramount, 2006), DVD.

2. Ibid.

3. Lentz, 11–13.

4. *Battle Hymn*, directed by Douglas Sirk (Universal-International Pictures, 1957).

5. D. Melissa Hilbish, "Battle Hymn (Autobiography-Film)," in *War and American Popular Culture: A Historical Encyclopedia*, M. Paul Holsinger, ed. (Westport, CT: Greenwood, 1999), 339–340. Another heroic portrayal of Air Force pilots is *Mission Over Korea* (1953). Naval aviators are the heroes of *Men of the Fighting Lady* (1954), based, in part, on the stories of James Mitchener, which were also made into the film *The Bridges of Toko-Ri* (1955). *Retreat, Hell!* (1952) focuses on the heroism of the Marine landing at Inchon and presents the retreat from the Chosin (Changjin) Reservoir as a "victory of spirit and determination," according to Hilbish. Ibid., 352.

6. *Battle Hymn*, directed by Douglas Sirk.

7. Review of *Battle Hymn*, *Time*, March 11, 1957, 98.

8. Lentz, 51.

9. Marya Mannes, "Junior Has a Craving," *New Republic*, February 17, 1947.

10. Savage, x.

11. Wright, 172.

12. "Man Alone," *Marines in Battle*, March 1958. Browne Popular Culture Library, BGSU.

13. "Another Thrilling Navy Combat Adventure Starring 'Torpedo Taylor,'" *Navy Combat*, August 1957; "The P.T. Strikes," *Navy Combat*, August 1958; "Shot Down," *Navy Combat*, August 1958, "Stand by to Attack," *Navy Combat*, August 1958. All from Browne Popular Culture Library, BGSU.

14. "Supply," *War*, July 1954. Browne Popular Library, BGSU.

15. Cameron, 218–219; Savage, 59.

16. *The Flying Leathernecks*, directed by Nicholas Ray (USA: RKO, 1951).

17. Howard Thompson, review of *Flying Leathernecks*, *New York Times*, September 20, 1951, 37.

18. Suid, *Guts & Glory*, 124.

19. *Go for Broke!* directed by Robert Pirosh (MGM, 1951).

20. Ibid.

21. Ibid.

22. Ibid.

23. Review of *Go for Broke!*, *Time*, May 28, 1951, 108.

24. Peter C. Rollins, "Victory at Sea: Cold War Epic," in *Television Histories: Shaping Collective Memory in the Media Age*, ed. Gary R. Edgerton and Peter C. Rollins (Lexington: University Press of Kentucky, 2001), 108–110, 118. *Victory at Sea* (NBC, 1952–1953).

25. Rollins, "Victory at Sea," 114.

26. J. Fred MacDonald, "The Cold War as Entertainment in 'Fifties Television," *Journal of Popular Film and Television* 7, no. 1 (1978), 12; MacDonald, *Television and the Red Menace*, 112–113; Rollins, "Victory at Sea," 106–107.

27. Public Opinion Surveys, Inc., "Attitudes of 16 to 20 Year Old Males," 33.

28. Ibid.

29. Public Opinion Surveys, Inc., "Attitudes of Adult Civilians," 24.

30. Jack Gould, "N.B.C. Video's 'Victory at Sea' Is a Compelling Drama of Navy Action with Rodgers Score," *New York Times*, October 27, 1952, 35.

31. Ibid.

32. Ibid.

33. *To Hell and Back*, directed by Jesse Hibbs (Universal-International Pictures, 1955).

34. Ibid.

35. In the film, Murphy mounts a tank because no tank destroyers were available.

36. "'To Hell and Back' Sells Enlistments for the Army," *Recruiting Journal of the U.S. Army and U.S. Air Force Recruiting Service* (October 1955), 13.

37. Ibid.

38. A. H. Weiler, review of *To Hell and Back*, *New York Times*, September 23, 1955, 21.

39. Ibid.

40. Review of *To Hell and Back*, *Time*, October 17, 1955. www.time.com (accessed October 2, 2009).

41. Ibid.

42. Public Opinion Surveys, "Attitudes of 16 to 20 Year Old Males," 42.

43. Ibid.

44. Ibid.

45. Public Opinion Surveys, "Attitudes of Adult Civilians," 34.

46. Public Opinion Surveys, "Attitudes of 16 to 20 Year Old Males," 42.

47. Public Opinion Surveys, "Attitudes of Adult Civilians," 34.

48. For discussions of Eisenhower's defense and nuclear policies, see Stephen E. Ambrose, *Eisenhower: Soldier and President* (New York: Simon and Schuster, 1990); Saki Dockrill, *Eisenhower's New Look National Security Policy* (New York: St. Martin's, 1996); Richard G. Hewlett and Jack M. Holl, *Atoms for Peace and War, 1953–1961* (Berkeley, CA: University of California Press, 1989).

49. United States Army Center of Military History, *American Military History*, revised ed. *Army Historical Series* (Washington, D.C.: GPO, 1989), 582.

50. A. J. Bacevich, *The Pentomic Era: The U.S. Army Between Korea and Vietnam* (Washington, D.C.: National Defense University Press, 1986), 15–16; United States Army Center of Military History, *American Military History*, 573.

51. Gallup, *The Gallup Poll*, vol. II, 1073. Some 53 percent supported technology coupled with a small standing force, while 27 percent supported large, standing forces.

52. Ibid., 1140. A full 74 percent of respondents supported maintaining the strength of the armed forces upon truce in the Korean War.

53. Ibid., 1429. Some 32 percent favored building more rockets and missiles, 20 percent favored building more bombers, 14 percent favored increasing ground troops, and 11 percent favored building more aircraft carriers.

54. Ibid., 1321. Just 4 percent responded the Army would be most important, 5 percent thought the Navy would be most important, 71 percent answered the Air Force would be most important, and 19 percent believed all three would be equally important.

55. William Walton, "Congress Chooses Air Power," *New Republic*, May 10, 1948, 9.

56. "Editorial: Eisenhower's Real Decision," *New Republic*, January 11, 1954, 10.

57. "Editorial: '…Be Candid Where We Can,'" *New Republic*, January 18, 1954, 6.

58. Dwight D. Eisenhower, Special Message to the Congress on National Security Requirements, January 13, 1955, in John T. Woolley and Gerhard Peters, *The American Presidency Project* [online],

Santa Barbara, CA, available at http://www.presidency.ucsb.edu/ws/?pid=10254 (accessed 29 June 2010).

59. Flynn, 161.

60. Dwight D. Eisenhower, Statement by the President Upon Signing the Reserve Forces Act of 1955, August 9, 1955, in John T. Woolley and Gerhard Peters, *The American Presidency Project* [online], Santa Barbara, CA, available from http://www.presidency.ucsb.ude/ws/?pid=10335 (accessed June 29, 2010).

61. U.S. Army Reserve, "Here's Your Plan Man!," Box 2, Recruiting Publicity Campaign Materials, 1950–67, Office of the Chief of the Army Reserve, Information Office, Chief of Staff, RG 319, NARA. Emphasis in the original.

62. U.S. Army Reserve, "You and the New Army Reserve," 1955, Box 2, Recruiting Publicity Materials, 1950–1967, Office of the Chief of Army Reserve, Information Office, Chief of Staff, RG 319, NARA.

63. U.S. Army Reserve, "Our Town's Leading Citizen," March 15, 1955, folder: volume 6 — USAR Publicity Materials FY 54-55, Box 1, Recruiting Publicity Campaign Materials, 1950–67, Office of the Army Reserve, Information Office, Chief of Staff, RG 319, NARA.

64. U.S. Army Reserve, "America's Strength in Reserve Begins in Our Town!" March 1, 1955, folder: volume 6 — USAR Publicity Materials FY 54-55, Box 1, Recruiting Publicity Campaign Materials, 1950–67, Office of the Army Reserve, Information Office, Chief of Staff, RG 319, NARA.

65. Flynn, 161.

66. Public Opinion Surveys, "Attitudes of 16 to 20 Year Old Males," 3–4.

67. Ibid.

68. Ibid.

69. Marling, Karal Ann, *As Seen on TV: The Visual Culture of Everyday Life in the 1950s* (Cambridge, MA: Harvard University Press, 1994), 166–168, 197.

70. Quoted in Peter Guralnick, *Careless Love: The Unmasking of Elvis Presley* (Boston: Little, Brown, 1999), 70.

71. Guralnick, 63.

72. Frank Tollman, "Which Patch on the German Uniform?" *New Republic*, December 28, 1953, 13.

73. J.F. Golay, "Germans with Guns Can't Be Trusted," *New Republic*, April 19, 1954, 9.

74. "Germany as an Ally," *New Republic*, November 1, 1954, 7.

75. James King, "A European Union Is Still Our Best Hope," *New Republic*, April 19, 1954, 15.

76. Frank Gorrell, "The Pentagon Shapes a New Plan," *New Republic*, November 9, 1953, 114. See also, "Germany as an Ally," *New Republic*, November 1, 1954, 7.

77. "A General Is Fired," *New Republic*, October 14, 1957, 9.

78. *Strategic Air Command*, directed by Anthony Mann (Paramount Pictures, 1955).

79. Suid, *Guts and Glory*, 220–221.

80. *Strategic Air Command*, directed by Anthony Mann.

81. Peter Biskind, *Seeing Is Believing: How Hollywood Taught Us to Stop Worrying and Love in the Fifties* (New York: Pantheon Books, 1983), 58–64. Biskind refers to this film as "the domestication of war." He argues that the movie restored the notion of public sacrifice last seen during World War II. Sally's private concerns about spending time with her husband appear petty compared to the important work he does defending the country. Public interest trumps personal life.

82. Bosley Crowther, review of *Strategic Air Command*, New York Times, April 21, 1955.

83. Crowther, review of *Strategic Air Command*; Russell E. Shain, "Effects of Pentagon Influence on War Movies," 1948–1970, *Journalism Quarterly*, vol. 49 (1972): 642; Suid, *Guts and Glory*, 221.

84. Review of *Strategic Air Command*, Time, May 2, 1955, 98.

85. Ibid.

86. Public Opinion Surveys, Inc., "Attitudes of 16 to 20 Year Old Males," 39.

87. Ibid.

88. Ibid.

89. Public Opinion Surveys, Inc., "Attitudes of Adult Civilians," 31.

90. Ibid.

91. "Democracy's Ace in the Hole," *Submarine Attack*, December 1959. Browne Popular Culture Library, BGSU.

92. "Intruders," *U.S. Air Force Comics*, February 1960. Browne Popular Culture Library, BGSU.

93. Ibid.

94. MacDonald, *Television and the Red Menace*, 111, 118–120.

95. Chester J. Pach, Jr., and Elmo Richardson, *The Presidency of Dwight D. Eisenhower*, revised ed. (Lawrence: University Press of Kansas, 1991), 170–171; T. A. Heppenheimer, *Countdown: A History of Spaceflight* (New York: John Wiley & Sons, 1997), 124–125; Walter A. McDougall, *...The Heavens and the Earth: A Political History of the Space Age* (New York: Basic, 1985), 118–124.

96. Arthur Krock, "The Effects of Sputnik Thus Far," *New York Times*, October 10, 1957, 32.

97. Heppenheimer, 127–129; Stephen Ambrose, *Eisenhower: Soldier and President* (New York: Simon & Schuster, 1990), 449–450.

98. Heppenheimer, 125.

99. Ambrose, *Eisenhower*, 453.

100. Quoted in Ambrose, *Eisenhower*, 453.

101. These shows include (with the number of episodes in parentheses): *Crusade in Europe* (26), *Crusade in the Pacific* (26), *The Big Picture* (828), *Victory at Sea* (26), *Navy Log* (102), *The Phil Silvers Show* (138), *Combat Sergeant* (13), *The West Point Story* (39), *Air Power* (26), *Men of Annapolis* (39), *Citizen Soldier* (39), *The Silent Service* (78), *Flight* (39), *Steve Canyon* (39), *Men into Space* (38), and *The Blue Angels* (39). Chart listed in MacDonald, *Television and the Red Menace*, 111.

102. *The Big Picture* appeared on several television outlets from 1951–71. The Army produced 828 episodes. MacDonald, *Television and the Red Menace*, 111.

103. "The Big Picture," *Recruiting Journal of the U.S. Army and U.S. Air Force Recruiting Service* (July 1954), 12.

104. Department of the Army, "The Big Picture: Blue Badge," October 1952, United States Army Audiovisual Center, Office of the Deputy Chief of Staff for Operations, RG 111, NARA.

105. For more on the troop information programs and service members' responses to them, see Christopher S. DeRosa, *Political Indoctrination in the U.S. Army from World War II to the Vietnam War* (Lincoln: University of Nebraska Press, 2006), 249–250.

106. Public Opinion Surveys Inc, "Attitudes of Adult Civilians," 28.

107. Ibid.

108. Ibid.

109. Ibid.

110. Quoted in Christopher S. DeRosa, *Political Indoctrination in the U.S. Army from World War II to the Vietnam War* (Lincoln: University of Nebraska Press, 2006), 251.

111. Brooks and Marsh, 557, 849; *Navy Log* (CBS, 1955–58).

112. "Web Feet," *Navy Log*, aired December 21, 1956 (UCLA Film and Television Archive).

113. "Incident at Formosa," *Navy Log*, aired December 5, 1956 (UCLA Film and Television Archive).

114. "Family Special," *Navy Log*, aired November 8, 1955 (UCLA Film and Television Archive).

115. Ibid.

116. Public Opinion Surveys, Inc., "Attitudes of 16 to 20 Year Old Males," 33–34.

117. Ibid.

118. Public Opinion Surveys, Inc., "Attitudes of Adult Civilians," 25.

119. Jeffrey S. Wilson and Terri Sabatos, "Reclaiming Duty, Honor, Country: West Point Story and America in the 1950s" (paper presented at the War in Film, Television, and History Conference, Dolce International Conference Center, Dallas/Fort Worth, November 12, 2004); Brooks and Marsh, 849; "TV Show 'West Point' Is Receiving Army Cooperation," *The Army Reservist*, December 1956, 21; *West Point Story* (USA: CBS, 1956–57).

120. Gallup, *The Gallup Poll*, vol. II, 1008–1009. According to a Gallup poll taken in August 1951, 82 percent of the respondents were aware of the scandal. Of those people, 37 percent thought the punishment had been too hard, 28 percent said just about right, 4 percent said not severe enough, and 13 percent had no opinion. "The Harder Right," *West Point Story*, aired May 24, 1957 (UCLA Film and Television Archive).

121. Ibid.

122. Brooks and Marsh, 337. *Hennesey* (CBS: 1959–62).

123. "Remember Pearl Harbor," *Hennesey*, aired December 4, 1961 (UCLA Film and Television Archive).

124. "Pilot," *Hennesey*, aired September 28, 1959 (UCLA Film and Television Archive); "Hennesey Joins the Marines," *Hennesey*, aired January 18, 1960 (UCLA Film and Television Archive); "Hennesey at Peyton Place," *Hennesey*, aired October 19, 1959 (UCLA Film and Television Archive).

125. "TV 'Hennesey' Good Navy Image," *Navy Recruiter* (Winter 1959), 10.

126. Cobbett Steinberg, *TV Facts* (New York: Facts on File, 1985), 179–180.

127. *The Phil Silvers Show* (CBS, 1955–59).

128. MacDonald, *Television and the Red Menace*, 114–115.

129. Ibid., 114.

130. Ibid.

131. Ibid., 191–196. Carl Boggs and Tom Pollard make similar claims for film in *The Hollywood War Machine*, as does David L. Robb in *Operation Hollywood*.

132. "Hillbilly Whiz," *The Phil Silvers Show*, aired October 1, 1957 (CBS and Paramount, 2006), DVD.

133. "The New Recruits," *The Phil Silvers Show*, aired September 20, 1955 (CBS and Paramount, 2006), DVD.

134. "Bilko's Cousin," *The Phil Silvers Show*, aired January 24, 1958 (CBS and Paramount, 2006), DVD.

135. Ibid.

136. Major Multissimus, "The Wear of the Army Green," *Army* (May 1957), 27.

137. Public Opinion Surveys, "Attitudes of 16 to 20 Year Old Males," 34.

138. Public Opinion Surveys, "Attitudes of Adult Civilians," 24–25.

139. Public Opinion Surveys, "Attitudes of 16 to 20 Year Old Males, 34, 36; Public Opinion Surveys, Inc., "Attitudes of Adult Civilians," 23–28.

140. Public Opinion Surveys, "Attitudes of Adult Civilians," 23–28.

141. Public Opinion Surveys, "Attitudes of 16 to 20 Year Old Males, 34, 36.

142. Steinberg, 169–175.

143. Savage, 58.

144. Quoted in Jeff Bacon, "Beetle at 60," *Army Times*, Off Duty, September 13, 2010, 6.

145. Huebner, *The Warrior Image*, 132; U.S. Census Bureau, Historical National Population Estimates, available at http://www.census.gov/popest/archives/1990s/popclockest.txt (accessed July 20, 2010).

146. Mort Walker, *50 Years of Beetle Bailey* (New York: Nanter, Beall, Minoustchine, 2000), 16.

147. Mort Walker, "Beetle Bailey," *Beetle Bailey*, May–July 1957. Browne Popular Culture Library, BGSU.

148. Mort Walker, "Caught on Guard," *Beetle Bailey*, August–September 1959. Browne Popular Culture Library, BGSU.

149. Mort Walker, *50 Years of Beetle Bailey*, 17. General Halftrack's bombshell secretary, Miss Buxley, does not appear in the comic until 1971.

150. Ibid.

151. Ibid.

152. Major Multissimus, 27.

153. Reprinted in Jeff Bacon, "Beetle at 60," *Army Times*, Off Duty, September 13, 2010, 6.

154. Tim J. Watts, "Beetle Bailey: Comic Strip by Mort Walker," in *Encyclopedia of War and American Society*, ed. Peter Karsten (Thousand Oaks, CA: Sage, 2006), 72.

155. Ibid.; Bacon, "Beetle at 60," 6–7. Beetle Bailey became the third most widely distributed comic of all time and was being published in 1,800 newspapers in 2010. King Features Syndicate, "About the Comic," 2010 available from http://www.kingfeatures.com/features/comics/bbailey/about.htm (accessed October 29, 2010).

156. Tim J. Watts, "Sad Sack," in *Encyclopedia of War and American Society*, ed. Peter Karsten (Thousand Oaks, CA: Sage, 2006), 761–763.

157. George Baker, "Qualifications," *Sad Sack*, April 1958. Browne Popular Culture Library, BGSU.

158. George Baker, "Sad Sack and the Sarge in 'Thoughts,'" *Sad Sack and the Sarge*, September 1958. Browne Popular Culture Library, BGSU.

159. George Baker, "Sadie Sack: Gone to Pot," *Sad Sack and the Sarge*, September 1958. Browne Popular Culture Library, BGSU.

160. Letter from Lt. Gen. John R. Hodge, HQ Third Army to Lt. Gen. J. E. Hull, Office of the Chief of Staff, 7 August 1951, Box 742, 341–350, Decimal File, 1951–1952, RG 319, NARA.

161. Ibid.

162. Commanding General of FMF Pacific and Marine Corps Base at Twentynine Palms, California, Memorandum to Commandant Marine Corps, RE: Enlistment Options, 7 November 1958, Box 142, January 1, 1956–October 15, 1961, P14-4–P14-5, Central Files, RG 127, NARA.

163. George Porter, "Elite," 1957, P-111, NAVMC 6652, Combat Art Records, Recruiting Poster Index, 1945–1970, Marine Corps Historical Center; George Porter, "Honor," 1957, P-157, NAVMC Series 6636, Published by Majestic Press, Combat Art Records, Recruiting Poster Index, 1945–1970, Marine Corps Historical Center; George Porter, "Pride," 1957, P-158, NAVMC 6635, Combat Art Records, Recruiting Poster Index, 1945–1970, Marine Corps Historical Center; George Porter, "Spirit," 1957, P-156, NAVMC Series 6637, Combat Art Records, Recruiting Poster Index, 1945–1970, Marine Corps Historical Center; George Porter, "Valor," 1957, P-9, Combat Art Records, Recruiting Poster Index, 1945–1970, Marine Corps Historical Center.

164. Commandant of the Marine Corps, Marine Corps Bulletin 1100, January 29, 1958, Box 142, January 1, 1956–October 15, 1961, P14-4–P14-5, Central Files, RG 127, NARA.

165. U.S. Air Force, "A Bright Future Becomes Real Where the Age of Space Is Real," *Senior Scholastic—Teacher Edition*, November 18, 1959.

166. Cover Photograph, *Navy Recruiter* (Spring 1960); "Space Age Specialists," *Navy Recruiter* (Winter 1959).

167. U.S. Air Force, "Hobbyists: Make Your Hobby the Key to a Real Future in the New Age of Space," *Popular Science*, September 1959, 245.

168. Dancer-Fitzgerald-Sample, Recommendations for the U.S. Army Reserve and ROTC Adver-

tising and Publicity Program FY '59, November 10, 1958, Box 9, Recruiting Publicity Campaign Materials, 1950–1967, Office of the Chief of the Army Reserve, Information Office, Chief of Staff, RG 319, NARA. Emphasis is mine.

169. Dancer-Fitzgerald-Sample, "Choice, Not Chance Copy Test," September 19, 1956, Box 7, FY-56 TC Series, Recruiting Publicity Campaign Materials, 1950–67, Office of the Chief, Army Reserve Information Office, RG 319, NARA.

170. U.S. Army, "Choose It Yourself Before Enlistment," *Popular Science*, November 1959, 241.

171. "Choose Your Field," *Navy Recruiter* (Fall 1959), 19.

172. Cabell Phillips, "Your Best Deal in Military Service," *Harper's Magazine*, July 1957, 54.

173. Ibid., 55.

174. Ibid.

175. W.R. Smedberg, III, Personal Letter to All Flag Officers, Unit Commanders, Commanding Officers in Charge RE: Selective Service Training and Retention (STAR) Program, August 2, 1960, Box 8, Central Files, 1961, Office of Information, RG 428, NARA.

176. Bacevich, *The Pentomic Era*, 123–24.

177. Director of Division of Recruiting, Performance of Women Recruiters Assigned to the Recruiting Service, 8 February, 1952, Box 141, P14-3/1–P14-4, July 1, 1950–December 31, 1955, Central Files, RG 127, NARA.

178. Winifred Quick Collins and Herbert M. Levine, *More Than a Uniform: A Navy Woman in a Navy Man's World* (Denton: University of North Texas Press, 1997), 163.

179. U.S. Marine Corps, "Serve," November 9, 1955, P114, NAVMC Series 6073, Combat Art Records, Marine Corps Historical Center.

180. U.S. Navy, "Serve with Pride and Patriotism," c. 1950s, Navy Art — Posters, Photographic Section, Navy Historical Center.

181. U.S. Navy, "Respected as an Officer, Honored as a Navy Nurse," c. 1950s, Navy Art — Posters, Photographic Section, Naval Historical Center.

182. U.S. Navy, "U.S. Navy Career Women," May 11, 1951, Box 53, Document Collection of the Technical Library, 1900–85, Administrative and Management Division, RG 24, NARA.

183. Ibid.

184. Ibid.

185. Ibid.

186. U.S. Marine Corps, "Elite," 1957, P-111, NAVMC Series 6652, Combat Art Records, Marine Corps Historical Center.

187. Commandant of the Marine Corps, Marine Corps Bulletin 1100, RE: Promotional Material, April 21, 1959, Box 1, January 1, 1959–December 31, 1959, Subject Correspondence, 1000–1200, RG 127, NARA.

188. Commandant of the Marine Corps, Memorandum: Direct Mail Program for Women High School Graduates, November 6, 1951, Box 141, P14-3/1–P14-4, July 1, 1950–December 31, 1955, Central Files, RG 127, NARA.

189. Commandant of the Marine Corps, Marine Corps Order 1100.49, Direct Mail Campaign, February 5, 1958, Box 142, January 1, 1956–October 15, 1961, P14-4–P14-5, Central Files, RG 127, NARA.

190. U.S. Army Reserve, "A Soldier's World for You," 1955, Box 2, Recruiting Publicity Campaign Materials, 1950–67, Information Office, Office of the Chief of the Army Reserve, Chief of Staff, RG 319, NARA.

191. Ibid.

192. Ibid.

193. Ibid.

194. U.S. Navy, "U.S. Navy Career Women."

195. Ibid.

196. Ibid.

197. Ibid.

198. ROC (W) Underway, April 13, 1951, Box 53, Document Collection of the Technical Library, 1900–85, Administrative and Management Division, RG 24, NARA.

199. U.S. Navy, *Judy Joins the WAVES*, July 15, 1951, folder: Misc. Women in the Navy Pamphlets, Box 53, Document Collection of the Technical Library 1900–85, Administrative and Management Division, RG 24, NARA.

200. Ibid.

201. Collins and Levine, 139; Captain F. B. C. Martin, Letter to Captain J.B. Hancock regarding Comments on Conclusion and Recommendations of Volunteer Composite Unit W-10 (WAVES), June 26, 1952, Box 501, General Correspondence, 1946–60, Administrative and Management Division, RG 24, NARA.

202. *Operation Petticoat*, directed by Blake Edwards (Universal-International Pictures, 1959).

203. Suid, *Sailing on the Silver Screen*, 141.

204. *Operation Petticoat*, directed by Blake Edwards.

205. Ibid.

206. Ibid.

207. Review of *Operation Petticoat, Time*, December 14, 1959, 96.

208. Ibid.

209. "Presenting the Navy's Story to the Public, Recruiters Profit by Tie-in with Feature Films," *Navy Recruiter*, vol. 14, no.2 (1960), 17–18.

210. Morden, 104

211. Picture caption, *Saturday Evening Post*, May 12, 1956, 113.

212. Collins and Levine, 129.

213. Ibid., 155.

214. Research Division of the Office of Armed Forces Information and Education, *Enlisted Women in the Services* (Washington, D.C.: Department of Defense, 1953), 98–99. Some 42 and 48 percent stated "favorable" for enlisted men and male officer attitudes, respectively. For civilian men of their age, 43 percent indicated a negative attitude and 24 percent perceived a mixed attitude. Of other civilian men, 32 percent said unfavorable and 28 percent indicated mixed attitudes.

215. Ibid., 100. An estimated 42 percent reported favorable attitudes from women of their own age, while only 22 percent stated favorable attitudes from other civilian women.

216. Attitude Research Branch, Armed Forces Information and Education Division, "Attitudes of Girls' Nation Toward Military Service for Women and Toward Recruiting Appeals," August 2 (and 6), 1952, Box 1009, Surveys on Troop Attitudes, 1942–June 1955, Research Division, Assistant Secretary of Defense (Manpower, Personnel & Reserves), RG 330, NARA. One-third of the respondents were 16 years old or younger, two-thirds were 17 years old, and one teenager was 18 years old.

217. Ibid.

218. See William H. Chafe, *The Paradox of Change: American Women in the 20th Century* (New York: Oxford University Press, 1991); Jane F. Gernard, *Desiring Revolution: Second-Wave Feminism and the Rewriting of American Sexual Thought, 1920 to 1982* (New York: Columbia University Press, 2001).

219. Attitude Research Branch, Armed Forces Information and Education Division, "Attitudes of Girls' Nation Toward Military Service for Women and Toward Recruiting Appeals."

220. Ibid.

221. Ibid.

222. Ibid.

223. Attitude Research Branch, Armed Forces Information and Education Division, "Women in the Air Force," January 1952, Box 1008, Surveys on Troop Attitudes, 1942–June 1955, Research Division, Assistant Secretary of Defense (Manpower, Personnel and Reserve), RG 330, NARA.

224. Ibid.

225. Attitude Research Branch, Armed Forces Information and Education Division, "Women in the WAC," May 1952, Box 1008, Surveys on Troop Attitudes, 1942–June 1955, Research Division, Assistant Secretary of Defense (Manpower, Personnel and Reserve), RG 330, NARA.

226. Research Division of the Office of Armed Forces Information and Education, *Enlisted Women in the Services*, 21, 96.

227. Ibid., 94–97.

228. United States Marine Corps Manpower Utilization Council, "Survey of Utilization of Manpower in the Electronics Field," 1952, Box 141, July 1, 1950–December 31, 1955, P14-3/1–P14-4, Central Files, RG 127, NARA.

229. Director of Personnel, Memorandum to Chief of Staff," October 6, 1952, Box 141, July 1, 1950–December 31, 1955, P14'3/1–P14-4, Central Files, RG 127, NARA.

230. Eli Ginzberg quoted in Holm, 159.

231. Public Opinion Surveys, "Attitudes of 16 to 20 Year Old Males," 6.

232. Public Opinion Surveys, "Attitudes of Adult Civilians," 7. Mark R. Grandstaff interprets the survey results to indicate rejection of the anti-standing military tradition. He asserts that the middle class came to view military service as an acceptable career. Advertising campaigns successfully convinced the public that the armed forces both protected the country and instilled American values and respect for authority in its members. He suggests that this new perspective overturned the traditional hostility toward military service and convinced Americans that enlistment meant a good job and a patriotic way of life. See Grandstaff, "Making the Military American," 299–323.

233. Public Opinion Surveys, Inc., "Attitudes of Adult Civilians," 7.

234. Morris Janowitz, *The Professional Soldier: A Social and Political Portrait* (Glencoe, IL: Free, 1960), 226.

235. "Draftee in a Peacetime Army," *Life*, July 11, 1995, 97.

236. Ibid.

237. Ibid.

238. Ibid.
239. "How to Make Marines," *Life*, October 8, 1951; "Draftee in a Peacetime Army," 101.
240. "Draftee in a Peacetime Army," 104.
241. Dancer-Fitzgerald-Sample, "Choice, Not Chance Copy Test," September 19, 1956, Box 7, FY-56 TV Series, Recruiting Publicity Campaign Materials, 1950–67, Office of the Chief, Army Reserve Information Office, RG 319, NARA.
242. Ibid.
243. John P. Roche, "Memoirs of a 'Subversive,'" *New Republic*, January 24, 1955, 22.
244. Ibid.

Chapter 4

1. *The Americanization of Emily*, directed by Arthur Hiller (MGM: 1964).
2. Ibid.
3. Ibid.
4. Ibid.
5. Flynn, 227; Richard W. Stewart, ed., *American Military History Volume II: The United States Army in a Global Era, 1917–2003* (Washington, D.C.: Center of Military History, United States Army), 371. Flynn states that in 1954 about 50 percent of the force was non-combat related, and by 1965, 60 percent of military jobs were non-combat in nature.
6. U.S. Army, "Choose It Yourself," *Popular Science* (March 1961), 25; United States Army, "Choose Your Job Training Then Learn by Doing," *Popular Science* (June 1961), 199.
7. U.S. Army. "In Today's World, What Does It Take to Feel Like a Man?" *Popular Science* (December 1962), 9.
8. U.S. Army, "One Army on Alert," *The Army Reservist* (September-October 1961), 11.
9. U.S. Navy, "Aviation Officer Candidate," *Navy Recruiter* (Summer 1961), inside-back cover.
10. U.S. Air Force, "Join the Aerospace Team," *Popular Science* (April 1962), 15.
11. See Walter A. McDougall, ...*The Heavens and the Earth: A Political History of the Space Age* (New York: Basic, 1985).
12. Marine Corps Bulletin 1100R, July 20, 1964, Box 1, January 1, 1964–December 31, 1964, Central Files 1000–1200, RG 127, NARA.
13. Ibid.
14. "Socio-Economic Survey No. 5," April 1963, Box 114, Recruiting Publicity Campaign Materials, 1950–1967, Information Office, Office of the Chief of the Army Reserve, Chief of Staff, RG 319, NARA.
15. James Mills, "Memo to the U.S. Army: Why Can't You Use This Man, in Trouble for Wanting to Be a Soldier?" *Life*, September 19, 1960, 60.
16. Flynn, 229.
17. Bailey, *America's Army*, 16.
18. Jack Raymonds, "Reserve Plan Touches on Sensitive Nerve," *New York Times*, December 20, 1964, E5.
19. Ibid.
20. Ibid.
21. Michael D. Doubler, *Civilian in Peace, Soldier in War: The Army National Guard 1636–2000* (Lawrence: University Press of Kansas, 2003), 255.
22. Godson, 190; Holm, 179–181; Morden, 171–216; Judith Hicks Stiehm, "The Generation of U.S. Enlisted Women," *Signs* 11, no. 1 (1985): 165.
23. U.S. Marine Corps, "Pride," 1961, P-115, NAVMC 6783, Combat Art Records, Marine Corps Historical Center.
24. U.S. Marine Corps, "Be a Woman Marine," June 6, 1964, Control Co. 99-99-297, Combat Art Records, Marine Corps Historical Center.
25. Morden, 233–234.
26. Holm, 181.
27. Collins and Levine, 171.
28. Ibid., 158.
29. Ibid., 172–175.
30. Morden, 189–192.
31. Godson, 190; Holm, 183–192.
32. Dancer-Fitzgerald-Sample, Inc., "Study of Motivation For and Against Joining the Army Nurse Corps," November 1962, Box 14, Recruiting Publicity Campaign Materials, 1950–67, Army Reserve Information Office, Office of the Chief, RG 319, NARA.
33. Ibid.
34. "Socio-Economic Survey No. 5," April 1963, Box 114, Recruiting Publicity Campaign Materials, 1950–67, Information Office, Office of the Chief of the Army Reserve, Chief of Staff, RG 319, NARA.

35. "Cinema: Operation Overblown," *Time*, October 19, 1962, available from http://www.time.com/printout/0,8816,827910,00.html (accessed September 28, 2010).

36. Richard Oulahan, Jr., "Filming 'The Longest Day' Produced the Longest Headache," *Life*, October 12, 1962, 114.

37. Ibid., 118.

38. *The Longest Day*, directed by Ken Annakin, Andrew Marton, Bernhard Wicki, and Darryl Zanuck (Twentieth Century–Fox, 1962).

39. Stephen E. Ambrose, "'The Longest Day' (1962: 'Blockbuster' History," *Historical Journal of Film, Radio, and Television* 14, no. 4 (1994): 422–423.

40. Ibid., 422.

41. Ibid., 426–427.

42. Bosley Crowther, review of *The Longest Day*, *New York Times*, October 5, 1962, 28.

43. Ibid.

44. Ibid.

45. "Cinema: Operation Overblown," *Time*, October 19, 1962.

46. Ibid.

47. Ibid.

48. "Cinema: October 26, 1962," *Time*, October 26, 1962, available from http://www.time.com/time/printout/0,8816,874500,00.html (accessed September 28, 2010).

49. *Hell Is for Heroes*, directed by Don Siegel (Paramount Pictures, 1962).

50. Ibid.

51. Ibid.

52. Ibid.

53. Basinger, *The World War II Combat Film*, 302–303.

54. *Hell Is for Heroes*, directed by Don Siegel (Paramount Pictures, 1962).

55. Eugene Archer, review of *Hell Is for Heroes*, *New York Times*, July 12, 1962, 19.

56. "The Dangerous Game of Numbers," *Life*, February 8, 1960, 51.

57. John L. Steele, "The Cold Hard Facts Just Don't Add Up ... but Tough-Minded Answers Do," *Life*, February 8, 1960, 52, 54; "Needed: A Mightier Shield," *Life*, February 15, 1960, 32.

58. John Lewis Gaddis, *We Now Know: Rethinking Cold War History* (New York: Oxford University Press, 1997), 262.

59. Allan R. Millett and Peter Maslowski, *For the Common Defense: A Military History of the United States of America*, revised and expanded ed. (New York: Free, 1994), 552–53. Taylor, the former Army chief of staff, resigned in protest of Eisenhower's budget cuts to the Army. He argued against the New Look, favoring a build-up of conventional forces and personnel to respond to low levels of aggression. See. Adam Yarmolinsky, "Flexible Response," *The Oxford Companion to American Military History* (New York: Oxford University Press, 1999), 270–71.

60. Millett and Maslowski, 560.

61. "United, We Must Advance," *Life*, August 4, 1961, 50.

62. Millett and Maslowski, 560.

63. Hanson W. Baldwin, "Informing the Troops," *New York Times*, December 17, 1961, 51.

64. Quoted in "United, We Must Advance," *Life*, August 4, 1961, 50.

65. Gaddis, 274.

66. David A. Welch, "Cuban Missile Crisis," in *The Oxford Companion to American Military History*, ed. John Whiteclay Chambers II (New York: Oxford University Press, 1999), 196. See also Gaddis, *We Now Know*, 274–80.

67. Welch, "The Cuban Missile Crisis," 196–197.

68. Lynn Spiegel, *Make Room for TV: Television and the Family Ideal in Postwar America* (Chicago: University of Chicago Press, 1992), 1.

69. MacDonald, *Television and the Red Menace*, 192. Military dramas, with number of episodes, included *The Americans* (17), *The Gallant Men* (26), *Combat!* (152), *The Lieutenant* (29), *Twelve O'Clock High* (78), *Convoy* (13), *Jericho* (16), *Court Martial* (26), *The Rat Patrol* (58), and *Garrison's Gorillas* (26). Military situation comedies included *Hennesey* (96), *McKeever & the Colonel* (26), *Ensign O'Toole* (26), *McHale's Navy* (138), *No Time for Sergeants* (34), *Broadside* (32), *Gomer Pyle U.S.M.C.* (150), *Mr. Roberts* (30), *The Wackiest Ship in the Army* (29), *F Troop* (65), *Hogan's Heroes* (168), and *I Dream of Jeannie* (139).

70. "Those Cool War Heroes," *Newsweek*, November 19, 1965, 77; MacDonald, *Television and the Red Menace*, 191.

71. MacDonald, *Television and the Red Menace*, 192. MacDonald describes the show as Sergeant Saunders spending five years "walking around the eucalyptus trees and potted plants of a Hollywood film lot, acting out a popular fantasy that war was somehow part moral crusade, part athletic event: (195–196). In contrast, Eric Worland argues that the best episodes dealt with complex issues and that the show did not buy into the heroic mythos of World War II. He asserts that the series showed the

human costs of war, with a predominance of anti-heroic themes and some which were anti-war. Eric John Worland, "The Other Living Room War: Evolving Cold War Imagery in Popular TV Programs of the Vietnam Era, 1960–1975" (Ph.D. diss., University of California, 1989), 212–227.

72. "Those Cool War Heroes," 77.

73. David Pierson, "ABC-TV's Combat, World War II, and the Enduring Image of the Combat Cold Warrior," *Film and History* 21, no. 2 (2001): 25; Steven Jay Rubin, *Combat Films: American Realism: 1945–1970* (Jefferson, NC: McFarland, 1981), 24–36, 173; Brooks and Marsh, *Complete Directory to Prime Time TV*, 161; MacDonald, *Television and the Red Menace*, vii, 192; "Those Cool War Heroes," 77; Worland, 227.

74. "Those Cool War Heroes," 77.

75. MacDonald, *Television and the Red Menace*, 191.

76. "Television: The New Season," *Time*, October 12, 1962, available at http://www.time.com/time/printout/0,8816,829292,00.html (accessed July 13, 2010).

77. "Point of View," *Combat!*, aired September 29, 1964 (UCLA Film and Television Archives).

78. "The Enemy," *Combat!*, aired January 5, 1965 (UCLA Film and Television Archives).

79. "The First Day," *Combat!*, aired September 21, 1965 (UCLA Film and Television Archives).

80. "Cat and Mouse," *Combat!*, aired December 4, 1962 (UCLA Film and Television Archives).

81. See also Andrew Huebner, *The Warrior Image* (Chapel Hill: University of North Carolina Press, 2008), 163. Huebner credits *Combat!* with "almost every disquieting aspect of the warrior image ... there were brutal orders from officers, violent rivalries between soldiers, breakdowns in teamwork, graphic wounds and death, psychological injuries," and more.

82. "Television: The New Season," *Time*, 12 October 1962, available at http://www.time.com/time/printout/0,8816,829292,00.html (accessed July 13, 2010).

83. "The Warriors," *The Gallant Men*, aired August 3, 1963 (UCLA Film and Television Archives).

84. "Retreat to Concord," *The Gallant Men*, aired October 12, 1962 (UCLA Film and Television Archives).

85. "The Hero," *Twelve O'Clock High*, aired May 7, 1965 (UCLA Film and Television Archives).

86. "The Sound of Distant Thunder," *Twelve O'Clock High*, aired May 14, 1965 (UCLA Film and Television Archives).

87. "Hot Shot," *Twelve O'Clock High*, aired April 18, 1966 (UCLA Film and Television Archives).

88. "To Kill a Man," *The Lieutenant*, aired April 18, 1964 (UCLA Film and Television Archives).

89. Ibid.

90. "To Set It Right," *The Lieutenant*, aired February 22, 1964 (UCLA Film and Television Archives).

91. Ibid.

92. "Corporal in Command," *Battlefield Action* (July 1962). Browne Popular Culture Library, BGSU. The author took some artistic license as a battlefield commission should have resulted in the rank of second lieutenant.

93. "Guadalcanal," *War Stories: Combat* (July–September 1963). Browne Popular Culture Library, BGSU.

94. "Every Man a Hero," *Marines Attack* (August 1964). Browne Popular Culture Library, BGSU.

95. "Germans in Arms Again — on Our Side," *Life*, May 16, 1960, 110.

96. Ibid.

97. Ibid.

98. Ibid., 116.

99. Moskos, 28.

100. John Bryant places *McHale's Navy* within the context of the "variant comedy" television series, which presents anti-authoritarian themes and provides a venue of controlled criticism for such issues as materialism, the generation gap, and social dissent. The military comedies poke fun at the conflict between authority and freedom. John Bryant, "Situation Comedy of the Sixties: The Evolution of a Genre," *Studies in American Humor* 7 (1989), 130–134.

101. Erik Barnouw, *Tube of Plenty: The Evolution of American Television*, second revised ed. (New York: Oxford University Press, 1990), 375.

102. "An Ensign for McHale," *McHale's Navy*, aired October 11, 1962 (UCLA Film and Television Archives).

103. Ibid.

104. "The Captain's Mission," *McHale's Navy*, aired January 10, 1963 (UCLA Film and Television Archives).

105. Brooks and Marsh, 108.

106. "Don't Make Waves," *Broadside*, aired September 20, 1964 (UCLA Film and Television Archives).

107. Brooks and Marsh, 229–230, 906. Ed Sullivan's show ran on CBS from 1948 to 1971.

108. *The Americanization of Emily*, directed by Arthur Hiller (MGM: 1964).

109. Ibid.

110. Ibid.

111. Ibid.

112. Suid, *Guts & Glory*, 206–209; James Wolcott, "From Fear to Eternity," *Vanity Fair*, March 2005, 227–228.

113. Bosley Crowther, review of *The Americanization of Emily*, *New York Times*, October 28, 1964, 51; Suid, *Guts and Glory*, 209.

114. See Paul Boyer, *By the Bomb's Early Light: American Thought and Culture at the Dawn of the Atomic Age* (New York: Pantheon, 1985).

115. *On the Beach*, directed by Stanley Kramer (United Artists, 1959).

116. Bosley Crowther, review of *On the Beach*, *New York Times*, December 18, 1959, 34.

117. Suid, *Sailing on the Silver Screen*, 162–164.

118. Review of *On the Beach*, *Time*, December 28, 1959. www.time.com (accessed October 2, 2009).

119. Stanley Kauffmann, "Waiting for the End," *New Republic*, December 14, 1959, 21.

120. *Fail-Safe*, written by Harvey Wheeler, was first serialized in the *Saturday Evening Post* during the Cuban Missile Crisis. As a novel, it became the sixth best seller in 1962. *Seven Days in May*, written by Fletcher Knebel and Charles W. Bailey II, was the seventh best seller in 1962. Whitfield, *Culture*, 213, 224.

121. Sherry, 242.

122. *Dr. Strangelove or: How I Stopped Worrying and Learned to Love the Bomb*, directed by Stanley Kubrick (Columbia Pictures, 1964).

123. Ibid.

124. Bosley Crowther, review of *Dr. Strangelove*, *New York Times*, January 30, 1964, 24.

125. Tom Prideaux, "Do They Hit the Target?," *Life*, December 20, 1963, 128.

126. Loudon Wainwright, "The Strange Case of Dr. Strangelove," *Life*, March 13, 1964, 15.

127. Review of *Dr. Strangelove, or: How I Learned to Stop Worrying and Love the Bomb*, *Time*, January 31, 1964, 69.

128. Wainwright, 15.

129. Florence Allen, "Letter to the Editor," *Life*, April 3, 1964, 26.

130. John E. Mullins, "Letter to the Editor," *Life*, April 3, 1964, 26.

131. Emily Kennedy, "Letter to the Editor," *Life*, April 3, 1964, 26.

132. Suid, *Guts and Glory*, 232–233; Wainwright, 15.

133. *Fail-Safe*, directed by Sidney Lumet (Columbia Pictures, 1964).

134. Ibid.

135. Ibid.

136. Ibid.

137. Bosley Crowther, Review of *Fail-Safe*, *New York Times*, September 16, 1964, 36.

138. Review of *Fail-Safe*, *Time*, October 9, 1964.

139. Richard Oulahan, "Doomsday Is Better as a Farce," *Life*, October 30, 1964, 12.

140. Stanley Kauffmann, "Less Funny but Less Serious," *New Republic*, September 12, 1964, 26–27.

141. William Burr, ed., "The Nuclear Vault: The Air Force Versus Hollywood," The National Security Archive available at http://www.gwu.edu/~nsarchiv/nukevault/ebb304/index.htm (accessed January 20, 2010).

142. Ibid. The era of détente began under the Johnson administration. Johnson signed eight agreements with the Soviet Union, including the Treaty on Non-Proliferation in July 1968. Bruce J. Schulman, *The Seventies: The Great Shift in American Culture, Society, and Politics* (Cambridge, MA: Da Capo Press, 2001), 6.

143. David Rossie, "Congress Remains in the Twilight Zone," *Binghamton Press & Sun Bulletin*, July 31, 2000.

144. *Seven Days in May*, directed by John Frankenheimer (Paramount Pictures, 1964).

145. Ibid.

146. Ibid.

147. Bosley Crowther, Review of *Seven Days in May*, *New York Times*, February 20, 1964, 22.

148. Review of *Seven Days in May*, *Time*, February 21, 1964, 94.

149. Erik Riker-Coleman, "Seven Days in May" in *Encyclopedia of War & American Society*, ed. Peter Karsten (Thousand Oaks, CA: Sage, 2006), 779.

150. Raymond D. Senter, "Rebellion in the Air Force?" *New Republic*, September 28, 1963, 13.

151. Ibid., 14.

152. Ibid.

153. Christopher S. DeRosa, *Political Indoctrination in the U.S. Army from World War II to the Vietnam War* (Lincoln: University of Nebraska Press, 2006), 176–79. See also Lori Lyn Bogle, *The Pentagon's Battle for the American Mind: The Early Cold War* (College Station: Texas A&M University Press, 2004).

154. DeRosa, 179–80.

155. Ibid., 181; Hanson Baldwin, "Gen. Walker Hints Legal Action Over Statements About Ouster," *New York Times*, September 11, 1961, 6.

156. DeRosa, 204.

157. Ibid., 205.

158. "Fair Play for Gen. Walker," *Life*, October 6, 1961, 4.

159. Ibid.

160. Ibid.

161. Frederic W. Collins, "Military Indoctrination of Civilians," *New Republic*, June 26, 1961, 13.

162. Ibid.

163. Quoted in Collins, "Military Indoctrination of Civilians," 14.

164. Collins, "Military Indoctrination of Civilians," 14.

165. Ibid.

165. Ibid.

166. William H. Honan, "War Games for Kids This Christmas," *New Republic*, December 19, 1964, 9.

167. Bill Mauldin, Cartoon, *New Republic*, December 19, 1964, 9.

Chapter 5

1. "This Crummy War," *Army War Heroes*, October 1968. Browne Popular Culture Library, BGSU.

2. The James Bond franchise began in 1962 with the film *Dr. No*, which starred Sean Connery. The series proved popular in the United States as well. Five spinoff films were produced during the 1960s, including *From Russia with Love, Goldfinger,* and *You Only Live Twice*. The series continued through the ensuing decades, resulting in over 20 films to date.

3. Barnouw, 367–68.

4. Ibid., 375.

5. "Request Permission to Escape," *Hogan's Heroes*, aired April 29, 1966 (UCLA Film and Television Archives).

6. "The Informer," *Hogan's Heroes*, aired September 17, 1965 (UCLA Film and Television Archives).

7. "Hogan Go Home," *Hogan's Heroes*, aired January 13, 1968 (UCLA Film and Television Archives).

8. "Top Hat, White Tie, and Bomb Sights," *Hogan's Heroes*, aired November 19, 1965 (UCLA Film and Television Archives).

9. "Request Permission to Escape," *Hogan's Heroes*.

10. "The Flame Grows Higher," *Hogan's Heroes*, aired April 29, 1966 (UCLA Film and Television Archives).

11. "Happiness Is a Warm Sergeant," *Hogan's Heroes*, aired November 26, 1965 (UCLA Film and Television Archives).

12. "The Assassin," *Hogan's Heroes*, aired April 8, 1966 (UCLA Film and Television Archives).

13. Brenda Scott Royce, *Hogan's Heroes: A Comprehensive Reference to the 1965–1971 Television Comedy Series, with Cast Biographies and an Episode Guide* (Jefferson, NC: McFarland, 1993), 1–3, 120.

14. Brooks and Marsh, 651; Eric John Worland, "The Other Living Room War: Evolving Cold War Imagery with Popular TV Programs of the Vietnam Era, 1960–1975" (Ph.D. diss., University of California, 1989), 238–40.

15. "Those Cool War Heroes, 77.

16. "David and Goliath Raid" *The Rat Patrol*, aired September 18, 1967 (UCLA Film and Television Archive).

17. "Those Cool War Heroes," 77.

18. Ibid.

19. Leslie Raddatz, "More British Than Big Ben," *TV Guide*, 29 July 1967, 16.

20. Suid, *Sailing on the Silver Screen*, 156–159.

21. *Battle of the Bulge*, directed by Ken Annakin (Warner Bros., 1965).

22. Ibid.

23. Ibid.

24. Bosley Crowther, review of *Battle of the Bulge*, *New York Times*, December 18, 1965, 36.

25. Ibid.

26. Ibid.

27. Review of *Battle of the Bulge*, *Time*, December 31, 1965, 77.

28. Suid, *Guts & Glory*, 196.

29. Quoted in Suid, *Guts & Glory*, 193.

30. Suid, *Guts & Glory*, 193; *In Harm's Way*, directed by Otto Preminger (Paramount Pictures, 1965).

31. *In Harm's Way*, directed by Otto Preminger.

32. Ibid.

33. Bosley Crowther, "John Wayne Starred in Preminger Film," *New York Times*, April 7, 1965, 36.

34. Ibid.

35. Ibid.

36. Ibid.

37. Ibid.

38. "Cinema: World War Twosome," *Time*, 9 April 9, 1965, available at http://www.time.com/mag azine/article/0,9171,898638,00.html (accessed July 9, 2010).

39. Ibid.

40. Kenneth M. Cameron, *America on Film: Hollywood and American History* (New York: Continuum, 1997), 158–63; David A. Horowitz and Peter N. Carroll, *On the Edge: The United States Since 1945*, 3rd ed. (Belmont, CA: Wadsworth, 2002), 169–73; Mitchell K. Hall, *Crossroads: American Popular Culture and the Vietnam Generation* (Lanham, MD: Rowman and Littlefield Publishers, 2005), 65–76, 86, 104, 118–36; MacDonald, *Television and the Red Menace*, 245–47.

41. Basinger, *The World War II Combat Film*, 181; Tom Englehardt, *The End of Victory Culture: Cold War America and the Disillusioning of a Generation* (Amherst: University of Massachusetts Press, 1995), 236.

42. *The Dirty Dozen*, directed by Robert Aldrich (MGM, 1967).

43. Ibid.

44. Ibid.

45. Bosley Crowther, review of *The Dirty Dozen*, *New York Times*, June 16, 1967, 36.

46. Ibid.

47. Ibid.

48. James A. Donovan, *Militarism, U.S.A.* (New York: Charles Scribner's Sons, 1970), 197.

49. Review of *The Dirty Dozen*, *Time*, June 30, 1967, 68.

50. Ibid.

51. Quoted in Donovan, *Militarism*, 198.

52. "Too Many Cooks Spoil the Troop," *F Troop*, aired March 29, 1966 (UCLA Film and Television Archives).

53. "A Fort's Best Friend Is Not a Mother," *F Troop*, aired April 19, 1966 (UCLA Film and Television Archives).

54. "Lieutenant O'Rourke, Front and Center," *F Troop*, aired April 26, 1966 (UCLA Film and Television Archives).

55. "For Whom the Bugle Tolls," *F Troop*, aired November 10, 1966 (UCLA Film and Television Archives); "Scourge of the West," *F Troop*, aired September 14, 1965 (UCLA Film and Television Archives); "Lieutenant O'Rourke, Front and Center," *F Troop*, aired April 26, 1966 (UCLA Film and Television Archives).

56. Barnouw, 375; James T. Coon, "Sixties Entertainment Television and Cold War Discourses" (Ph.D. diss. BGSU, 1994), 144.

57. Brinkley, 446–47.

58. Huebner, 187, 197. For a study of the media and Vietnam see William M. Hammond, *Reporting Vietnam: Media and Military at War* (Lawrence: University Press of Kansas, 1998).

59. Huebner, 188.

60. Wright, 194.

61. Ibid., 199.

62. George C. Herring, *America's Longest War: The United States and Vietnam, 1950–1975*, 2nd ed. (New York: McGraw-Hill, Inc., 1986), 56–57, 70.

63. "Homecoming," *Fightin' Marines*, April 1963. Brown Popular Culture Library, BGSU.

64. George Gallup, *The Gallup Poll: Public Opinion, 1935–1971*, vol. III, 1959–1971 (New York: Random House, 1972), 1882. An April 1964 poll revealed that only 37 percent of respondents had given "any attention to developments in South Vietnam," compared to the 63 percent who had given little or no attention to it. Among the informed respondents, only 42 percent believed the U.S. was "handling affairs in South Vietnam as well as could be expected," while 46 percent thought events were going badly.

65. "Riding Shotgun," *Fightin' Army*, January 1964. Browne Popular Culture Library, BGSU.

66. Walter J. Boyne, *Beyond the Wild Blue: A History of the U.S. Air Force* (New York: St. Martin's Griffin, 1997), 152–156; Herring, 118–31.

67. "The Protégé," *Fightin' Marines*, September 1965. Browne Popular Culture Library, BGSU.

68. "The Hit and Run War," *Army War Heroes*, October 1966. Browne Popular Culture Library, BGSU.

69. "Fighting Air in Viet-Nam," *Fightin' Army*, April–May 1966. Browne Popular Culture Library, BGSU.

70. *The Ugly American* (Universal Pictures, 1963) substituted a fictitious country for Vietnam. The film came out before major ground combat operations in Vietnam and before many Americans paid close attrition to U.S. policy there. Hall, 180–181.

71. David Farber, *The Age of Great Dreams: America in the 1960s* (New York: Hill and Wang, 1994), 138; Garry Wills, *John Wayne's America* (New York: Simon and Schuster, 1997), 228.

72. I deliberately chose not to focus this chapter on the anti-war movement, as this history has been covered by others. Instead, I am focusing on other elements of anti-militarism in American culture. For a history of the anti-war movement, see Melvin Small, *Antiwarriors: The Vietnam War and the Battle for America's Hearts and Minds* (Wilmington, DE: SR, 2002).

73. Scholars across many fields have analyzed the film for its politics and propaganda support of the Vietnam War, and there are many works that cover this topic in detail, including Ivan Butler, *The War Film* (South Brunswick, NJ: A.S. Barnes, 1974), 131–134; Ronald Davis, *Duke: The Life and Times of John Wayne* (Norman: University of Oklahoma Press, 1986); John Hellman, *American Myth and the Legacy of Vietnam* (New York: Columbia University Press, 1986), 53–93; Bonnie S. Jefferson, "John Wayne: American Icon, Patriotic Zealot and Cold War Ideologue," in *War and Film in America: Historical and Critical Essays*, ed. Marilyn J. Matelski and Nancy Lynch Street (Jefferson, NC: McFarland, 2003), 25–42; Randy Roberts and James D. Olson, *John Wayne: American* (Lincoln: University of Nebraska Press, 1995); Sherry, *In the Shadow of War*, 289–99; Richard Slotkin, *Gunfighter Nation: The Myth of the Frontier in Twentieth-Century America* (New York: Athenaeum, 1992), 520–32; Suid, *Guts & Glory*, 247–56.

74. Rod Paschall, "Special Operations Forces: Army Special Forces," in *The Oxford Companion to American Military History*, ed. John Whiteclay Chambers II (New York: Oxford University Press, 1999), 670; Millett and Maslowski, 561.

75. Moskos, 23; Wills, 229.

76. Suid, *Guts & Glory*, 247; Wills, 229–231.

77. Wills, 229–231.

78. J.W. Fulbright, *The Pentagon Propaganda Machine* (New York: Liveright, 1970), 120.

79. *The Green Berets*, directed by Ray Kellogg and John Wayne (Warner Bros., 1968).

80. Wills, 232; Hammond, 126, 226–230. Hammond observes that most media spokesmen on network television favored the Vietnam War.

81. Suid, *Guts and Glory*, 254.

82. Renata Adler, Review of *The Green Berets*, *New York Times*, June 20, 1968, 49.

83. Englehardt, 234–235; Hellman, 91.

84. Wills, 233.

85. Slotkin, 531.

86. Gallup, *The Gallup Poll*, vol. III, 1925.

87. "Fooling the People," *New Republic*, August 13, 1966, 6.

88. Bill Mauldin, "Spirit of '66," *New Republic*, August 13, 1966, 6.

89. Erskine, 141.

90. Ibid.

91. Farber, 156–168.

92. Hammond, 159.

93. Ibid.

94. Farber, 214.

95. Erskine, 141.

96. "To Re-Enlist or Not to Re-Enlist," *Gomer Pyle U.S.M.C.*, aired February 15, 1967 (cable syndication rerun); "The Recruiting Poster," *Gomer Pyle U.S.M.C.*, aired September 15, 1967 (UCLA Film and Television Archives); "A Star Is Born," *Gomer Pyle U.S.M.C.*, aired February 11, 1966 (cable syndication rerun).

97. "Gomer Pyle U.S.M.C.," *The Andy Griffith Show*, aired May 18, 1964 (cable syndication rerun).

98. Ibid.

99. "PFC Gomer Pyle," *Gomer Pyle U.S.M.C.*, aired September 17, 1965 (cable syndication rerun); "Leader of Men," *Gomer Pyle U.S.M.C.*, aired September 29, 1967 (cable syndication rerun).

100. "A Visit from Aunt Bee," *Gomer Pyle U.S.M.C.*, aired September 8, 1967 (UCLA Film and Television Archives).

101. "Corporal Carol," *Gomer Pyle U.S.M.C.*, aired September 22, 1967 (cable syndication rerun).

102. Ibid.

103. Barnouw, 375, 432.

104. Ronald Searle, "The Irrepressible, Indestructible, Instant Peasant Gomer Pyle," *TV Guide*, August 26, 1967, 16.

105. National Sales Aids, *Recruiting and Career Counseling Journal*, November 1967, 12–13.

106. "Newest Ad Series Follows Same Theme," *Recruiting and Career Counseling Journal*, April 1968, 8.

107. U.S. Department of the Army, "Executive Summary: Provide: Project Volunteer in Defense of the Nation," vol. 1, U.S. Army Center of Military History, 7–8.

108. H. L. Miller, Chief of Information, Memorandum for the Secretary of the Navy, Re: Impact of Public Affairs on Enlistment and Retention of Personnel," February 1, 1968, Box 6, Central Subject Files, Office of Information, RG 428, NARA. Emphasis in the original.

109. Public Opinion Surveys, "Attitudes of Adult Civilians," 10–12; Public Opinion Surveys, Inc., "Attitudes of 16 to 20 Year Old Males," 10–12.

110. United States Army Recruiting Command, "Comments by USAREC on PROVIDE," August 9, 1969, Folder: 208-01 Op Planning File 69, Box 1, WDWW Z-38, RG 319, NARA.

111. U.S. Army, "Executive Summary: Provide," 11.

112. U.S. Army, "5 Things You Should Do About the Draft," *Popular Science*, October 1965, 33.

113. U.S. Army, "New Set of Wheels? I Hit the Jackpot!" *Popular Science*, November 1965, 28–29.

114. U.S. Army, "This Is the Day You Learn About Guts!" *Popular Science*, April 1966, 10–11.

115. U.S. Army, "When a Crack Electronics Expert Is Needed Fast, You're the Guy They Call," *Popular Science*, November 1966, 66–67.

116. "Complete Your Education. Learn to Command," *Recruiting and Career Counseling Journal*, April 1970, 19.

117. "One Man," *Recruiting and Career Counseling Journal*, April 1970, 18. "An Army of One" was the U.S. Army's recruiting slogan from 2001–06.

118. Ibid.

119. U.S. Army Reserve, "Reservists Wear Man-Size," *Army Reserve Magazine*, September-October 1965, 31.

120. United States Army Reserve, "60 Great in '68," *Army Reserve Magazine*, April 1968, 16.

121. Bailey, 15.

122. Doubler, 259.

123. U.S. Marine Corps, "The Marine Corps Builds Men," 1965, P-65, NAVMC Series 6954, Combat Art Records, Marine Corps Historical Center.

124. U.S. Marine Corps, "Be a Leader of Men (2)," 1965, P-118, NAVMC Series 6946, Combat Art Records, Marine Corps Historical Center.

125. U.S. Navy, "And Never Store Avocados Too Long," *Navy Recruiter*, December 1967, 14–15.

126. U.S. Navy, "Action with the Fleet," c. 1960s, Navy Art — Posters, Photographic Section, Naval Historical Center.

127. U.S. Navy, "Travel," c. 1960s, Navy Art — Posters, Photographic Section, Naval Historical Center.

128. U.S. Air Force, "About-Face!" *Popular Science*, April 1968, 71.

129. Assistant Chief of Staff G-1, Memorandum Re: Project Volunteer; Enclosure: Marine Corps Paper on Project Volunteer (Draft), June 19, 1969, Box 2, Central Files, 1080/1–1200/1, RG 127, NARA.

130. U.S. Marine Corps, "Ask a Marine," June 6, 1970, P-159, NAVMC Series 7107, Combat Art Records, Marine Corps Historical Center.

131. U.S. Army, "Learn a Skill. Make a Future," *Popular Science*, November 1968.

132. U.S. Army, "Enroll in the Army," *Popular Science*, October 1968.

133. U.S. Navy, "And Never Store Avocados Too Long," 14.

134. "Nervous? You bet I was," *Recruiting and Career Counseling Journal*, May 1965.

135. Westheider, 120–22.

136. "End the Draft and Pay the Soldiers," *New Republic*, July 11, 1964, 4–5.

137. Ibid.

138. Englehardt, 248; Westheider, 35; Bailey, 95.

139. Alfred B. Fitt, Memorandum for the Acting Secretary of the Army (M&RA), the Deputy Under Secretary of the Navy (Manpower), and the Acting Assistant Secretary of the Air Force (M&RA) Re: Initiation of Intensified Recruitment Program, February 20, 1968, Box 1, Correspondence, 1968, General Files, Administration and Management Division, RG 24, NARA.

140. R.G. Zimmermann, Memorandum from Chief of Naval Personnel Re: Intensified Recruiting Program in Poverty Sections of Cities, March 22, 1968, Box 1 Correspondence 1968, General Files, Administration and Management Division, RG 24, NARA.

141. R.G. Zimmerman, Memorandum from Chief of Naval Personnel Re: Intensified Recruitment Program in Poverty Sections of Cities; Implementation of 18 Additional Cities, May 28, 1968, Box 1 Correspondence 1968, General Files, Administration and Management Division, RG 24, NARA.

142. Bailey, 107.

143. Ibid., 98.

144. Morden, 193, 216, 224; "Newest Ad Series Follows Same Theme," *Recruiting and Career Counseling Journal*, April 1968, 8–9.

145. U.S. Army Reserve, "The Little Guy Doesn't Know It, but the Lady Is a Captain," *Missouri*

Nurse, June 1967, 13; see also "Army Nurses—Serving Humanity," *Recruiting and Career Counseling Journal*, February 1967, cover.

146. U.S. Army Reserve, "Promising Careers: Nurses," June 1966, Box 22, Recruiting Publicity Campaign Materials, 1950–1967, Information Office, Office of the Chief of the Army Reserve, Chief of Staff, RG 319, NARA.

147. U.S. Army, "Where Can You Find 10,000 Young Women Who Agree? In the Women's Army Corps," *TV Guide*, June 3, 1967, 18.

148. "Discover a Young World of People Like You," *Recruiting and Career Counseling Journal*, May 1969, 9.

149. "WAC Enlisted — Cape Cod," *Recruiting and Career Counseling Journal*, November 1967, 13.

150. U.S. Army, "Are WAC Officers Being Spoiled for Civilian Life?," *TV Guide*, July 1, 1967, 14.

151. U.S. Navy, "The Navy — WAVES OFFICER," c. 1970s, Navy Art — Posters, Photographic Section, Naval Historical Center.

152. U.S. Navy, "This Is Linn Anderson, WAVES Officer," c. 1970, Navy Art — Posters, Photographic Section, Naval Historical Center.

153. U.S. Marine Corps, "Share a Proud Tradition" June 6, 1968, Control No. 99-99-161, Combat Art Records, Marine Corps Historical Center.

154. Quoted in Morden, 242.

155. "Nurses Urgently Needed," *Recruiting and Career Counseling Journal*, February 1967.

156. Holm, 239.

157. Shelby Stanton, *U.S. Uniforms of the Vietnam War* (Harrisburg, PA: Stackpole, 1989), 85, 90.

158. Jake Schuffert, *No Sweat: A Collection of Jake Schuffert Cartoons from Army Times, Air Force Times, Navy Times*, 4the ed. (Washington, D.C.: Army Times, 1970), 40. Browne Popular Culture Library, BGSU.

159. Major Claudia Ramsay, "Why Do Women Join the Army?" *Recruiting and Career Counseling Journal*, May 1968, 3. According to Beth Bailey, less than 1.5 percent of Army positions were open to enlisted women in 1967, which probably has to do with the 2 percent ceiling on women in the armed forces that was still in effect at that time. Bailey, 141.

160. Bailey, 141.

161. Morden, 231.

162. Directorate of Personnel Studies and Research, Office of the Deputy Chief of Staff for Personnel, U.S. Army, "Provide: Project Volunteer in Defense of the Nation, Volume II: Support Analysis," 1969, RG: 330, NARA. The other benefits included camaraderie, medical benefits, job security, and career opportunities.

163. Ibid.

164. Directorate of Personnel Studies and Research, "Provide: Volume II: Support Analysis."

165. Ibid.

166. Quoted in the Directorate of Personnel Studies and Research, "Provide: Volume II: Support Analysis."

167. Jerome Johnson and Jerald G. Bachman, "Young Men Look at Military Service: A Preliminary Report (Ann Arbor, MI: Institute for Social Research, University of Michigan, June 1970), Folder: Youth in Transition—1969 (ISR), Box 1, Entry A1 1055, RG 330, NARA.

168. Erskine, 134.

169. Ibid. Italics in the original.

170. Johnson and Bachman, "Young Men Look at Military Service."

171. "Keeping the Draft," *New Republic*, May 29, 1965, 7.

172. Flynn, 219.

173. "Multiple Choice," *New Republic*, May 28, 1966, 5.

174. Flynn, 19, 78.

175. Bailey, 21.

176. Ibid., 21, 38.

177. "Draft Scandal," *New Republic*, December 25, 1965, 7.

178. Quoted in "Draft Scandal," 7.

179. Flynn, 226.

180. Quoted in Flynn, 226.

181. Quoted in Flynn, 266.

182. Blair Clark, "The Question Is What Kind of Army?" *Harper's Magazine* 239, no. 1492 (September 1969), 83.

183. Ibid., 82.

184. Ibid.

185. Ibid., 81.

186. Bailey, 29.

187. Bailey, 31; Flynn, 237.

188. Flynn, 237–238. For the transition to the All Volunteer Force see Bailey, *America's Army* and Robert K. Griffith, Jr., The U.S. Army's Transition to the All-Volunteer Force, 1968–1974 (Washington, D.C.: U.S. Army Center of Military History, 1997).

189. U.S. Department of the Army, "Executive Summary: Provide," v.

190. U.S. Department of the Army, "Executive Summary: Provide," vi; Godson, 208; Morden, 227–228.

191. Quoted in Leonard Sloane, "Makers of Military Toys Are Picketed by Mothers," *New York Times*, March 8, 1966, 49, 57.

192. Quoted in Sloane, "Makers of Military Toys," 49, 57.

193. Hall, 84; Gerald Mast and Bruce F. Kawin, *A Short History of the Movies*, 6th. ed. (Boston: Allyn and Bacon, 1996), 469.

194. Butler, 141; Bernard F. Dick, *The Star-Spangled Screen: The American World War II Film* (Lexington: The University Press of Kentucky, 1985), 248; Wetta and Curley, 6–7; Lawrence Suid does not consider *MASH* a war film. Suid, *Guts and Glory*, 279.

195. Huebner, 246.

196. *MASH*, directed by Robert Altman (Twentieth Century–Fox, 1970).

197. Ibid.

198. Ibid.

199. Review of *MASH*, *Time*, January 26, 1970, 78.

200. Ibid.

201. Vincent Canby, "Blood, Blasphemy and Laughs," *New York Times*, February 1, 1970, 1.

202. Richard Corliss, "I Admit It, I Didn't Like M*A*S*H," *New York Times*, March 22, 1970, 19.

203. Ibid.

204. Ibid.

205. *Catch-22*, directed by Mike Nichols (Paramount Pictures, 1970).

206. Joseph Heller, *Catch-22* (New York: Dell, 1961); Suid, *Guts and Glory*, 280; Whitfield, *Culture*, 214; Stephen J. Whitfield, "Still the Best Catch There Is: Joseph Heller's *Catch-22*," in *Rethinking Cold War Culture*, Peter J. Kuznick and James Gilbert, eds. (Washington, D.C.: Smithsonian Institution, 2001), 176.

207. *Catch-22*, directed by Mike Nichols.

208. Ibid.

209. Ibid.

210. Vincent Canby, Review of *Catch-22*, *New York Times*, June 25, 1970, 54; Whitfield, "Joseph Heller's 'Catch 22,'" 184.

211. "Some Are More Yossarian Than Others," *Time*, June 15, 1970, 66. *How I Won the War* (1967) is a British film featuring John Lennon and Michael Crawford about a bumbling British World War II commander and his soldiers in North Africa and Europe.

212. *Patton*, directed by Franklin Schaffner (Twentieth Century–Fox, 1970).

213. Ibid.

214. Ibid.

215. Ibid.

216. Ibid.

217. Ibid.

218. Suid, *Guts and Glory*, 274.

219. "Old Blood and Guts," *Time*, February 9, 1970, 78.

220. Vincent Canby, review of *Patton*, *New York Times*, February 5, 1970, 33.

221. Vincent Canby, review of *Patton*, *New York Times*, February 8, 1970, 1.

222. Suid, *Guts and Glory*, 274.

223. Peter Schejeldahl, "Is 'Patton' a Lie?," *New York Times*, June 14, 1970, 11. Bernard Dick believes any anti-war sentiment in *Patton* is something eager student activists devised "to find non-existent analogies with Vietnam." Dick, 248. For further commentary on the pro-war and anti-war aspects of the film, see Rubin, 201–02 and Wetta and Curley, 10.

224. Schejeldahl, 11.

225. Roger J. Spiller, foreword to *Celluloid Wars: A Guide to Film and the American Experience of War* by Frank J. Wetta and Stephen J. Curley (New York: Greenwood, 1992), xii.

226. Tom Roberts, "A Company of Soldiers," in *Frontline* (PBS, 2005).

Conclusion

1. Weigley, xii.

2. Ibid.

3. Peter Karsten, "The American Democratic Citizen-Soldier: Triumph or Disaster?" *Military Affairs* 30, no. 1 (1966), 39–40.

4. Stewart, *American Military History*, Vol. II, 369.

5. Ibid., 369–374; Millett and Masklowski, 597–98.

6. Schulman, 221.

7. Ibid.

8. Andrew J. Bacevich, *The New American Militarism: How Americans Are Seduced by War* (New York: Oxford University Press, 2005), 5–6. For more perspectives on American militarism, see Peter D. Feaver and Christopher Gelpi, *Choosing Your Battles: American Civil-Military Relations and the Use of Force* (Princeton, NJ: Princeton University Press, 2004), Jason K. Dempsey, *Our Army: Soldiers, Politics, and American Civil-Military Relations* (Princeton, NJ: Princeton University Press, 2010), and Richard E. Rubenstein, *Reasons to Kill: Why Americans Choose War* (New York: Bloomsbury, 2010).

9. Bacevich, *New American Militarism*, 6.

10. Ibid., 105–11.

11. Charles M. Province, Northeast Kansas Korean War Memorial, available at http://pattonhq.com/koreamemorial.html (accessed July 13, 2010). Emphasis in the original.

12. U.S. Department of Labor Veterans' Employment and Training Service, *Transition Assistance Program Workshop Participant Manual* (Washington, D.C.: U.S. Department of Labor, November 2002), back cover.

13. Cooper, *Rise of the National Guard*, xv. Cooper notes, "Today, the federal government provides 95 percent of the National Guard's funding and exerts such control over state military forces that some scholars contend, with only slight exaggeration, that the Army and Air National Guards are federal forces on loan to the states."

14. Lisa M. Mundey, "Citizen-Soldiers or Warriors: Language for a Democracy," in *Semiotics 2008: Specialization, Semiosis, Semiotics, Proceedings of the 33rd Annual Meeting of the Semiotic Society of America*, eds. John Deely and Leonard G. Sbrocchi (New York: Legas, 2009): 130–39.

15. Gallup, Inc., "In U.S., Military Ranks Best, Congress Worst," *Gallup* http://www.gallup.com/video/108130/us-military-ranks-best-congress-worst.aspx (accessed September 2, 2010).

16. Bacevich, *The New American Militarism*, 170.

17. See John Bodnar, "Saving Private Ryan and Postwar Memory in America," *The American Historical Review*, vol. 106, No. 3 (June 2001): 805–817.

18. Quoted in Jeff Bacon, "Beetle at 60," *Army Times*, Off Duty, September 13, 2010, 7.

19. Margaret Aikens, "Is Avatar Anti-Military?" *Atlanta Military Families Examiner*, December 30, 2009, available at http://www.examiner.com (accessed July 18, 2010); Mike Parker, "Chicago Alderman Declares War on 'Avatar,'" CBS Broadcasting, Inc., January 7, 2010, available from http://cbs2chicago.com/local/Avatar.Balcer.negative.2.1412100.html (accessed July 18, 2010).

20. Mort Walker and Greg Walker, "Beetle Bailey," September 3, 2010, available from http://www.kingfeatures.com/features/comics/bbailey/about.htm (accessed October 29, 2010).

BIBLIOGRAPHY

Primary Sources

Archives
Browne Popular Culture Library, Bowling Green State University, Bowling Green, Ohio.
   Graphic Arts Collection
U.C.L.A. Film and Television Archives, University of California, Los Angeles.
U.S. Department of the Navy, Naval Historical Center, Washington Naval Yard, Washing-
   ton, D.C.
   Photographic Section, Navy Art — Posters
U.S. Marine Corps, Marine Corps Historical Center, Washington Naval Yard, Washington,
   D.C.
   Combat Art Records
U.S. National Archives and Records Administration, College Park, Maryland.
   Record Group 24: Bureau of Naval Personnel
   Record Group 111: Records of the Office of the Chief Signals Officer
   Record Group 127: Headquarters Marine Corps
   Record Group 319: Records of the Army Chief of Staff
   Record Group 330: Records of the Secretary of Defense
   Record Group 340: Records of the Secretary of the Air Force
   Record Group 342: Records of the U.S. Air Force Commands
   Record Group 428: Records of the Secretary of the Navy

Films
Aldrich, Robert. *The Dirty Dozen*. 145 min. MGM, 1967.
Altman, Robert. *MASH*. 116 min. Twentieth Century–Fox, 1970.
Annakin, Ken. *Battle of the Bulge*. 167 min. Warner Bros., 1965.
Annakin, Ken, Andrew Marton, Bernhard Wicki, and Darryl F. Zanuck. *The Longest Day*.
    178 min. Twentieth Century–Fox, 1962.
Cromwell, John. *Since You Went Away*. 177 min. MGM, 1944.
Dmytryk, Edward. *The Caine Mutiny*. 124 min. Columbia Pictures, 1954.
Dwan, Allan. *Sands of Iwo Jima*. 100 min. Republic Pictures, 1949.
Edwards, Blake. *Operation Petticoat*. 122 min. Universal Pictures, 1959.
Fleischer, Richard. *Tora! Tora! Tora!* 144 min. Twentieth Century–Fox, 1970.
Ford, John. *They Were Expendable*. 135 min. MGM, 1945.
Ford, John, and Mervyn LeRoy. *Mister Roberts*. 123 min. Warner Bros., 1955.
Frankenheimer, John. *The Manchurian Candidate*. 126 min. United Artists, 1962.
_____. *Seven Days in May*. 118 min. Paramount Pictures, 1964.
Fuller, Samuel. *The Steel Helmet*. 85 min. Lippert Pictures, 1951.
Garnett, Tay. *Bataan*, 114 min. MGM, 1943.

Griffith, D. W. *The Birth of a Nation*, 187 min. David W. Griffith Corp., 1915
Hibbs, Jesse. *To Hell and Back*. 106 min. Universal Pictures, 1955.
Hiller, Arthur. *The Americanization of Emily*. 115 min. MGM, 1964.
Kellogg, Ray, and John Wayne. *The Green Berets*. 141 min. Warner Bros., 1968.
King, Henry. *Twelve O'Clock High*. 132 min. Twentieth Century–Fox, 1949.
Kramer, Stanley. *On the Beach*. 134 min. United Artists, 1959.
Kubrick, Stanley. *Dr. Strangelove, or: How I Stopped Worrying and Learned to Love the Bomb*. 93 min. Columbia Pictures, 1964.
Lumet, Sidney. *Fail-Safe*. 112 min. Columbia Pictures, 1964.
Mann, Anthony. *Strategic Air Command*. 112 min. Paramount Pictures, 1955.
McLaglen, Andrew. *The Devil's Brigade*. 130 min. Wolper Pictures, 1968.
Milestone, Lewis. *All Quiet on the Western Front*. 131 min. Universal Pictures, 1930.
_____. *The Halls of Montezuma*. 113 min. Twentieth Century–Fox, 1950.
_____. *Pork Chop Hill*. 97 min. United Artists, 1959.
_____. *A Walk in the Sun*. 117 min. Twentieth Century–Fox, 1945.
Nichols, Mike. *Catch-22*. 122 min. Paramount Pictures, 1970.
Pirosh, Robert. *Go for Broke!* 92 min. MGM, 1951.
Preminger, Otto. *In Harm's Way*. 165 min. Paramount Pictures, 1965.
Ray, Nicholas. *The Flying Leathernecks*. 102 min. RKO, 1951.
Robson, Mark. *The Bridges at Toko-Ri*. 102 min. Paramount Pictures, 1955.
Schaffner, Franklin. *Patton*. 170 min. Twentieth Century–Fox, 1970.
Selander, Lesley. *Flat Top*. 83 min. Monogram Pictures Corporation, 1952.
Siegal, Don. *Hell Is for Heroes*. 90 min. Paramount Pictures, 1962.
Sirk, Douglas. *Battle Hymn*. 108 min. Universal-International Pictures, 1957.
Wellman, William. *Battleground*. 118 min. MGM, 1949.
_____. *The Story of G.I. Joe*. 108 min. United Artists, 1945.
Wilder, Billy. *Stalag 17*. 120 min. Paramount Pictures, 1953.
Wyler, William. *The Best Years of Our Lives*. 172 min. RKO, 1946.
Zinnemann, Fred. *From Here to Eternity*. 118 min. Columbia Pictures, 1953.

Periodicals

The Army Reservist, 1954–1961.
The Army Reserve Magazine, 1965–1968.
Life, 1945–1970.
Navy Recruiter, 1959–1960, 1967.
The New Republic, 1945–1970.
New York Times, 1945–1970.
Newsweek, 19 November 1965.
Popular Science, 1948–1970.
Saturday Evening Post, 1946–1970.
Senior Scholastic — Teacher Edition, October 21, 1959.
TV Guide, 1960–1970.

Published Primary Sources

Baldwin, Hanson W. *Great Mistakes of the War*. New York: Harper and Brothers, 1949. Facsimile print, Ann Arbor, MI: University Microfilms International, 1978.
_____. "What's Wrong with the Regulars?" *Saturday Evening Post*, October 31, 1953.
Caputo, Philip. *A Rumor of War*. New York: Ballantine, 1977.
Collins, Winifred Quick, and Herbert M. Levine. *More Than a Uniform: A Navy Woman in a Navy Man's World*. Denton: University of North Texas Press, 1997.
Erskine, Hazel. "The Polls: Is War a Mistake?" *The Public Opinion Quarterly* 34. no. 1 (Spring 1970): 134–150.
Fulbright, J. W. *The Pentagon Propaganda Machine*. New York: Liveright, 1970.
Fussell, Paul. *Wartime: Understanding and Behavior in the Second World War*. New York: Oxford University Press, 1989.

Gallup, George. *The Gallup Poll: Public Opinion, 1935–1971, Vol. I, 1935–1948.* New York: Random House, 1972.

_____. *The Gallup Poll: Public Opinion, 1935–1971, Vol. II, 1949–1958.* New York: Random House, 1972.

_____. *The Gallup Poll: Public Opinion, 1935–1971, Vol. III, 1959–1971.* New York: Random House, 1972.

Harrison, William H., Jr. "As We See It." *The National Guardsman,* December 1959.

Janowitz, Morris. *The Professional Soldier: A Social and Political Portrait.* Glencoe, IL: Free, 1960.

Kovic, Ron. *Born on the Fourth of July.* New York: Pocket, 1976.

Little, Roger W. "Solidarity Is the Key to the Mass Army." *The Army Combat Forces Journal,* February 1955.

Mauldin, Bill. *Bill Mauldin's Army: Bill Mauldin's Greatest World War II Cartoons.* Novato, CA: Presidio, 1983.

Michener, James. "The Bridges at Toko-Ri." *Life,* July 6, 1953.

Murphy, Audie. *To Hell and Back.* New York: Bantam, 1949, reprint 1979.

O'Sullivan, John, and Alan M. Meckler, eds. *The Draft and Its Enemies.* Urbana: University of Illinois Press, 1974.

Phillips, Cabell. "Your Best Deal in Military Service." *Harper's Magazine,* July 1957.

"The Quarter's Polls." *The Public Opinion Quarterly* 9, no. 4 (1945–1946): 510–38.

Raddatz, Leslie. "More British Than Big Ben." *TV Guide,* July 29, 1967.

Research Division of the Office of Armed Forces Information and Education. "Enlisted Women in the Services." Washington, D.C.: Department of Defense, 1953.

Roberts, Tom. "A Company of Soldiers." In *Frontline.* USA: PBS, 2005.

Schuffert, Jake. *No Sweat: A Collection of Jake Schuffert Cartoons from Army Times, Air Force Times, Navy Times,* 4th ed. Washington, D.C.: Army Times, 1970.

Searle, Ronald. "The Irrepressible, Indestructible, Instant Peasant Gomer Pyle." *TV Guide,* August 26, 1967.

Somit, Albert. "The Military Hero as Presidential Candidate." *The Public Opinion Quarterly* 12, no. 2 (1948).

Stouffer, Samuel A., Arthur A. Lumsdaine, Marion Harper Lumsdaine, Robin M. Williams, Jr., M. Brewster Smoth, Irving L. Janis, Shirley A. Star, and Leonard S. Cottrell, Jr. *The American Soldier: Combat and Its Aftermath, Vol. II.* New York: John Wiley, 1949; reprint, Manhattan, KS: *Military Affairs* with permission of Princeton University Press, 1977.

Suchman, Edward A., Rose K. Goldsen, and Robin M. Williams, Jr. "Attitudes Toward the Korean War." *The Public Opinion Quarterly* 17, no. 2 (1953): 171–84.

_____. "Student Reaction to Impending Military Service." *American Sociological Review* 18, no. 3 (June 1953): 293–304.

Sumrall, Master Sergeant. "Take a Barracks Bride? Not Me!" *U.S. Lady,* September 1955.

United States Army Recruiting Service. "You've Got to be Good." *Flying Aces,* March 1944.

United States Army Reserve. "The Little Guy Doesn't Know It, but the Lady Is a Captain." *Missouri Nurse,* June 1967.

United States Department of Labor Veterans' Employment and Training Service. *Transition Assistance Program Workshop Participant Manual.* Washington, D.C.: U.S. Department of Labor, 2002.

Walker, Mort. *50 Years of Beetle Bailey.* New York: Nanter, Beall, Minoustchine, 2000.

Wallace, Terry. *Bloods: An Oral History of the Vietnam War by Black Veterans.* New York: Random House, 1984.

Television Series

Broadside, 30 min. ABC, 1964.

Combat!, 60 min. ABC, 1962–67.

Crusade in Europe, 30 min. ABC, 1949.

Crusade in the Pacific, 30 min. ABC, 1951.

F Troop, 30 min. ABC, 1965–67.
The Gallant Men, 60 min. ABC, 1962–63.
Gomer Pyle U.S.M.C., 30 min. CBS, 1964–69.
Hennesey, 30 min. CBS, 1959–62.
Hogan's Heroes, 30 min. CBS, 1965–71.
I Dream of Jeannie, 30 min. NBC, 1965–70.
The Lieutenant, 60 min. CBS, 1963–64.
McHale's Navy, 30 min. ABC, 1962–66.
Navy Log, 30 min. CBS, 1955–58.
The Phil Silvers Show, 30 min. CBS, 1955–59.
The Rat Patrol, 30 min.— ABC, 1966–68.
Twelve O'Clock High, 60 min.— ABC, 1964–67.
Victory at Sea, 30 min.— NBC, 1952–53.
West Point Story, 30 min.— CBS, 1956–57.

Unpublished Primary Sources

Public Opinion Surveys Inc. "Attitudes of Adult Civilians Toward the Military Service as a Career." Princeton, NJ: Public Opinion Surveys, 1955.
_____. "Attitudes of 16 to 20 Year Old Males Toward the Military Service as a Career." Princeton, NJ: Public Opinion Surveys, 1955.

Secondary Sources

Alpers, Benjamin L. "This Is the Army: Imagining a Democratic Military in World War II." *Journal of American History* 85, no. 1 (1998): 129–63.
Ambrose, Stephen E. *Citizen Soldiers.* New York: Simon & Schuster, 1997.
_____. *D-Day, June 6, 1944: The Climatic Battle of World War II.* New York: Simon & Schuster, 1994.
_____. *Eisenhower: Soldier and President.* New York: Simon & Schuster, 1990.
_____. "'The Longest Day' (1962): 'Blockbuster' History." *Historical Journal of Film, Radio and Television* 14, no. 4 (1994): 421–31.
Appy, Christian G. "'We'll Follow the Old Man': The Strains of Sentimental Militarism in Popular Films of the Fifties." In *Rethinking Cold War Culture*, edited by Peter J. Kuznick and James Gilbert. Washington, D.C.: Smithsonian Institution, 2001.
Bacevich, Andrew J. *The New American Militarism: How Americans Are Seduced by War.* New York: Oxford University Press, 2005.
_____. *The Pentomic Era: The U.S. Army Between Korea and Vietnam.* Washington, D.C.: National Defense University Press, 1986.
Bailey, Beth. *America's Army: Making the All Volunteer Force.* Cambridge, MA: Belknap Press of Harvard University Press, 2009.
Barnouw, Erik. *Tube of Plenty: The Evolution of American Television*, 2d rev. ed. New York: Oxford University Press, 1990.
Barson, Michael. "Propaganda." *Entertainment Weekly*, April 4, 2003.
Basinger, Jeanine. *A Woman's View: How Hollywood Spoke to Women, 1930–1960.* New York: Alfred A. Knopf, 1993.
_____. *The World War II Combat Film: Anatomy of a Genre.* New York: Columbia University Press, 1986.
_____. *The World War II Combat Film: Anatomy of a Genre.* Updated ed. Middletown, CT: Wesleyan University Press, 2003.
Beidler, Philip D. *The Good War's Greatest Hits: World War II and American Remembering.* Athens: University of Georgia Press, 1998.
Berghahn, Volker Rolf. *Militarism: The History of an International Debate, 1861–1979.* New York: St. Martin's, 1982.
Bindas, Kenneth J., and Kenneth J. Heineman. "Image Is Everything? Television and the

Counterculture Message in the 1960s." *Journal of Popular Film and Television* 22, no. 1 (1994): 22–37.

Biskind, Peter. *Seeing Is Believing: How Hollywood Taught Us to Stop Worrying and Love the Fifties.* New York: Pantheon, 1983.

Boddy, William. *Fifties Television: The Industry and Its Critics.* Urbana: University of Illinois Press, 1990.

Bodnar, John. "Saving Private Ryan and Postwar Memory in America," *The American Historical Review* 106, no. 3 (June 2001): 805–17.

Boettcher, Thomas D. *First Call: The Making of the Modern U.S. Military, 1945–1953.* Boston: Little, Brown, 1992.

Boggs, Carl, and Tom Pollard. *The Hollywood War Machine: U.S. Militarism and Popular Culture.* Boulder, CO: Paradigm, 2007.

Bogle, Lori Lyn. *The Pentagon's Battle for the American Mind: The Early Cold War.* College Station: Texas A&M University Press, 2004.

Bowers, William T., William M. Hammond, and George L. MacGarrigle. *Black Soldier, White Army: The 24th Infantry Regiment in Korea.* Washington, D.C.: United States Army Center of Military History, 1996.

Boyer, Paul. *By the Bomb's Early Light: American Thought and Culture at the Dawn of the Atomic Age.* New York: Pantheon, 1985.

Boyne, Walter J. *Beyond the Wild Blue: A History of the U.S. Air Force.* New York: St. Martin's Griffin, 1997.

Brinkley, Alan. *The Publisher: Henry Luce and His American Century.* New York: Alfred A. Knopf, 2010.

Brokaw, Tom. *The Greatest Generation.* New York: Dell, 2001.

Brooks, Tim, and Earle Marsh. *The Complete Directory to Prime Time Network TV Shows, 1946–Present,* 4th ed. New York: Ballantine, 1988.

Bryant, John. "Situation Comedy of the Sixties: The Evolution of a Genre." *Studies in American Humor* 7 (1989): 118–39.

Builder, Carl H. *The Masks of War: American Military Styles in Strategy and Analysis.* Baltimore: Johns Hopkins University Press, 1989.

Buote, Brenda J. "New Warriors Wanted, Recruiters Tap Patriotism to Add to Military Ranks." *The Boston Globe,* April 13, 2003.

Butler, Ivan. *The War Film.* South Brunswick, NJ: A.S. Barnes, 1974.

Cameron, Craig M. *American Samurai: Myth, Imagination, and the Conduct of Battle in the First Marine Division, 1941–1951.* New York: Cambridge University Press, 1994.

Cameron, Kenneth M. *America on Film: Hollywood and American History.* New York: Continuum, 1997.

Cantor, Muriel G., and Joel M. Cantor. *Prime-Time Television: Content and Control,* 2d ed. Newbury Park, CA: Sage, 1992.

Chafe, William H. *The Paradox of Change: American Women in the 20th Century.* New York: Oxford University Press, 1991.

Coon, James T. "Sixties Entertainment Television and Cold War Discourses." Ph.D. diss, Bowling Green State University, 1994.

Cooper, Jerry. *The Rise of the National Guard: The Evolution of the American Militia, 1865–1920.* Lincoln: University of Nebraska Press, 1997.

Cragin, Thomas J. "America's D-Day Comes to France: The French Reception of *The Longest Day* and *Saving Private Ryan.*" Paper presented at the War in Film, Television, and History, Dolce International Conference Center, Dallas/Ft. Worth, November 13, 2004.

Cunliffe, Marcus. *Soldiers and Civilians: The Martial Spirit in America, 1775–1865.* New York: Free, 1973.

Curtin, Michael. *Redeeming the Wasteland: Television Documentary and Cold War Politics.* New Brunswick, NJ: Rutgers University Press, 1995.

Dalfiume, Richard M. *Desegregation of the U.S. Armed Forces: Fighting on Two Fronts, 1939–1953.* Columbia: University of Missouri Press, 1969.

Davidson, James West, and Mark Hamilton Lytle. *After the Fact: The Art of Historical Detection*, 5th ed., vol. II. Boston: McGraw Hill, 2005.

Davis, Ronald. *Duke: The Life and Times of John Wayne*. Norman: University of Oklahoma Press, 1998.

DePastino, Todd. *Bill Mauldin: A Life Up Front*. New York: W.W. Norton, 2008.

DeRosa, Christopher S. *Political Indoctrination in the U.S. Army from World War II to the Vietnam War*. Lincoln: University of Nebraska Press, 2006.

Dick, Bernard F. *The Star-Spangled Screen: The American World War II Film*. Lexington: University Press of Kentucky, 1985.

Dockrill, Saki. *Eisenhower's New Look National Security Policy*. New York: St. Martin's, 1996.

Doherty, Thomas. *Projections of War: Hollywood, American Culture, and World War II*. New York: Columbia University Press, 1993.

Donnelly, William M. "'The Best Army that Can Be Put in the Field in the Circumstances': The U.S. Army, July 1951–July 1953." *Journal of Military History* 71, no. 3 (2007): 809–47.

_____. *Under Army Orders: The Army National Guard During the Korean War*. College Station: Texas A&M University Press, 2001.

Donovan, James A. *Militarism, U.S.A.* New York: Scribner's, 1970.

Doubler, Michael D. *Civilian in Peace, Soldier in War: The Army National Guard, 1636–2000*. Lawrence: University Press of Kansas, 2003.

_____. *Closing with the Enemy: How GIs Fought the War in Europe, 1944–1945*. Lawrence: University Press of Kansas, 1994.

Douglas, Susan. *Where the Girls Are: Growing Up Female with the Mass Media*. New York: Random House, 1994.

Dower, John W. *War Without Mercy: Race and Power in the Pacific War*. New York: Pantheon, 1987.

Dudziak, Mary L. *Cold War Civil Rights: Race and the Image of American Democracy*. Princeton: Princeton University Press, 2000.

Ekirch, Arthur A., Jr. *The Civilian and the Military: A History of the American Antimilitarist Tradition*. Paperback ed. Colorado Springs: Ralph Myles, 1972.

Engelhardt, Tom. *The End of Victory Culture: Cold War America and the Disillusioning of a Generation*. Amherst: University of Massachusetts Press, 1995.

Farber, David. *The Age of Great Dreams: America in the 1960s*. New York: Hill and Wang, 1994.

Flynn, George Q. *The Draft, 1940–1973*. Lawrence: University Press of Kansas, 1993.

French, Shannon E. *The Code of the Warrior: Exploring Warrior Values Past and Present*. New York: Rowman and Littlefield, 2003.

Fussell, Paul. *The Great War and Modern Memory*. New York: Oxford University Press, 1975.

Gaddis, John Lewis. *We Now Know: Rethinking Cold War History*. New York: Oxford University Press, 1997.

Godson, Susan H. *Serving Proudly: A History of Women in the U.S. Navy*. Annapolis, MD: Naval Institute, 2001.

Graham, Don. *No Name on the Bullet: A Biography of Audie Murphy*. New York: Viking Penguin, 1989.

Grandstaff, Mark R. "Making the Military American: Advertising, Reform, and the Demise of an Antistanding Military Tradition, 1945–1955." *Journal of Military History* 60, no. 2 (1996): 299–323.

Griffith, Robert K., Jr. *The U.S. Army's Transition to the All-Volunteer Force, 1968–1974*. Edited by Jeffrey J Clarke, *Army Historical Series*. Washington, D.C.: U.S. Army Center of Military History, 1996.

Guralnick, Peter. *Careless Love: The Unmasking of Elvis Presley*. Boston: Little, Brown, 1999.

Hall, Mitchell K. *Crossroads: American Popular Culture and the Vietnam Generation*. Lanham, MD: Rowman and Littlefield, 2005.

Hammond, William M. *Reporting Vietnam: Media and Military at War.* Lawrence: University Press of Kansas, 1998.

Hellmann, John. *American Myth and the Legacy of Vietnam.* New York: Columbia University Press, 1986.

Heppenheimer, T. A. *Countdown: A History of Spaceflight.* New York: John Wiley, 1997.

Herrera, Ricardo. "Self-Governance and the American Citizen as Soldier, 1775–1861." *The Journal of Military History* 65 (January 2001): 21–52.

Herring, George C. *America's Longest War: The United States and Vietnam, 1950–1975,* 2nd ed. New York: McGraw-Hill, 1986.

Hess, Stephen, and Sandy Northrop. *Drawn and Quartered: The History of American Political Cartoons.* Montgomery, AL: Elliott and Clark, 1996.

Hewlett, Richard G., and Jack M. Holl. *Atoms for Peace and War, 1953–1961.* Berkeley: University of California Press, 1989.

Holm, Jeanne. *Women in the Military: An Unfinished Revolution,* rev. ed. Novato, CA: Presidio, 1992.

Horowitz, David A., and Peter N. Carroll. *On the Edge: The United States Since 1945,* 3rd ed. Belmont, CA: Wadsworth, 2002.

Holsinger, M. Paul, ed. *War and American Popular Culture: A Historical Encyclopedia.* Westport, CT: Greenwood, 1999.

Huebner, Andrew J. *The Warrior Image: Soldiers in American Culture from the Second World War to the Vietnam Era.* Chapel Hill: University of North Carolina Press, 2008.

Hynes, Samuel. *The Soldiers' Tale: Bearing Witness to Modern War.* New York: Penguin, 1997.

Jefferson, Bonnie S. "John Wayne: American Icon, Patriotic Zealot and Cold War Ideologue." In *War and Film in America: Historical and Critical Essays,* edited by Marilyn J. Matelski and Nancy Lynch Street. Jefferson, NC: McFarland, 2003.

Kalisch, Philip A., Beatrice J Kalisch, and Margaret Scobey. *Images of Nurses on Television.* New York: Springer, 1983.

Kemble, C. Robert. *The Image of the Army Officer in America.* Westport, CT: Greenwood, 1973.

Kindsvatter, Peter S. *American Soldier: Ground Combat in the World Wars, Korea, and Vietnam.* Lawrence: University Press of Kansas, 2003.

Kohn, Richard H. "The Danger of Militarization in an Endless 'War' on Terrorism." *The Journal of Military History* 73, no. 1 (January 2009): 177–208.

Koppes, Clayton R., and Gregory D. Black. *Hollywood Goes to War: How Politics, Profits, Propaganda Shaped World War II Movies.* New York: Free, 1987.

Kuznick, Peter J., and James Gilbert. "U.S. Culture and the Cold War." In *Rethinking Cold War Culture,* edited by Peter J. Kuznick and James Gilbert, 1–13. Washington, D.C.: Smithsonian Institution, 2001.

Leed, Eric J. *No Man's Land: Combat and Identity in World War I.* New York: Cambridge University Press, 1979.

Lenihan, John H. "Hollywood Laughs at the Cold War, 1947–1961." In *Hollywood as Mirror: Changing Views of "Outsiders" and "Enemies" in American Movies,* edited by Robert Brent Toplin. Westport, CT: Greenwood, 1993.

Lentz, Robert J. *Korean War Filmography.* Jefferson, NC: McFarland, 2003.

Linderman, Gerald F. *The World Within War: America's Combat Experience in World War II.* New York: Free, 1997.

Lindsay, Robert. *This HIGH Name: Public Relations and the U.S. Marine Corps.* Madison: University of Wisconsin Press, 1956.

Loring, Lorna McCabe. "Making a Home for the Military Family: The Institutionalization of Postwar Domesticity in the United States Military, 1945–1965." Kansas State University, 2002.

MacDonald, J. Fred. "The Cold War As Entertainment in 'Fifties' Television." *Journal of Popular Film and Television* 7, no. 1 (1978).

_____. *Television and the Red Menace: The Video Road to Vietnam.* New York: Praeger, 1985.

Marling, Karal Ann. *As Seen on TV: The Visual Culture of Everyday Life in the 1950s*. Cambridge, MA: Harvard University Press, 1994.

_____, and John Wetenhall. *Iwo Jima: Monuments, Memories, and the American Hero*. Cambridge, MA: Harvard University Press, 1991.

Mast, Gerald, and Bruce F. Kawin. *A Short History of the Movies*, 6th ed. Boston: Allyn and Bacon, 1996.

May, Elaine Tyler. *Homeward Bound: American Families in the Cold War Era*, rev. and updated ed. New York: Basic Books, 1999.

Mayland, Charles. "*Dr. Strangelove* (1964): Nightmare Comedy and the Ideology of Liberal Consensus." In *Hollywood as Historian: American Film in a Cultural Context*, edited by Peter C. Rollins, 190–210. Lexington: University Press of Kentucky, 1983.

McAdams, Frank. *The American War Film: History and Hollywood*. Westport, CT: Praeger, 2002.

McLuhan, Marshall. *Understanding Media: The Extensions of Man*. New York: McGraw-Hill, 1964.

Menand, Louis. "Paris, Texas: How Hollywood Brought the Cinema Back from France." *The New Yorker*, February 17 and 24, 2003.

Miller, Douglas T., and Marion Nowak. *The Fifties: The Way We Really Were*. Garden City, NY: Doubleday, 1977.

Miller, John Jackson, Maggie Thompson, Peter Bickford, and Brent Frankenhoff. *The Standard Catalog of Comic Books*. Iola, WI: Krause, 2002.

Millett, Allan R. *Semper Fidelis: The History of the United States Marine Corps*. New York: Macmillan, 1980.

_____. *The War for Korea, 1950–1951: They Came from the North*. Lawrence: University Press of Kansas, 2010.

_____, and Peter Maslowski. *For the Common Defense: A Military History of the United States of America*. Revised and Expanded ed. New York: Free, 1994.

Morden, Bettie J. *The Women's Army Corps, 1945–1978, Army Historical Series*. Washington, D.C.: Government Printing Office, 1990.

Moskos, Charles C., Jr. *The American Enlisted Man: The Rank and File in Today's Military*. New York: Russell Sage Foundation, 1970.

Mundey, Lisa M. "Citizen-Soldiers or Warriors: Language for a Democracy," in *Semiotics 2008: Specialization, Semiosis, Semiotics," Proceedings of the 33rd Annual Meeting of the Semiotic Society of America*. Edited by John Deely and Leonard G. Sbrocchi. New York: Legas, 2009.

Murray, Williamson, and Allan R. Millett. *A War to Be Won: Fighting the Second World War*. Cambridge, MA: Belknap Press of Harvard University Press, 2001.

Nalty, Bernard C. *Strength for the Fight: A History of Black Americans in the Military*. New York: Free, 1986.

Navasky, Victor S. *Naming Names*. New York: Penguin, 1991.

O'Connor, John E., ed. *American History/American Television*. New York: Frederick Ungar, 1983.

_____. *Image as Artifact: The Historical Analysis of Film and Television*. Malabar, FL: Robert E. Krieger, 1990.

Pach, Chester J., and Elmo Richardson. *The Presidency of Dwight D. Eisenhower*. Lawrence: University of Kansas Press, 1991.

Parillo, Mark P., ed. *We Were in the Big One: Experiences of the World War II Generation*. Wilmington, DE: Scholarly Resources, 2002.

Peterson, Arthur Hews. "An Investigation of the United States Army and United States Air Force Recruiting Organization and Program." MS, Columbia University, 1948.

Pierson, David. "ABC-TV's *Combat!*, World War II, and the Enduring Image of the Combat Cold Warrior." *Film and History* 21, no. 2 (2001): 25–32.

Prior, Robin, and Trevor Wilson. "Paul Fussell at War." *War in History* 1, no. 1 (1994): 63–80.

Quart, Leonard, and Albert Auster. *American Film and Society Since 1945*, 2d ed. New York: Praeger, 1991.

Robb, David L. *Operation Hollywood: How the Pentagon Shapes and Censor the Movies.* Amherst, NY: Prometheus, 2004.

Roberts, Randy, and James S. Olson. *John Wayne, American.* Lincoln: University of Nebraska Press, 1995.

Rollins, Peter C. "Victory at Sea: Cold War Epic." In *Television Histories: Shaping Collective Memory in the Media Age,* edited by Gary R. Edgerton and Peter C. Rollins, 103–22. Lexington: University Press of Kentucky, 2001.

Royce, Brenda Scott. *Hogan's Heroes: A Comprehensive Reference to the 1965–1971 Television Comedy Series, with Cast Biographies and an Episode Guide.* Jefferson, NC: McFarland, 1993.

Rubin, Steven Jay. *Combat Films: American Realism, 1945–1970.* Jefferson: McFarland, 1981.

Savage, William W., Jr. *Comic Books and America, 1945–1954.* Norman: University of Oklahoma Press, 1990.

Sayre, Nora. *Running Time: Films of the Cold War.* New York: Dial, 1982.

Schafer, Elizabeth. "Press (Western) and the Korean War," In *The Korean War: An Encyclopedia,* edited by Stanley Sandler, 269–71. New York: Garland, 1995.

Schulman, Bruce J. *The Seventies: The Great Shift in American Culture, Society, and Politics.* Cambridge, MA: Da Capo, 2001.

Segal, David R. *Recruiting for Uncle Sam: Citizenship and Military Manpower Policy.* Lawrence: University Press of Kansas, 1989.

Shain, Russell E. "Effects of Pentagon Influence on War Movies, 1948–1970." *Journalism Quarterly* 49 (1972): 641–47.

_____. "Hollywood's Cold War." *Journal of Popular Film* 3, no. 4 (1974): 334–49.

Shea, Nancy. *The Army Wife,* 3d rev. ed. New York: Harper and Brothers, 1954.

_____. *The Waacs.* New York: Harper and Brothers, 1943.

Sherry, Michael S. *In the Shadow of War: The United States Since the 1930s.* New Haven, CT: Yale University Press, 1995.

Shindler, Colin. *Hollywood Goes to War: Films and American Society, 1939–1952.* Boston: Routledge and Kegan Paul, 1979.

Simmons, Edwin H. *The United States Marines, 1775–1975.* New York: Viking, 1976.

Simpson, Harold B. *Audie Murphy, American Soldier.* Hillsboro, TX: Hill Junior College Press, 1975.

Sklar, Robert. *Movie-Made America: A Social History of American Movies.* New York: Random House, 1975.

_____. *Prime-Time America: Life On and Beyond the Television Screen.* New York: Oxford University Press, 1980.

Slayton, Robert A. *Arms of Destruction: Ranking the World's Best Land Weapons of WWII.* New York: Citadel Press, 2004.

Slotkin, Richard. *Gunfighter Nation: The Myth of the Frontier in Twentieth-Century America.* New York: Atheneum, 1992.

Spiegel, Lynn. *Make Room for TV: Television and the Family Ideal in Postwar America.* Chicago: University of Chicago Press, 1992.

_____, and Michael Curtin, eds. *The Revolution Wasn't Televised.* New York: Routledge, 1997.

Spiller, Roger J. "Foreword." In *Celluloid Wars: A Guide to Film and the American Experience of War,* edited by Frank J. Wetta and Stephen J. Curley, xi–xiii. New York: Greenwood, 1992.

Stanton, Shelby. *U.S. Army Uniforms of the Cold War, 1948–1973.* Mechanicsburg, PA: Stackpole, 1994.

_____. *U.S. Army Uniforms of the Korean War.* Harrisburg, PA: Stackpole, 1992.

_____. *U.S. Army Uniforms of the Vietnam War.* Harrisburg, PA: Stackpole, 1989.

Steinberg, Cobbett. *TV Facts.* New York: Facts on File, 1985.

Sterling, Christopher H., and John Michael Kittross. *Stay Tuned: A History of American Broadcasting,* 3d ed. Mahwah, NJ: Lawrence Erlbaun, 2002.

Stewart, Richard W. *American Military History Volume II: The United States Army in a*

Global Era, 1917–2003. Washington, D.C.: Center of Military History, United States Army, 2005.

Stiehm, Judith Hicks. "The Generations of U.S. Enlisted Women." *Signs* 11, no. 1 (1985): 155–75.

Suid, Lawrence H. *Guts and Glory: The Making of the American Military Image in Film*, rev. and expanded ed. Lexington: University Press of Kentucky, 2002.

_____. *Sailing on the Silver Screen: Hollywood and the U.S. Navy*. Annapolis, MD: Naval Institute, 1996.

Tobin, James. *Ernie Pyle's War: America's Eyewitness to World War II*. Lawrence: University Press of Kansas, 1997.

Toplin, Robert Brent. *Reel History: In Defense of Hollywood*. Lawrence: University Press of Kansas, 2002.

_____, ed. *Hollywood as Mirror: Changing Views of "Outsiders" and "Enemies" in American Movies*. Westport, CT: Greenwood, 1993.

Treadwell, Mattie E. *The Women's Army Corps*. Washington, D.C.: Government Printing Office, 1990.

United States Army Center of Military History. *American Military History*, rev. ed., Army Historical Series. Washington, D.C.: Government Printing Office, 1989.

Vagts, Alfred. *A History of Militarism: Romance and Realities of a Profession*. New York: W. W. Norton, 1937.

Varhola, Michael J. *Fire and Ice: The Korean War, 1950–1953*. Mason City, IA: Savas, 2000.

Voeltz, Richard. "Film, Television, and Literature of the Korean War." In *The Korean War: An Encyclopedia*, edited by Stanley Sandler, 111–13. New York: Garland, 1995.

Watts, Tim J. "Beetle Bailey: Comic Strip by Mort Walker." In *Encyclopedia of War and American Society*, edited by Peter Karsten, 71–73. Thousand Oaks, CA: Sage, 2006.

Weigley, Russell F. *History of the United States Army*. New York: Macmillan, 1967.

Westheider, James E. *Fighting on Two Fronts: African Americans and the Vietnam War*. New York: New York University Press, 1997.

Wetta, Frank J., and Stephen J. Curley. *Celluloid Wars: A Guide to Film and the American Experience of War*. New York: Greenwood, 1992.

Whitfield, Stephen J. *The Culture of the Cold War*, 2d ed. Baltimore: Johns Hopkins University Press, 1996.

_____. "Still the Best Catch There Is: Joseph Heller's *Catch-22*." In *Rethinking Cold War Culture*, edited by Peter J. Kuznick and James Gilbert, 175–200. Washington, D.C.: Smithsonian Institution, 2001.

Whittebols, James. *Watching M*A*S*H, Watching America: A Social History of the 1972–1983 Television Series*. Jefferson, NC: McFarland, 1998.

Wills, Gary. *John Wayne's America*. New York: Simon and Schuster, 1997.

Wilson, Jeffrey S., and Terri Sabatos. "Reclaiming Duty, Honor, Country: West Point Story and America in the 1950s." Paper presented at the War in Film, Television, and History Conference, Dolce International Conference Center, Dallas/Ft. Worth, November 12, 2004.

Wolcott, James. "From Fear to Eternity." *Vanity Fair*, March 2005.

Wool, Harold. *The Military Specialist: Skilled Manpower for the Armed Forces*. Baltimore: Johns Hopkins University Press, 1968.

Worland, Eric John. "The Other Living Room War: Evolving Cold War Imagery in Popular TV Programs of the Vietnam Era, 1960–1975." Ph.D. diss., University of California, 1989.

Wright, Bradford W. *Comic Book Nation: The Transformation of Youth Culture in America*. Baltimore, MD: Johns Hopkins University Press, 2001.

INDEX

Page numbers in **bold italics** indicate illustrations.

9 780786 466504